The Architect's Responsibilities

In The Project Delivery Process

By H.L. Murvin, AIA

Third Edition

Thanks to the following persons who assisted in the preparation of this manual.

Editing: R. Fraatz

Typing: G. Goulet, C. Moser

Proofing: J. Romano, C. Babbitt

Typesetting: A. McAllister

Library of Congress Catalog Card Number: In Processing
I S B N: 0-9608498-3-1

Printed in the United States of America

It should be noted that the author has incorporated samples of filled out forms and other documents used on an architectural project in order to give the reader illustrations of these elements which go into the delivery process of a hypothetical project. In actual practice, the architect's responsibilities are based on requirements of the owner's specific project, laws of the place of building, professional judgment, and local building regulations. Actual forms and documents selected should be reviewed by the owner's attorney to assure the owner that his needs will be met, since there are variations in needs from project to project and locality to locality. The author, therefore, disclaims any responsibility for the use of forms, documents and the description of the architect's responsibilities presented in this manual for any purpose other than study material in conjunction with educational use of this publication. The purpose of this manual is to be an educational tool to develop and present in an orderly way the project delivery process of a representative architectural project.

Introduction

The architect is responsible for imparting distinctive aesthetic qualities to our buildings, yet his realm is not buildings alone. The proper fulfillment of the architect's responsibilities requires competent, ethical, and impartial service, not only on behalf of the client, but also in the public interest. Seldom does a building affect only its owner, nor does it stand alone. For this reason, the architect is responsible for designing buildings that protect the health, safety, and welfare of all who use them and also enhance the environment by taking due regard for the natural environment, existing physical factors, and circulatory patterns. In addition, the architect designs a building for efficient and economical operation and utilizes materials and equipment most appropriate for their particular application. In this way, our communities develop logically and intelligently; their architecture has a positive impact on society and is a source of satisfaction to the client and all who use it.

In addition to the moral responsibility the architect owes to his profession and the general public, the architect has direct legal responsibilities which begin with the preparation of a legal instrument, the contract between architect and owner. In accepting a commission, both owner and architect should clearly understand their responsibilities during the course of the project. This manual will describe the architect's responsibilities in the project delivery process during the various phases of a representative architectural project.

Specimen American Institute of Architects Documents have been filled out by the author and incorporated in this manual for use as study material. This material illustrates the application of various documents required in a hypothetical construction project. Furthermore, these documents provide background information since they form the context for a description of the architect's responsibilities. The names, dates, locations and data used on the sample forms are fictitious and are for illustrative purposes only.

These forms have become the standard of the industry. The AIA is to be commended for its efforts in developing these forms. Their use has not only standardized construction procedures but also has reduced misunderstandings and errors. Use of these forms is highly recommended in all cases since they are of benefit to owner, contractor and architect alike.

This material should not be construed to be legal or insurance advice. Furthermore, information given here is not meant to supersede the AIA documents; but rather, it is intended to be used in conjunction with the AIA documents. Every effort has been made by the author to ensure that the information in this manual is accurate and correct; however, consult the AIA documents for detailed explanations of specific questions. The Construction Specifications Institute is also to be commended for its efforts in developing its "Masterformat" which has become widely accepted and is used almost exclusively throughout the United States today. Their recommendations consist of a standardized project manual arrangement; standard specification divisions, section titles and numbers; and a standardized three part format for specification writing. This excellent system has reduced errors and omissions and greatly enhanced the architect's ability to communicate large amounts of technical information effectively in a standardized format. The use of the CSI Masterformat is also highly recommended since it has reduced misunderstandings and is of benefit to owner, contractor and architect alike.

The material discussed in this manual pertains to private projects and does not necessarily apply to governmental projects in all cases. The architect should familiarize himself with specific requirements for governmental projects. The federal, state and local governments usually provide their own printed forms that differ from the AIA documents.

Table of Contents

Sample Documents and Exhibits

Sample Documents and Exhibits

Foreword

The architect's responsibilities described in this manual are those of the traditional design-award-build project delivery process. There are several methods of project delivery but this method is used most frequently and is relatively straightforward. This process is characterized by clearly defined, linear phases, with the award of the contract occurring between design and construction. The responsibilities and relationships of the owner, architect and contractor during the construction phase have been established through experience gained by the use of this method through the years.

Other approaches to project delivery differ in that major phases of the project delivery process occur simultaneously. The major benefit is a reduction in time required for completion of the project. In addition, the contractor for construction often enters the process at an earlier stage. Thus, construction expertise is included in the pre-construction phases.

The non-traditional approaches can best be understood with the background of a clear understanding of the architect's responsibilities in the traditional project delivery process, since these other approaches are, generally speaking, a variation on the traditional approach. Furthermore, a basic complement of professional services is required in the delivery process for any project. Each approach to project delivery includes these essential professional services to one extent or the other. Therefore, a definite understanding of the architect's responsibilities in the traditional project delivery process is important in all cases.

Architect-Client Contract

The legal and professional relationship between the architect and the client (owner) is stipulated in the Owner-Architect Agreement. This document not only states the basis for the architect's compensation but also states in detail the obligations of both parties to the agreement.

The architect agrees to furnish professional services to the client, and the client agrees to provide compensation for these services. The Standard Form of Agreement Between Owner and Architect, published by The American Institute of Architects (AIA), divides the architect's basic services into five phases:

1) Schematic Design Phase
2) Design Development Phase
3) Construction Documents Phase
4) Bidding or Negotiation Phase
5) Construction Phase-Administration of the Construction Contract

The architect's primary responsibility is to act as the client's professional adviser. He develops his best solution for the project based on the owner's criteria; prepares preliminary estimates of construction cost; advises on selection of materials, systems and equipment; advises on selection of contractors and acts as the owner's representative during construction of the project.

The client must clearly describe his requirements for the project, provide necessary information about the site and budget, and give prompt and thorough attention to the drawings and other documents submitted to him by the architect. The initial step in an architectural project is the pre-contractual conference between client and architect. After receiving notification that he is considered the architect for the project, the architect completes several tasks prior to the execution of the Owner-Architect Agreement.

The architect verifies that his professional liability insurance is valid in the project locality and that he meets all licensing requirements. He negotiates tentative compensation with all consultants required for the project and verifies their professional liability insurance coverage and professional licensing.

He reviews the client's objectives in regard to time limitations for project completion, project budget and program of requirements to determine if they are consistent with a reasonable production schedule. In addition, he considers the project scope and building type and determines if these factors are compatible with the budget.

He defines the project constraints such as special economic considerations, zoning ordinances and planning regulations, unusual site shape or topography, and other special requirements that will influence project completion and in-house production costs.

The architect reviews the Contract Documents. He determines what constitutes basic services; additional services that will be required on the project, if any; and their method of compensation. He verifies the method contemplated by the owner for award of the construction contract. He verifies the form of General Conditions to be utilized on the project. The architect should obtain this information at the earliest possible point. A form used for the purpose of gathering this information is AIA Document 611, Owner's Instructions Regarding Bidding Documents and Procedures.

This document should be filled out by the owner with the assistance of his attorney. Obviously, the type of Owner-Contractor Agreement that will be utilized and other such items will affect the amount of time and cost of the architectural services required for the project. Therefore, after obtaining this information, the architect takes these items into account, prepares the Owner-Architect Agreement Form and submits it to the owner. This is a relatively straightforward process if AIA documents are to be used. However, if the client wishes to provide his own forms, the architect may be required to review these with legal counsel. In addition, if the owner requires special provisions these should also be reviewed by an attorney prior to execution of the agreement.

There are four basic types of agreements between owner and architect. Their main differences are in the method by which the architect's compensation is determined. The compensation may be based on a percentage of the project's construction cost, a stipulated sum, a multiple of direct personnel expense, or a professional fee plus expense. Any one of the four types of agreements may be used with the standard form available from the AIA (Document B141).

In the "Percentage of the Construction Cost of the Project Agreement," the owner agrees to pay a fee consisting of a stipulated percentage of the cost of the construction work to the architect for his services. This frequently used form is best suited to typical construction projects of definite scope requiring complete professional services where bids are to be taken prior to the beginning of construction.

The "Stipulated Sum Agreement" is often referred to as a lump sum agreement. In this form of agreement, a fixed amount (lump sum) is set forth as the total payment for the performance of the basic services outlined in the contract. It is best used when there is a well defined scope of work. Obviously, it rewards efficiency on the part of the architect. Furthermore, it does not penalize the architect for judicious reductions in construction cost as does the "Percentage of the Construction Cost Agreement." In addition, the "Stipulated Sum Agreement" is easy to invoice and in essence, the fee is based on the value to the client of the services received. However, as opposed to the "Percentage of Construction Cost Agreement" where fees increase automatically with inflation as construction costs increase, fee increases with the "Stipulated Sum Agreement" are often difficult to obtain.

In the "Multiple of Direct Personnel Expense Agreement," the compensation for services is determined by multiplying the regular rates of pay plus benefits times a multiplier (usually between two and one-half and three and one-half). A multiple of the expense of consultants for normal professional services is also included. Coordinating the work of consultants is a direct personnel expense of the architect. The architect's multiple on the services of consultants covers both administrative costs and the liability the architect must assume for their services. Reimbursable expenses, payments, owner's responsibilities, accounting records and other general provisions are the same as in the "Percentage of Construction Cost Agreement." This type of agreement is best used when the scope of the project must remain flexible. Other uses are when unusual procedures for planning and awarding of construction contracts are followed or when only partial professional services are required.

In the "Professional Fee Plus Expense Agreement" the compensation is based on a combination of a fixed fee for the architect's personal services plus a multiple for direct personnel expense and consultant's services. By having a fixed fee which is predetermined on the basis of the anticipated personal services and complexity of the project, the architect is free to give advice without having his compensation affected by the cost of the project. The scope of the project, not its cost, becomes the basis for the fixed fee. All other expenses for direct personnel costs and consulting fees as well as other articles and provisions are similar to those in the above noted agreements. This type of contract is best utilized for projects of special purpose requiring the architect's close personal attention.

The initial articles of the AIA Owner-Architect Agreement define the extent of the architect's responsibilities in regard to providing basic professional services for schematic design, design development, preparation of construction documents and bidding documents, providing preliminary estimates of construction cost and administering the construction contract. In addition, project representation beyond basic services and additional services are defined.

Article 4 defines the owner's responsibilities. The owner agrees to provide full information on the requirements of the project; designate authorized representatives for the project; furnish a site survey; furnish the services of geotechnical engineers for the preparation of a soil report, evaluations of hazardous materials and appropriate professional recommendations when requested by the architect; and pay for legal, accounting, auditing and insurance counseling services as are required for the project. Further, the owner is required to furnish the services of consultants other than geotechnical engineers when such services are reasonably required and are requested by the architect. Such consultant's services are in addition to the normal structural, mechanical, and electrical engineering services furnished by the architect as a part of the architect's basic services.

As outlined in paragraph 4.9 of the AIA Owner-Architect Agreement, the architect may rely upon the accuracy and completeness of the above noted services, surveys, reports, etc. furnished by the owner and therefore cannot be held liable for errors contained in this information.

Further paragraphs under the owner's responsibilities article contain important provisions that define the owner's duties and responsibilities or clarify the rights and obligations of the parties under the agreement. For example, the architect is often asked by the owner to sign certificates. When these are required of the architect or the architect's consultants, they must be submitted at least fourteen days prior to execution in order to give the architect ample time to review the provision of the certificate. In addition, the architect may wish to review such certifications with his attorney during this time period. Furthermore, the owner may not request certifications of the architect that would require knowledge or services beyond the scope of the agreement. Further articles define the project construction cost and the extent of the work on which this cost is based; responsibility for construction cost; use and ownership of the architect's drawings, specifications and other documents; provisions for arbitration; termination, suspension or abandonment of the project by either the owner or architect; miscellaneous provisions; payments to the architect related to direct personnel expense, reimbursable expenses, basic services, and additional services; and the availability of the architect's accounting records to the owner.

As defined under provisions of Article 6, "Use of Architect's Drawings, Specifications and Other Documents," the architect owns the copyright on all drawings and specifications. This provision is further extended to include documents other than drawings and specifications. In essence, the owner is prevented from using the documents on other projects unless agreed upon by the architect. Obviously, codes, zoning, soil conditions, loading conditions and numerous other factors may be different in other localities. For this reason the architect must take into account these important considerations and make modifications as required if the documents are to be reused on another project. Therefore, the documents are reused only with the architect's written agreement and with appropriate compensation to the architect. The exception to this is if the architect is "adjudged" to be in default under the agreement. The word "adjudged" has the implicit meaning in this case that the architect must be found to be in default by a court or arbitration panel, and not merely declared in default by the owner.

Under the provisions of Article 8, "Termination, Suspension or

Abandonment", full compensation for services performed before notice of suspension is required to be paid to the architect if the project is suspended by the owner for more than thirty days. If the project is abandoned by the owner for more than ninety consecutive days, the architect may terminate the agreement upon written notice. Further, if the owner does not make payment to the architect when it is due, the architect may suspend services upon seven days' written notice to the owner. In this case, the architect has no liability to the owner for delay.

As outlined under the "Miscellaneous Provisions" article, the architect and the architect's consultants have no responsibility for the discovery, removal or disposal of hazardous materials. Nor does the architect have responsibility for exposure of persons to hazardous materials. In essence, the primary responsibility for dealing with hazardous materials such as asbestos or polychlorinated biphenyl (PCB), etc. has been assigned to the owner. The owner furnishes the services of geotechnical engineers for tests for hazardous materials, and for reports and recommendations when requested by the architect. As appropriate, the architect requests such services in writing at the outset of the project. Further, since the architect is generally not trained in this area, he should avoid performing inspections, preparing reports or devising the manner of testing himself.

Further paragraphs under "Miscellaneous Provisions" describe the architect's rights regarding professional credit. The architect may include photographs and other representations of the project in his promotional materials. However, the owner may designate specific information as confidential or proprietary by notifying the architect in writing. In addition, the owner must provide credit for the architect on the construction sign and promotional materials for the project.

Under the provisions of Article 10, "Payments to the Architect", the architect is entitled to various reimbursable expenses in addition to compensation for basic and additional services. These include out of town travel, long distance calls, reproductions, postage, overtime work authorized by owner, renderings, models, additional insurance requested by the owner, and computer-aided design and drafting equipment time. The architect may wish to consider adding other items to the list of reimbursable expenses such as: photographic drawing production techniques, photography services, photographs, and the development and enlargement of prints used for the project or on the owner's behalf.

Paragraph 10.5 provides protection for the architect against payments withheld by the owner: no deductions may be withheld from the architect's compensation due to penalties or other amounts withheld from payments to contractors. Further, no deductions may be made because of changes in the work other than those for which the architect has been found to be liable. The architect may wish to consider adding other clauses for additional protection. For example, the architect may wish to stipulate that the architect's invoice will be considered accurate unless the owner has notified the architect to the contrary within two weeks from the date of receipt of the invoice.

Articles 11 and 12 define the owner's responsibilities regarding the architect's compensation for basic services and additional services. Basic services are the five phases of the architect's services defined in the initial articles of the agreement. The architect is compensated for these services as stipulated in the Owner-Architect Agreement under "Basis of Compensation." Here, the amount of initial payment to the architect and the compensation for basic services is typed on the form.

Compensation for additional services for the architect, the architect's employees, and consultants is also typed on the form. Additional services are often compensated on a multiple of direct personnel expense basis. There are three types of additional services outlined in Article 3 of the Owner-Architect Agreement:

1) Project Representation Beyond Basic Services—Here, the architect provides one or more project representatives to carry out on-site duties if more extensive on-site representation is required by the owner than that described under "Basic Services". These services are provided only if authorized in writing by the owner.

2) Contingent Additional Services—Here, services are required for the project due to circumstances beyond the architect's control. In this case, the architect notifies the owner before commencing the services. If the owner determines that such services are not required, the owner must give prompt written notice to the architect. Then, the architect has no obligation to provide these services. An example of such services is the evaluation of substitutions of construction products proposed by the contractor in lieu of those specified. In addition, approval of such products often requires revision of drawings and specifications. Such services would be compensated as additional services if the architect notifies the owner that he is proceeding with the work on a certain date and the owner does not notify the architect that these services are not required.

3) Optional Additional Services—Here, these services are provided only if authorized or confirmed by the owner in writing. In general, these services are either not absolutely necessary for the project or they could be performed by someone other than the architect. An example of such services is analyzing the owner's needs and programming the requirements of the project. It is the owner's responsibility to provide this information. This information could be compiled by the owner's staff, an outside consultant, or the architect. If the owner requests the architect to perform such services, the owner must confirm the request for these services in writing and they are compensated as an additional service. In summary, it is the owner's decision who

perform Optional Additional Services and whether these services are required at all.

Many of the potential problems related to architectural projects can be avoided by understanding the fundamental concepts of the Owner-Architect Agreement. Those articles that define the rights, duties and responsibilities of the parties are of particular importance. An awareness of these concepts will guide the architect's actions and decisions as the project progresses through the various phases. The architect should make an item by item review of the provisions prior to execution of the agreement. Since each project and each client is generally unique, the architect cannot rely solely on standard forms without first ascertaining how they apply to a particular project.

Further, the owner may propose modifications to the standard AIA Owner Architect Agreement. Particular attention should be paid to these modifications and their legal implications. Therefore, the architect may wish to hold detailed discussions of the modifications proposed with his attorney to determine how such modifications will effect the architect's legal position.

There are three general categories of obligations that architects owe to their clients and the general public on a project:

1) Regulatory Laws—These are a set of professional obligations to which mandatory and strict adherence is required. Examples of such laws are building codes, handicapped codes, energy codes, and zoning ordinances. They have been adopted by the government to protect the health, safety and welfare of the general public.

2) Contractual Obligations—These are the terms that the architect

and owner have agreed upon in a contract such as the AIA Owner-Architect Agreement.

3) Standard of Care—This important obligation is the essence of professional responsibility. The architect is required to practice in a manner meeting a reasonable standard of care. This entails taking actions that another reasonably prudent architect would take in the same community, given the same time and the same or similar circumstances.

While the law sets a reasonable standard of care, this standard can be modified by contract language. These modifications could raise the law's expectations for the performance of the architect's duties. For example, some clients do not understand that architects are not required to perform perfectly. Such clients may propose modifications to the standard AIA Owner-Architect Agreement which will in essence provide guarantees. It should be pointed out in these cases that buildings are generally one of a kind and cannot be tested as mass produced manufactured products can be. Therefore, the architect is only required to exercise a degree of effort, skill and care equivalent to what may be reasonably required of another architect, given the same time, locality and circumstances. Similarly, doctors do not guarantee good health and attorneys do not guarantee their clients they will win the case.

The architect's actions on a project are examined in the perspective of this reasonable standard of care. What complicates this issue is that each project has its own unique set of acceptable actions, procedures and decisions. Therefore, there is no precise legal definition of the architect's exact duties for a project in advance. The standard of care is a general principle. Therefore, the courts and arbitration panels must define comprehensively what was required after the act in each case.

The architect is not required to design a perfect floor plan. Neither is there a guarantee that the drawings and specifications will be perfect. The law requires, however, that they will be prepared in accordance with a reasonable standard of care. Further, the law does not accept standards of practice that do not meet the needs of the general public in regard to health, safety and welfare.

The standard of care may appear to be a rather ill defined area. However, in actual practice, the principle works in a rather straightforward manner if a dispute related to this issue develops and cannot be settled in an informal manner. Should a lawsuit become necessary, each side brings expert witnesses into court for testimony. The expert witnesses are generally design professionals with experience in similar projects. They review the facts and give testimony as to whether or not they believe that the architect's actions met a reasonable standard of care in the particular situation. In situations where acceptable professional decisions or actions can be easily determined in advance, these have been set forth in codes, ordinances and regulations and are, in general, always required to meet the reasonable standard of care. These form the standards for professional practice for a community. However, there are many areas where the best course of action is less clear, and here is where disputes may develop over what constitutes prudent professional practice.

While the legal concept regarding professional behavior only requires a "reasonable" standard of care, the architect can inadvertently alter the situation by raising the standard of care that will be applied on the project. For example, the architect could sign a lending institution's form certifying that the completed project will meet all applicable codes and regulations. The architect may wish to consider inserting words such as "to the best of the architect's knowledge, information and belief" into all required certificates in order to reduce the possible expectation of performance higher than the reasonable standard of care. Another example would be that the architect could sign a document prepared by the owner stating that the roof will not leak. The architect, in essence, has provided a guarantee in these cases and unknowingly raised the standard of care. Further, the architect can inadvertently expand the standard of care. For example, the architect visits the job site and responds to the contractor's inquiries related to construction techniques for a caisson foundation system. Since construction means, methods and techniques are the contractor's responsibility, the architect has unknowingly expanded the standard of care.

The architect should make every effort to clarify the scope of services and discuss the reasonable standard of care with the owner. However, recognize that some owners will intentionally add certain words to increase the architect's required performance and shift liability for the project onto the architect. Words that are particularly ambiguous which may increase the architect's standard of care should be avoided, and where possible, eliminated from the Owner-Architect Agreement. Such words include the following: insures, assures, ensures, guarantees, warrants, represents, certifies, the highest standard, all, every, always, any, solely, documents, of every nature and description, with no exceptions, and "etc." Note that most professional liability insurance policies do not insure for claims against architects who have agreed to perform services that exceed the reasonable standard of care. Agreements that contain provisions requiring a standard of performance that exceeds those described in the AIA Owner-Architect Agreement should also be avoided unless the compensation is adequate to justify such additional risks.

The owner may also ask the architect to meet a rather rigid schedule for document production. Note that professional liability insurance generally does not cover claims against the architect for not meeting schedules or for time delays. The architect may wish to state that he will simply endeavor to meet a reasonable schedule. Secondly, he may wish to state that any delays caused by the owner for the approval process, changes or other decisions will cause the architect's schedule to be extended by a commensurate amount.

In some cases, the owner may provide the Owner-Architect Agreement. Generally, the owner will also furnish the General Conditions that describe the architect's services during the Construction Phase of the project. The architect should carefully review these General Conditions to ensure that all services required in the General Conditions are satisfactory and if so, they are outlined in the Owner-Architect Agreement. Obviously, the architect's compensation should reflect fees for such services.

Note that owner furnished agreements often require that the architect perform in accordance with the "highest professional standards." The architect should avoid signing an agreement with such provisions since, in the owner's opinion, there will generally be something "higher" than the services provided. Therefore, these standards are unattainable. Note that the "highest standards" would also require the highest costing materials which are often incompatible with the owner's budget. For example, the highest standards would require copper flashing rather than galvanized metal flashing that is obviously acceptable and less costly.

Furthermore, the owner often asks for indemnification from liability except for items "solely" caused by the owner. Note that in this case the owner could be 99% responsible for a problem and the architect only 1% responsible. Here, the architect would still have to pay for all liability because the owner is not "solely" responsible. Conversely, the owner could provide indemnification for liability to the architect. Recognize that such indemnification is only as good as the assets of the owner that are backing the indemnification.

Expanding or raising the standard of care needlessly increases the architect's liability exposure. The architect may inadvertently become responsible for more than the law normally requires. It is unwise for the architect to expand or raise the standard of care applied to professional services without understanding the alternatives. First, the architect may deem the risk unreasonably high and avoid such action entirely.

Alternatively, the architect may wish to knowingly assume such risks with appropriate compensation for them. In either case, the decision should be a conscious one after considering the consequences. Basically, to show liability the claimant must first prove the architect had a duty and then prove that the duty was breached by the architect.

AIA Document B141

Standard Form of Agreement Between Owner and Architect

1987 EDITION

THIS DOCUMENT HAS IMPORTANT LEGAL CONSEQUENCES; CONSULTATION WITH AN ATTORNEY IS ENCOURAGED WITH RESPECT TO ITS COMPLETION OR MODIFICATION.

SAMPLE

AGREEMENT

made as of the   First   day of   June   in the year of Nineteen Hundred and Eighty Seven.

BETWEEN the Owner:
(Name and address)

Typical Manufacturing Company
950 Broadway Blvd., Oakland, California

and the Architect:
(Name and address)

A B C Architects
600 Main St., San Francisco, California

For the following Project:
(Include detailed description of Project, location, address and scope.)

Typical Manufacturing Company's new
Industrial Plant and Office
100 Industrial Blvd.
Hayward, California

The Owner and Architect agree as set forth below.

ARTICLE 1
ARCHITECT'S RESPONSIBILITIES

1.1 ARCHITECT'S SERVICES

1.1.1 The Architect's services consist of those services performed by the Architect, Architect's employees and Architect's consultants as enumerated in Articles 2 and 3 of this Agreement and any other services included in Article 12.

1.1.2 The Architect's services shall be performed as expeditiously as is consistent with professional skill and care and the orderly progress of the Work. Upon request of the Owner, the Architect shall submit for the Owner's approval a schedule for the performance of the Architect's services which may be adjusted as the Project proceeds, and shall include allowances for periods of time required for the Owner's review and for approval of submissions by authorities having jurisdiction over the Project. Time limits established by this schedule approved by the Owner shall not, except for reasonable cause, be exceeded by the Architect or Owner.

1.1.3 The services covered by this Agreement are subject to the time limitations contained in Subparagraph 11.5.1.

ARTICLE 2
SCOPE OF ARCHITECT'S BASIC SERVICES

2.1 DEFINITION

2.1.1 The Architect's Basic Services consist of those described in Paragraphs 2.2 through 2.6 and any other services identified in Article 12 as part of Basic Services, and include normal structural, mechanical and electrical engineering services.

2.2 SCHEMATIC DESIGN PHASE

2.2.1 The Architect shall review the program furnished by the Owner to ascertain the requirements of the Project and shall arrive at a mutual understanding of such requirements with the Owner.

2.2.2 The Architect shall provide a preliminary evaluation of the Owner's program, schedule and construction budget requirements, each in terms of the other, subject to the limitations set forth in Subparagraph 5.2.1.

2.2.3 The Architect shall review with the Owner alternative approaches to design and construction of the Project.

2.2.4 Based on the mutually agreed-upon program, schedule and construction budget requirements, the Architect shall prepare, for approval by the Owner, Schematic Design Documents consisting of drawings and other documents illustrating the scale and relationship of Project components.

2.2.5 The Architect shall submit to the Owner a preliminary estimate of Construction Cost based on current area, volume or other unit costs.

2.3 DESIGN DEVELOPMENT PHASE

2.3.1 Based on the approved Schematic Design Documents and any adjustments authorized by the Owner in the program,
schedule or construction budget, the Architect shall prepare, for approval by the Owner, Design Development Documents consisting of drawings and other documents to fix and describe the size and character of the Project as to architectural, structural, mechanical and electrical systems, materials and such other elements as may be appropriate.

2.3.2 The Architect shall advise the Owner of any adjustments to the preliminary estimate of Construction Cost.

2.4 CONSTRUCTION DOCUMENTS PHASE

2.4.1 Based on the approved Design Development Documents and any further adjustments in the scope or quality of the Project or in the construction budget authorized by the Owner, the Architect shall prepare, for approval by the Owner, Construction Documents consisting of Drawings and Specifications setting forth in detail the requirements for the construction of the Project.

2.4.2 The Architect shall assist the Owner in the preparation of the necessary bidding information, bidding forms, the Conditions of the Contract, and the form of Agreement between the Owner and Contractor.

2.4.3 The Architect shall advise the Owner of any adjustments to previous preliminary estimates of Construction Cost indicated by changes in requirements or general market conditions.

2.4.4 The Architect shall assist the Owner in connection with the Owner's responsibility for filing documents required for the approval of governmental authorities having jurisdiction over the Project.

2.5 BIDDING OR NEGOTIATION PHASE

2.5.1 The Architect, following the Owner's approval of the Construction Documents and of the latest preliminary estimate of Construction Cost, shall assist the Owner in obtaining bids or negotiated proposals and assist in awarding and preparing contracts for construction.

2.6 CONSTRUCTION PHASE—ADMINISTRATION OF THE CONSTRUCTION CONTRACT

2.6.1 The Architect's responsibility to provide Basic Services for the Construction Phase under this Agreement commences with the award of the Contract for Construction and terminates at the earlier of the issuance to the Owner of the final Certificate for Payment or 60 days after the date of Substantial Completion of the Work, unless extended under the terms of Subparagraph 10.3.3.

2.6.2 The Architect shall provide administration of the Contract for Construction as set forth below and in the edition of AIA Document A201, General Conditions of the Contract for Construction, current as of the date of this Agreement, unless otherwise provided in this Agreement.

2.6.3 Duties, responsibilities and limitations of authority of the Architect shall not be restricted, modified or extended without written agreement of the Owner and Architect with consent of the Contractor, which consent shall not be unreasonably withheld.

2.6.4 The Architect shall be a representative of and shall advise and consult with the Owner (1) during construction until final payment to the Contractor is due, and (2) as an Additional Service at the Owner's direction from time to time during the correction period described in the Contract for Construction. The Architect shall have authority to act on behalf of the Owner only to the extent provided in this Agreement unless otherwise modified by written instrument.

2.6.5 The Architect shall visit the site at intervals appropriate to the stage of construction or as otherwise agreed by the Owner and Architect in writing to become generally familiar with the progress and quality of the Work completed and to determine in general if the Work is being performed in a manner indicating that the Work when completed will be in accordance with the Contract Documents. However, the Architect shall not be required to make exhaustive or continuous on-site inspections to check the quality or quantity of the Work. On the basis of on-site observations as an architect, the Architect shall keep the Owner informed of the progress and quality of the Work, and shall endeavor to guard the Owner against defects and deficiencies in the Work. *(More extensive site representation may be agreed to as an Additional Service, as described in Paragraph 3.2.)*

2.6.6 The Architect shall not have control over or charge of and shall not be responsible for construction means, methods, techniques, sequences or procedures, or for safety precautions and programs in connection with the Work, since these are solely the Contractor's responsibility under the Contract for Construction. The Architect shall not be responsible for the Contractor's schedules or failure to carry out the Work in accordance with the Contract Documents. The Architect shall not have control over or charge of acts or omissions of the Contractor, Subcontractors, or their agents or employees, or of any other persons performing portions of the Work.

2.6.7 The Architect shall at all times have access to the Work wherever it is in preparation or progress.

2.6.8 Except as may otherwise be provided in the Contract Documents or when direct communications have been specially authorized, the Owner and Contractor shall communicate through the Architect. Communications by and with the Architect's consultants shall be through the Architect.

2.6.9 Based on the Architect's observations and evaluations of the Contractor's Applications for Payment, the Architect shall review and certify the amounts due the Contractor.

2.6.10 The Architect's certification for payment shall constitute a representation to the Owner, based on the Architect's observations at the site as provided in Subparagraph 2.6.5 and on the data comprising the Contractor's Application for Payment, that the Work has progressed to the point indicated and that, to the best of the Architect's knowledge, information and belief, quality of the Work is in accordance with the Contract Documents. The foregoing representations are subject to an evaluation of the Work for conformance with the Contract Documents upon Substantial Completion, to results of subsequent tests and inspections, to minor deviations from the Contract Documents correctable prior to completion and to specific qualifications expressed by the Architect. The issuance of a Certificate for Payment shall further constitute a representation that the Contractor is entitled to payment in the amount certified. However, the issuance of a Certificate for Payment shall not be a representation that the Architect has (1) made exhaustive or continuous on-site inspections to check the quality or

quantity of the Work, (2) reviewed construction means, methods, techniques, sequences or procedures, (3) reviewed copies of requisitions received from Subcontractors and material suppliers and other data requested by the Owner to substantiate the Contractor's right to payment or (4) ascertained how or for what purpose the Contractor has used money previously paid on account of the Contract Sum.

2.6.11 The Architect shall have authority to reject Work which does not conform to the Contract Documents. Whenever the Architect considers it necessary or advisable for implementation of the intent of the Contract Documents, the Architect will have authority to require additional inspection or testing of the Work in accordance with the provisions of the Contract Documents, whether or not such Work is fabricated, installed or completed. However, neither this authority of the Architect nor a decision made in good faith either to exercise or not to exercise such authority shall give rise to a duty or responsibility of the Architect to the Contractor, Subcontractors, material and equipment suppliers, their agents or employees or other persons performing portions of the Work.

2.6.12 The Architect shall review and approve or take other appropriate action upon Contractor's submittals such as Shop Drawings, Product Data and Samples, but only for the limited purpose of checking for conformance with information given and the design concept expressed in the Contract Documents. The Architect's action shall be taken with such reasonable promptness as to cause no delay in the Work or in the construction of the Owner or of separate contractors, while allowing sufficient time in the Architect's professional judgment to permit adequate review. Review of such submittals is not conducted for the purpose of determining the accuracy and completeness of other details such as dimensions and quantities or for substantiating instructions for installation or performance of equipment or systems designed by the Contractor, all of which remain the responsibility of the Contractor to the extent required by the Contract Documents. The Architect's review shall not constitute approval of safety precautions or, unless otherwise specifically stated by the Architect, of construction means, methods, techniques, sequences or procedures. The Architect's approval of a specific item shall not indicate approval of an assembly of which the item is a component. When professional certification of performance characteristics of materials, systems or equipment is required by the Contract Documents, the Architect shall be entitled to rely upon such certification to establish that the materials, systems or equipment will meet the performance criteria required by the Contract Documents.

2.6.13 The Architect shall prepare Change Orders and Construction Change Directives, with supporting documentation and data if deemed necessary by the Architect as provided in Subparagraphs 3.1.1 and 3.3.3, for the Owner's approval and execution in accordance with the Contract Documents, and may authorize minor changes in the Work not involving an adjustment in the Contract Sum or an extension of the Contract Time which are not inconsistent with the intent of the Contract Documents.

2.6.14 The Architect shall conduct inspections to determine the date or dates of Substantial Completion and the date of final completion, shall receive and forward to the Owner for the Owner's review and records written warranties and related documents required by the Contract Documents and assembled by the Contractor, and shall issue a final Certificate for Payment upon compliance with the requirements of the Contract Documents.

2.6.15 The Architect shall interpret and decide matters concerning performance of the Owner and Contractor under the requirements of the Contract Documents on written request of either the Owner or Contractor. The Architect's response to such requests shall be made with reasonable promptness and within any time limits agreed upon.

2.6.16 Interpretations and decisions of the Architect shall be consistent with the intent of and reasonably inferable from the Contract Documents and shall be in writing or in the form of drawings. When making such interpretations and initial decisions, the Architect shall endeavor to secure faithful performance by both Owner and Contractor, shall not show partiality to either, and shall not be liable for results of interpretations or decisions so rendered in good faith.

2.6.17 The Architect's decisions on matters relating to aesthetic effect shall be final if consistent with the intent expressed in the Contract Documents.

2.6.18 The Architect shall render written decisions within a reasonable time on all claims, disputes or other matters in question between the Owner and Contractor relating to the execution or progress of the Work as provided in the Contract Documents.

2.6.19 The Architect's decisions on claims, disputes or other matters, including those in question between the Owner and Contractor, except for those relating to aesthetic effect as provided in Subparagraph 2.6.17, shall be subject to arbitration as provided in this Agreement and in the Contract Documents.

ARTICLE 3
ADDITIONAL SERVICES

3.1 GENERAL

3.1.1 The services described in this Article 3 are not included in Basic Services unless so identified in Article 12, and they shall be paid for by the Owner as provided in this Agreement, in addition to the compensation for Basic Services. The services described under Paragraphs 3.2 and 3.4 shall only be provided if authorized or confirmed in writing by the Owner. If services described under Contingent Additional Services in Paragraph 3.3 are required due to circumstances beyond the Architect's control, the Architect shall notify the Owner prior to commencing such services. If the Owner deems that such services described under Paragraph 3.3 are not required, the Owner shall give prompt written notice to the Architect. If the Owner indicates in writing that all or part of such Contingent Additional Services are not required, the Architect shall have no obligation to provide those services.

3.2 PROJECT REPRESENTATION BEYOND BASIC SERVICES

3.2.1 If more extensive representation at the site than is described in Subparagraph 2.6.5 is required, the Architect shall provide one or more Project Representatives to assist in carrying out such additional on-site responsibilities.

3.2.2 Project Representatives shall be selected, employed and directed by the Architect, and the Architect shall be compensated therefor as agreed by the Owner and Architect. The duties, responsibilities and limitations of authority of Project Representatives shall be as described in the edition of AIA Document B352 current as of the date of this Agreement, unless otherwise agreed.

3.2.3 Through the observations by such Project Representatives, the Architect shall endeavor to provide further protection for the Owner against defects and deficiencies in the Work, but the furnishing of such project representation shall not modify the rights, responsibilities or obligations of the Architect as described elsewhere in this Agreement.

3.3 CONTINGENT ADDITIONAL SERVICES

3.3.1 Making revisions in Drawings, Specifications or other documents when such revisions are:

  .1 inconsistent with approvals or instructions previously given by the Owner, including revisions made necessary by adjustments in the Owner's program or Project budget;

  .2 required by the enactment or revision of codes, laws or regulations subsequent to the preparation of such documents; or

  .3 due to changes required as a result of the Owner's failure to render decisions in a timely manner.

3.3.2 Providing services required because of significant changes in the Project including, but not limited to, size, quality, complexity, the Owner's schedule, or the method of bidding or negotiating and contracting for construction, except for services required under Subparagraph 5.2.5.

3.3.3 Preparing Drawings, Specifications and other documentation and supporting data, evaluating Contractor's proposals, and providing other services in connection with Change Orders and Construction Change Directives.

3.3.4 Providing services in connection with evaluating substitutions proposed by the Contractor and making subsequent revisions to Drawings, Specifications and other documentation resulting therefrom.

3.3.5 Providing consultation concerning replacement of Work damaged by fire or other cause during construction, and furnishing services required in connection with the replacement of such Work.

3.3.6 Providing services made necessary by the default of the Contractor, by major defects or deficiencies in the Work of the Contractor, or by failure of performance of either the Owner or Contractor under the Contract for Construction.

3.3.7 Providing services in evaluating an extensive number of claims submitted by the Contractor or others in connection with the Work.

3.3.8 Providing services in connection with a public hearing, arbitration proceeding or legal proceeding except where the Architect is party thereto.

3.3.9 Preparing documents for alternate, separate or sequential bids or providing services in connection with bidding, negotiation or construction prior to the completion of the Construction Documents Phase.

3.4 OPTIONAL ADDITIONAL SERVICES

3.4.1 Providing analyses of the Owner's needs and programming the requirements of the Project.

3.4.2 Providing financial feasibility or other special studies.

3.4.3 Providing planning surveys, site evaluations or comparative studies of prospective sites.

3.4.4 Providing special surveys, environmental studies and submissions required for approvals of governmental authorities or others having jurisdiction over the Project.

3.4.5 Providing services relative to future facilities, systems and equipment.

3.4.6 Providing services to investigate existing conditions or facilities or to make measured drawings thereof.

3.4.7 Providing services to verify the accuracy of drawings or other information furnished by the Owner.

3.4.8 Providing coordination of construction performed by separate contractors or by the Owner's own forces and coordination of services required in connection with construction performed and equipment supplied by the Owner.

3.4.9 Providing services in connection with the work of a construction manager or separate consultants retained by the Owner.

3.4.10 Providing detailed estimates of Construction Cost.

3.4.11 Providing detailed quantity surveys or inventories of material, equipment and labor.

3.4.12 Providing analyses of owning and operating costs.

3.4.13 Providing interior design and other similar services required for or in connection with the selection, procurement or installation of furniture, furnishings and related equipment.

3.4.14 Providing services for planning tenant or rental spaces.

3.4.15 Making investigations, inventories of materials or equipment, or valuations and detailed appraisals of existing facilities.

3.4.16 Preparing a set of reproducible record drawings showing significant changes in the Work made during construction based on marked-up prints, drawings and other data furnished by the Contractor to the Architect.

3.4.17 Providing assistance in the utilization of equipment or systems such as testing, adjusting and balancing, preparation of operation and maintenance manuals, training personnel for operation and maintenance, and consultation during operation.

3.4.18 Providing services after issuance to the Owner of the final Certificate for Payment, or in the absence of a final Certificate for Payment, more than 60 days after the date of Substantial Completion of the Work.

3.4.19 Providing services of consultants for other than architectural, structural, mechanical and electrical engineering portions of the Project provided as a part of Basic Services.

3.4.20 Providing any other services not otherwise included in this Agreement or not customarily furnished in accordance with generally accepted architectural practice.

ARTICLE 4
OWNER'S RESPONSIBILITIES

4.1 The Owner shall provide full information regarding requirements for the Project, including a program which shall set forth the Owner's objectives, schedule, constraints and criteria, including space requirements and relationships, flexibility, expandability, special equipment, systems and site requirements.

4.2 The Owner shall establish and update an overall budget for the Project, including the Construction Cost, the Owner's other costs and reasonable contingencies related to all of these costs.

4.3 If requested by the Architect, the Owner shall furnish evidence that financial arrangements have been made to fulfill the Owner's obligations under this Agreement.

4.4 The Owner shall designate a representative authorized to act on the Owner's behalf with respect to the Project. The Owner or such authorized representative shall render decisions in a timely manner pertaining to documents submitted by the Architect in order to avoid unreasonable delay in the orderly and sequential progress of the Architect's services.

4.5 The Owner shall furnish surveys describing physical characteristics, legal limitations and utility locations for the site of the Project, and a written legal description of the site. The surveys and legal information shall include, as applicable, grades and lines of streets, alleys, pavements and adjoining property and structures; adjacent drainage; rights-of-way, restrictions, easements, encroachments, zoning, deed restrictions, boundaries and contours of the site; locations, dimensions and necessary data pertaining to existing buildings, other improvements and trees; and information concerning available utility services and lines, both public and private, above and below grade, including inverts and depths. All the information on the survey shall be referenced to a project benchmark.

4.6 The Owner shall furnish the services of geotechnical engineers when such services are requested by the Architect. Such services may include but are not limited to test borings, test pits, determinations of soil bearing values, percolation tests, evaluations of hazardous materials, ground corrosion and resistivity tests, including necessary operations for anticipating subsoil conditions, with reports and appropriate professional recommendations.

4.6.1 The Owner shall furnish the services of other consultants when such services are reasonably required by the scope of the Project and are requested by the Architect.

4.7 The Owner shall furnish structural, mechanical, chemical, air and water pollution tests, tests for hazardous materials, and other laboratory and environmental tests, inspections and reports required by law or the Contract Documents.

4.8 The Owner shall furnish all legal, accounting and insurance counseling services as may be necessary at any time for the Project, including auditing services the Owner may require to verify the Contractor's Applications for Payment or to ascertain how or for what purposes the Contractor has used the money paid by or on behalf of the Owner.

4.9 The services, information, surveys and reports required by Paragraphs 4.5 through 4.8 shall be furnished at the Owner's expense, and the Architect shall be entitled to rely upon the accuracy and completeness thereof.

4.10 Prompt written notice shall be given by the Owner to the Architect if the Owner becomes aware of any fault or defect in the Project or nonconformance with the Contract Documents.

4.11 The proposed language of certificates or certifications requested of the Architect or Architect's consultants shall be submitted to the Architect for review and approval at least 14 days prior to execution. The Owner shall not request certifications that would require knowledge or services beyond the scope of this Agreement.

AIA DOCUMENT B141 • OWNER-ARCHITECT AGREEMENT • FOURTEENTH EDITION • AIA® • ©1987
THE AMERICAN INSTITUTE OF ARCHITECTS, 1735 NEW YORK AVENUE, N.W., WASHINGTON, D.C. 20006

ARTICLE 5
CONSTRUCTION COST

5.1 DEFINITION

5.1.1 The Construction Cost shall be the total cost or estimated cost to the Owner of all elements of the Project designed or specified by the Architect.

5.1.2 The Construction Cost shall include the cost at current market rates of labor and materials furnished by the Owner and equipment designed, specified, selected or specially provided for by the Architect, plus a reasonable allowance for the Contractor's overhead and profit. In addition, a reasonable allowance for contingencies shall be included for market conditions at the time of bidding and for changes in the Work during construction.

5.1.3 Construction Cost does not include the compensation of the Architect and Architect's consultants, the costs of the land, rights-of-way, financing or other costs which are the responsibility of the Owner as provided in Article 4.

5.2 RESPONSIBILITY FOR CONSTRUCTION COST

5.2.1 Evaluations of the Owner's Project budget, preliminary estimates of Construction Cost and detailed estimates of Construction Cost, if any, prepared by the Architect, represent the Architect's best judgment as a design professional familiar with the construction industry. It is recognized, however, that neither the Architect nor the Owner has control over the cost of labor, materials or equipment, over the Contractor's methods of determining bid prices, or over competitive bidding, market or negotiating conditions. Accordingly, the Architect cannot and does not warrant or represent that bids or negotiated prices will not vary from the Owner's Project budget or from any estimate of Construction Cost or evaluation prepared or agreed to by the Architect.

5.2.2 No fixed limit of Construction Cost shall be established as a condition of this Agreement by the furnishing, proposal or establishment of a Project budget, unless such fixed limit has been agreed upon in writing and signed by the parties hereto. If such a fixed limit has been established, the Architect shall be permitted to include contingencies for design, bidding and price escalation, to determine what materials, equipment, component systems and types of construction are to be included in the Contract Documents, to make reasonable adjustments in the scope of the Project and to include in the Contract Documents alternate bids to adjust the Construction Cost to the fixed limit. Fixed limits, if any, shall be increased in the amount of an increase in the Contract Sum occurring after execution of the Contract for Construction.

5.2.3 If the Bidding or Negotiation Phase has not commenced within 90 days after the Architect submits the Construction Documents to the Owner, any Project budget or fixed limit of Construction Cost shall be adjusted to reflect changes in the general level of prices in the construction industry between the date of submission of the Construction Documents to the Owner and the date on which proposals are sought.

5.2.4 If a fixed limit of Construction Cost (adjusted as provided in Subparagraph 5.2.3) is exceeded by the lowest bona fide bid or negotiated proposal, the Owner shall:

  .1 give written approval of an increase in such fixed limit;

  .2 authorize rebidding or renegotiating of the Project within a reasonable time;

  .3 if the Project is abandoned, terminate in accordance with Paragraph 8.3; or

  .4 cooperate in revising the Project scope and quality as required to reduce the Construction Cost.

5.2.5 If the Owner chooses to proceed under Clause 5.2.4.4, the Architect, without additional charge, shall modify the Contract Documents as necessary to comply with the fixed limit, if established as a condition of this Agreement. The modification of Contract Documents shall be the limit of the Architect's responsibility arising out of the establishment of a fixed limit. The Architect shall be entitled to compensation in accordance with this Agreement for all services performed whether or not the Construction Phase is commenced.

ARTICLE 6
USE OF ARCHITECT'S DRAWINGS, SPECIFICATIONS AND OTHER DOCUMENTS

6.1 The Drawings, Specifications and other documents prepared by the Architect for this Project are instruments of the Architect's service for use solely with respect to this Project and, unless otherwise provided, the Architect shall be deemed the author of these documents and shall retain all common law, statutory and other reserved rights, including the copyright. The Owner shall be permitted to retain copies, including reproducible copies, of the Architect's Drawings, Specifications and other documents for information and reference in connection with the Owner's use and occupancy of the Project. The Architect's Drawings, Specifications or other documents shall not be used by the Owner or others on other projects, for additions to this Project or for completion of this Project by others, unless the Architect is adjudged to be in default under this Agreement, except by agreement in writing and with appropriate compensation to the Architect.

6.2 Submission or distribution of documents to meet official regulatory requirements or for similar purposes in connection with the Project is not to be construed as publication in derogation of the Architect's reserved rights.

ARTICLE 7
ARBITRATION

7.1 Claims, disputes or other matters in question between the parties to this Agreement arising out of or relating to this Agreement or breach thereof shall be subject to and decided by arbitration in accordance with the Construction Industry Arbitration Rules of the American Arbitration Association currently in effect unless the parties mutually agree otherwise.

7.2 Demand for arbitration shall be filed in writing with the other party to this Agreement and with the American Arbitration Association. A demand for arbitration shall be made within a reasonable time after the claim, dispute or other matter in question has arisen. In no event shall the demand for arbitration be made after the date when institution of legal or equitable proceedings based on such claim, dispute or other matter in question would be barred by the applicable statutes of limitations.

7.3 No arbitration arising out of or relating to this Agreement shall include, by consolidation, joinder or in any other manner, an additional person or entity not a party to this Agreement, except by written consent containing a specific reference to this Agreement signed by the Owner, Architect, and any other person or entity sought to be joined. Consent to arbitration involving an additional person or entity shall not constitute consent to arbitration of any claim, dispute or other matter in question not described in the written consent or with a person or entity not named or described therein. The foregoing agreement to arbitrate and other agreements to arbitrate with an additional person or entity duly consented to by the parties to this Agreement shall be specifically enforceable in accordance with applicable law in any court having jurisdiction thereof.

7.4 The award rendered by the arbitrator or arbitrators shall be final, and judgment may be entered upon it in accordance with applicable law in any court having jurisdiction thereof.

ARTICLE 8
TERMINATION, SUSPENSION OR ABANDONMENT

8.1 This Agreement may be terminated by either party upon not less than seven days' written notice should the other party fail substantially to perform in accordance with the terms of this Agreement through no fault of the party initiating the termination.

8.2 If the Project is suspended by the Owner for more than 30 consecutive days, the Architect shall be compensated for services performed prior to notice of such suspension. When the Project is resumed, the Architect's compensation shall be equitably adjusted to provide for expenses incurred in the interruption and resumption of the Architect's services.

8.3 This Agreement may be terminated by the Owner upon not less than seven days' written notice to the Architect in the event that the Project is permanently abandoned. If the Project is abandoned by the Owner for more than 90 consecutive days, the Architect may terminate this Agreement by giving written notice.

8.4 Failure of the Owner to make payments to the Architect in accordance with this Agreement shall be considered substantial nonperformance and cause for termination.

8.5 If the Owner fails to make payment when due the Architect for services and expenses, the Architect may, upon seven days' written notice to the Owner, suspend performance of services under this Agreement. Unless payment in full is received by the Architect within seven days of the date of the notice, the suspension shall take effect without further notice. In the event of a suspension of services, the Architect shall have no liability to the Owner for delay or damage caused the Owner because of such suspension of services.

8.6 In the event of termination not the fault of the Architect, the Architect shall be compensated for services performed prior to termination, together with Reimbursable Expenses then due and all Termination Expenses as defined in Paragraph 8.7.

8.7 Termination Expenses are in addition to compensation for Basic and Additional Services, and include expenses which are directly attributable to termination. Termination Expenses shall be computed as a percentage of the total compensation for Basic Services and Additional Services earned to the time of termination, as follows:

   .1 Twenty percent of the total compensation for Basic and Additional Services earned to date if termination occurs before or during the predesign, site analysis, or Schematic Design Phases; or

   .2 Ten percent of the total compensation for Basic and Additional Services earned to date if termination occurs during the Design Development Phase; or

   .3 Five percent of the total compensation for Basic and Additional Services earned to date if termination occurs during any subsequent phase.

ARTICLE 9
MISCELLANEOUS PROVISIONS

9.1 Unless otherwise provided, this Agreement shall be governed by the law of the principal place of business of the Architect.

9.2 Terms in this Agreement shall have the same meaning as those in AIA Document A201, General Conditions of the Contract for Construction, current as of the date of this Agreement.

9.3 Causes of action between the parties to this Agreement pertaining to acts or failures to act shall be deemed to have accrued and the applicable statutes of limitations shall commence to run not later than either the date of Substantial Completion for acts or failures to act occurring prior to Substantial Completion or the date of issuance of the final Certificate for Payment for acts or failures to act occurring after Substantial Completion.

9.4 The Owner and Architect waive all rights against each other and against the contractors, consultants, agents and employees of the other for damages, but only to the extent covered by property insurance during construction, except such rights as they may have to the proceeds of such insurance as set forth in the edition of AIA Document A201, General Conditions of the Contract for Construction, current as of the date of this Agreement. The Owner and Architect each shall require similar waivers from their contractors, consultants and agents.

9.5 The Owner and Architect, respectively, bind themselves, their partners, successors, assigns and legal representatives to the other party to this Agreement and to the partners, successors, assigns and legal representatives of such other party with respect to all covenants of this Agreement. Neither Owner nor Architect shall assign this Agreement without the written consent of the other.

9.6 This Agreement represents the entire and integrated agreement between the Owner and Architect and supersedes all prior negotiations, representations or agreements, either written or oral. This Agreement may be amended only by written instrument signed by both Owner and Architect.

9.7 Nothing contained in this Agreement shall create a contractual relationship with or a cause of action in favor of a third party against either the Owner or Architect.

9.8 Unless otherwise provided in this Agreement, the Architect and Architect's consultants shall have no responsibility for the discovery, presence, handling, removal or disposal of or exposure of persons to hazardous materials in any form at the Project site, including but not limited to asbestos, asbestos products, polychlorinated biphenyl (PCB) or other toxic substances.

9.9 The Architect shall have the right to include representations of the design of the Project, including photographs of the exterior and interior, among the Architect's promotional and professional materials. The Architect's materials shall not include the Owner's confidential or proprietary information if the Owner has previously advised the Architect in writing of

AIA DOCUMENT B141 • OWNER-ARCHITECT AGREEMENT • FOURTEENTH EDITION • AIA® • ©1987
THE AMERICAN INSTITUTE OF ARCHITECTS, 1735 NEW YORK AVENUE, N.W., WASHINGTON, D.C. 20006

the specific information considered by the Owner to be confidential or proprietary. The Owner shall provide professional credit for the Architect on the construction sign and in the promotional materials for the Project.

ARTICLE 10
PAYMENTS TO THE ARCHITECT

10.1 DIRECT PERSONNEL EXPENSE

10.1.1 Direct Personnel Expense is defined as the direct salaries of the Architect's personnel engaged on the Project and the portion of the cost of their mandatory and customary contributions and benefits related thereto, such as employment taxes and other statutory employee benefits, insurance, sick leave, holidays, vacations, pensions and similar contributions and benefits.

10.2 REIMBURSABLE EXPENSES

10.2.1 Reimbursable Expenses are in addition to compensation for Basic and Additional Services and include expenses incurred by the Architect and Architect's employees and consultants in the interest of the Project, as identified in the following Clauses.

10.2.1.1 Expense of transportation in connection with the Project; expenses in connection with authorized out-of-town travel; long-distance communications; and fees paid for securing approval of authorities having jurisdiction over the Project.

10.2.1.2 Expense of reproductions, postage and handling of Drawings, Specifications and other documents.

10.2.1.3 If authorized in advance by the Owner, expense of overtime work requiring higher than regular rates.

10.2.1.4 Expense of renderings, models and mock-ups requested by the Owner.

10.2.1.5 Expense of additional insurance coverage or limits, including professional liability insurance, requested by the Owner in excess of that normally carried by the Architect and Architect's consultants.

10.2.1.6 Expense of computer-aided design and drafting equipment time when used in connection with the Project.

10.3 PAYMENTS ON ACCOUNT OF BASIC SERVICES

10.3.1 An initial payment as set forth in Paragraph 11.1 is the minimum payment under this Agreement.

10.3.2 Subsequent payments for Basic Services shall be made monthly and, where applicable, shall be in proportion to services performed within each phase of service, on the basis set forth in Subparagraph 11.2.2.

10.3.3 If and to the extent that the time initially established in Subparagraph 11.5.1 of this Agreement is exceeded or extended through no fault of the Architect, compensation for any services rendered during the additional period of time shall be computed in the manner set forth in Subparagraph 11.3.2.

10.3.4 When compensation is based on a percentage of Construction Cost and any portions of the Project are deleted or otherwise not constructed, compensation for those portions of the Project shall be payable to the extent services are performed on those portions, in accordance with the schedule set forth in Subparagraph 11.2.2, based on (1) the lowest bona fide bid or negotiated proposal, or (2) if no such bid or proposal is received, the most recent preliminary estimate of Construction Cost or detailed estimate of Construction Cost for such portions of the Project.

10.4 PAYMENTS ON ACCOUNT OF ADDITIONAL SERVICES

10.4.1 Payments on account of the Architect's Additional Services and for Reimbursable Expenses shall be made monthly upon presentation of the Architect's statement of services rendered or expenses incurred.

10.5 PAYMENTS WITHHELD

10.5.1 No deductions shall be made from the Architect's compensation on account of penalty, liquidated damages or other sums withheld from payments to contractors, or on account of the cost of changes in the Work other than those for which the Architect has been found to be liable.

10.6 ARCHITECT'S ACCOUNTING RECORDS

10.6.1 Records of Reimbursable Expenses and expenses pertaining to Additional Services and services performed on the basis of a multiple of Direct Personnel Expense shall be available to the Owner or the Owner's authorized representative at mutually convenient times.

ARTICLE 11
BASIS OF COMPENSATION

The Owner shall compensate the Architect as follows:

11.1 AN INITIAL PAYMENT of   ten thousand   Dollars ($10,000.00   )
shall be made upon execution of this Agreement and credited to the Owner's account at final payment.

11.2 BASIC COMPENSATION

11.2.1 FOR BASIC SERVICES, as described in Article 2, and any other services included in Article 12 as part of Basic Services, Basic Compensation shall be computed as follows:

(Insert basis of compensation, including stipulated sums, multiples or percentages, and identify phases to which particular methods of compensation apply, if necessary.)

Compensation shall be based on one of the following Percentages of Construction Cost, as defined in Article 5: For portions of the Project to be awarded under:

A single stipulated-sum construction contract: 7%; A single cost-plus const. contract: 10%;
Separate stipulated-sum construction contract: 9%; Separate cost-plus const. contracts: 12%

11.2.2 Where compensation is based on a stipulated sum or percentage of Construction Cost, progress payments for Basic Services in each phase shall total the following percentages of the total Basic Compensation payable:

(Insert additional phases as appropriate.)

Schematic Design Phase:	Fifteen	percent (15%)
Design Development Phase:	Twenty	percent (20%)
Construction Documents Phase:	Forty	percent (40%)
Bidding or Negotiation Phase:	Five	percent (5%)
Construction Phase:	Twenty	percent (20%)

Total Basic Compensation: one hundred percent (100%)

11.3 COMPENSATION FOR ADDITIONAL SERVICES

11.3.1 FOR PROJECT REPRESENTATION BEYOND BASIC SERVICES, as described in Paragraph 3.2, compensation shall be computed as follows:

Employees' time at a multiple of three (3.0) times their Direct Personnel Expense as defined in Article 10.1.1. Principal's time shall be billed at eighty-five dollars ($85.00) per hour. Consultants' services shall be billed at a multiple of one and one-tenth (1.10) times the amounts billed to the Architect for such services.

11.3.2 FOR ADDITIONAL SERVICES OF THE ARCHITECT, as described in Articles 3 and 12, other than (1) Additional Project Representation, as described in Paragraph 3.2, and (2) services included in Article 12 as part of Additional Services, but excluding services of consultants, compensation shall be computed as follows:

(Insert basis of compensation, including rates and/or multiples of Direct Personnel Expense for Principals and employees, and identify Principals and classify employees, if required. Identify specific services to which particular methods of compensation apply, if necessary.)

Employees' time at a multiple of three (3.0) times their Direct Personnel Expense as defined in Article 10.1.1. Principal's time shall be billed at eighty-five dollars ($85.00) per hour.

11.3.3 FOR ADDITIONAL SERVICES OF CONSULTANTS, including additional structural, mechanical and electrical engineering services and those provided under Subparagraph 3.4.19 or identified in Article 12 as part of Additional Services, a multiple of One and one-tenth (1.10) times the amounts billed to the Architect for such services.
(Identify specific types of consultants in Article 12, if required.)

11.4 REIMBURSABLE EXPENSES

11.4.1 FOR REIMBURSABLE EXPENSES, as described in Paragraph 10.2, and any other items included in Article 12 as Reimbursable Expenses, a multiple of One and one-tenth (1.10) times the expenses incurred by the Architect, the Architect's employees and consultants in the interest of the Project.

11.5 ADDITIONAL PROVISIONS

11.5.1 IF THE BASIC SERVICES covered by this Agreement have not been completed within twenty-four (24) months of the date hereof, through no fault of the Architect, extension of the Architect's services beyond that time shall be compensated as provided in Subparagraphs 10.3.3 and 11.3.2.

11.5.2 Payments are due and payable thirty (30) days from the date of the Architect's invoice. Amounts unpaid sixty (60) days after the invoice date shall bear interest at the rate entered below, or in the absence thereof at the legal rate prevailing from time to time at the principal place of business of the Architect.

(Insert rate of interest agreed upon.) Eight percent (8%) annually

(Usury laws and requirements under the Federal Truth in Lending Act, similar state and local consumer credit laws and other regulations at the Owner's and Architect's principal places of business, the location of the Project and elsewhere may affect the validity of this provision. Specific legal advice should be obtained with respect to deletions or modifications, and also regarding requirements such as written disclosures or waivers.)

AIA DOCUMENT B141 • OWNER-ARCHITECT AGREEMENT • FOURTEENTH EDITION • AIA® • ©1987
THE AMERICAN INSTITUTE OF ARCHITECTS, 1735 NEW YORK AVENUE, N.W., WASHINGTON, D.C. 20006

11.5.3 The rates and multiples set forth for Additional Services shall be annually adjusted in accordance with normal salary review practices of the Architect.

ARTICLE 12
OTHER CONDITIONS OR SERVICES

(Insert descriptions of other services, identify Additional Services included within Basic Compensation and modifications to the payment and compensation terms included in this Agreement.)

It is understood that the following additional services are to be performed: Interior design services required for selection, procurement, and installation of furniture for corporate offices, conference room and product showroom. The Architect's total compensation for these services shall not exceed thirty thousand dollars ($30,000).

This Agreement entered into as of the day and year first written above.

OWNER
Typical Manufacturing Co.
950 Broadway Blvd.
Oakland, California

ARCHITECT
A B C Architects
600 Main St.
San Francisco, California

_____
(Signature) William Jones, President

_____
(Printed name and title)

_____
(Signature) Frank Smith, Principal

_____
(Printed name and title)

Design, Working Drawings and Specifications

The project delivery process begins when the architect enters into a contractual agreement with the owner. By executing the agreement the architect assumes certain legal responsibilities which he endeavors to carry out to the utmost of his capabilities. He agrees to furnish certain basic professional services to a client for which the client compensates him according to the Owner-Architect Agreement. These basic services include design and preparation of working drawings and specifications which the architect provides for the project.

In accordance with the agreement, the parties proceed through the various project stages. The American Institute of Architects' Standard Form of Agreement Between Owner and Architect, Document B141, stipulates the architect's responsibilities in the preparation of design documents in the Schematic Design Phase and the Design Development Phase, and in the execution of working drawings and specifications in the Construction Documents Phase.

As stated in the terms and conditions of the AIA Owner-Architect Agreement, it is the architect's responsibility to obtain the owner's approval of each phase of the work before proceeding to subsequent phases. This procedure clarifies the intentions of the owner, architect, and user before the next phase begins and reduces the necessity for changes in the later stages of design and the execution of working drawings.

In essence, the procedure for design and execution of working drawings specifications is as follows:

First, the architect reviews the program furnished by the owner to determine the requirements of the project and confirms these requirements with the owner. Based upon a mutual understanding of the requirements, the architect prepares Schematic Design Studies. These consist of conceptual drawings and other documents illustrating the functional relationship of the elements and the scale of the project. These are submitted for approval by the owner. In addition, the architect submits to the owner a preliminary estimate of construction cost.

Next, the architect prepares from the approved Schematic Design Studies, for approval by the owner, the Design Development Documents. These consist of drawings and other documents which establish the scope and characteristics of the entire project. These documents illustrate structural, mechanical, and electrical systems, materials, and other essentials as may be required. In addition, the architect advises the owner of any adjustments to the preliminary estimate of construction cost.

Upon entering the Construction Document Phase, the architect prepares from the approved Design Development Documents, for approval by the owner, detailed drawings and specifications. These documents fix and describe the requirements for construction of the entire project including the necessary bidding information. During this phase, the architect also assists the owner in the preparation of bidding forms, the conditions of the construction contract, and the form of agreement between owner and contractor.

In addition, the architect advises the owner of any adjustments in the previous preliminary estimate of construction cost indicated by changes in requirements or general market conditions. Furthermore, the architect assists the owner in filing the required documents for approval of governmental authorities having jurisdiction over the project.

The working drawings and specifications form the largest part of the Contract Documents. The working drawings describe graphically how the building is to be built. In general, working drawings show what to do and specifications tell how to do it. It is the architect's responsibility to ensure that these documents are complete and indicate correctly all dimensions, materials and equipment required for estimating purposes and for preparation of manufacturer's shop drawings. They must also accurately serve as a guide for the contractor's performance of the work. In addition, they must be definite and precise in order to form the basis of a legal contract which may, if a dispute arises, be tested in court.

It should be noted that the conceptual drawings of the Schematic Design Phase are intended primarily for the client and other non-technical people. The drawings of the Design Development Phase are for professional and construction industry personnel as well as for non-technical people. Working drawings and specifications form the medium by which the design drawings, models and related documents are translated into an actual building or structure. The working drawings and specifications are prepared almost entirely for persons working regularly in the construction industry. Thus, the prime function of working drawings is to convey specific and detailed information in a concise and logical manner rather than to be presentation drawings of a design concept.

More time and effort is devoted to the preparation of working drawings and specifications than to any other phase of the architect's services. Generally, forty to fifty percent of the architect's fee is allocated to the Construction Document Phase, whereas twenty-five to thirty-five percent usually goes to the Bidding Phase and Administration of the Construction Contract Phase. If thirty-five percent of the fee is assigned to design, much of the detailed investigation of structural systems and material selection is done in the design phase. Therefore, some of the work required later for the working drawings and specifications is reduced.

A more detailed description of the architect's responsibilities toward the client and the public in the area of design and execution of working drawings and specifications will be covered in the following sections of this book.

Conferences With the Client

The success of a project depends in large part on a solid base of cooperation and understanding established by the architect in conferences with the client. As the client's professional advisor, the architect holds regular and timely conferences with the client and assists him in achieving the best solution to his problem.

In these conferences, the architect discusses with the client alternative project design solutions, the estimated cost of the work, selection of materials and construction systems, and many other related matters. In addition, the architect obtains necessary information from the client, such as his goals and objectives, space needs, detailed requirements and project budget.

Since the process of reading drawings, sketches, and specifications is almost always unfamiliar to the client, as the work proceeds the architect should make every effort to hold regular conferences with the client to ensure the client's understanding and approval of the sketches, drawings, specifications, and other documents.

The minutes of such conferences should be recorded in writing, summarized in a report and distributed to those attending. This avoids the possibility of misunderstandings and costly changes in later stages of the project. In addition, these reports should be dated and properly filed by the architect for future reference.

A successful client-architect relationship is largely dependent upon whether or not the client fully understands the scope and extent of the architect's services and the time required to perform these services. Furthermore, mutually agreed upon deadlines for completion of the various phases of architectural services should be established. In addition, the responsibilities of both architect and client in the project delivery process must be fully understood by both parties.

These responsibilities are specifically stated in the standard AIA Owner-Architect Agreement (client-architect contract) and should be discussed in conferences at the outset of the project. Because the range of services needed to design and complete the client's project often varies from project to project, a review of the services in each phase should be made before execution of the agreement. Additional services not covered by the standard form of agreement should be agreed upon and compensation for these services established.

It is important that the architect does not create expectations in conferences with the client that contradict the protective language in the AIA Owner-Architect Agreement. Responses to questions posed by the owner may give the impression that the architect will deliver more than required by the agreement or the reasonable standard of care. Therefore, the architect may simply wish to call to the owner's attention various paragraphs in the AIA Owner-Architect Agreement in response to certain questions. For example, the architect may wish to respond to questions related to the accuracy of the preliminary estimate of construction cost by referring to provisions of paragraph 5.2.1 and 5.2.2 of the AIA Owner-Architect Agreement. In this way, the architect can ensure that the owner understands that preliminary estimates of construction costs are not guaranteed and that the preliminary estimate of construction cost is not a promise to design the project within a fixed limit of construction cost.

Other questions that often come up are related to work performed by the contractor. To avoid unrealistic expectations, the architect may wish to call to the owner's attention the numerous paragraphs of article 2.6 of the AIA Owner-Architect Agreement that describe the architect's services in detail for the owner. To be certain that the owner understands that the architect does not guarantee the contractor's performance, the architect may wish to point out provisions of paragraph 2.6.6 which state that the architect is not responsible for construction means, methods or techniques or for safety precautions; nor does the architect have control over acts or omissions of the contractor. In this way, the owner can clearly see the difference between the services that the architect intends to perform and those of the contractor.

An estimate for time required for the project should also be discussed in conferences. The client should fully understand that timely completion of the project is a cooperative endeavor. The time required for architectural services varies according to the client's decisions. Therefore, estimates of time should be periodically reviewed by the architect and client in regularly held conferences.

At various stages throughout the project delivery process the client will need to provide specific information and take action on his own part as defined in the AIA Owner-Architect Agreement and the AIA General Conditions of the Contract for Construction. These items should be discussed in regularly held conferences. The client must understand that the project is expedited by his prompt action on all questions, approvals, Change Orders and Certificates for Payment.

During conferences, the client may direct that changes be made to drawings that have been previously approved. The architect should make sure that all changes affecting architectural fees, the cost of the project, the design concept, or the scope of the project are confirmed in writing. Further, the architect should have the client date and initial diagrams or sketches that are generated in conferences to document such changes. In addition, drawings and other documents should be approved by the client in writing at the end of the various phases of the architect's services.

Furthermore, in conferences, the client may propose changes in architectural services to be performed. The architect should be sure that any changes in services are put in writing and made only as an amendment to the original agreement. Recognize that the architect should use caution in modifying the standard provisions of the AIA Owner-Architect Agreement. In general, the architect should first consult with an attorney concerning the effect of such modifications. Also, the architect should check with his professional liability insurance carrier to determine the effects such modifications may have on his insurance coverage.

Note that paragraph 9.6 of the AIA Owner-Architect Agreement deals with the issue of modifications to the agreement. This provision states that the AIA Owner-Architect Agreement represents the entire agreement and supersedes all prior negotiations, either written or oral. Further, the agreement may only be amended by written instrument signed by both owner and architect.

In addition to regularly held conferences with the client, other conferences are held at appropriate stages in the project delivery process. The pre-bid conference is held prior to receiving bids, the pre-construction conference is held prior to start of construction and weekly job conferences are held on a regularly scheduled basis once the construction is under way. These conferences will be discussed in other sections of this manual. The pre-bid conference is discussed in the section entitled "Acceptance of Bids." The pre-construction conference and the weekly job conferences are discussed in the section entitled "Administration of Construction Contract."

Preliminary Design

The architect's responsibility to the client to provide preliminary design services falls within the first two phases of the work he has contracted to perform. These are the Schematic Design Phase and the Design Development Phase. These terms are used to describe the two design and planning processes which establish the size and character of the project.

The Schematic Design Phase starts with conferences with the client concerning the building program. Next, the architect inspects the site and reviews the program of requirements, space needs, geotechnical report, and land survey, all furnished by the owner. Then, using the owner's statement of space needs and program requirements, the architect determines tentative space and volume requirements, and obtains the owner's written approval. At this point, the architect enters into architectural programming.

Note that the AIA Owner-Architect Agreement assumes that the owner will furnish the program. (Any services required by the architect to prepare a program are considered additional services.) Often the owner will simply furnish a list of square footages along with a geotechnical report and land survey. However, recognize that a program furnished by an owner seldom contains a complete evaluation of data obtained from all the sources necessary to truly summarize the project requirements. For instance, rarely would the building code requirements or zoning regulation analysis be included in an owner furnished program. For this reason, the architect generally must integrate owner furnished data with his own research, investigations and evaluations in order to obtain the final written program.

Programming is the problem-seeking process that leads to problem solving in design. The programming should proceed in an objective manner to: establish goals and objectives in order to clarify the owner's requirements; determine project constraints that include governmental codes, zoning ordinances, and regulations, project budget, site conditions, pedestrian and vehicular access, and time limitations; gather information that considers such factors as departmental functions, systems and procedures, movement of materials, personnel and the public, and desired adjacencies; and organize and analyze facts which include tabulations of existing square footages and populations, future expansion, special equipment requirements and in general determine the needs of the owner and the people for whom the facility is designed. In addition, the architect verifies that the program of space requirements is in balance with the budget.

The architect is now ready to state the problem. After evaluating all the information from the previous steps, the architect must arrive at the most important statements concerning the program. Thus, the programming process concludes by defining the problem which must, ultimately, be solved through the design process.

Note that paragraph 2.2.1 of the AIA Owner-Architect Agreement states that the architect reviews the program of requirements furnished by the owner in order to arrive at a mutual understanding of the requirements. Recognize that if the owner does not furnish a program or if the program is sketchy or incomplete, the architect may provide analyses of the owner's needs and program the requirements of the project as an Optional Additional Service as outlined in paragraph 3.4.1. However, these services are provided only if authorized in writing by the owner as outlined in paragraph 3.1.1. If the architect does prepare such a program of requirements, they should be approved in writing by the owner. In any case, the architect should not proceed with the design until a specific program has been both established and also approved by the owner in writing.

Without such a written program the architect could incur liability by not solving all the owner's requirements. If the architect performs programming, a definite checklist of possible wants and needs should be developed by the architect and discussed with the owner. Further, if the owner provides the program, the architect should be aware that it may not be complete. Therefore, the architect should ask questions as may be required to clarify areas and ascertain exact requirements. Then, when the architect has completed defining the problem more concisely, the owner should approve any additions or clarifications in writing. In this case, if the owner has approved the program in writing, the program provides a basis for increases in architectural fees if changes are required by the owner in later phases of the project.

Further, in accordance with paragraph 2.2.2 of the AIA Owner-Architect Agreement, the architect evaluates the owner's program, schedule and budget in terms of each other and subject to the limitations of paragraph 5.2.1. This paragraph states that the architect does not guarantee that costs will not vary from the owner's budget. However, the architect should make recommendations to the owner which will assist the owner's decisions related to balancing the scope, quality and cost of the project.

The actual design results from a combination of intuition, insight, and experienced judgment. Having comprehended the program, the architect generates design studies in the form of sketches and models. A series of alternatives is developed to study the possibilities of the problem and to find an acceptable solution within the project budget.

It is the architect's responsibility to see that the project is designed according to applicable codes regardless of plan checking and permit approval by regulatory agencies such as the Building Department, Zoning Commission and Planning Commission. For this reason the architect should research building code, zoning ordinance and regulatory requirements and check for compliance both before starting to design and also after each design phase as the project proceeds. The review should include not only the building code in the project locality but also any specific regulations pertaining to a particular occupancy type. For instance, a hospital may be governed by both state and local regulations.

If the architect has questions regarding an interpretation of the requirements of the building code or any other regulations governing the project, he should meet with the appropriate governmental officials to discuss the problem. The minutes of the meeting and the architect's understanding of the official's interpretation may then be sent to the official at such agency and the project owner. This allows the parties to respond if they disagree. Therefore, the architect has not only documented the decision making process but also reduced the chances of problems developing at a later date.

Not only will the project be affected by governmental officials involved in protecting public health, safety and welfare, but also by lending institutions, future tenants and other users of the structure. It is important that the architect obtains their input at the earliest possible point in order to maintain an orderly project delivery process.

Based on a mutual understanding of the requirements of the project, the architect prepares and submits Schematic Design Studies consisting of conceptual drawings, sketches, and other documents illustrating the scale and relationships of the project components for approval by the owner. The architect also submits to the owner a preliminary estimate of construction cost based on current area, volume, or other unit costs for the owner's approval.

Upon the client's written approval of the Schematic Design Studies, the preliminary estimate of construction cost and his written authority to proceed, the architect enters the Design Development Phase. This phase is a further refinement by the architect of the Schematic Design Studies.

The architect reviews the owner's specific requirements along with the program and verifies compliance. He re-checks all documents against the legal requirements of the codes, ordinances, and local regulations. In addition, as the documents develop, he obtains tentative project approval from regulatory agencies such as the Building Department, Zoning Commission, and Planning Commission.

The architect then prepares Design Development Documents consisting of more detailed drawings, a site plan, floor plans, sections, elevations, schedules, outline specifications, and other documents to establish in greater detail the extent and character of the entire project as to structural, mechanical, and electrical systems, materials, and other essentials. These documents, as well as an adjusted preliminary estimate of construction costs, are submitted to the owner for written approval before the architect proceeds to the Construction Documents Phase.

During the preliminary design process, alternatives may be developed for overall design concepts or for much smaller items such as possible selections of materials or systems. Recognize that the architect acts as the owner's professional advisor in this capacity and makes recommendations. The owner makes the final decision. When alternatives develop, the architect should discuss specific details with the owner and present such items in terms of the owner's objectives, initial and long term cost, and so on. Once the presentation is made, the architect should let the owner make the decision and then document the decision in writing. Therefore, if problems develop in the future, the owner is less likely to dispute a decision in which he was closely involved. If litigation does develop, the architect can document his presentation of each alternative and the owner's approval of the item in question.

The preliminary estimate of construction cost is important to both the owner and architect alike. The architect is obliged by the Owner-Architect Agreement to design within the project budget if agreed upon in writing. However, with the rapid escalation of the cost of construction, the architect is seldom willing to agree in writing to bring the project in within a fixed limit budget. Nonetheless, the architect does have a professional responsibility to his client to make reasonable selections of materials and equipment which will be suitable with the owner's budget. Therefore, the initial cost estimates guide the architect's thinking as to project scope and material selection. In addition, at an early stage the owner is informed of the type and size of building he can reasonably expect for a given cost.

Selection of Materials

The selection of materials and equipment is the responsibility of the architect. He must determine which materials best suit the design and fulfill the requirements of the program within the economic limitations established by the client.

First, all work must satisfy the building code and other governmental regulations protecting the public health, safety, and welfare. Next, the architect considers such factors as functional requirements, relationship to adjacent materials and assemblies, long-term maintenance, appearance and availability.

The cost of the project is directly affected by the materials selected. The relative cost of materials can change radically due to increases in energy costs, supply and demand, transportation costs, etc. Therefore, the architect must select materials with an awareness of the current market situation. Similarly, materials and the cost of labor to install them will vary widely from one location to another. Further, many materials are available in several thicknesses, grades and finishes. Knowing the performance of these variables will help the architect in the selection of the least expensive grade, finish, or thickness to achieve the desired result. Using a grade of lesser quality and cost is valid only when adequate performance can be assured.

As important as cost control may be, it is the architect's responsibility to make a realistic appraisal of not only initial cost, but also the ultimate cost of using a particular material. An inexpensive material subject to early replacement or expensive maintenance is generally less desirable than more expensive materials or equipment with greater long-range economy. As the owner's professional advisor, the architect must clarify these cost relationships during the selection of materials and encourage the owner to make decisions in light of the total annual cost for the design life of the building.

It should be noted that architects can become involved in litigation due to performance failure of construction products and incorrect use of materials. For example, a problem can develop due to the use of a new product or system that fails. This is because manufacturers are continually developing new products in order to utilize new technology or lower cost. In some cases, these new products have not been fully tested by the manufacturer and do not perform as expected. In other cases, a problem can develop due to misapplication or improper investigation of a new product or system.

Any reduction in the cost of construction or benefit to the completed project through the use of a new product or system is primarily for the benefit of the owner. The architect receives little, if any, benefit from specifying a new product or system. In spite of this, it is quite possible that an architect who specified a product or system that failed will become involved in litigation along with the manufacturer. Often, owners seek to shift a portion of the cost of damages, repairs or replacement to the architect. A great deal of protection can be given to the architect if it can be substantiated that the use of materials conformed concisely to the manufacturer's system and recommended installation procedures. Therefore, it is of great importance to avoid misapplication or incorrect usage of products or systems. It should be noted that many manufacturer's have disclaimers to protect themselves from litigation in the event a rated system has been compromised through the substitution of materials or improper installation procedures.

Another issue is the degree to which the architect must investigate a new product, material or system before specifying it or recommending it to the owner. Courts have not concisely defined what a reasonable investigation of a new product, material or system is. In general, these cases are judged by the reasonable standard of care on an individual basis. However, note that the architect should obtain literature, manufacturer's recommendations, test results and certifications on a material, product, or system. The architect should not rely solely on the manufacturer's sales literature regarding the suitability of new materials, products or systems. Further, the architect should not rely on test reports furnished by the manufacturer unless the scope of the test and the reputation of the testing source is known.

For this reason, the architect may wish to check references from owners of other projects where the material, product or system has been used. Also, the architect may wish to review articles in professional magazines and trade journals that evaluate the item before specifying or recommending its use. Furthermore, the architect must use his own professional judgment concerning the suitability of the use of a product, material or system on a particular project. Also, it is important to recognize that the materials, products and systems selected should have received the approval of building code officials prior to being utilized. For example, wood frame structural connections such as metal post bases or metal column caps should have an approval number of building code officials and be rated for allowable loads, bolt values, and so on.

Obviously, the items that are most crucial to the effective performance of a building are those that lead to the highest potential for litigation in the event of failure. For example, such items include fire protection; structural integrity; the watertight sealing of roofs and walls; and prevention of sound transmission. To obtain the performance required, these systems should be selected and materials installed according to manufacturer's recommendations that are based on test results and reports. Further, such systems should be checked against code requirements for approved assemblies in the project locality to ensure that the system meets regulatory requirements.

For example, if test results indicate that a certain type of party wall consisting of certain products, accessories and installation details will provide a sound transmission coefficient rating of 40, then the architect may reasonably expect that he can obtain the same results from a comparable installation in a project. This will require field observation of installation techniques to insure the contractor has conformed to recommended installation procedures and making sure the same products used in the test are specified and also incorporated in the work.

Even though metal studs, clips, gypsum wall board and insulation from various sources may appear both similar and suitable, the architect would have no evidence that would hold up in court that an untested combination of materials from various manufacturers will provide the same sound transmission coefficient as the tested wall. In the event of unsatisfactory results, the architect would have no proof of which product caused the partition to perform less well than expected.

It is unlikely that the prudent architect will specify unconventional materials or installation procedures. However, material substitutions are often proposed by the contractor in order to reduce costs. Also, questionable installation procedures may occur in the field for the sake of expediency. If the architect has approved such substitutions or installation procedures, he may be held responsible for any resulting lack of performance that may occur. Further, it should be noted that if a product or system fails, the consequential damage claims of third parties such as employees, tenants, the general public, adjacent property owners and so on, can be in excess of the property damage claims of the owner. For this reason, liability to third parties should also be considered when utilizing new products or contemplating cost savings through substitution of products, even if the owner requires the use of a new product or substitution to reduce costs. In this case, the architect may wish to request a written indemnity and hold-harmless agreement from the owner against all claims related to such products or systems. Note, however, that some states prohibit the indemnification of architects for negligent acts.

Where appropriate, the architect may also wish to make written recommendations to the owner concerning the retention of consultants to assist the architect in selection of materials, systems or equipment in certain critical areas of the project. While the architect provides structural, mechanical and electrical engineering consultants as a part of the architect's basic service, other consultants may be required for other critical areas of the project. In accordance with paragraph 4.6.1 of the AIA Owner-Architect Agreement, the owner shall furnish other consultants when reasonably required and requested by the architect. Examples of such consultants include roofing consultants, acoustical consultants, indoor air quality consultants, energy consultants, and elevator consultants.

In some cases, the owner is not willing to approve the expense of retaining such consultants. Further, even if the consultant is hired, recommendations by the consultant may add a significant increase in the cost of the project. For example, an air-quality consultant may recommend monitoring systems to detect indoor air pollution that are designed to last over the life of the building. The owner may determine that such a system is cost prohibitive. Note that in the event the owner rejects the architect's recommendations to retain a consultant or, in the event that the owner rejects the consultant's recommendations, these recommendations can help protect the architect in the event of litigation related to that area of the project. For instance, if a claim for damages for indoor air pollution or contamination was made in the above example, it would be not only less likely that the architect would be involved in the litigation, but also easier for the architect to prove he was not at fault if he does become involved.

Estimates of Cost

As outlined in the AIA Owner-Architect Agreement, the architect submits to the owner a preliminary estimate of construction cost based on current unit cost analysis. The first estimate of cost is submitted at the end of the Schematic Design Phase of the architect's services. The architect also notifies the owner of any adjustments to prior preliminary estimates of construction cost after the Design Development Phase and after the Construction Document Phase. These adjustments may be due to changes in requirements, general market conditions, or changes in the scope of the project.

Providing an accurate preliminary estimate of construction cost is one of the most important aspects of the architect's services. The accuracy and reliability of these estimates is of great importance to the client since there is generally a direct relationship between construction cost and the viability of the project. Furthermore, these estimates are of great importance to the architect since they directly affect his decisions in determining the quality of materials, design elements, and construction systems.

As outlined in paragraph 5.2.1 of the AIA Owner-Architect Agreement, no cost estimate provided by the architect is "guaranteed." He makes a professional analysis of the estimated cost of construction of the project using his best judgment and the most current sources of information available. It is the architect's duty to ensure that the owner understands the basis and limitations of cost estimating and to inform him in writing concerning estimated construction costs to the best of his knowledge and ability, without providing guarantees. The architect should obtain the owner's written approval of the preliminary estimate of construction cost at the conclusion of each phase, in addition to approval of the drawings and other documents. It should also be noted that preparation of detailed cost estimates is provided by the architect only as an additional service.

Furthermore, in accordance with paragraph 5.2.2 of the AIA Owner-Architect Agreement, no fixed limit of construction cost is established by the furnishing of a project budget, unless the fixed limit is agreed upon in writing and signed by both the owner and the architect. In spite of the protective language offered by paragraphs 5.2.1 and 5.2.2, when the construction cost substantially exceeds the preliminary estimate of construction cost, the owner may contend that the architect is responsible for the additional cost, or that the drawings were "worthless", and the architect will become involved in litigation. This could result in a loss of fees or a requirement that the architect make revisions at no additional cost to meet the owner's budget. Further problems may develop if the architect fails to perform his contractual obligation to adjust the preliminary estimate of construction cost and advise the owner of increases in cost as the project develops. Adding to this problem of possible liability exposure is the fact that typical professional liability insurance policies exclude coverage for claims of inaccurate cost estimates.

In addition, the architect should keep the client informed of increases from previous estimates and propose revisions or alternatives to adjust the cost downward if the client requires such changes. It is far more desirable to make such changes at the outset of the project. Making changes after the Construction Documents are completed is not only inefficient but also carries a great deal of liability risk for the architect due to possible errors in coordination among the documents. Therefore, determining the owner's priorities and establishing what is absolutely necessary for a successful project at the outset of the project reduces the chances of overdesigning and provides the architect with a strong defense if the owner contends that the cost is too high at a later date.

Also, the architect should maintain communication with the owner by documenting, in writing, the effect on the project cost of each change the owner makes during the design phases. Owners seldom understand the implications of changes they propose on the construction cost, the production schedule or the cost of the architects services. Note that paragraph 3.3.1 of the AIA Owner-Architect Agreement indicates that making revisions in documents is a Contingent Additional Service when the revisions are inconsistent with approvals previously given by the owner. This also includes revisions made necessary by adjustments in the owner's program or project budget. As outlined in paragraph 3.1.1 of the AIA Owner-Architect Agreement, the architect must notify the owner prior to commencing such services. Furthermore, if the owner determines that such services are not required, he must give prompt written notice. In this case, the architect has no obligation to perform the services. A prompt notification to the owner of each additional cost will not only notify the owner of an increase in architectural fee but will provide the opportunity to document changes that affect the estimated construction cost.

Recognize that it is important to require the owner to approve the drawings, specifications and cost estimates in writing, before proceeding to the next design phase. The architect should not proceed until the approval is received. It should be noted that the owner could temporarily suspend the architect's work by withholding such approval. Paragraph 4.4 of the AIA Owner-Architect Agreement addresses this issue and requires that the owner render decisions on documents submitted in a timely manner to avoid unreasonable delay to the architect. The architect may wish to consider adding a provision to the Owner-Architect Agreement indicating procedures to be followed in the event the owner does not approve the documents. In this case, the architect may wish to require the owner to submit a list of all objections and provide the architect with a reasonable extension of time during which the architect will address the owner's listed objections.

If litigation does develop regarding cost limitations on a project, one of the first issues that must be addressed is the extent to which the architect has undertaken the duty to design within such limitations. If the owner can establish that meeting the cost limitations is required as a condition of the architect receiving payment, failure to meet such a condition may mean that the architect's fees are denied. The main contention of the owner in such cases is that producing drawings and specifications capable of being constructed within the owner's budgetary requirements was an implied condition of the owner's obligation to pay for the architect's services.

Further, if the architect has agreed in writing to design within a fixed limit of construction cost as a part of his contractual obligations, the architect could be held responsible to the owner for damages resulting from costs over such a fixed limit. In this case, the reasonable standard of care is generally applied. This usually allows the architect some excess over the fixed amount. Courts have often allowed up to 10% without imposing liability on the architect. Nevertheless, it should be noted that when the standard of care is applied, cases are based on the circumstances of each individual case. Note that it can also be argued that when bids exceed the preliminary estimate and the owner proceeds with the project, the increased costs reflect the actual value of the structure, and for this reason there is no damage.

In essence, the AIA Owner-Architect Agreement paragraph 5.2.1 endeavors to make it difficult for the owner to require the architect to make accurate cost estimates as a condition of payment. Note that the architect should be careful not to negate this protective language through making oral or written statements that the cost estimates are accurate. Secondly, if a fixed limit of construction cost is established as outlined in paragraph 5.2.2, there are many limitations on the owner. For example, the architect may include contingencies for price escalation; determine materials, equipment and other features; make adjustments in the scope of the project; and include alternates in the bid in order to adjust the construction cost to the fixed limit. Further, if a fixed limit of construction cost is exceeded, the owner is offered four options: (1) give written approval of the increase; (2) authorize rebidding within a reasonable time; (3) abandon the project and terminate the contract in accordance with the terms of the agreement; (4) cooperate in revising the scope and quality of the project to reduce the cost. If the owner elects to take the fourth option and have the architect redesign the project, paragraph 5.2.5 indicates that the architect shall modify the documents without additional fee and this is the limit of the architect's responsibility.

If the architect does not have the expertise to provide reasonably accurate preliminary estimates of construction cost, he may wish to request that the owner provides an independent cost estimating service. The service would provide cost data and preliminary estimates of construction cost at the end of each phase of the architect's design services. Further, such a service may be used to monitor the cost of changes proposed by the owner and be required to keep the owner and architect informed of budget deviations.

The preliminary estimates of construction cost furnished by the architect should be carefully considered in advance. Since the AIA Owner-Architect Agreement requires adjustments at the end of both the Design Development Phase and the Construction Document Phase, these are important responsibilities also. While the protective language in the document is important, it will not protect the architect in all cases, particularly if there is a substantial cost discrepancy and periodic adjustments to the preliminary estimate of construction cost were not made.

There are several ways of obtaining the estimated construction cost of a proposed building. The most frequently used approaches are the area method, the volume method, and the comparative method.

In the area method, the projected number of square feet of the building is multiplied by an estimated cost per square foot. This method is accurate in the case for which cost data are available on a comparable building which has recently been built having similar soil conditions and in the same locality.

In the volume method, the number of cubic feet computed to be contained within the outer surfaces of the building is multiplied by an estimated cost per cubic foot. Again, accuracy depends upon availability of valid cost data on similar buildings. For many types of buildings this may be the more accurate method since the cost per cubic foot for equipment for heating and air conditioning is often directly related to volume.

The comparative method is used when a proposed facility corresponds almost exactly to a facility recently built for which cost data are available. In this approach a cost per office, per classroom, per workstation, etc. is calculated for the existing building and multiplied by the number of workstations, etc. in the proposed facility. Obviously, the proposed workstations or rooms must be identical in size, dimensions, etc. to the existing workstations for this method to be valid.

Seldom are cost data available on an existing comparable building which corresponds exactly to the proposed building. Therefore, accuracy in these methods depends on assigning reasonably correct prices per cubic foot or per square foot and adjusting the unit prices to special conditions of the project. The many variables concerning the cost analysis which must be considered include the following: size of the project; shape of the building; height of the structure; type and quality of construction and finish materials; and unusual foundation problems, if any. In addition, variations in unit costs due to location should be made by using index numbers.

The purpose of the preliminary estimate of construction cost is to correlate the design with the owner's budget. The project budget is not to be confused with the preliminary estimate of construction cost. The project budget is the total development cost and reflects all anticipated costs throughout the project. The amount available in the owner's project budget for construction costs is found by subtracting all other development costs from the total project budget.

The following items are included in a typical project budget: construction costs consisting of the building costs, site work and construction contingency; professional fees for architectural, engineering, landscaping and interior design services; cost of geotechnical reports, the site survey, construction testing and inspection; landscaping and irrigation; equipment and furniture; cost of the land; financing; insurance; taxes and permits; and legal fees.

In summary, the funds in the project budget available for construction should be correlated with the owner's space requirements and the current unit cost of construction in the project locality. An approximate construction cost is arrived at by multiplying the total area of the building by the adjusted unit cost of construction and adding estimated costs for site work and construction contingency. If the owner's requirements are more extensive than can be supported by available funds for construction, a decision must be made by the owner either to reduce requirements or provide additional funds. Often, an acceptable compromise can be achieved by a discussion of space requirements with the owner and a reduction in the scope of the project where careful analysis indicates it can best be made. In addition, the judicious selection of materials and equipment often brings the project further in line with available funds.

CONSTRUCTION COST AND CONSTRUCTION CONTINGENCY

The construction cost is defined in paragraph 5.1.1 of the AIA Owner-Architect Agreement as the total cost or estimated cost to the owner of all elements of the project designed or specified by the architect. Also, paragraph 5.1.2 states that the cost of construction includes labor, materials and equipment furnished by the owner and designed, specified or selected by the architect. Further, the construction cost includes a "reasonable allowance" for contingencies for changes in market conditions and for "changes in the work during construction."

The architect may wish to add a supplement to paragraph 5.1.2 that will define what a "reasonable allowance" for contingencies is and that "changes in the work during construction" includes changes for the architect's errors and omissions. An amount that some firms use for such an allowance for the architect's errors and omissions is 2% - 5% of the construction cost. This amount is justifiable because the architect is required to perform his services only in accordance with the degree of ordinary and reasonable skill and care exercised by other competent architects performing services similar to those required by the agreement. Since most projects are prototypes, utilizing ordinary and reasonable skill and care in the preparation of construction documents will invariably produce some errors and omissions. Therefore, these modifications are aimed at informing the owner in advance of the reasonable standard of care and creating a standard that is capable of determination with less chance of dispute. Further, by incorporating contract language that simply requires professional skill and judgment similar to that reasonably expected from other architects performing similar services, the risk of potential liability is not excessively burdensome on the architect.

Engineering Consultants

The architect's contact with engineering consultants starts in the Schematic Design Phase when he negotiates, prepares, and executes agreements with consultants for various services as required to supplement his own skills and knowledge. Consultation may be necessary on such items as mechanical, electrical, structural and civil engineering; roofing; arts; acoustics; or elevators. Prior to executing an agreement, the architect requests evidence of professional licensing and a certificate of adequate professional liability insurance coverage from all consultants.

There are two types of architect-consultant working relationships. In the indirect relationship, the owner retains the consultant as an advisor on specific needs and special requirements of the project or to compile a better program of project requirements. In the more typical direct relationship, the architect retains the consultant directly to supplement his own knowledge. In this case, the architect must accept responsibility for the consultant's work to the owner, contractor, and the public. The direct architect-consultant relationship is used most frequently. It gives the architect both the responsibility and the authority to control and coordinate the various aspects of the project.

In the direct relationship, the agreement covering a consultant's services should make him legally responsible to the architect for his work. An engineering consultant should be selected with great care, and the agreement should outline the consultant's responsibility for errors and omissions and define his obligation to work within stated budget limitations.

In accordance with paragraph 4.5 of the AIA Owner-Architect

Agreement, the owner furnishes a site survey that is generally prepared by a licensed surveyor or civil engineer. As outlined in paragraph 4.6, the owner furnishes the services of a geotechnical engineer who provides services that include soil tests and evaluations of hazardous materials along with reports and recommendations. Both the surveyor and geotechnical engineer are retained by the owner. This relationship makes them legally responsible to the owner for their reports, surveys and tests. The architect reviews their reports, tests and recommendations but is not responsible to the owner for their content. As outlined in paragraph 4.8 of the AIA Owner-Architect Agreement, the owner furnishes such services, surveys and reports at his expense, and the architect may rely upon their accuracy and completeness.

As described in paragraph 4.6.1 of the AIA Owner-Architect Agreement, the owner is required to furnish the services of consultants other than surveyors or geotechnical engineers when these services are reasonably requested by the architect. An example of such a consultant is an air quality consultant. These services are in addition to normal structural, mechanical and electrical engineering services furnished by the architect as a part of the architect's basic services described in paragraph 2.1.1 of the AIA Owner-Architect Agreement.

Note that the architect typically retains the structural, mechanical and electrical consultants under direct contract. Therefore, the architect is legally responsible to the owner for all working drawings, specifications and other Contract Documents prepared by his consultants for structural, mechanical and electrical portions of the work. The architect's consultants are in turn responsible for their services to the architect. For this reason, the architect should carefully select consulting engineers based on their competence, past experience on projects of a similar nature, and ability to provide good services on the specific project. Further, the architect should check to see that the consultant has sufficient personnel to maintain the production schedule and complete the documents required in a timely manner.

During the Schematic Design Phase the architect confers with consultants to obtain information such as analyses of comparative systems and estimates of their costs based on a square foot or other unit cost basis. The consultants also provide the architect with such items as approximate space requirements and suitable locations for facilities or equipment, an outline of the general scheme of the design, and a description of systems recommended. Furthermore, the architect requires that the consultants examine the site and inform him of their requirements for investigations and tests. In addition, the architect obtains any other information from his consultants for their phase of services that may be required for the coordination and execution of his work.

During the Design Development Phase the consultants prepare design development layouts as required to illustrate and describe the work for their portion of the project. The architect also requires that the consultants investigate and confirm in writing the conformance of their portion of the project with all applicable public and utility regulations. The consultants should request written approval for utility connections. The architect reviews the consultants' layouts, drawings, and outline specifications to confirm adequate provisions for all systems. He reviews the consultants' preliminary estimates of construction costs and estimates of operating costs for their portion of the project. He reviews the results from investigations and tests and forwards the information to appropriate consultants. The consultants' layouts are submitted along with the architect's Design Development Documents for approval by the owner.

During the Construction Documents Phase the consultants prepare working drawings, final specifications, and adjust the preliminary estimate of cost for their portion of the work. The architect checks all work to ensure that all documents have been revised to accomplish the changes ordered. Note that the consultants retain ownership and the copyright on documents they have prepared for their portion of the work in accordance with paragraph 6.1 of the AIA Architect-Consultant Agreement. During the Bidding or Negotiation Phase, the consultants assist the architect and owner in evaluating bids.

During the Construction Administration Phase, the consultants assist the architect by visiting the site and performing field observations for their portion of the work. Just like the architect, the consultants do not have control over construction means, methods or techniques. The consultants assist the architect in determining the payments due the contractor for their portion of the work. Further, upon written request, the consultant makes interpretations of the documents that were prepared by the consultant. The consultants reject work for their parts of the project. In addition, they review and approve the contractor's submittals for their portion of the work. The consultants also assist the architect in preparing Change Orders and Construction Change Directives for their portion of the work. In addition, the consultants assist the architect in determining the date of substantial completion and the date of final completion for their part of the project.

The architect should be certain that the work performed by consultants is under written agreement. The AIA Architect-Consultant Agreement, Document C141, is expressly prepared for this purpose. This document clearly outlines the consultant's scope of responsibility for his portion of the work that in essence parallels the responsibilities of the architect as defined in the AIA Owner-Architect Agreement.

As outlined in the AIA Owner-Consultant Agreement, the architect is under no obligation to pay the consultant until the architect is paid by the owner for the consultant's services. Paragraph 10.3.6 states that payments to consultants will be made "after the architect is paid by the owner." Furthermore, such payments are to be in proportion to the amounts received by the architect that are attributable to the consultant's services.

Since the architect is legally responsible for the work of his consultants, the architect generally requires the consultants to carry various types of insurance coverage. The types of coverage are outlined in paragraphs 10.6.1 and 10.6.2 of the AIA Architect-Consultant Agreement. The amounts of coverage are inserted in paragraph 11.5 of the agreement. The exact requirements and amounts of coverages should be determined after consultation with insurance counsel. Note that paragraph 10.6.4 requires the consultant to submit certificates of insurance coverage to the architect evidencing that the types of insurance required by paragraphs 10.6.1 and 10.6.2 are in force. Further, the coverages indicated on the certificate should be in the amounts required by paragraph 11.5.

In addition, the insurance certificates are required to contain statements that at least 30 days' prior written notice will be given to the architect in the event of cancellation, reduction in or non-renewal of the insurance. The architect may wish to add a clause to paragraph 11.5 to take care of such problems if they arise. For example, the architect may wish to consider adding a provision to paragraph 11.5 such as: should the consultant fail to procure and maintain insurance in the form acceptable to the architect, the architect may, but shall not be obligated to procure and maintain insurance for the consultant. The consultant shall pay the cost thereof and shall furnish all necessary information to make effective such insurance.

Article 12 of the Architect-Consultant Agreement is for the insertion of other conditions or services. Here, the architect may wish to consider adding a provision such as: the services of professional subconsultants engaged by the consultant shall be subject to prior written approval of the architect. In addition, the architect may wish to consider adding an indemnification clause. Such a clause could be added to protect the architect against errors and omissions of the consultant. For instance, the provision could state that the architect and engineer indemnify and hold each other harmless from claims and damages, including legal fees and court costs, resulting from errors, omissions or negligent acts for which either party is legally responsible to the other. Provisions being considered for insertion into the Architect-Consultant Agreement should be reviewed by an attorney prior to execution of the agreement.

4. This Document is intended for use as a "consumable" (consumables are further defined by Senate Report 94-473 on the Copyright Act of 1976). This Document is not intended to be used as "model language" (language taken from an existing document and incorporated, without attribution, into a newly-created document). Rather, it is a standard form which is intended to be modified by appending separate amendment sheets and/or filling in provided blank spaces.

AIA Document C141

Standard Form of Agreement Between Architect and Consultant
1987 EDITION

Recommended for use with the current editions of standard AIA agreement forms and documents.

THIS DOCUMENT HAS IMPORTANT LEGAL CONSEQUENCES; CONSULTATION WITH AN ATTORNEY IS ENCOURAGED WITH RESPECT TO ITS COMPLETION OR MODIFICATION.

AGREEMENT

made as of the   Third   day of   June   in the year of Nineteen Hundred and Eighty Seven.

BETWEEN the Architect:
(Name and address)
   A B C Architects
   600 Main St.
   San Francisco, California

and the Consultant:
(Name and address)
   D E F Engineers
   800 Second St.
   San Francisco, California

Consultant's Discipline or Services: Structural Engineering

The Architect has made an agreement dated   June 1, 1987   with the Owner: Typical Manufacturing Co.
    950 Broadway Blvd., Oakland, California

For the following Project:
(Include detailed description of Project, location, address and scope.)
Typical Manufacturing Co.'s new
Industrial Plant & Office
100 Industrial Blvd.
Hayward, California

which agreement is hereinafter referred to as the Prime Agreement and which provides for furnishing professional services in connection with the Project described therein. A copy of the Prime Agreement (from which compensation amounts may be deleted) is attached, made a part hereof and marked Exhibit A.

The Architect and the Consultant agree as set forth below.

I. THE CONSULTANT shall provide for the Architect, in accordance with the Terms and Conditions of this Agreement, the following professional services, which the Architect is required to provide for the Owner under the attached copy of the Prime Agreement:

(Describe the type of consulting services.)

```
Structural Engineering Services
```

The part of the Project for which the Consultant is to provide such services is hereinafter called This Part of the Project.

The Consultant is an independent contractor for This Part of the Project, responsible for methods and means used in performing the Consultant's services under this Agreement, and is not an employee, agent or partner of the Architect.

II. THE ARCHITECT shall be the general administrator of the professional services for the Project, and shall facilitate the exchange of information among the consultants retained by the Architect for the Project as necessary for the coordination of This Part of the Project.

Except as authorized by the Architect, all communication between the Consultant and the Owner, Contractor or other consultants for the Project shall be forwarded through the Architect.

ARTICLE 1
CONSULTANT'S RESPONSIBILITIES

1.1 CONSULTANT'S SERVICES

1.1.1 The Consultant's services consist of those services performed by the Consultant and Consultant's employees as enumerated in Articles 2 and 3 of this Agreement and any other services included in Article 12.

1.1.2 The Consultant's services shall be performed according to this Agreement with the Architect in the same manner and to the same extent that the Architect is bound by the attached Prime Agreement to perform such services for the Owner. Except as set forth herein, the Consultant shall not have any duties or responsibilities for any other part of the Project.

1.1.3 The Consultant shall designate, when necessary, a representative authorized to act in the Consultant's behalf with respect to This Part of the Project.

1.1.4 The Consultant's services shall be performed in manner, sequence and timing so that they will be coordinated with those of the Architect and other consultants for the Project.

1.1.5 The Consultant shall recommend to the Architect that appropriate investigations, surveys, tests, analyses and reports be obtained as necessary for the proper execution of the Consultant's services.

1.1.6 The Consultant shall provide progress copies of drawings, reports, specifications and other necessary information to the Architect and other consultants for coordination and review. All aspects of the Work designed by the Consultant shall be coordinated by the Consultant, and the Consultant shall also become familiar with the Work designed by the Architect and other consultants as necessary for the proper coordination of This Part of the Project.

1.1.7 The Consultant shall cooperate with the Architect in determining the proper share of the construction budget to be allocated to This Part of the Project.

1.1.8 The Consultant shall not be responsible for the acts or omissions of the Architect, Architect's other consultants, Contractor, Subcontractors, their agents or employees, or other persons performing any of the Work.

1.1.9 The Consultant's services shall be performed as expeditiously as is consistent with professional skill and care and the orderly progress of the Work. Upon request of the Architect, the Consultant shall submit for the Architect's approval a schedule for the performance of the Consultant's services which may be adjusted as the Project proceeds, and shall include allowances for periods of time required for the Owner's and Architect's review and for approval of submissions by authorities having jurisdiction over the Project. Time limits established by this schedule and approved by the Architect shall not, except for reasonable cause, be exceeded by the Consultant or Architect. The Consultant shall not be responsible for delays beyond the Consultant's control.

ARTICLE 2
SCOPE OF CONSULTANT'S BASIC SERVICES

2.1 DEFINITION

2.1.1 The Consultant's Basic Services consist of those services described in Paragraphs 2.2 through 2.6 and other services identified in Article 12 as part of Basic Services.

2.2 SCHEMATIC DESIGN PHASE

2.2.1 The Consultant shall ascertain the requirements for This Part of the Project and shall confirm such requirements to the Architect.

2.2.2 The Consultant shall review alternative systems with the Architect, attend necessary conferences, prepare necessary analyses, drawings and other documents, be available for general consultation, and make recommendations regarding basic systems for This Part of the Project. When necessary, the Consultant shall consult with public agencies and other organizations concerning utility services and requirements.

2.2.3 The Consultant shall prepare and submit to the Architect a preliminary estimate of Construction Cost of This Part of the Project based on current area, volume or other unit costs, as directed by the Architect.

2.3 DESIGN DEVELOPMENT PHASE

2.3.1 When authorized by the Architect, the Consultant shall prepare Design Development Documents from the Schematic Design Studies approved by the Owner and confirmed by the Architect. The Design Development Documents shall consist of drawings and other documents to fix and describe This Part of the Project, including materials, equipment, component systems and types of construction as may be appropriate, all of which are to be approved by the Owner and Architect.

2.3.2 The Consultant shall advise the Architect of adjustments to the preliminary estimate of Construction Cost for This Part of the Project.

2.4 CONSTRUCTION DOCUMENTS PHASE

2.4.1 When authorized by the Architect, the Consultant shall prepare, from the Design Development Documents approved by the Owner and confirmed by the Architect, Drawings and Specifications setting forth in detail the requirements for the construction of This Part of the Project, all of which are to be approved by the Owner and Architect. The Consultant shall prepare the Drawings and Specifications in such format as the Architect may reasonably require.

2.4.2 The Consultant shall advise the Architect of adjustments to previous preliminary estimates of Construction Cost for This Part of the Project indicated by changes in requirements or general market conditions.

2.4.3 The Consultant shall assist the Architect as necessary in connection with the Owner's responsibility for filing the documents concerning This Part of the Project required for the approval of governmental authorities having jurisdiction over the Project.

2.5 BIDDING OR NEGOTIATION PHASE

2.5.1 If required by the Architect, the Consultant shall assist the Architect and Owner in obtaining and evaluating bids or negotiated proposals, and assist in awarding and preparing contracts for construction.

2.6 CONSTRUCTION PHASE—ADMINISTRATION OF THE CONSTRUCTION CONTRACT

2.6.1 The Consultant's responsibility to provide Basic Services for the Construction Phase under this Agreement commences with the award of the Contract for Construction and terminates at the earlier of the issuance to the Owner of the final Certificate for Payment or 60 days after the date of Substantial Completion of the Work, unless extended under terms of Subparagraph 10.3.4.

2.6.2 The Consultant shall assist the Architect in the administration of the Contract for Construction with respect to This Part of the Project, as set forth below and in the edition of AIA Document A201, General Conditions of the Contract for Construction, identified in the Prime Agreement, unless otherwise provided in this Agreement.

2.6.3 The Consultant shall visit the site at intervals appropriate to the stage of construction for This Part of the Project, or as otherwise agreed with the Architect in writing, to become generally familiar with the progress and quality of the Work completed for This Part of the Project and to determine in general if the Work is being performed in a manner indicating that the Work, when completed, will be in accordance with the Contract Documents. However, the Consultant shall not be required to make exhaustive or continuous on-site inspections to check the quality or quantity of the Work for This Part of the Project. On the basis of such on-site observations as a consultant, the Consultant shall keep the Architect informed of the progress of the Work for This Part of the Project and shall endeavor to guard the Owner against defects and deficiencies in such Work. *(More extensive site representation may be agreed to as an Additional Service, as described in Paragraph 3.2.)*

2.6.4 The Consultant shall not have control over or charge of and shall not be responsible for construction means, methods, techniques, sequences or procedures, or for safety precautions and programs in connection with the Work for This Part of the Project, since these are solely the Contractor's responsibility under the Contract for Construction. The Consultant shall not be responsible for the Contractor's or a Subcontractor's schedule or failure to carry out the Work in accordance with the Contract Documents. The Consultant shall not have control over or charge of acts or omissions of the Contractor, Subcontractors, their agents or employees or other persons performing portions of the Work.

2.6.5 The Consultant shall at all times have access to the Work for This Part of the Project, wherever it is in preparation or progress.

2.6.6 Based on the Consultant's observations and evaluations of the Contractor's Applications for Payment, the Consultant shall assist the Architect in determining the amounts due the Contractor for This Part of the Project and shall certify such amounts to the Architect in writing.

2.6.7 Certification for payment by the Consultant to the Architect of the amounts due the Contractor shall constitute a representation to the Architect based on the Consultant's observations at the site as provided in Subparagraph 2.6.3 and on the data comprising the Contractor's Application for Payment, that the Work for This Part of the Project has progressed to the point indicated and that, to the best of the Consultant's knowledge, information and belief, the quality of the Work is in accordance with the Contract Documents. The foregoing representations are subject to an evaluation of such Work for conformance with the Contract Documents upon Substantial Completion, to results of subsequent tests and inspections, to minor deviations from the Contract Documents correctable prior to completion, and to specific qualifications expressed by the Consultant.

2.6.8 Upon written request of the Architect, the Consultant shall furnish to the Architect, with reasonable promptness, in writing or in the form of drawings, interpretations of the Contract Documents prepared by the Consultant, if, in the opinion of the Architect, such interpretations are necessary for the proper execution or progress of the Work.

2.6.9 The Consultant shall within a reasonable time render written recommendations on claims, disputes and other matters in question between the Owner and Contractor relating to the execution or progress of This Part of the Project as provided by the Contract Documents.

2.6.10 The Consultant shall assist the Architect in determining whether the Architect shall reject Work for This Part of the Project which does not conform to the Contract Documents or whether additional inspection or testing is required.

2.6.11 The Consultant shall review and approve, or take other appropriate action upon and forward to the Architect for final disposition, Contractor's submittals such as Shop Drawings, Product Data and Samples with respect to This Part of the Project; but only for the limited purpose of checking for conformance with information given and the design concept expressed in the Contract Documents. The Consultant's action will be taken with such reasonable promptness as to cause no delay in the construction of the Owner or of separate contractors, while allowing sufficient time in the Consultant's professional judgment to permit adequate review. Review of such submittals is not conducted for the purpose of determining the accuracy and completeness of other details such as dimensions and quantities, or for substantiating instructions for installation or performance of equipment or systems designed by the Contractor, all of which remain the responsibility of the Contractor, to the extent required for This Part of the Project by the Contract Documents. The Consultant's review shall not constitute approval of safety precautions or, unless otherwise specifically stated by the Consultant, of construction means, methods, techniques, sequences or procedures. The Consultant's approval of a specific item shall not indicate approval of an assembly of which the item is a component. When professional certification of performance characteristics of materials, systems or equipment is required by the Contract Documents, the Consultant shall be entitled to rely upon such certifications to establish that the materials, systems or equipment will meet the performance criteria required by the Contract Documents.

2.6.12 The Consultant shall assist the Architect in preparing Change Orders for This Part of the Project for the Owner's approval and execution in accordance with the Contract Documents, including those pursuant to Construction Change Directives, and may recommend to the Architect minor changes in the Work not involving an adjustment in the Contract Sum or an extension of the Contract Time which are not inconsistent with the intent of the Contract Documents.

AIA DOCUMENT C141 • ARCHITECT-CONSULTANT AGREEMENT • SIXTH EDITION • AIA® • ©1987
THE AMERICAN INSTITUTE OF ARCHITECTS. 1735 NEW YORK AVENUE, N.W., WASHINGTON, D.C. 20006

2.6.13 The Consultant shall assist the Architect in conducting inspections, with respect to This Part of the Project, to determine the date or dates of Substantial Completion and the date of final completion, and shall review and approve, or take other appropriate action on, the Contractor's list of items to be completed or corrected, and shall forward the list to the Architect for final disposition. The Consultant shall assist the Architect in receiving and forwarding to the Owner for the Owner's review and records written warranties and related documents required by the Contract Documents assembled by the Contractor with respect to This Part of the Project. If requested, the Consultant shall issue to the Architect a final certification in writing with respect to final payment for This Part of the Project.

ARTICLE 3
ADDITIONAL SERVICES

3.1   GENERAL

3.1.1   The services described in this Article 3 are not included in Basic Services unless identified in Article 12 and shall only be provided if authorized or confirmed in writing by the Architect.

3.2   PROJECT REPRESENTATION BEYOND BASIC SERVICES

3.2.1   If more extensive representation at the site than is described under Subparagraph 2.6.3 is required for This Part of the Project, the Consultant shall, if requested by the Architect, provide one or more Project Representatives to assist the Consultant in carrying out such additional on-site responsibilities.

3.2.2   Project Representatives shall be selected, employed and directed by the Consultant, and the Consultant shall be compensated therefor as agreed by the Architect and Consultant. The duties, responsibilities and limitations of authority of Project Representatives shall be as described in an exhibit to this Agreement.

3.2.3   Through the observations by such Project Representatives, the Consultant shall endeavor to provide further protection for the Owner against defects and deficiencies in the Work for This Part of the Project, but the furnishing of such project representation shall not modify the rights, responsibilities or obligations of the Consultant as described elsewhere in this Agreement.

3.3   CONTINGENT ADDITIONAL SERVICES

3.3.1   Making revisions in Drawings, Specifications or other documents when such revisions are:

   .1   inconsistent with approvals or instructions previously given by the Owner, including revisions made necessary by any adjustments in the program or Project budget;

   .2   required by the enactment or revision of codes, laws or regulations subsequent to the preparation of such documents; or

   .3   required as a result of the Owner's failure to render decisions in a timely manner.

3.3.2   Providing services required because of significant changes for This Part of the Project including, but not limited to, changes in size, quality and complexity, Owner's schedule, method of bidding or negotiating and contracting for construction Work.

3.3.3   Preparing Drawings, Specifications and other documentation and supporting data, and providing other services in connection with Change Orders and Construction Change Directives, other than those required as a result of negligent error or omission by the Consultant.

3.3.4   Providing services in connection with evaluating substitutions proposed by the Contractor and making subsequent revisions to Drawings, Specifications and other documentation resulting therefrom.

3.3.5   Providing consultation concerning replacement of Work damaged by fire or other cause during construction, and furnishing services required in connection with the replacement of such Work.

3.3.6   Providing services made necessary by the default of the Contractor, or by major defects or deficiencies in the Work of the Contractor, or by failure of performance of either the Owner or Contractor under the Contract for Construction.

3.3.7   Providing services in evaluating an extensive number of claims submitted by the Contractor or others in connection with the Work for This Part of the Project.

3.3.8   Providing services in connection with a public hearing, arbitration proceeding or legal proceeding.

3.4   OPTIONAL ADDITIONAL SERVICES

3.4.1   Providing analyses of the Owner's needs, and programming the requirements for This Part of the Project.

3.4.2   Providing financial feasibility or other special studies.

3.4.3   Providing planning surveys, site evaluations or comparative studies of prospective sites.

3.4.4   Providing special surveys, environmental studies and submissions required for approvals of governmental authorities or others having jurisdiction over the Project.

3.4.5   Providing services relative to future facilities, systems and equipment.

3.4.6   Providing services to investigate existing conditions or facilities, or to make measured drawings thereof.

3.4.7   Providing services to verify the accuracy of drawings or other information furnished by the Architect.

3.4.8   Providing coordination of construction performed by separate contractors or by the Owner's own forces and coordination of services required in connection with construction performed and equipment supplied by the Owner.

3.4.9   Providing services in connection with the work of a construction manager or separate consultants retained by the Owner.

3.4.10   Providing detailed estimates of Construction Cost.

3.4.11   Providing detailed quantity surveys or inventories of material, equipment and labor.

3.4.12   Providing analyses of owning and operating costs.

3.4.13   Providing services or special consultants related to interior design services and other similar services required for, or in connection with, the selection, procurement or installation of furniture, furnishings and related equipment.

3.4.14   Providing services for planning tenant or rental spaces.

3.4.15 Making investigations, inventories of materials or equipment or valuations, and detailed appraisals of existing facilities.

3.4.16 Preparing a set of reproducible record drawings showing significant changes in the Work for This Part of the Project made during construction, based on marked-up prints, drawings and other data furnished by the Contractor to the Architect.

3.4.17 Providing assistance in the utilization of equipment or systems, such as initial start-up or testing, adjusting and balancing, preparation of operation and maintenance manuals, training personnel for operation and maintenance, and consultation during operation.

3.4.18 Providing services after issuance to the Owner of the final Certificate for Payment, or in the absence of a final Certificate for Payment, more than 60 days after the date of Substantial Completion of the Work for This Part of the Project.

3.4.19 Providing services of subconsultants for other than the normal consulting services for This Part of the Project provided as part of Basic Services.

3.4.20 Providing coordination of Work in connection with equipment supplied by the Owner.

3.4.21 Providing any other services not otherwise included in this Agreement or not customarily furnished in accordance with generally accepted consulting practice for This Part of the Project.

ARTICLE 4
ARCHITECT'S RESPONSIBILITIES

4.1 The Architect shall, with reasonable promptness, provide available information regarding requirements for This Part of the Project.

4.2 The Architect may designate a representative authorized to act on the Architect's behalf with respect to This Part of the Project. The Architect or such authorized representative shall render decisions in a timely manner pertaining to documents submitted by the Consultant in order to avoid unreasonable delay in the orderly and sequential progress of the Consultant's services.

4.3 If the Consultant considers it necessary for This Part of the Project, the Architect shall request that the Owner furnish the services of other consultants when such services are reasonably required by the scope of the Project, including surveys describing physical characteristics, legal limitations and utility locations for the site of the Project and a written legal description of the site. The surveys and legal information shall include, as applicable, grades and lines of streets, alleys, pavements and adjoining property and structures; adjacent drainage; rights-of-way, restrictions, easements, encroachments, zoning, deed restrictions, boundaries and contours of the site; locations, dimensions and necessary data pertaining to existing buildings, other improvements and trees; and information concerning available utility services and lines both public and private, above and below grade, including inverts and depths. All information on the survey shall be referenced to a project benchmark.

4.4 On the Consultant's request for This Part of the Project, the Architect shall furnish to the Consultant, with reasonable promptness, (1) detailed layouts showing the location of connections, and (2) tabulations giving sizes and loads of equip-

ment designed, specified or furnished by others for incorporation into other parts of the Project.

4.5 On the Consultant's request for This Part of the Project, the Architect shall request the Owner to furnish, with reasonable promptness, the services of geotechnical engineers. Such services may include, but are not limited to, test borings, test pits, determinations of soil bearing values, percolation tests, evaluations of hazardous materials, ground corrosion and resistivity tests, including necessary operations for anticipating subsoil conditions, with reports and appropriate professional recommendations.

4.6 On the Consultant's request for This Part of the Project, the Architect shall request the Owner to furnish structural, mechanical, chemical, air and water pollution tests, tests for hazardous materials and other laboratory and environmental tests, inspections and reports required by law or the Contract Documents.

4.7 The services, information, surveys and reports required by Paragraphs 4.3 through 4.6 shall be furnished at no expense to the Consultant who shall be entitled to rely upon the accuracy and completeness thereof.

4.8 Prompt written notice shall be given by the Architect to the Consultant if the Architect becomes aware of any fault or defect with respect to This Part of the Project or nonconformance with the Contract Documents.

4.9 The Architect shall confer with the Consultant before issuing interpretations or clarifications of documents prepared by the Consultant and shall request the recommendation of the Consultant before providing interpretations or clarifications of Shop Drawings, Product Data, Samples or other submissions of the Contractor, or of Change Orders and Construction Change Directives affecting This Part of the Project.

4.10 The Architect shall furnish to the Consultant a copy of preliminary estimates of Construction Cost or detailed estimates of Construction Cost as submitted to the Owner, bidding documents, bid tabulations, negotiated proposals and Contract Documents, including Change Orders and Construction Change Directives as issued, to the extent that they pertain to This Part of the Project.

4.11 The Architect shall advise the Consultant of the identity of other consultants participating in the Project and the scope of their services.

4.12 The Architect shall review the Consultant's work for compliance with the Owner's program and for overall coordination with the architectural and engineering requirements.

ARTICLE 5
CONSTRUCTION COST

5.1 DEFINITION

5.1.1 The Construction Cost shall be the total cost or estimated cost to the Owner of all elements of the Project designed or specified by the Architect or the Architect's consultants. The Construction Cost of This Part of the Project shall be the total cost or estimated cost to the Owner of all elements of the Project designed or specified by the Consultant.

5.1.2 The Construction Cost or the Construction Cost of This Part of the Project shall include the cost at current market rates of labor and materials furnished by the Owner and equipment designed, specified, selected or specially provided for by the

AIA DOCUMENT C141 • ARCHITECT-CONSULTANT AGREEMENT • SIXTH EDITION • AIA® • ©1987
THE AMERICAN INSTITUTE OF ARCHITECTS, 1735 NEW YORK AVENUE, N.W., WASHINGTON, D.C. 20006

Architect or Consultant, plus a reasonable allowance for the Contractor's overhead and profit. In addition, a reasonable allowance for contingencies shall be included for market conditions at the time of bidding and for changes in the Work during construction.

5.1.3 Construction Cost does not include the compensation of the Architect and Architect's consultants, the costs of the land, rights-of-way and financing, or other costs which are the responsibility of the Architect as provided in Article 4 of this Agreement, or which are the responsibility of the Owner as defined in the Prime Agreement.

5.2 RESPONSIBILITY FOR CONSTRUCTION COST

5.2.1 Evaluations of the Owner's Project budget, preliminary estimates of Construction Cost and detailed estimates of Construction Cost, if any, prepared by the Consultant for This Part of the Project, represent the Consultant's best judgment as a professional familiar with the construction industry. It is recognized, however, that neither the Consultant nor Architect has control over the cost of labor, materials or equipment, over the Contractor's methods of determining bid prices, or over competitive bidding, market or negotiating conditions. Accordingly, the Consultant cannot and does not warrant or represent that bids or negotiated prices for This Part of the Project will not vary from the Owner's Project budget or from any estimate of Construction Cost or evaluation prepared or agreed to by the Consultant.

5.2.2 The Architect and Consultant shall establish, if practicable, a fixed limit of Construction Cost for This Part of the Project, which may be fixed independently of the limit, if any, established in the Prime Agreement. If such a fixed limit has been established, the Consultant, after conferring with the Architect, shall be permitted to include contingencies for design, bidding and price escalation, to determine what materials, equipment, component systems and types of construction are to be included in the Contract Documents with respect to This Part of the Project, to make reasonable adjustments in the scope of This Part of the Project and to include in the Contract Documents alternate bids to adjust the Construction Cost to the fixed limit for This Part of the Project. Such fixed limit shall be increased in the amount of any increase in the Contract Sum related to This Part of the Project occurring after execution of the Contract for Construction.

5.2.3 If the Bidding or Negotiation Phase for This Part of the Project has not commenced within 90 days after the Architect submits the Construction Documents to the Owner, any Project budget or fixed limit of Construction Cost for This Part of the Project established as a condition of this Agreement shall be adjusted to reflect changes in the general level of prices in the construction industry between the date of submission of the Construction Documents to the Owner and the date on which bids or proposals are sought.

5.2.4 If a fixed limit of Construction Cost for This Part of the Project (adjusted as provided in Subparagraph 5.2.3) is exceeded by the lowest bona fide bid or negotiated proposal, the Architect may require the Consultant, without additional charge, to modify the Consultant's Drawings, Specifications and other documents for This Part of the Project as necessary to bring the Construction Cost thereof within such fixed limit for This Part of the Project. If it was not practicable to establish a fixed limit of Construction Cost for This Part of the Project, and if the lowest bona fide bid or negotiated proposal, the detailed estimate of Construction Cost or the preliminary estimate of Construction Cost established for the entire Project (including

the bidding contingency) exceeds the fixed limit of Construction Cost of the entire Project and the budget for This Part of the Project is exceeded, the Architect may require that the Drawings, Specifications and other documents prepared by the Consultant be modified without additional compensation to the Consultant, so that the Consultant may bear a reasonable portion of the burden of reducing the Construction Cost of This Part of the Project so that the fixed limit of Construction Cost for the entire Project is not exceeded. The providing of such service shall be the limit of the Consultant's responsibility in this regard, and having done so, the Consultant shall be entitled to compensation for all services performed in accordance with this Agreement.

ARTICLE 6
USE OF CONSULTANT'S DRAWINGS, SPECIFICATIONS AND OTHER DOCUMENTS

6.1 Except for reference and coordination purposes in connection with future additions or alterations to the Work, Drawings, Specifications and other documents prepared by the Consultant are instruments of the Consultant's service for use solely with respect to this Project and, unless otherwise provided, the Consultant shall be deemed the author of these documents and shall retain all common law, statutory and other reserved rights, including the copyright. The Architect and Owner shall be permitted to retain copies, including reproducible copies, of the Consultant's Drawings, Specifications and other documents for information and reference. The Consultant's Drawings, Specifications or other documents shall not be used by the Architect or others on other projects, or for completion of this Project by others, unless the Consultant is adjudged to be in default under this Agreement, except by agreement in writing and with appropriate compensation to the Consultant.

6.2 The Architect and Consultant shall not make changes in each other's Drawings, Specifications and other documents without written permission of the other party.

6.3 The Consultant shall maintain on file and make available to the Architect design calculations for This Part of the Project, and shall furnish copies thereof to the Architect on request.

6.4 Submission or distribution of Consultant's documents to meet official regulatory requirements or for similar purposes in connection with This Part of the Project is not to be construed as publication in derogation of the Consultant's reserved rights.

ARTICLE 7
ARBITRATION

7.1 Claims, disputes or other matters in question between the parties to this Agreement arising out of or relating to this Agreement or the breach thereof, shall be subject to and decided by arbitration in accordance with the Construction Industry Arbitration Rules of the American Arbitration Association currently in effect unless the parties mutually agree otherwise.

7.2 Demand for arbitration shall be filed in writing with the other party to this Agreement and with the American Arbitration Association. A demand for arbitration shall be made within a reasonable time after the claim, dispute or other matter in question has arisen. In no event shall the demand for arbitration be made after the date when institution of legal or equitable proceedings based on such claim, dispute or other matter in question would be barred by the applicable statutes of limitations.

7.3 No arbitration arising out of or relating to this Agreement shall include, by consolidation, joinder or in any other manner, an additional person or entity not a party to this Agreement except by written consent containing a specific reference to this Agreement and signed by the Architect, Consultant and any other person or entity sought to be joined. Consent to arbitration involving an additional person or entity shall not constitute consent to arbitration of any claim, dispute or other matter in question not described in the written consent or with a person or entity not named or described therein. The foregoing agreement to arbitrate and other agreements to arbitrate with an additional person or entity duly consented to by the parties to this Agreement shall be specifically enforceable in accordance with applicable law in any court having jurisdiction thereof.

7.4 The award rendered by the arbitrator or arbitrators shall be final, and judgment may be entered upon it in accordance with applicable law in any court having jurisdiction thereof.

ARTICLE 8
TERMINATION, SUSPENSION OR ABANDONMENT

8.1 This Agreement may be terminated at such time as the Prime Agreement is terminated. The Architect shall promptly notify the Consultant of such termination.

8.2 If the Project is suspended for more than 30 consecutive days, for reasons other than the fault of the Consultant, the Consultant shall be compensated for services performed prior to notice of such suspension. When the Project is resumed, the Consultant's compensation shall be equitably adjusted to provide for expenses incurred in the interruption and resumption of the Consultant's services.

8.3 If the Project is abandoned by the Architect because of the Owner's abandonment of the Project for more than 90 consecutive days, the Consultant may terminate this Agreement by giving written notice.

8.4 This Agreement may be terminated by either party upon not less than seven days' written notice should the other party fail substantially to perform in accordance with the terms of this Agreement through no fault of the party initiating the termination.

8.5 If the Prime Agreement is terminated through no fault of the Consultant, the Consultant's compensation for This Part of the Project, for services performed and expenses incurred prior to the date of termination, and Termination Expenses, if any, shall be limited to a proportional share of payment received by the Architect.

ARTICLE 9
MISCELLANEOUS PROVISIONS

9.1 Unless otherwise provided, this Agreement shall be governed by the law of the principal place of business of the Architect.

9.2 Terms in this Agreement shall have the same meanings as those in AIA Document A201, General Conditions of the Contract for Construction, current as of the date identified in the Prime Agreement.

9.3 Causes of action between the parties to this Agreement pertaining to acts or failures to act shall be deemed to have accrued and the applicable statutes of limitations shall commence to run not later than either the date of Substantial Completion for acts or failures to act occurring prior to Substantial

Completion or the date of issuance of the final Certificate for Payment for acts or failures to act occurring after Substantial Completion.

9.4 The Architect and Consultant waive all rights against each other and against the contractors, consultants, agents and employees of the other for damages, but only to the extent covered by property insurance during construction, except such rights as they may have to the proceeds of such insurance as set forth in the edition of AIA Document A201, General Conditions of the Contract for Construction, current as of the date identified in the Prime Agreement. The Consultant and Architect shall require similar waivers from the Consultant's contractors, consultants and agents.

9.5 The Architect and Consultant, respectively, bind themselves, their partners, successors, assigns and legal representatives to the other party to this Agreement and to the partners, successors, assigns and legal representatives of such other party with respect to all covenants of this Agreement. Neither Architect nor Consultant shall assign this Agreement without written consent of the other.

9.6 This Agreement represents the entire and integrated agreement for This Part of the Project between the Architect and Consultant and supersedes all prior negotiations, representations or agreements, either written or oral. This Agreement may be amended only by written instrument signed by both Architect and Consultant.

9.7 Nothing contained in this Agreement shall create a contractual relationship with or a cause of action in favor of a third party against either the Architect or Consultant.

9.8 Unless otherwise provided in this Agreement, the Architect and Consultant shall have no responsibility for the discovery, presence, handling, removal, or disposal of or exposure of persons to hazardous materials in any form at the Project site, including but not limited to asbestos, asbestos products, polychlorinated biphenyl (PCB) or other toxic substances.

ARTICLE 10
PAYMENTS TO THE CONSULTANT

10.1 DIRECT PERSONNEL EXPENSE AND DIRECT SALARY EXPENSE

10.1.1 Direct Personnel Expense is defined as the direct salaries of the Consultant's personnel engaged on the Project, and the portion of the cost of their mandatory and customary contributions and benefits related thereto, such as employment taxes and other statutory employee benefits, insurance, sick leave, holidays, vacations, pensions, and similar contributions and benefits.

10.1.2 Direct Salary Expense is defined as the direct salaries of the Consultant's personnel engaged on the Project, but does not include the cost of related mandatory and customary contributions and benefits.

10.2 REIMBURSABLE EXPENSES

10.2.1 Reimbursable Expenses are in addition to compensation for Basic and Additional Services and include expenses incurred by the Consultant and Consultant's employees and subconsultants in the interest of the Project, to the extent they are reimbursable by the Owner under the Prime Agreement, as identified in the following Clauses.

AIA DOCUMENT C141 • ARCHITECT-CONSULTANT AGREEMENT • SIXTH EDITION • AIA® • ©1987
THE AMERICAN INSTITUTE OF ARCHITECTS, 1735 NEW YORK AVENUE, N.W., WASHINGTON, D.C. 20006

10.2.1.1 Expense of transportation in connection with the Project; expenses in connection with authorized out-of-town travel; long-distance communications; and fees paid for securing approvals of authorities having jurisdiction over the Project.

10.2.1.2 Expense of reproductions, postage and handling of Drawings, Specifications and other documents.

10.2.1.3 If authorized in advance by the Architect, expense of overtime work requiring higher than regular rates.

10.2.1.4 Expense of renderings, models and mock-ups requested by the Architect.

10.2.1.5 Expense of additional insurance coverage or limits, including professional liability insurance in excess of the requirements of Paragraph 11.5.

10.2.1.6 Expense of computer-aided design and drafting equipment time when used in connection with This Part of the Project.

10.3 PAYMENTS ON ACCOUNT OF SERVICES

10.3.1 Payments for Basic Services, Additional Services and Reimbursable Expenses shall be made on the basis set forth in Article 11.

10.3.2 The Architect shall disclose to the Consultant, prior to the execution of this Agreement, contingent or other special provisions relative to compensation that are included in the Architect's understanding with the Owner or in the Prime Agreement.

10.3.3 The Consultant shall submit invoices for Basic Services, Additional Services and Reimbursable Expenses in accordance with the provisions of the Prime Agreement. The Architect shall review such invoices and, if they are considered incorrect or untimely, the Architect shall review the matter with the Consultant and confirm in writing to the Consultant within ten days from receipt of the Consultant's billing the Architect's understanding of the disposition of the issue.

10.3.4 If and to the extent that the time initially established in Subparagraph 11.4.1 of this Agreement is exceeded or extended through no fault of the Consultant, compensation for services rendered during the additional period of time shall be computed in the matter set forth in Paragraph 11.2.

10.3.5 When compensation is based on a percentage of Construction Cost, and portions of the Project are deleted or otherwise not constructed, compensation for those portions of the Project shall be payable to the extent services are performed on those portions, in accordance with the schedule set forth in Subparagraph 11.1.2, based on (1) the lowest bona fide bid or negotiated proposal, or (2) if no such bid or proposal is received, the most recent preliminary estimate of Construction Cost or detailed estimate of Construction Cost for This Part of the Project.

10.3.6 Payments to the Consultant will be made promptly after the Architect is paid by the Owner under the Prime Agreement. The Architect shall exert reasonable and diligent efforts to collect prompt payment from the Owner. The Architect shall pay the Consultant in proportion to amounts received from the Owner which are attributable to the Consultant's services rendered.

10.4 PAYMENTS WITHHELD

10.4.1 No deductions shall be made from the Consultant's compensation on account of penalty, liquidated damages or other sums withheld from payments to contractors, or on account of the cost of changes in the Work other than those for which the Consultant has been found to be liable.

10.5 CONSULTANT'S ACCOUNTING RECORDS

10.5.1 Records of Reimbursable Expenses and expenses pertaining to Additional Services and services performed on the basis of a multiple of Direct Personnel Expense shall be available to the Architect or Architect's authorized representative at mutually convenient times.

10.6 INSURANCE

10.6.1 If required by the Architect, the Consultant shall obtain insurance covering claims arising out of the performance of professional services under this Agreement and caused by errors, omissions, or negligent acts for which the Consultant is legally liable. This insurance, if available, shall be maintained in force by the Consultant for a reasonable period after the date of Substantial Completion of the Project as agreed to by the Architect and Consultant.

10.6.2 Unless otherwise agreed, the Architect and Consultant shall each provide insurance to protect themselves from claims under workers' or workmen's compensation acts; from claims for damages because of bodily injury, including personal injury, sickness, disease, or death of any employees or of any other person; from claims for damages because of injury to or destruction of property including loss of use resulting therefrom; and from damage to or destruction of property including valuable papers and records coverage and including loss of use resulting therefrom.

10.6.3 The insurance required pursuant to Subparagraphs 10.6.1 and 10.6.2 shall be in not less than the minimum limits required by law or by Paragraph 11.5.

10.6.4 The Consultant shall furnish to the Architect Certificates of Insurance evidencing the insurance required by Subparagraphs 10.6.1 and 10.6.2, including appropriate evidence that each type of insurance includes appropriate coverage for this specific Project. Certificates shall contain provisions that at least 30 days' prior written notice will be given to the Architect in the event of cancellation, reduction in or nonrenewal of the insurance.

ARTICLE 11
BASIS OF COMPENSATION

The Architect shall compensate the Consultant as follows:

11.1 BASIC COMPENSATION

11.1.1 FOR BASIC SERVICES, as described in Paragraphs 2.2 through Subparagraph 2.6.13 and other services included in Article 12 as part of Basic Services, Basic Compensation shall be computed as follows:

(Insert basis of compensation, including stipulated sums, multiples or percentages, and identify phases to which particular methods of compensation apply, if necessary.)

Compensation shall be based on one of the following Percentages of Construction Cost as defined in Article 5: For portions of the Project to be awarded under: A single stipulated-sum construction contract:0.75%; A single cost-plus const. contract: 1.0% Separate stipulated-sum construction contract:0.90%; Separate cost-plus const. contracts;1.2%

11.1.2 Where compensation is based on a stipulated sum or percentage of Construction Cost for This Part of the Project, progress payments for Basic Services in each phase shall total the following percentages of the total Basic Compensation payable:

(Insert additional phases as appropriate.)

Schematic Design Phase:	Fifteen	percent (15 %)
Design Development Phase:	Twenty	percent (20 %)
Construction Documents Phase:	Forty	percent (40 %)
Bidding or Negotiation Phase:	Five	percent (5 %)
Construction Phase:	Twenty	percent (20 %)
Total Basic Compensation		one hundred percent (100%)

11.2 COMPENSATION FOR ADDITIONAL SERVICES

11.2.1 FOR PROJECT REPRESENTATION BEYOND BASIC SERVICES, as described in Paragraph 3.2, compensation shall be computed as follows:

Employees' time at a multiple of three (3.0) times their Direct Personnel Expense as defined in Article 10.1.1. Principal's time shall be billed at eighty dollars ($80.00) per hour. Subconsultants' services shall be billed at a multiple of one and one-tenth (1.10) times the amounts billed to the Consultant for such services.

11.2.2 FOR ADDITIONAL SERVICES OF THE CONSULTANT, as described in Article 3, other than (1) Additional Project Representation described in Subparagraphs 3.2.1 through 3.2.3, (2) services required to meet a budget modified by the Owner and (3) services excluding services of subconsultants for other than the normal consulting services for This Part of the Project, compensation shall be computed as follows:

(Insert basis of compensation, including rates and/or multiples of Direct Personnel Expense for Principals and employees, and identify Principals and classify employees, if required. Identify specific services to which particular methods of compensation apply, if necessary.)

Employees' time at a multiple of three (3.0) times their Direct Personnel Expense as defined in Article 10.1.1. Principal's time shall be billed at eighty dollars ($80.00) per hour.

AIA DOCUMENT C141 • ARCHITECT-CONSULTANT AGREEMENT • SIXTH EDITION • AIA® • ©1987
THE AMERICAN INSTITUTE OF ARCHITECTS, 1735 NEW YORK AVENUE, N.W., WASHINGTON, D.C. 20006

11.2.3 FOR ADDITIONAL SERVICES OF SUBCONSULTANTS for other than normal consulting services for This Part of the Project, as provided under Subparagraph 11.2.2 or identified in Article 12 as Additional Services, a multiple of one and one-tenth (1.10) times the amounts billed to the Consultant for such services.

(Identify specific types of subconsultants in Article 12, if required.)

11.3 REIMBURSABLE EXPENSES

11.3.1 FOR REIMBURSABLE EXPENSES, as described in Paragraph 10.2, a multiple of one and one-tenth (1.10) times the expenses incurred by the Consultant, Consultant's employees and subconsultants in the interest of This Part of the Project.

11.4 ADDITIONAL PROVISIONS

11.4.1 IF BASIC SERVICES covered by this Agreement have not been completed within twenty-four (24) months of the date hereof, through no fault of the Consultant for This Part of the Project, extension of the Consultant's services beyond that time shall be considered Additional Services and the amounts of compensation set forth in this Agreement shall be equitably adjusted as provided in Subparagraph 11.2.2.

11.4.2 The rates and multiples set forth for Additional Services shall be annually adjusted in accordance with normal salary review practices of the Consultant.

11.4.3 PAYMENT PROVISIONS

(Insert provisions as to conditions, contingencies, times, manner and other particulars concerning payments, including any provisions for the payment of interest.)

Payments shall be made monthly and shall be in proportion to services performed within each phase of service, on the basis set forth in Subparagraph 11.1.2.

Payments are due and payable thirty days from date of Engineer's invoice. Amounts unpaid sixty days after the invoice shall bear interest at the rate of eight percent (8%) annually.

11.5 INSURANCE COVERAGES

(After consultation with insurance counsel for the Architect and Consultant, insert the minimum limits of insurance required for each type of insurance required in Subparagraphs 10.6.1 and 10.6.2, and other coverages which may be necessary to protect them. If insurance required is in excess of what the Consultant normally carries, the Consultant will be reimbursed if the Architect is reimbursed by the Owner.)

(Author's note: The following insurance requirements are for study material only. The architect must not give insurance advice. The requirements and amounts of insurance coverages should be inserted only after consultation with insurance counsel for the Architect and Consultant.)

Before commencing the performance of the Consultant's services under this Agreement, the Consultant shall procure and maintain, at the Consultant's own expense, until one year after the date of Substantial Completion of the Project, at least the following insurance in the form and with such limits as are agreeable to the Architect:
(A) Professional Liability Insurance covering claims made at any time during or subsequent to completion of the Consultant's services with a limit of not less than $_____ and with a deductible of not more than $_____ per claim.
(B) Worker's Compensation and Employers' Liability Insurance, in accordance with the laws of the state in which the Consultant's services are performed. (C) Broad Form Comprehensive Liability and Property Insurance, naming the Architect as an additional insured. (D) Automobile Public Liability and Property Damage Insurance, including non-owned automobiles, naming the Architect as an additional insured. The Consultant shall furnish the Architect with appropriate certificates from the Consultant's insurance company in accordance with subparagraph 10.6.4. Should the Consultant fail to procure and maintain such insurance in the form acceptable to the Architect, the Architect may, but shall not be obligated to procure and maintain such insurance for the Consultant. The Consultant shall pay the cost thereof and shall furnish all necessary information to make effective such insurance.

ARTICLE 12
OTHER CONDITIONS OR SERVICES

(Insert descriptions of other services, identify specific types of subconsultants, identify Additional Services included within Basic Compensation and modifications to the payment and compensation terms included in this Agreement.)

Services of professional subconsultants engaged by the Consultant shall be subject to prior written approval of the Architect.

This Agreement entered into as of the day and year first written above.

	A B C Architects		D E F Engineers
ARCHITECT	600 Main St.	CONSULTANT	800 Second St.
	San Francisco, California		San Francisco, California

_____   _____
(Signature)   (Signature)

        Frank Smith, Principal   Gerald Johnson, Principal
_____   _____
(Printed name and title)   (Printed name and title)

Working Drawings

Working drawings must be neat, clear and well presented but they employ different techniques and methods of presentation than those utilized for Schematic Design Drawings and Design Development Drawings. Each phase of the architect's basic services is intended to present a building or structure as it is to be. However, each phase is for different purposes and is directed toward different persons. Working drawings are directed primarily toward those persons working regularly in the construction industry. Working drawings start from a background of Design Development Drawings, material and color schedules, outline specifications, and a preliminary estimate of construction cost, all approved by the owner. In addition, several other important documents are required which are furnished by the owner. These documents include the site survey, geotechnical reports, the program of detailed requirements and often financial feasibility studies and other market data. It is up to the architect to see that this necessary background is established in initial phases of the project delivery process. Furthermore, it is the architect's responsibility to investigate items that include the following: materials utilized; construction methods; structural, mechanical and electrical systems; zoning ordinances; building codes; state laws and other regulatory requirements.

The architect's responsibility in obtaining this background of information prior to preparing working drawings cannot be underestimated. The working drawing stage is the final drawing stage and therefore the final decision stage. Every line placed on the tracing paper represents a decision made. The sum of these decisions represents the drawings for the finished project.

Upon reviewing the preliminary design and analyzing the necessary background information the architect prepares working drawings and final specifications which set forth in technical detail the requirements for construction of the project materials, equipment, workmanship, and finishes required for the architectural portion of the work, related site work, and special equipment. All work is coordinated with structural, mechanical, and electrical layouts. Final material and color schedules are discussed with the owner.

The purpose of working drawings is to provide detailed graphic representations of the characteristics and scope of the project for the bidding and construction process. To accomplish this the architect produces scaled drawings which include a site plan, floor plans, sections, elevations, details, notes, and schedules. These drawings depict graphically all work to be done with respect to dimensions; arrangement; location of materials and equipment; structural, mechanical, and electrical systems siting; and all other relevant information regarding the elements of the work. To facilitate this, the drawings must be arranged in a logical sequence. The plans, elevations, sections, and details should be free from redundant or conflicting notes. The drawings should be drawn to scale and should be dimensioned completely and precisely, and the linework should be clear and legible, with all notes lettered neatly.

In order to reduce possible liability exposure, the architect may wish to establish a systematic quality control program. By developing a checklist for virtually all areas of practice and regularly using such checklists on the project, the chances of problems developing are greatly reduced. Extensive use of standard details can further reduce errors and enhance the architect's accuracy on the preliminary estimate of construction cost. Further, evaluations of details, specifications and procedures from previous projects are a critical part of any quality control system. Such information should be carefully documented, filed, and periodically updated for use on subsequent projects.

Generally speaking, the working drawings form a concise legal document which graphically fixes and describes locations, limits, relationships and dimensions. In addition, they classify and name materials and include explanatory notes which amplify the drawings. Usually, these notes are not intended to explain the quality of materials and workmanship and therefore should not be written to contradict, duplicate or complicate the information that is given in the specifications.

The coordination required during the production of working drawings is twofold: between the drawings and specifications for the entire project, and between the drawings produced by the architect and the drawings produced by the engineering consultants working on the project. The architect must ensure that all decisions and changes are properly accounted for in both working drawings and specifications and with his consultants.

Upon completion of final plans and specifications by both the architect and his consultants for the complete set of working drawings required for bidding and construction, the architect checks all completed documents for coordination, compliance with program and codes, and accuracy. The checking of drawings is a very important responsibility of the architect. This very important procedure is necessary for correct, complete, and correlated drawings. In addition, the architect advises the owner of any adjustments to previous preliminary estimates of construction cost and the time schedule resulting from requirement changes or general market conditions.

The architect prepares final area and volume calculations and submits the working drawings and preliminary estimates of construction cost to the owner for his written approval. Upon approval, the architect places the necessary architect's seals and signatures on the documents required by reviewing authorities and obtains the same from his engineering consultants.

Specifications and the Project Manual

The specifications describe in written detail the architect's selection and the quality of materials and equipment. The method of installation and quality of workmanship are also precisely described. The preparation of the specifications is one of the critical elements of the architect's responsibilities. The accuracy of cost estimates, the smooth functioning of the contractor's operations, and the effectiveness of the finished product can all be related in part to the quality of the specifications.

The purpose of specifications is to augment and amplify the working drawings and other Construction Documents by enumerating and describing in concise written detail, each item included within the scope of the performance of the work. In addition, for contracts competitively awarded, the specifications establish a single, definite basis for competition. Furthermore, during the construction process, they furnish a compact book of instructions for the architect's field observations, consulting engineers, laboratory technicians, contractors and all others engaged in performing, supervising, inspecting or observing the work.

The first step in the specification writing process is the preparation of outline specifications. This should be pursued concurrently with the design effort. After the Owner's approval of the Schematic Design Studies, the architect expands and revises the preliminary outline specifications and coordinates them with the evolving Design Development Documents.

The outline specifications should clearly describe items that include the following: the site work and demolition, if any; type and quality of interior and exterior finish materials; the structural, mechanical and electrical systems; and all other major systems and equipment to be used. These outline specifications generally do not include installation procedures or a high degree of detail. They serve as a guide in establishing the basic quality of building to be expected under the budget. The final specifications which are prepared later are a detailed extension of this basic outline. (See Illustration 1, "Sample—Four Pages of Outline Specifications.")

During the Construction Document Phase, it is the architect's responsibility to prepare complete, clear, and concise final specifications with adequate descriptions of the various classes of work segregated under the proper divisions, sections, and articles in accordance with established standards. By using established standards, the architect reduces chances for duplication, omission or contradiction of information. For private sector work, most firms prepare a Project Manual organized in accordance with an established format recommended by the Construction Specifications Institute. Note that government projects and some private projects may have different requirements.

The Project Manual usually is a bound 8-1/2" x 11" volume assembled specifically for a particular construction project. (See Illustration 2, "Construction Documents.") Note that the Project Manual includes four document groupings:

1) Bidding Requirements: Invitation to Bid, Instructions to Bidders, prebid information, the Bid Form and the Bid Bond.

2) Contract Forms: The Agreement Between Owner and Contractor, Performance Bond, Payment Bond and certificates.

3) Contract Conditions: General Conditions and Supplementary Conditions.

4) Specifications: Written documents for the various portions of the work generally following the recommended organizational concept of the Construction Specifications Institute.

The contents of the first three groupings are based on related contractual elements that have definite legal implications. Since the architect's advice must not be construed to be legal advice, these groupings require input from the owner and the owner's legal counsel. These documents are not specifications and should not be used or modified without the guidance of the owner's legal counsel and the written approval of the owner.

The Project Manual for most private sector projects is arranged and organized in accordance with the Construction Specification Institute's system entitled "Masterformat". (See Illustration 3, "Project Manual Arrangement.") This is a standardized system for arranging, titling and numbering all parts of a Project Manual. Further, the system is used for automated data filing, data retrieval and cost accounting. "Masterformat" consists of two portions. The first portion consists of groupings 1 — 3 listed above: Bidding Requirements, Contract Forms and Contract Conditions. As mentioned, these first three groupings of the Project Manual are not specifications and are referred to as "documents" instead of sections. The titles for forms and documents under these three Project Manual groupings have been assigned five digit numbers, the first two of which are zeros. These numbers are used primarily for the purpose of filing and for coordination of the form or document with the other portions of "Masterformat". (See Illustration 4, "Bidding Requirements, Contract Forms, and Conditions of the Contract.")

The second portion of the "Masterformat" system consists of the specifications. The specifications are divided into sixteen "divisions." The divisions are basic categories of related construction information that logically lend themselves to convenient subdivision. These sixteen divisions are fixed in both number and title. Therefore, these divisions are always the same. For example, Division 4 will always be "Masonry" regardless of the building type or the location of the project.

Each division is broken down further into a group of related "sections". Each section covers one portion of the total work or requirements for the project. For example, an individual section may describe a particular product such as carpet and its installation methods. The number of sections within a particular division vary from division to division. This would be expected since each division covers rather diverse categories. For example, Site Work is specified in Division 2 and Finishes are specified in Division 9. (See Illustration 5, "Bidding Requirements, Contract Forms, and Conditions of the Contract" with the 16 Division Broadscope Specification Format.) Note that the sections listed here under each of the 16 divisions are "Broadscope" sections. These will be discussed later in this chapter.

The architect selects particular sections from a division that are applicable to the architect's selection of materials for the project. Obviously, many of the titles listed in "Masterformat" are not used on a specific project. Further, if there are no sections of work within a Division such as Division 4—Masonry, that division is not used in the specification. However, it should be noted that the remaining divisions are never renumbered. The Table of Contents for the Project Manual simply lists all divisions and notes those that are not used by placing "Not In Use" below the division title. (See Illustration 6, "Typical Manufacturing Company—Specifications.")

Each specification section that is prepared is divided into a standard "Three Part Section Format" in accordance with a CSI recommended system. This simple organizational concept facilitates placement of related information within each individual section and provides a logical standardized arrangement that enables the user to find information quickly. Each part of this format contains several standard headings called "articles" that follow a regular sequence. Obviously, every article will not be applicable for every section and therefore will not be used in all cases. The architect should not use the articles that do not apply as these can result in contradictions in the specifications which can cause the architect to incur liability. Further, new articles are introduced as required by the pertinent conditions of the project. The "Three Part Section Format" is as follows:

Part 1—General: The scope of work is described in general terms along with related work in other sections that is necessary to understand prior to fabrication and installation. Further, references to codes, regulations and standards, quality assurance, and so on are set forth in this part.

Part 2—Products: The materials, equipment, fixtures or products to be used are clearly described. Descriptions of the manufacturing process used in the development of products may also be described. This may include mixing of concrete, for example, or the fabrication of hollow metal door frames, etc.

Part 3—Execution: The workmanship, erection, installation and application procedures are described in detail.

(See Illustration 7, "Three Part Section Format Outline.") Note that articles consist of one or more paragraphs. In general, these paragraphs should be quite short and deal only with one topic or point.

Each section of the specifications defines or clarifies requirements for administration, procedures or units of work for the project. Although the CSI "Masterformat" section titles and numbers relate to specific work categories, it should be noted that the specifications should not attempt to define or imply trade jurisdiction. For example, each contractor that bids on a project will subdivide the work differently among subcontractors. Therefore, the specifications are always addressed to the contractor and not to subcontractors. Since the contractor signs an agreement with the owner to construct the project, responsibility for the total construction is with the contractor regardless of how the work is divided among the contractor's subcontractors.

The sections are organized on the basis of a five digit numbering system. Standard titles are used for all sections. The first two numbers of a section are the division numbers. For example, the first two numbers of divisions 1 — 9 are numbered as 01, 02, etc., divisions 10 — 16 are numbered as 10, 11, etc. The first two numbers of the five digit number indicate the location of sections in "Masterformat" much like letters indicate the locations of words in a dictionary. For example, 03100 refers to Concrete Formwork under Division 3 — Concrete. Similarly, 08100 refers to Metal Doors and Frames under Division 8 — Doors and Windows.

"Masterformat" also identifies three levels of complexity of section scope. These are Broadscope, Mediumscope and Narrowscope sections. (See Illustration 8, "Division 3 — Concrete.") Note that Broadscope Explanations are on the right and that Mediumscope Numbers and Titles are on the left. These are defined as follows.

Broadscope: These are very general and encompassing sections. For example, Broadscope Section 03200 is Concrete Reinforcement. Reinforcing steel, welded wire fabric, stressing tendons, and fibrous reinforcing could all be specified under this one broadscope section. However, if all these items were being used on a project, a single broadscope section might become too complex. Therefore, this specification could be broken down into several mediumscope sections. Furthermore, note that the CSI "Masterformat" indicates that concrete reinforcement may be specified in various other sections such as: 02500 — Paving and Surfacing, 03300 — Cast-in-Place Concrete, 03400 — Precast Concrete, and 03500 — Cementitious Decks. Also, notice that a "Masterformat" note indicates that stressing tendons are usually specified in 03365 — Post-Tensioned Concrete. The Broadscope Section 03200 — Concrete Reinforcement would be most applicable on a simple project and might include, for example, reinforcing steel and welded wire fabric.

Mediumscope: These are sections covering units of work of a more limited scope. For example, "Masterformat" identifies three mediumscope sections under Broadscope Section 03100, Concrete Formwork.

03110   Structural Cast-in-Place Concrete Formwork
03120   Architectural Cast-in-Place Concrete Formwork
03130   Permanent Forms

Generally, as the complexity of the project increases, more mediumscope sections are used.

Narrowscope: These are sections covering a very specific and extremely limited scope. Therefore, smaller units of work can be covered in greater detail. For example, "Masterformat" identifies two narrowscope sections under section 03130, Permanent Forms.

Permanent Steel Forms
Prefabricated Stair Forms

Further, narrowscope sections are used for special areas of a project That contain unusual features that must be custom fabricated. For example, specially designed wood molding and trim for a conference room could be a narrowscope section.

"Masterformat" identifies all broadscope and mediumscope sections with fixed numbers and titles. However, titles only are identified for narrowscope sections. Within a range, the architect can assign numbers for any narrowscope section used. Numerical intervals have been intentionally left between broadscope and mediumscope fixed numbers so that narrowscope numbers, within a range and in sequence, may be placed between two existing fixed section numbers. For example, the narrowscope sections mentioned above could be identified as:

03131   Permanent Steel Forms
03132   Prefabricated Stair Forms

Further, the architect may add additional narrowscope titles even if there is no listing of such a title in "Masterformat." This may be the case for special work of a custom nature.

Division 1 consists of general requirements for administration and procedural items that are only superficially covered in standard General Conditions and Supplementary Condition such as submittals, substitutions, temporary facilities and project meetings. Further, this division also provides a means of specifying items that relate to all sections. Therefore, the need to repeat standard paragraphs in each section is eliminated. For example, typical sizes of material samples, size and number of copies of shop drawings and content of warranties are generally included in Division 1, thereby eliminating the placement of these standards throughout the other sections. (See Illustration 9, "Division 1 — General Requirements.")

Divisions 2 — 16 consist of specific requirements for units of work. Selection of what comprises a unit of work is left somewhat to the discretion of each specifier. However, the CSI "Masterformat" provides a degree of guidance. Obviously, the first decision that must be made is the selection of section titles that are applicable to the materials and items of work used on the project. The architect's decision as to which section numbers and titles to use of the many options available in "Masterformat" depends on many things. Basic considerations are: whether the project is large or small, whether the project is simple or complex, whether systems or products are to be specified, and whether the project is to be bid on a single lump sum basis or as several smaller contracts for various portions of the work.

The architect may use broadscope sections, mediumscope sections, narrowscope sections or a combination of all three types of sections on one project. A mix is acceptable and is often desirable to fulfill the needs of the project. Generally, the use of numerous narrowscope sections should be limited to very large and complex construction projects. Broadscope sections provide the greatest range of possibilities in describing a unit of work and may be all that is required on a relatively simple project. For example, a system utilizing concrete formwork, concrete reinforcing, and cast-in-place concrete may be specified in the single Broadscope Section 03300 — Cast-in-Place Concrete. Alternatively, these items could be specified in three broadscope sections:

03100	Concrete Formwork
03200	Concrete Reinforcing
03300	Cast-in-Place Concrete

The choice as to which option to use depends upon the complexity of the project. For example, a single section 03300 might be used for a small single story building. The use of three, generally more detailed sections, might be used for a larger project, such as, a three story commercial building. The choice, however, will always depend upon the pertinent facts related to a particular project.

A mediumscope section covers a unit of work more limited in scope than the broadscope section. These are generally required as the complexity of the work increases. More complex work requires a larger number of more detailed sections for clarity. Therefore, mediumscope, and if required, narrowscope sections are utilized. The architect can make a section all-inclusive by combining several narrowscope sections into one mediumscope section. Or several shorter sections can be written that are coordinated and located together in accordance with the "Masterformat" numbering system.

For example, the specification for concrete for a four story cast-in-place concrete building could be organized as all broadscope:

03100	Concrete Formwork
03200	Concrete Reinforcement
03300	Cast-in-Place Concrete

Or the specification could be organized using both broadscope and mediumscope sections:

    03110   Structural Cast-in-Place Concrete Formwork
    03120   Architectural Cast-in-Place Concrete Formwork
    03200   Concrete Reinforcement
    03310   Structural Concrete
    03330   Architectural Concrete

Also, Mediumscope Section 03310 — Structural Concrete could be broken down still further into narrowscope sections as follows:

    03312   Normalweight Structural Concrete
    03314   Lightweight Structural Concrete

The main advantages of breaking the longer sections down into shorter sections are as follows:

1)   The architect's task of assembling the Project Manual is usually made easier. Further, last minute revisions such as the deletion of a material are made simpler since the architect can generally remove an entire section more easily than revising an all-inclusive section.

2)   The specifications are easier to use and are easier to coordinate during writing. Further, by adding titles, rather than adding information to an all-inclusive section, it is easier to check to see that all items have been properly included in the specification.

However, the disadvantages of breaking down the longer sections into shorter sections should be carefully considered. These include the following:

1)   Writing narrowscope sections the first time may take considerably more time than writing broadscope sections. Obviously, the amount of data will be longer.

2) Further, sections must be carefully cross referenced. This will also add time since there is more cross referencing to do.

3) Part 1 section material must be repeated more times. This adds to the possibility of error. Further, a simple narrowscope section becomes quite long since information is often repeated in sections covering similar materials.

4) Narrowscope sections require more space in a Project Manual for the reasons mentioned above. A large Project Manual may cause bidders to increase their bid price because they assume that there are more restrictions than may actually be the case.

In summary, the specifications are organized as follows:

Divisions 1 — 16: Divisions are organized in accordance with the Construction Specification Institute 16 Division Format.

Sections: Only sections relevant to the specific project are included in the Project Manual. Sections are organized under appropriate categories in the CSI 16 Division Format. Sections are titled and numbered in accordance with the CSI "Masterformat" list of section numbers and titles. Sections may be broadscope, mediumscope or narrowscope.

Section Parts: The parts of each section are organized in accordance with the CSI "Three Part Section Format."

Part 1 — General
Part 2 — Products
Part 3 — Execution

Articles: The category titles for major related articles within each part are organized in accordance with recommendations of the CSI "Three Part Format."

Paragraphs: The paragraphs are not explicitly defined by the CSI. However, the CSI does recommend that each paragraph should describe only one point or idea. One or more paragraphs form an article.

SPECIFICATION WRITING

Specifications must be technically adequate for the purpose intended. They must be definite and concise in regard to requirements, conditions and stipulations. In addition, good specifications require clear and unambiguous phrasing and expressions and must be equitable in purpose and application to all parties of the contract. Furthermore, specifications must be fundamentally economical in operation. Also, they must be legally enforceable with a minimum of friction and misunderstanding since they form a significant part of the contract between the owner and the contractor.

Although architects still refer to "writing" specifications, actually most sections are assembled from existing data consisting of carefully worded paragraphs. This method entails editing a standard "office master" specification section. Where no office master specification is available, use of the same section from another project can be helpful. However, the architect must spend additional time assuring materials, references and methods are both up-to-date and pertinent to the specific needs of the project.

Where no office master or previous project section is available, the architect often uses a commercially available guide specification. Use of these guide specifications can help limit the potential for accidentally forgetting to include an important item. The Construction Specification Institute's "Spectext", The American Institute of Architects' "Masterspec", and Hans Meier's "Library of Specifications" are some of the commercially available guide specifications for private sector projects. Federal Guide Specifications, The General Services Administration's Public Building Service Guide Specifications, the Naval Facilities Command's "NAVFAC Guide Specifications" and the Army Corps of Engineers' "Military Specifications" are commercially available for governmental projects.

The commercially available guide specifications can be used to assist the architect in developing office master specifications. The guide specifications provide the basis for office masters through combining text directly from the guide with supplements consisting of specific office requirements. Further, provisions in the guide specifications that do not apply are carefully edited out of the office master specifications.

The guides are also used as a reference for additional technical information. They provide a clear and concise method for specifying a particular requirement and reduce the time required to prepare specifications. In general, guide specifications are available on computer disks and can be edited electronically with automated equipment. This further reduces production time and allows specialists in specification writing to handle more projects.

Another important advantage in the use of guide specifications is that they often improve the architect's legal liability position. For most commercially available guide specifications, the content is formally reviewed by technical committees of users and specialists. Therefore, the risk from sole authorship is reduced. Charges of ambiguous language or faulty documentation of requirements are more difficult to substantiate since the guide specifications use language that is a standard for design professionals. In addition, the guide specifications are generally sponsored by professional organizations. Further, most systems give subscribers quarterly updates on new products, technology and regulations.

For example, the AIA's "Masterspec" Basic Version includes the most commonly used sections for typical projects. These serve either as a ready to edit specification system or as references for the preparation of office masters. Each section has a Cover Sheet, Specification Text Sheets, and Drawing Coordination Sheets. The Cover Sheets give the architect a brief description of the contents, including material added at the latest update. The Specification Text Sheets are the actual specifications ready to edit to fit the needs of a specific project or for use in preparation of an office master specification section. Editing instructions are provided in the form of retain/delete provisions, multiple choice selections, or revisions. Evaluation Sheets provide a qualitative overview of products that would be both difficult and time consuming to obtain from product literature. The relative merits of competitive products are discussed without manufacturers' claims. This aids the architect in selecting the right product for the job quickly and logically on the basis of pertinent facts. Also included with each section are Drawing Coordination Sheets that offer the architect assistance in quality control in coordinating drawings with specifications. (See Illustration 11.)

Often, the guide specifications are used to develop office master specifications. These are developed for each product or system that is commonly used on a particular building type in an office. The office masters are then utilized as the basis for the specifications for the specific type of projects that are typically done by that office. Office master specifications should include selections of particular products, systems and standards that reflect the quality of work generally done by the office. In addition, they should include specific local code and regulatory requirements, reflect local construction practices, and should include special specification requirements based on the previous experience of the office.

However, the office master is not a compilation of old project specifications. Further, the office master should not be an unmodified commercial guide specification. Office masters necessitate careful research and review. They are tailored for the specific needs of a particular office in a specific project locality. Secondly, they require periodic revision based on updated information concerning new products, regulations, and modifications based on the use of the specifications on actual projects. Thirdly, the office master must still be edited and supplemented for each individual project. No fixed set of requirements will achieve a reasonable standard of care for all projects. It is a basic premise that most projects are unique. Further, each architect, consulting engineer, owner, and building site is unique. Consequently, the specification requirements will vary from project to project.

The advantages of the use of office master specifications are that they establish a format for project specifications, incorporate accepted language and terminology (often based on commercially available guide specifications), exemplify typical methods for a firm's specifying, and provide basic procedural decisions for project specifications. Further, the available office masters applicable to a project are generally edited first. Thus, a considerable amount of comprehensive technical information is generated for the project in an efficient manner. Secondly, by editing the office masters first, new personnel involved in the specification preparation process can familiarize themselves with the manner in which the office prefers its specifications to be written.

The architect utilizes both reference material and specific project information when preparing the specifications for a project. It is critical that both types of information be readily available when editing or writing a specification section. Reference material includes commercial guide specifications with their accompanying technical information sheets, codes, regulations, manufacturer's literature, trade association standards, and technical reference books. Specific project information includes drawings, outline specifications, checklists and notes. The checklists and notes contain information relevant to decisions made regarding specific project requirements. This information is often obtained directly from the owner or the owner's project representative in conferences or interviews. The architect generally uses previously prepared checklists to obtain the owner's preferences in regard to materials, colors, textures and so on. This information is generally filed in accordance with the CSI Format. All information must be kept organized and be regularly referred to in order to assure that each section fully reflects grades, types and classes of materials appropriate to the project.

Furthermore, each specification section should include a statement such as, "The General Conditions, Supplementary Conditions, and Division 1, General Requirements, are a part of this section and the contract for this work and apply to this section fully as if repeated here." This statement has legal significance since some subcontracts are based on requirements of only certain sections of the specification. This statement may be the only means by which the General Conditions, etc. are made a part of the subcontract.

Government agencies and some corporate clients that do large amounts of construction may have their own master specifications. In this case, they require the architect to prepare specifications using their master specifications. These are often referred to as client guide specifications. The architect will generally require more time to prepare project specifications from client guide specifications than would be required to prepare specifications from the firm's own office masters. The method for developing specifications from client guide specifications is generally the same as developing a section from an office master. However, more time must be spent to review new products and materials in order to provide the quality expected by the client. In addition, the architect must incorporate local code requirements and construction practices into the sections.

To summarize, the specifications must be precisely written regardless of whether the basis of the section is a commercially available guide specification, an office master specification, a client guide specification, or a sole authorship specification. In all cases, the architect is ultimately responsible for coordination with the drawings, addition of supplemental information, deletion of information that does not apply, internal coordination within the specifications themselves and of course, the end result. Errors in wording, omissions, lack of coordination, ambiguous or contradictory language can cause the architect to incur large amounts of liability. For example, errors in the wording of a stucco specification on a large college campus construction project caused failure of the finish within three years and resulted in a fifteen million dollar lawsuit.

The following example for a hypothetical project has been devised to provide a sample specification section as study material. The project is described as follows:

A medium sized corporation, Typical Manufacturing Company, has decided to construct an industrial plant and offices to house the manufacturing plant, sales force, and administrative operations of its company. In accordance with the Owner/Architect Agreement (AIA Document B141), the owner provided a program of requirements for the project that included employee dressing facilities with lockers and benches.

Based on the owner's program of requirements and an interview with the owner's authorized project representative, the architect prepared outline specifications during the design phases of the project. These were subsequently approved by the owner. As mentioned earlier in this section, the architect generally uses a previously prepared checklist for the interview with the owner's project representative. This not only saves time, but also reduces the possibility of overlooking an important item. (See Illustration 10, "Sample Specifications Checklist.")

Outline Specification - Metal Lockers:

Provide metal lockers with concrete base in areas shown on drawings. Lockers shall be single-tier wardrobe lockers with recessed handles, and sloping metal tops. Each locker to have hat shelf, hooks, number plate, and built-in combination lock. Locker finish shall be baked on enamel selected from manufacturer's standard colors. Provide trim and closers for exposed ends. Provide standard manufacturer's benches in areas shown on drawings.

Upon receiving written approval of the outline specifications from the owner, the architect proceeded to prepare the final specification section for mental lockers. (For this sample, a section from the AIA's "Masterspec" was used.) Based on information from above and that contained in the editing instructions, the reasons for editing decisions should be self-evident. In general, what is involved in this particular section is deleting out inapplicable requirements. One exception is a short supplement added by the architect requiring that the sloping tops be hipped on exposed ends. Note that other sections may require far more extensive modifications and supplements to meet the project requirements. (See Illustration 11, "Sample — Edited Specification Section." See also Illustration 12, "Sample — Final Specification Section.")

1

TYPICAL MANUFACTURING CO.   OUTLINE SPECIFICATIONS
INDUSTRIAL PLANT & OFFICES   PAGE 1 OF 20
HAYWARD, CALIFORNIA

THE OUTLINE SPECIFICATIONS ARE TO BE USED AS A GUIDE IN ESTABLISHING THE
SCOPE AND QUALITY OF THIS PROJECT BUT DO NOT PRESUME TO BE COMPLETE TO THE
LAST DETAIL. ALL WORK SHALL COMPLY WITH APPLICABLE LOCAL CODES AND
REGULATIONS AND SHALL BE OF FINISH QUALITY, ACCEPTABLE AS COMMON PRACTICE
IN THE CONSTRUCTION INDUSTRY.

GENERAL CONDITIONS

GENERAL CONDITIONS OF THE CONTRACT SHALL BE AIA FORM 201 (1987) WITH
SUITABLE SUPPLEMENTARY CONDITIONS.

DIVISION 2 - SITEWORK

SECTION 02050 - DEMOLITION

THE DEMOLITION INCLUDES THE COMPLETE WRECKING OF STRUCTURES AS SHOWN ON
DRAWINGS AND REMOVAL AND DISPOSAL OF DEMOLISHED MATERIALS.

SECTION 02110 - SITE CLEARING

REMOVE CONCRETE WALLS, CURBS, SLABS, AND ASPHALT PAVEMENT THAT ARE NOT
TO BE USED; BRUSH; VEGETATION; BILLBOARDS AND SIMILAR SURFACE
OBSTRUCTIONS; AND ABANDONED UNDERGROUND UTILITY LINES WITHIN THE
BOUNDARIES OF THE SITE. CLEAR ALL RUBISH AND DEBRIS. UTILITY LINES
WITHIN THE UTILITY EASEMENT AT THE SOUTHEAST CORNER OF THE SITE SHALL
REMAIN.

SECTION 02200 - EARTHWORK

A. STRIP ANY REMAINING VEGETATION AND ALL SURFACE SOILS CONTAINING
ORGANIC MATTER (APPROXIMATELY 4 INCHES).

B. PREPARE AREAS TO RECEIVE PAVING, ENGINEERED FILLS, FOOTINGS AND
FOUNDATIONS IN ACCORDANCE WITH REQUIREMENTS OF THE GEOTECHNICAL REPORT.

C. EXCAVATE AS REQUIRED FOR FOUNDATIONS AND FOOTINGS. EXCESS MATERIALS
FROM THE EXCAVATION SHALL BE REMOVED FROM THE SITE.

D. FOUNDATION EXCAVATIONS, ENGINEERED FILLS AND COMPACTION SHALL BE
OBSERVED BY THE GEOTECHNICAL ENGINEER. COSTS FOR SUCH OBSERVATIONS WILL
BE PAID FOR BY THE OWNER.

SECTION 02500 - PAVING AND SURFACING

A. VEHICLE ENTRANCE ROADS, LOADING AREAS, AND PARKING AREAS SHALL RECEIVE ASPHALT PAVING OVER AN AGGREGATE BASE AND AGGREGATE SUBBASE. ASPHALT PAVING SECTIONS AS PER THE RECOMMENDATIONS OF THE GEOTECHNICAL ENGINEER. (REFER TO GEOTECHNICAL REPORT.)

B. PROVIDE PRE-CAST CONCRETE PARKING BUMPERS FOR PARKING STALLS.

C. PROVIDE 3" WIDE YELLOW PAINTED LINES AND TRAFFIC MARKINGS.

SECTION 02825 - FOUNTAIN AND POOL

CUSTOM DESIGN BY ARCHITECT.

SECTION 02900 - LANDSCAPING

LANDSCAPING WORK SHALL BE IN ACCORDANCE WITH DRAWINGS AND SPECIFICATIONS PREPARED BY THE LANDSCAPE ARCHITECT. LANDSCAPE WORK INCLUDES SOIL, TREES, PLANT MATERIALS, CARE OF EXISTING TREES TO REMAIN, REINFORCED PRECAST CONCRETE PLANTERS, AND IRRIGATION SYSTEM.

DIVISION 3 - CONCRETE

SECTION 03100 - CONCRETE FORMWORK

CONCRETE FORMWORK SHALL CONFORM WITH APPLICABLE REQUIREMENTS OF THE UNIFORM BUILDING CODE, CHAPTER 26, AND THE AMERICAN CONCRETE INSTITUTE, "RECOMMENDED PRACTICE FOR CONCRETE FORMWORK."

SECTION 03200 - CONCRETE REINFORCEMENT

REINFORCING BARS SHALL MEET THE REQUIREMENTS OF ASTM, GRADE 60. REINFORCEMENT AND PLACEMENT SHALL CONFORM WITH APPLICABLE REQUIREMENTS OF THE UNIFORM BUILDING CODE, CHAPTER 26, AND THE CONCRETE REINFORCING STEEL INSTITUTE, "MANUAL OF PRACTICE."

SECTION 03300 - CAST IN PLACE CONCRETE

A. SIDEWALKS AND ON-GRADE SLABS: BAR-REINFORCED, REGULAR WEIGHT CONCRETE. 2500 P.S.I.

SAMPLE - FOUR PAGES OF OUTLINE SPECIFICATIONS

    SECTION 03300 - CAST IN PLACE CONCRETE

B. FOUNDATION SYSTEM: SPREAD FOOTINGS. BAR-REINFORCED, REGULAR WEIGHT
CONCRETE. 4000 P.S.I.

C. FORMED CONCRETE: BAR-REINFORCED, REGULAR WEIGHT CONCRETE. 4000
P.S.I.

    SECTION 03345 - CONCRETE FINISHING

A. SIDEWALKS: MEDIUM BROOM FINISH WITH SMOOTH TROWELLED BANDS.

B. ON-GRADE SLABS AND TYPICAL FLOORS: SMOOTH TROWELLED FINISH.

C. FORMED CONCRETE: INTEGRALLY COLORED, BOARD FORMED, ROUGH TEXTURED
WITH UNIFORMLY AND REGULARLY SPACED, PLASTIC CONE SNAPTIES WITH
PRE-CAST CONCRETE PLUGS.

    SECTION 03400 - PRECAST CONCRETE

WALL PANELS SHALL BE FIBERGLASS REINFORCED, PRECAST CONCRETE, AND SHALL
BE SHOP FABRICATED BY A FIRM EXPERIENCED IN THE BUSINESS OF PROVIDING
ARCHITECTURAL PRECAST CONCRETE WALL PANELS. COLOR SHALL BE AS PRODUCED
BY WHITE PORTLAND CEMENT AND LIGHT COLORED AGGREGATES. SANDBLAST AND
APPLY WATER REPELLENT TREATMENT.

DIVISION 4 - MASONRY

    (NOT IN USE.)

DIVISION 5 - METALS

    STRUCTURAL WORK SHALL BE IN CONFORMANCE WITH DRAWINGS AND
    SPECIFICATIONS PREPARED BY THE STRUCTURAL ENGINEER. DESIGN LOADS WILL
    COMPLY WITH THE UNIFORM BUILDING CODE. MATERIALS TESTING AND INSPECTION
    COSTS WILL BE PAID BY THE OWNER.

    SECTION 05120 - STRUCTURAL STEEL

    COLUMNS, GIRDERS AND BEAMS SHALL BE A-36, SHOP PRIMED, STRUCTURAL
    STEEL. WELDED AND BOLTED CONNECTIONS AS PER DRAWING REQUIREMENTS.
    COMPLY WITH UNIFORM BUILDING CODE, CHAPTER 27 AND AMERICAN INSTITUTE OF
    STEEL CONSTRUCTION'S "MANUAL OF STEEL CONSTRUCTION."

SAMPLE - FOUR PAGES OF OUTLINE SPECIFICATIONS

TYPICAL MANUFACTURING CO.   OUTLINE SPECIFICATIONS
INDUSTRIAL PLANT AND OFFICES   PAGE 4 OF 20
HAYWARD, CALIFORNIA

SECTION 05300 - METAL DECKING

TYPICAL FLOORS: 3" CELLULAR METAL DECK WITH 2-1/2" REGULAR WEIGHT
CONCRETE FILL.

SECTION 05400 - COLD FORMED METAL FRAMING

A. PARTITIONS AND WALLS SHALL BE OF 3-5/8" 25 GAUGE NON-LOADBEARING,
SCREW-TYPE METAL STUDS WITH GYPSUM WALLBOARD FINISH. THE NUMBER OF
LAYERS AND THICKNESS AS REQUIRED BY FIRE RESISTANCE RATINGS.

B. 16 GAUGE STRUCTURAL STUDS SHALL BE USED FOR SUPPORT OF LAVATORY
COUNTERS AND OTHER WALL SUPPORTED ITEMS.

C. SOUND INSULATED PARTITIONS SHALL HAVE TOP AND BOTTOM PLATES, WALL
STUDS ABUTTING COLUMNS OR INTERSECTING PARTITIONS, OUTLET BOXES AND
OTHER PENETRATIONS SEALED AIRTIGHT WITH ACOUSTICAL SEALANT.

D. STRUCTURE HIGH PARTITIONS SHALL HAVE STUDS INSTALLED WITH PROVISIONS
FOR DEFLECTION OF BUILDING FLOOR CONSTRUCTION WITHOUT DAMAGE TO
PARTITIONS.

SECTION 05500 - METAL FABRICATIONS

A. PROVIDE METAL STAIRS AND PLATFORMS, METAL RAILINGS, WALL MOUNTED
HANDRAILS, LADDERS, FLOOR GRATINGS, ELEVATOR EQUIPMENT BEAMS, ELEVATOR
PIT SCREENS AND SUPPORTS FOR LAVATORY COUNTERS AS SHOWN ON DRAWINGS.

B. STAIRS AND PLATFORMS: WELDED STEEL CHECKERPLATE TREADS AND OPEN
RISERS WITH CHANNEL STRINGERS, SHOP PRIMED AND PAINTED.

C. METAL RAILINGS AND WALL MOUNTED HANDRAILS: STEEL PIPE WITH WELDED
FITTINGS AND WALL BRACKETS, SHOP PRIMED AND PAINTED.

D. LADDERS: WELDED STEEL, SHOP PRIMED AND PAINTED.

E. FLOOR GRATINGS: STEEL BAR TYPE, GALVANIZED, UNPAINTED.

F. ELEVATOR EQUIPMENT BEAMS: A-36 STEEL SECTIONS, SHOP PRIMED.

G. ELEVATOR PIT SCREENS: WOVEN WIRE DIAMOND MESH, SHOP PRIMED AND
PAINTED.

H. SUPPORTS FOR LAVATORY COUNTERS: GALVANIZED STEEL SECTIONS.

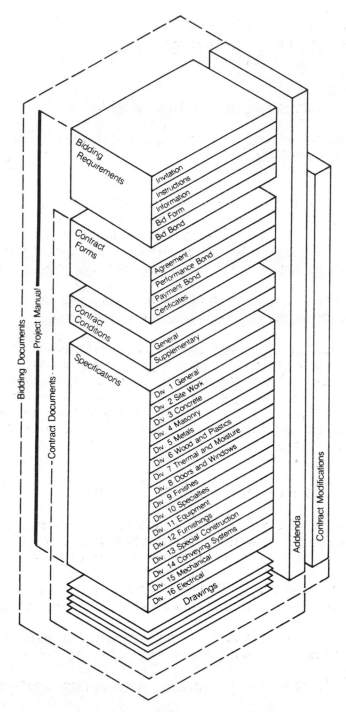

—ELEMENTS OF A PROJECT MANUAL

Construction Documents

(Reproduced by permission of the Construction Specifications Institute)

3

INTRODUCTORY PAGES

Cover Page
Title Page
Certification and Seals Page
Table of Contents Page

BIDDING REQUIREMENTS

00100	**INSTRUCTIONS TO BIDDERS**
-120	Supplementary Instructions to Bidders
-130	Pre-Bid Conferences
00200	**INFORMATION AVAILABLE TO BIDDERS**
-210	Preliminary Construction Schedule
	Preliminary Network Schedule
	Preliminary Phasing Network Schedule
-220	Geotechnical Data
	Owner's Disclaimer
	Soil Boring Data
	Geotechnical Report
-230	Existing Conditions
	Description of Existing Site
	Description of Existing Buildings
	Property Survey
00300	**BID FORMS**
00400	**SUPPLEMENTS TO BID FORMS**
-410	Bid Security Form
-420	Bidders Qualification Form
-430	Subcontractor List
-440	Substitution List
-450	Equipment Suppliers List
-460	List of Alternates/Alternatives
-470	List of Estimated Quantities
-480	Noncollusion Affadavit

CONTRACT DOCUMENTS

00500	**AGREEMENT FORMS**
00600	**BONDS AND CERTIFICATES**
-610	Performance Bonds
-620	Labor and Materials Payment Bond
-630	Guaranty Bond
-640	Maintenance Bond
-650	Certificates of Insurance
-660	Certificates of Compliance with Applicable Laws and Regulations
	Equal Employment Opportunity
	Wage Rates
	Non-segregated Facilities
	Air and Water Acts
00700	**GENERAL CONDITIONS**
00800	**SUPPLEMENTARY CONDITIONS**
-810	Modifications to General Conditions
-820	Additional Articles
	Equal Employment Opportunity Requirements
	Wage Rate Requirements
	Non-segregated Facilities Requirements
	Specific Project Requirements
	Statutory Declarations
-830	Wage Determination Schedule
00850	**DRAWINGS AND SCHEDULES**
-860	List of Drawings
-870	Schedules and Tables
-880	Details
00900	**ADDENDA AND MODIFICATIONS**

DIVISION 1 GENERAL REQUIREMENTS

DIVISIONS 2-16

Project Manual Arrangement

BIDDING REQUIREMENTS, CONTRACT FORMS*, AND CONDITIONS OF THE CONTRACT*

Document Number	Title
00010	**PRE-BID INFORMATION**
-020	Invitation to Bid
-030	Advertisement for Bids
-040	Prequalification Forms

Broadscope Explanation

00010 — PRE-BID INFORMATION

Invitation to Bid or Advertisement for Bids. Describes project and provides basic information concerning bidding.

> *Related Requirements:*
> Bid preparation information: Document 00100.

> **Note:** *The Pre-Bid Information is not a part of the Contract Documents, unless incorporated by the Agreement or by the Conditions of the Contract.*

00100	**INSTRUCTIONS TO BIDDERS**
-120	Supplementary Instructions to Bidders
-130	Pre-Bid Conferences

00100 — INSTRUCTIONS TO BIDDERS

Requirements for preparation and submission of bids. Includes information or conditions affecting award of contract and may include references to Division I for information required when submitting substitution proposals during bidding period.

> *Related Requirements:*
> Pre-Bid Information: Document 00010.
> Procedures for substitutions: Section 01600.

> **Note:** *The Instructions to Bidders is not a part of the Contract Documents unless incorporated by the Agreement or by the Conditions of the Contract.*

00200	**INFORMATION AVAILABLE TO BIDDERS**
-210	Preliminary Construction Schedule
	Preliminary Network Schedule
	Preliminary Phasing Network Schedule
-220	Geotechnical Data
	Owner's Disclaimer
	Soil Boring Data
	Geotechnical Report
-230	Existing Conditions
	Description of Existing Site
	Description of Existing Buildings
	Property Survey

00200 — INFORMATION AVAILABLE TO BIDDERS

Information that is available to bidders.

> *Related Requirements:*
> Subsurface investigation by Contractor: Section 02010.

> **Note:** *Information Available to Bidders is not a part of the Contract Documents unless incorporated by the Agreement or by the Conditions of the Contract.*

00300	**BID FORMS**

00300 — BID FORMS

Forms upon which bids are submitted.

> *Related Requirements:*
> Bid security: Document 00400.

> **Note:** *Bid Forms are not part of the Contract Documents unless incorporated by the Agreement or by the Conditions of the Contract.*

00400	**SUPPLEMENTS TO BID FORMS**
-410	Bid Security Form
-420	Bidders Qualification Form
-430	Subcontractor List
-440	Substitution List
-450	Equipment Suppliers List
-460	List of Alternates/Alternatives
-470	List of Estimated Quantities
-480	Noncollusion Affadavit

00400 — SUPPLEMENTS TO BID FORMS

Attachments to Bid Forms required to be submitted with bids.

> **Note:** *Supplements to Bid Forms are not part of the Contract Documents unless incorporated by the Agreement or by the Conditions of the Contract.*

00500	**AGREEMENT FORMS***

00500 — AGREEMENT FORMS*

Forms upon which Contractor/Owner Agreement is executed and that legally binds the signing parties. Includes identification of parties, statement of work to be performed, statement of considerations, time of performance, and signatures.

> **Note:** *Standard forms* published by various organizations are usually utilized for agreement forms.*

(Reproduced by permission of the Construction Specifications Institute)

Document Number	Title		Broadscope Explanation

00600 — BONDS AND CERTIFICATES*

00600	**BONDS AND CERTIFICATES***
-610	Performance Bonds
-620	Labor and Materials Payment Bond
-630	Guaranty Bond
-640	Maintenance Bond
-650	Certificates of Insurance
-660	Certificates of Compliance with Applicable Laws and Regulations

Equal Employment Opportunity
Wage Rates
Non-segregated Facilities
Air and Water Acts

00600 — BONDS AND CERTIFICATES*
Forms for bonds and certificates.

> *Note:* *Standard forms* published by various organizations are usually utilized for bonds and certificates.*

| 00700 | **GENERAL CONDITIONS*** |

00700 — GENERAL CONDITIONS*
General definition of the relationships and responsibilities of the parties to the contract and the design professional and how the contract is to be administered.

> *Related Requirements:*
> *Supplementary Conditions: Document 00800.*
> *Administrative and procedural items: Division 1.*

> *Note:* *Standard General Conditions* published by various organizations are usually used for General Conditions. Canadian standard forms of contract often include the Agreement, Definitions, and Conditions of the Contract in one document.*

00800	**SUPPLEMENTARY CONDITIONS***
-810	Modifications to General Conditions
-820	Additional Articles

Equal Employment Opportunity Requirements
Wage Rate Requirements
Non-segregated Facilities Requirements
Specific Project Requirements
Statutory Declarations

| -830 | Wage Determination Schedule |

00800 — SUPPLEMENTARY CONDITIONS*
Modifications, deletions, and additions to standard General Conditions*.

> *Related Requirements:*
> *General Conditions: Document 00700.*
> *Administrative and procedural items: Division 1.*

00850	**DRAWINGS AND SCHEDULES**
-860	List of Drawings
-870	Schedules and Tables
-880	Details

00850 — DRAWINGS AND SCHEDULES
be included.

> *Note:* *If detail drawings and schedules are to be included in the Project Manual, they are included in this location. Detail drawings and schedules may be included as a separate volume of the Project Manual. Schedules relating to only one specification section are included in that section.*

| 00900 | **ADDENDA AND MODIFICATIONS** |

00900 — ADDENDA AND MODIFICATIONS
Addenda issued before the execution of the Agreement; and modifications, deletions, and additions to the Contract Documents issued after the execution of the Agreement.

> *Note:* *Since addenda and modifications are usually issued after the initial issue of the Project Manual is assembled and bound, they may be put into a separate Project Manual volume. Certain construction procedures and contract methods, including fast-track or phased construction, may require several "editions" of a Project Manual. In such cases, the subsequently issued "editions" of the Project Manual may contain the Addenda and Modifications applicable to the previous editions. In those instances they should be located here in the Project Manual.*

---

* These documents have important legal consequences. Initiation or modifications without explicit approval and guidance of Owner or Owner's Counsel is not recommended.

5

BIDDING REQUIREMENTS, CONTRACT FORMS, AND CONDITIONS OF THE CONTRACT

00010 PRE-BID INFORMATION
00100 INSTRUCTIONS TO BIDDERS
00200 INFORMATION AVAILABLE TO BIDDERS
00300 BID FORMS
00400 SUPPLEMENTS TO BID FORMS
00500 AGREEMENT FORMS
00600 BONDS AND CERTIFICATES
00700 GENERAL CONDITIONS
00800 SUPPLEMENTARY CONDITIONS
00850 DRAWINGS AND SCHEDULES
00900 ADDENDA AND MODIFICATIONS

Note: Since the items listed above are not specification sections, they are referred to as "Documents" in lieu of "Sections" in the Master List of Section Titles, Numbers, and Broadscope Explanations.

SPECIFICATIONS

DIVISION 1—GENERAL REQUIREMENTS

01010 SUMMARY OF WORK
01020 ALLOWANCES
01025 MEASUREMENT AND PAYMENT
01030 ALTERNATES/ALTERNATIVES
01040 COORDINATION
01050 FIELD ENGINEERING
01060 REGULATORY REQUIREMENTS
01070 ABBREVIATIONS AND SYMBOLS
01080 IDENTIFICATION SYSTEMS
01090 REFERENCE STANDARDS
01100 SPECIAL PROJECT PROCEDURES
01200 PROJECT MEETINGS
01300 SUBMITTALS
01400 QUALITY CONTROL
01500 CONSTRUCTION FACILITIES AND TEMPORARY CONTROLS
01600 MATERIAL AND EQUIPMENT
01650 STARTING OF SYSTEMS/COMMISSIONING
01700 CONTRACT CLOSEOUT
01800 MAINTENANCE

DIVISION 2—SITEWORK

02010 SUBSURFACE INVESTIGATION
02050 DEMOLITION
02100 SITE PREPARATION
02140 DEWATERING
02150 SHORING AND UNDERPINNING
02160 EXCAVATION SUPPORT SYSTEMS
02170 COFFERDAMS
02200 EARTHWORK
02300 TUNNELING
02350 PILES AND CAISSONS
02450 RAILROAD WORK
02480 MARINE WORK
02500 PAVING AND SURFACING
02600 PIPED UTILITY MATERIALS
02660 WATER DISTRIBUTION
02680 FUEL DISTRIBUTION
02700 SEWERAGE AND DRAINAGE
02760 RESTORATION OF UNDERGROUND PIPELINES
02770 PONDS AND RESERVOIRS
02780 POWER AND COMMUNICATIONS
02800 SITE IMPROVEMENTS
02900 LANDSCAPING

DIVISION 3—CONCRETE

03100 CONCRETE FORMWORK
03200 CONCRETE REINFORCEMENT
03250 CONCRETE ACCESSORIES
03300 CAST-IN-PLACE CONCRETE
03370 CONCRETE CURING
03400 PRECAST CONCRETE
03500 CEMENTITIOUS DECKS
03600 GROUT
03700 CONCRETE RESTORATION AND CLEANING
03800 MASS CONCRETE

DIVISION 4—MASONRY

04100 MORTAR
04150 MASONRY ACCESSORIES
04200 UNIT MASONRY
04400 STONE
04500 MASONRY RESTORATION AND CLEANING
04550 REFRACTORIES
04600 CORROSION RESISTANT MASONRY

DIVISION 5—METALS

05010 METAL MATERIALS
05030 METAL FINISHES
05050 METAL FASTENING
05100 STRUCTURAL METAL FRAMING
05200 METAL JOISTS
05300 METAL DECKING
05400 COLD-FORMED METAL FRAMING
05500 METAL FABRICATIONS
05580 SHEET METAL FABRICATIONS
05700 ORNAMENTAL METAL
05800 EXPANSION CONTROL
05900 HYDRAULIC STRUCTURES

DIVISION 6—WOOD AND PLASTICS

06050 FASTENERS AND ADHESIVES
06100 ROUGH CARPENTRY
06130 HEAVY TIMBER CONSTRUCTION
06150 WOOD-METAL SYSTEMS
06170 PREFABRICATED STRUCTURAL WOOD
06200 FINISH CARPENTRY
06300 WOOD TREATMENT
06400 ARCHITECTURAL WOODWORK
06500 PREFABRICATED STRUCTURAL PLASTICS
06600 PLASTIC FABRICATIONS

DIVISION 7—THERMAL AND MOISTURE PROTECTION

07100 WATERPROOFING
07150 DAMPPROOFING
07190 VAPOR AND AIR RETARDERS
07200 INSULATION
07250 FIREPROOFING
07300 SHINGLES AND ROOFING TILES
07400 PREFORMED ROOFING AND CLADDING/SIDING
07500 MEMBRANE ROOFING
07570 TRAFFIC TOPPING
07600 FLASHING AND SHEET METAL
07700 ROOF SPECIALTIES AND ACCESSORIES
07800 SKYLIGHTS
07900 JOINT SEALERS

DIVISION 8—DOORS AND WINDOWS

08100 METAL DOORS AND FRAMES
08200 WOOD AND PLASTIC DOORS
08250 DOOR OPENING ASSEMBLIES
08300 SPECIAL DOORS
08400 ENTRANCES AND STOREFRONTS
08500 METAL WINDOWS
08600 WOOD AND PLASTIC WINDOWS
08650 SPECIAL WINDOWS
08700 HARDWARE
08800 GLAZING
08900 GLAZED CURTAIN WALLS

DIVISION 9—FINISHES

09100 METAL SUPPORT SYSTEMS
09200 LATH AND PLASTER
09230 AGGREGATE COATINGS
09250 GYPSUM BOARD
09300 TILE
09400 TERRAZZO
09500 ACOUSTICAL TREATMENT
09540 SPECIAL SURFACES
09550 WOOD FLOORING
09600 STONE FLOORING
09630 UNIT MASONRY FLOORING
09650 RESILIENT FLOORING
09680 CARPET
09700 SPECIAL FLOORING
09780 FLOOR TREATMENT
09800 SPECIAL COATINGS
09900 PAINTING
09950 WALL COVERINGS

DIVISION 10—SPECIALTIES

10100	CHALKBOARDS AND TACKBOARDS
10150	COMPARTMENTS AND CUBICLES
10200	LOUVERS AND VENTS
10240	GRILLES AND SCREENS
10250	SERVICE WALL SYSTEMS
10260	WALL AND CORNER GUARDS
10270	ACCESS FLOORING
10280	SPECIALTY MODULES
10290	PEST CONTROL
10300	FIREPLACES AND STOVES
10340	PREFABRICATED EXTERIOR SPECIALTIES
10350	FLAGPOLES
10400	IDENTIFYING DEVICES
10450	PEDESTRIAN CONTROL DEVICES
10500	LOCKERS
10520	FIRE PROTECTION SPECIALTIES
10530	PROTECTIVE COVERS
10550	POSTAL SPECIALTIES
10600	PARTITIONS
10650	OPERABLE PARTITIONS
10670	STORAGE SHELVING
10700	EXTERIOR SUN CONTROL DEVICES
10750	TELEPHONE SPECIALTIES
10800	TOILET AND BATH ACCESSORIES
10880	SCALES
10900	WARDROBE AND CLOSET SPECIALTIES

DIVISION 11—EQUIPMENT

11010	MAINTENANCE EQUIPMENT
11020	SECURITY AND VAULT EQUIPMENT
11030	TELLER AND SERVICE EQUIPMENT
11040	ECCLESIASTICAL EQUIPMENT
11050	LIBRARY EQUIPMENT
11060	THEATER AND STAGE EQUIPMENT
11070	INSTRUMENTAL EQUIPMENT
11080	REGISTRATION EQUIPMENT
11090	CHECKROOM EQUIPMENT
11100	MERCANTILE EQUIPMENT
11110	COMMERCIAL LAUNDRY AND DRY CLEANING EQUIPMENT
11120	VENDING EQUIPMENT
11130	AUDIO-VISUAL EQUIPMENT
11140	SERVICE STATION EQUIPMENT
11150	PARKING CONTROL EQUIPMENT
11160	LOADING DOCK EQUIPMENT
11170	SOLID WASTE HANDLING EQUIPMENT
11190	DETENTION EQUIPMENT
11200	WATER SUPPLY AND TREATMENT EQUIPMENT
11280	HYDRAULIC GATES AND VALVES
11300	FLUID WASTE TREATMENT AND DISPOSAL EQUIPMENT
11400	FOOD SERVICE EQUIPMENT
11450	RESIDENTIAL EQUIPMENT
11460	UNIT KITCHENS
11470	DARKROOM EQUIPMENT
11480	ATHLETIC, RECREATIONAL AND THERAPEUTIC EQUIPMENT
11500	INDUSTRIAL AND PROCESS EQUIPMENT
11600	LABORATORY EQUIPMENT
11650	PLANETARIUM EQUIPMENT
11660	OBSERVATORY EQUIPMENT
11700	MEDICAL EQUIPMENT
11780	MORTUARY EQUIPMENT
11850	NAVIGATION EQUIPMENT

DIVISION 12—FURNISHINGS

12050	FABRICS
12100	ARTWORK
12300	MANUFACTURED CASEWORK
12500	WINDOW TREATMENT
12600	FURNITURE AND ACCESSORIES
12670	RUGS AND MATS
12700	MULTIPLE SEATING
12800	INTERIOR PLANTS AND PLANTERS

DIVISION 13—SPECIAL CONSTRUCTION

13010	AIR SUPPORTED STRUCTURES
13020	INTEGRATED ASSEMBLIES
13030	SPECIAL PURPOSE ROOMS
13080	SOUND, VIBRATION, AND SEISMIC CONTROL
13090	RADIATION PROTECTION
13100	NUCLEAR REACTORS
13120	PRE-ENGINEERED STRUCTURES
13150	POOLS
13160	ICE RINKS
13170	KENNELS AND ANIMAL SHELTERS
13180	SITE CONSTRUCTED INCINERATORS
13200	LIQUID AND GAS STORAGE TANKS
13220	FILTER UNDERDRAINS AND MEDIA
13230	DIGESTION TANK COVERS AND APPURTENANCES
13240	OXYGENATION SYSTEMS
13260	SLUDGE CONDITIONING SYSTEMS
13300	UTILITY CONTROL SYSTEMS
13400	INDUSTRIAL AND PROCESS CONTROL SYSTEMS
13500	RECORDING INSTRUMENTATION
13550	TRANSPORTATION CONTROL INSTRUMENTATION
13600	SOLAR ENERGY SYSTEMS
13700	WIND ENERGY SYSTEMS
13800	BUILDING AUTOMATION SYSTEMS
13900	FIRE SUPPRESSION AND SUPERVISORY SYSTEMS

DIVISION 14—CONVEYING SYSTEMS

14100	DUMBWAITERS
14200	ELEVATORS
14300	MOVING STAIRS AND WALKS
14400	LIFTS
14500	MATERIAL HANDLING SYSTEMS
14600	HOISTS AND CRANES
14700	TURNTABLES
14800	SCAFFOLDING
14900	TRANSPORTATION SYSTEMS

DIVISION 15—MECHANICAL

15050	BASIC MECHANICAL MATERIALS AND METHODS
15250	MECHANICAL INSULATION
15300	FIRE PROTECTION
15400	PLUMBING
15500	HEATING, VENTILATING, AND AIR CONDITIONING (HVAC)
15550	HEAT GENERATION
15650	REFRIGERATION
15750	HEAT TRANSFER
15850	AIR HANDLING
15880	AIR DISTRIBUTION
15950	CONTROLS
15990	TESTING, ADJUSTING, AND BALANCING

DIVISION 16—ELECTRICAL

16050	BASIC ELECTRICAL MATERIALS AND METHODS
16200	POWER GENERATION
16300	HIGH VOLTAGE DISTRIBUTION (Above 600-Volt)
16400	SERVICE AND DISTRIBUTION (600-Volt and Below)
16500	LIGHTING
16600	SPECIAL SYSTEMS
16700	COMMUNICATIONS
16850	ELECTRIC RESISTANCE HEATING
16900	CONTROLS
16950	TESTING

6

TYPICAL MANUFACTURING COMPANY - SPECIFICATIONS

SECTION   TITLE

DIVISION 1 - GENERAL REQUIREMENTS

01010   SUMMARY OF THE WORK
01030   ALTERNATES
01040   COORDINATION
01200   PROJECT MEETINGS
01300   SUBMITTALS
01400   QUALITY CONTROL
01500   CONSTRUCTION FACILITIES & TEMP. CONTROLS
01630   PRODUCT OPTIONS & SUBSTITUTIONS
01650   STARTING OF SYSTEMS/COMMISSIONING
01700   CONTRACT CLOSEOUT
01710   FINAL CLEANING
01720   PROJECT RECORD DOCUMENTS
01740   WARRANTIES & BONDS

DIVISION 2 - SITEWORK

02050   DEMOLITION
02110   SITE CLEARING
02200   EARTHWORK
02500   PAVING & SURFACING
02825   FOUNTAIN & POOL
02900   LANDSCAPING

DIVISION 3 - CONCRETE

03100   CONCRETE FORMWORK
03200   CONCRETE REINFORCEMENT
03300   CAST-IN-PLACE CONCRETE
03345   CONCRETE FINISHING
03400   PRECAST CONCRETE

DIVISION 4 - MASONRY

(NOT IN USE.)

DIVISION 5 - METALS

05120   STRUCTURAL STEEL
05300   METAL DECKING
05400   COLD-FORMED METAL FRAMING
05500   METAL FABRICATIONS

DIVISION 6 - WOOD & PLASTICS

06100   CARPENTRY, ROUGH
06240   PLASTIC LAMINATE

DIVISION 7 - THERMAL & MOISTURE PROTECTION

07265   MINERAL FIBER FIREPROOFING
07510   BUILT-UP BITUMINOUS ROOFING
07600   FLASHING & SHEET METAL
07900   JOINT SEALERS

DIVISION 8 - DOORS & WINDOWS

08100   METAL DOORS & FRAMES
08210   WOOD DOORS
08305   ACCESS DOORS
08330   COILING DOORS
08410   ALUMINUM ENTRANCES & STOREFRONT
08710   FINISH HARDWARE
08800   GLAZING

DIVISION 9 - FINISHES

09250   GYPSUM BOARD
09650   RESILIENT FLOORING
09680   CARPET
09900   PAINTING
09960   VINYL WALL COVERING

DIVISION 10 - SPECIALITIES

10500   METAL LOCKERS

DIVISION 11 - EQUIPMENT

11160   LOADING DOCK EQUIPMENT

DIVISION 12 - FURNISHINGS

12300   MANUFACTURED CASEWORK

DIVISION 13 - SPECIAL CONSTRUCTION

13400   INDUSTRIAL & PROCESS CONTROL SYSTEMS

DIVISION 14 - CONVEYING SYSTEMS

14200   ELEVATORS
14585   PNEUMATIC TUBE SYSTEM

DIVISION 15 - MECHANICAL

15010   BASIC MECHANICAL REQUIREMENTS
15055   BASIC PIPING MATERIALS & METHODS
15125   EXPANSION COMPENSATION
15140   SUPPORTS & ANCHORS
15190   MECHANICAL IDENTIFICATION
15250   MECHANICAL INSULATION
15420   DRAINAGE & VENT SYSTEM
15500   HEATING, VENTILATING & AIR CONDITIONING
15990   TESTING, ADJUSTING & BALANCING

DIVISION 16 - ELECTRICAL

16010   BASIC ELECTRICAL REQUIREMENTS
16050   BASIC ELECTRICAL MATERIALS & METHODS
16500   LIGHTING
16720   ALARM & DETECTION EQUIPMENT
16740   TELEPHONE SYSTEMS

SECTION FORMAT OUTLINE

PART 1 GENERAL

SUMMARY
Section Includes
Products Furnished but not
  Installed Under this Section
Products Installed but not
  Furnished Under this Section
Related Sections
Allowances
Unit Prices
Alternates/Alternatives*

REFERENCES

DEFINITIONS

SYSTEM DESCRIPTION
Design Requirements
Performance Requirements

SUBMITTALS
Product Data
Shop Drawings
Samples
Quality Control Submittals
  Design Data
  Test Reports
  Certificates
  Manufacturer's Instructions
  Manufacturer's Field Reports
Contract Closeout Submittals
  Project Record Documents
  Operation and Maintenance
    Data Warranty

QUALITY ASSURANCE
Qualifications
Regulatory Requirements
Certifications
Field Samples
Mock-Ups
Pre-Installation Conference

DELIVERY, STORAGE, AND HANDLING
Packing and Shipping
Acceptance at Site
Storage and Protection

PROJECT/SITE* CONDITIONS
Environmental Requirements
Existing Conditions
Field Measurements

SEQUENCING AND SCHEDULING

WARRANTY
Special Warranty

MAINTENANCE
Maintenance Service
Extra Materials

PART 2 PRODUCTS

MANUFACTURERS

MATERIALS

MANUFACTURED UNITS

EQUIPMENT

COMPONENTS

ACCESSORIES

MIXES

FABRICATION
Shop Assembly
Shop/Factory/Finishing
Tolerances

SOURCE QUALITY CONTROL
Tests
Inspection
Verification of Performance

PART 3 EXECUTION

EXAMINATION
Verification of Conditions

PREPARATION
Protection
Surface Preparation

ERECTION
INSTALLATION
APPLICATION

Special Techniques
Interface with Other Products
Tolerances

FIELD QUALITY CONTROL
Tests
Inspection
Manufacturer's Field Service

ADJUSTING

CLEANING

DEMONSTRATION

PROTECTION

SCHEDULES

(Reproduced by permission of the Construction Specifications Institute)

DIVISION 3—CONCRETE

| Section Number | Title | | Broadscope Explanation |

03100   CONCRETE FORMWORK
-110   Structural Cast-in-Place Concrete Formwork
    Slip-Forming
-120   Architectural Cast-in-Place Concrete Formwork
-130   Permanent Forms
    Permanent Steel Forms
    Prefabricated Stair Forms

03200   CONCRETE REINFORCEMENT
-210   Reinforcing Steel
-220   Welded Wire Fabric
-230   Stressing Tendons
-240   Fibrous Reinforcing

03250   CONCRETE ACCESSORIES
    Anchors and Inserts
    Expansion and Contraction Joints
    Waterstops

03300   CAST-IN-PLACE CONCRETE
-310   Structural Concrete
    Normalweight Structural Concrete
    Heavyweight Structural Concrete
    Lightweight Structural Concrete
    Shrinkage Compensating Concrete
-320   Concrete Topping
-330   Architectural Concrete
    Normalweight Architectural Concrete
    Lightweight Architectural Concrete
-340   Low Density Concrete
-345   Concrete Finishing
-350   Special Concrete Finishes
    Blasted Concrete
    Colored Concrete
    Exposed Aggregate Concrete
    Grooved Surface Concrete
    Heavy-Duty Concrete Floor Finishes
    Tooled Concrete
-360   Specially Placed Concrete
    Shotcrete
-365   Post-Tensioned Concrete

03370   CONCRETE CURING

Broadscope Explanation

03100 — CONCRETE FORMWORK
Permanent forms and temporary formwork for placing of structural and architectural cast-in-place concrete including formliners, coatings, form ties, and accessories.

> *Related Work:*
> Forms for precast concrete: Section 03400.
> Cementitious deck form boards: Section 03500.
> Metal Decking: Section 05300.

03200 — CONCRETE REINFORCEMENT
Reinforcing steel, welded wire fabric, and stressing tendons. Includes fibrous reinforcing.

> *Related Work:*
> Concrete paving: Section 02500.
> Post-tensioned concrete: Section 03300.
> Cementitious deck reinforcement: Section 03500.
> Reinforcement in masonry: Sections 04150 and 04200.

> *Note:*   Concrete reinforcement may be specified in Sections 02500, 03300, 03400, and 03500. Stressing tendons are usually specified in Section 03365.

03250 — CONCRETE ACCESSORIES
Expansion and contraction joints, anchors, inserts, and waterstops.

> *Related Work:*
> Form ties and accessories: Section 03100.
> Expansion joint covers: Section 05800.

> *Note:*   This section is used primarily for data filing of concrete accessories. Concrete accessories may be specified here or in Sections 03100, 03300, 03400, or 03500. Anchors for items attached or anchored to concrete are furnished under other Divisions and installed under this Division.

03300 — CAST-IN-PLACE CONCRETE
Concrete cast-in-place, including normal finishing.

> *Related Work:*
> Granular sub-base: Section 02200.
> Portland cement concrete paving: Section 02500.
> Concrete Formwork: Section 03100.
> Concrete Reinforcement: Section 03200.
> Concrete accessories: Section 03250.
> Concrete Curing: Section 03370.
> Gypsum concrete: Section 03500.
> Vapor retarders: Section 07190.
> Floor Treatment: Section 09780.

> *Note:*   Concrete reinforcement, concrete accessories, and concrete formwork may be specified in this section. Stressing tendons are usually specified in this section. Granular sub-base and vapor retarders for slabs on grade are often specified in this section.

03370 — CONCRETE CURING
Various methods of curing concrete including water, sand, paper, compounds, etc.

> *Note:*   This section is used mostly for data filing of concrete curing materials and methods. Concrete curing is often specified in Section 03300.

DIVISION 3—CONCRETE *Continued*

Section Number	Title
03400	**PRECAST CONCRETE**
-410	Structural Precast Concrete (Plant Cast)
	Precast Concrete Hollow-Core Planks
	Precast Concrete Slabs (Deck)
	Structural Precast Pretensioned Concrete (Plant Cast)
-420	Structural Precast Post-Tensioned Concrete (Plant Cast)
-430	Structural Precast Concrete (Site Cast)
	Lift-Slab Concrete
	Precast Post-Tensioned Concrete (Site Cast)
	Structural Precast Pretensioned Concrete (Site Cast)
-450	Architectural Precast Concrete (Plant Cast)
	Faced Architectural Precast Concrete
	Glass Fiber Reinforced Precast Concrete
-460	Architectural Precast Concrete (Site Cast)
-470	Tilt-Up Precast Concrete
-480	Precast Concrete Specialties
	Manholes
	Parking Bumpers
	Pavers
	Storage Tanks
	Vaults
03500	**CEMENTITIOUS DECKS**
-510	Gypsum Concrete
	Gypsum Concrete Floor Underlayment
	Gypsum Concrete Roof Deck
-520	Lightweight Insulating Concrete Deck
-530	Cementitious Wood Fiber Systems
	Cementitious Wood Fiber Plank and Tile
-540	Composite Concrete and Insulation Deck
03600	**GROUT**
	Catalyzed Metallic Grout
	Epoxy Grout
	Nonmetallic Grout
03700	**CONCRETE RESTORATION AND CLEANING**
-710	Concrete Cleaning
-720	Concrete Resurfacing
-730	Concrete Rehabilitation
03800	**MASS CONCRETE**

Broadscope Explanation

03400 — PRECAST CONCRETE

Concrete cast in forms before final placement (may be onsite or off-site). Also includes architectural precast concrete faced with stone, tile, masonry or other materials. Metal fasteners and welding of precast concrete elements are also included.

> **Related Work:**
> Installation of precast concrete elements as masonry units: Division 4.
> Glass fiber reinforced concrete composite panels: Section 07400.
>
> **Note:** Furnishing of veneer stone facing for architectural precast concrete panels may be specified in Section 04400. Furnishing of unit masonry facing for architectural precast concrete panels may be specified in Section 04200. Furnishing of tile facing for architectural precast composite panels may be specified in Section 09300. Precast storage tanks, parking bumpers, pavers and splashblocks are usually specified in Division 2. Roof walks are usually specified in Division 7.

03500 — CEMENTITIOUS DECKS

Poured and prefabricated cementitious floor and roof decks and fill. Includes form boards, reinforcement, and support members when specified as a system.

> **Related Work:**
> Low-density concrete: Section 03300.
> Precast concrete decks: Section 03400.
> Asphaltic thermal-setting insulating fill: Section 07200.
>
> **Note:** Corrugated permanent metal forms may be specified with the insulation fill as a system.

03600 — GROUT

Thin, fluid, shrink-resistant mortar-like material for filling joints and cavities and setting and anchoring items in masonry and concrete.

> **Related Work:**
> Masonry grout: Section 04100.
>
> **Note:** Shrink-resistant grout may be specified in Sections where it is used in installation of items such as structural metal framing, metal fabrications, and ornamental metal in, or on, concrete.

03700 — CONCRETE RESTORATION AND CLEANING

Epoxy injected crack repair is included in this section.

> **Note:** Normal cleaning of new concrete is usually specified in Sections 03300 and 03400.

03800 — MASS CONCRETE

Large volume placement of cast-in-place concrete, as in dams and other heavy construction, with dimensions large enough to require special construction techniques and procedures to cope with the generation of heat and attendant volume change to minimize cracking.

9

SPECIFICATIONS—DIVISIONS 1-16

DIVISION 1—GENERAL REQUIREMENTS

Section Number	Title

01010	**SUMMARY OF WORK**
	Work Covered by Contract Documents
	Contracts
	Work Under Other Contracts
	Future Work
	Work Sequence
	Contractor Use of Premises
	Occupancy
	   Owner Occupancy
	   Partial Occupancy
	   Continued Occupancy
	   Maintenance of Operation
	Pre-ordered Products
	Owner-furnished Items

01020
-021
 	
-024
	ALLOWANCES
	Cash Allowances
	  Inspection and Testing Allowances
	  Contingency Allowance
	Quantity Allowances

01025	**MEASUREMENT AND PAYMENT** *Unit Prices* *Application for Payment* *Change Order Procedures*
01030	**ALTERNATES/ALTERNATIVES**
01040 -041 -042 -043 -045	**COORDINATION** Project Coordination Mechanical and Electrical Coordination Job Site Administration Cutting and Patching
01050	**FIELD ENGINEERING**
01060	**REGULATORY REQUIREMENTS**

Broadscope Explanation

01010 — SUMMARY OF WORK

Identifies the project and the work covered by the contract documents. Establishes the type of contract (or contracts in the case of multiple contracts) and any separate contracts on the project.

    Related Requirements:
        Statement of work to be performed: Document 00500.

    Note: *Under separate or segregated contracts, the scope of work under each contract should be specified here. Since Summary of Work is normally written as a single section, numbers have not been assigned.*

01020 — ALLOWANCES

Identifies and schedules cash allowances included in the Contract Sum for products, testing services, and contingencies allowance. Also defines the Contractor's costs, included in the Contract Sum, and the administrative procedures for the selection of products under the allowance.

    Related Requirements:
        Adjustment of costs: Document 00700.
        Unit prices: Section 01025.

    Note: *Sections affected by allowances should contain a reference to this section.*

01025 — MEASUREMENT AND PAYMENT

Procedures and submittal requirements for: unit prices or lump sum items, applications for payment, and change order processing.

    Related Requirements:
        Allowances: Section 01020.
        Unit costs: Document 00300.

    Note: *Spaces for Bidder listing of unit prices or prices on lump sum items are located in the Bid Form.*

01030 — ALTERNATES/ALTERNATIVES

Identifies each alternate, describing the changes of work included in each, with references to the various specification sections involved. Rooms, areas, or portions of the work may be described to clarify changes.

    Related Requirements:
        Alternate Costs: Document 00300.

    Note: *Alternatives is a Canadian term. Spaces for Bidder listing of alternate costs are located in the Bid Form. Alternates sometimes require descriptions on the Drawings in order to define the scope properly. Sections affected by Alternates/Alternatives should contain a reference to this section.*

01040 — COORDINATION

Describes coordination of work under the Contract; work under separate contracts, coordination of multiple contract work, and coordination of various parts of the Work.

    Related Requirements:
        Work under separate contracts: Section 01010.
        Alteration project procedures: Section 01100.

01050 — FIELD ENGINEERING

Describes survey work and engineering responsibilities of the Contractor.

    Related Requirements:
        Owner's property survey: Document 00200.

    Note: *Surveys provided by the Owner should not be included in the Contract Documents. Work included here is by the Contractor only.*

01060 — REGULATORY REQUIREMENTS

Lists building codes, mechanical codes and fees, electrical codes and fees, and regulations applicable to the project.

    Related Requirements:
        Codes and regulations: Document 00010.

DIVISION 1—GENERAL REQUIREMENTS *Continued*

Section Number	Title

Broadscope Explanation

01070   **ABBREVIATIONS AND SYMBOLS**

01070 — ABBREVIATIONS AND SYMBOLS
Lists and explains abbreviations and symbols used in the Contract Documents.

> ***Note:*** *Abbreviations and symbols are often included on the drawings.*

01080   **IDENTIFICATION SYSTEMS**

01080 — IDENTIFICATION SYSTEMS
General procedural requirements for identifying elements of systems and equipment by such methods as paint, bands, tags, or signboards.

> ***Related Requirements:***
> *Painted signs: Section 09900.*
> *Identifying Devices: Section 10400.*
> *Equipment: Divisions 2 and 11.*
> *Special Construction: Division I3.*
> *Mechanical Systems: Division I5.*
> *Electrical Systems: Division 16.*

> ***Note:*** *Signs for the public and occupants of a building are included in Sections 09900 and 10400. Specific requirements and procedures should be included in the section where the identification systems are specified.*

01090   **REFERENCE STANDARDS**

01090 — REFERENCE STANDARDS
Establishes edition dates of standards not otherwise referenced in the Project Manual. Includes abbreviations, names, and addresses of organizations whose standards are referenced in the Project Manaul.

> ***Note:*** *Specific standards are referenced in appropriate specification sections.*

01100   **SPECIAL PROJECT PROCEDURES**
-110   Airport Project Procedures
-120   Alteration Project Procedures
       Hazardous Materials Procedures
-130   Detention Project Procedures
-140   Hospital Project Procedures
-150   Industrial Project Procedures
-160   Nuclear Project Procedures

01100 — SPECIAL PROJECT PROCEDURES
Describes special procedures required for additions and alterations projects for very complex projects and for handling hazardous materials such as Asbestos or PCB.

> ***Related Requirements:***
> *Coordination: Section 01040.*
> *Minor demolition for remodeling: Section 02050.*

> ***Note:*** *This section includes procedures only. If alterations or restoration work requires the specifying of sundry minor products for accomplishing the work consider using Section 13990 - Minor Alterations Work.*

01200   **PROJECT MEETINGS**
-210   Preconstruction Conferences
-220   Progress Meetings

01200 — PROJECT MEETINGS
Administrative and procedural requirements for meetings required for the Contractor's management of the Construction Contract.

> ***Related Requirements:***
> *Pre-bid conferences: Document 00100.*
> *Coordination: Section 01040.*

> ***Note:*** *Excluded from this section are pre-bid conferences and additional duties required for project coordination by the Contractor or Construction Manager responsible for coordination in multiplecontract work.*

01300   **SUBMITTALS**
-310   Progress Schedules
       Network Analysis Schedules
-320   Progress Reports
-330   Survey Data
-340   Shop Drawings, Product Data, and Samples
-350   Field Samples
-360   Layout Data
-370   Schedule of Values
-380   Construction Photographs

01300 — SUBMITTALS
General procedures and requirements for submittals. Specific requirements for submittals are included in the individual sections (Divisions 2-16).

> ***Related Requirements:***
> *Mock ups: Section 01400.*
> *Project closeout submittals: Section 01700.*

> ***Note:*** *Affected sections should contain a reference to this section. General procedures and requirements that are applicable to all sections are included in this section.*

01400   **QUALITY CONTROL**
-410   Testing Laboratory Services
-420   Inspection Services
-430   Mock-ups
-440   Contractor's Quality Control

01400 — QUALITY CONTROL
Inspection and testing laboratory qualifications, duties and responsibilities. Contractor's quality control requirements. Also includes mock-ups of products or systems for testing and operations

> ***Note:*** *Affected sections should contain a reference to this section.*

DIVISION 1—GENERAL REQUIREMENTS *Continued*

Section Number	Title

Broadscope Explanation

01500   **CONSTRUCTION FACILITIES AND TEMPORARY CONTROLS**
- -505   Mobilization
- -510   Temporary Utilities
  - *Temporary Electricity*
  - *Temporary Lighting*
  - *Temporary Heating, Cooling and Ventilating*
  - *Temporary Telephone*
  - *Temporary Water*
  - *Temporary Sanitary Facilities*
  - *Temporary Fire Protection*
- -520   Temporary Construction
  - *Interim Bridges*
  - *Interim Decking*
  - *Interim Overpasses*
  - *Interim Runarounds*
- -525   Construction Aids
  - *Construction Elevators and Hoists*
  - *Scaffolding and Platforms*
  - *Swing Staging*
  - *Temporary Enclosures*
- -530   Barriers and Enclosures
  - *Barricades*
  - *Fences*
  - *Tree and Plant Protection*
- -540   Security
  - *Protection of Work and Property*
- -550   Access Roads and Parking Areas
  - *Access Roads*
  - *Parking Areas*
- -560   Temporary Controls
  - *Construction Cleaning*
  - *Dust Control*
  - *Erosion and Sediment Control*
  - *Noise Control*
  - *Pest Control*
  - *Pollution Control*
  - *Rodent Control*
  - *Surface Water Control*
- -570   Traffic Regulation
  - *Construction Parking Control*
  - *Flagmen*
  - *Flares and Lights*
  - *Haul Routes*
  - *Traffic Signals*
- -580   Project Identification and Signs
- -590   Field Offices and Sheds

01600   **MATERIAL AND EQUIPMENT**
- -610   Transportation and Handling
- -620   Storage and Protection
- -630   Product Options and Substitutions

01650   **STARTING OF SYSTEMS/COMMISSIONING**
- -660   Testing, Adjusting, and Balancing of Systems
- -670   Systems Demonstrations

01500 — CONSTRUCTION FACILITIES AND TEMPORARY CONTROLS

Temporary utilities and miscellaneous temporary facilities required during construction. Sections include requirements for installation, maintenance, and removal. Job mobilization requirements for large construction and heavy civil engineering projects are also included.

> *Related Requirements:*
> *Final cleaning: Section 01700.*
> *Permanent Erosion Control: Section 02270.*

> **Note:** *Payments of costs involved are not specified in this Section. The Contractor-single contract projects-has this responsibility by stipulation in General Conditions. However, under other contractual arrangements, the responsibilities are covered under Section 01010. Some construction facilities and sanitary and safety requirements are required under General Conditions by applicable laws and regulations. These requirements need not be specified in detail in the Specifications. "Construction Aids" under this Broadscope section are primarily for Contractor's filing and cost accounting system.*

01600 — MATERIAL AND EQUIPMENT

General requirements for transportation, handling, storage, and protection of materials and equipment. Contractor's options in selection of products and manufacturers and procedures for consideration of proposal substitutions.

> *Related Requirements:*
> *Substitutions proposed during bidding: Document 00100.*

> **Note:** *Instructions to Bidders may contain a reference to this section to establish information required for consideration of substitution proposals made during bidding. Requirements for substitution submittals applicable only during the bidding period should be included in the Instructions to Bidders and not included in this section.*

01650 — STARTING OF SYSTEMS/COMMISSIONING

General procedural requirements for starting and placing in service systems and equipment. Specific requirements and procedures for starting of systems; testing, adjusting, and balancing; and demonstration of systems should be included in the Division where the system is specified. This Division 1 section should contain only the basic procedural requirements applying to all systems.

> *Related Requirements:*
> *Sitework: Division 2.*
> *Equipment: Division 11.*
> *Special Construction: Division 13.*
> *Conveying Systems: Division 14.*
> *Mechanical Systems: Division 15.*
> *Electrical Systems: Division 16.*

> **Note:** *Commissioning is a Canadian term. Sections with affected systems should contain a reference to this section.*

DIVISION 1—GENERAL REQUIREMENTS *Continued*

**Section
Number**   **Title**

Broadscope Explanation

01700	**CONTRACT CLOSEOUT**
-710	Final Cleaning
-720	Project Record Documents
-730	Operating and Maintenance Data
-740	Warranties and Bonds
-750	Spare Parts and Maintenance Materials

01700 — CONTRACT CLOSEOUT
Specific administrative procedures, closeout submittals, and forms to be used at substantial completion and at final completion of the work.

> *Related Requirements:*
> Submittals: Section 01300.
> Periodic construction cleaning: Section 01500.

> **Note:** Affected sections should contain a reference to this section.

01800   **MAINTENANCE**

01800 — MAINTENANCE

10

SAMPLE - SPECIFICATION CHECKLIST

ITEM: LOCKERS

DATE: Sept. 1, 1987

PROJECT:

TYPICAL MANUFACTURING CO.
INDUSTRIAL PLANT & OFFICES
100 INDUSTRIAL BLVD.
HAYWARD, CALIFORNIA

INTERVIEW WITH:

    Jim Robertson
    Project Representative
    Typical Manufacturing Co.

ABC ARCHITECTS
600 MAIN ST.
SAN FRANCISCO, CA

TYPE:

    -X- STANDARD
    --- COIN OPERATED
    --- PURSE LOCKER

MATERIAL:

    -X- EXPANDED METAL
    --- PERFORATED METAL
    --- PLASTIC LAMINATE

COLOR:

    -X- MANUFACTURER'S STANDARD
    --- CUSTOM
        COLOR PREFERENCE: DARK BLUE

TIERS:

    -X- 1 TIER
    --- 2 TIER
    --- 3 TIER

VENTILATION:

    -X- STANDARD
    --- FULL FRONT

LOCKS:

    --- NONE - (USER PROVIDES PADLOCK)
    --- KEY OPERATED
    -X- COMBINATION TYPE

TOP:

    -X- FLAT
    --- SLOPED

BASE:

    -X- CONCRETE CURB MOUNTED
    --- OPEN
    --- METAL TRIM

HANDLE:

    -X- RECESSED
    --- PROJECTING

CONFIGURATION:

    -X- WALL RECESSED
    --- FREESTANDING

FEATURES:

    -X- SHELF
    -X- NUMBER PLATES
    -X- COAT HOOKS

BENCH:

    --- NONE
    -X- MANUFACTURER'S STANDARD
    --- WOOD
    --- PLASTIC LAMINATE

COMMENTS:
        Baked-on-enamel finish
        Specify concrete curb in Division 3

DELETE FROM PROJECT SPECS

SECTION 10500 - METAL LOCKERS

PART 1 - GENERAL

RELATED DOCUMENTS:

Drawings and general provisions of Contract, including General and Supplementary Conditions and Division-1 Specification sections, apply to work of this section.

DELETE ALL NOTES TO EDITOR FROM PROJECT SPECS

DESCRIPTION OF WORK:

Extent of metal lockers is shown on drawings.

DELETE OR REVISE BELOW TO SUIT PROJECT.

Types of products in this section include the following:

Standard wardrobe lockers.

Single-tier lockers.

~~Double-tier lockers.~~

~~Multi-tier lockers.~~

~~Athletic lockers.~~

~~Single-tier lockers.~~

~~Double-tier lockers.~~

~~Multi-tier lockers.~~

Locker room benches.

Concrete base for lockers is specified in Division 3.

~~Masonry base for lockers is specified in Division 4.~~

~~Wood sleepers are specified in Division 6.~~

QUALITY ASSURANCE:

Uniformity: Provide each type of metal locker as produced by a single manufacturer, including necessary mounting accessories, fittings, and fastenings.

PLACE FOOTING AT BOTTOM OF EACH PAGE & ALIGN

TYPICAL MANUFACTURING CO.
INDUSTRIAL PLANT & OFFICES

SUBMITTALS:

Product Data: Submit manufacturer's technical data and installation instructions for metal locker units.

> DELETE BELOW IF NOT REQUIRED, OR MODIFY TO SUIT OFFICE PRACTICE. COORDINATE WITH DWGS.

Samples: Submit color samples on squares of same metal to be used for fabrication of lockers.

> DELETE BELOW IF NOT REQUIRED.

Shop Drawings: Submit shop drawings for metal lockers, verifying dimensions affecting locker installations. Show lockers in detail, method of installation, fillers, trim, base, and accessories. Include locker numbering sequence information.

> DELETE BELOW IF NO BUILT-IN COMBINATION LOCKS.

Combination Listing: Submit listings for combination locks and their respective locker numbers. Coordinate with shop drawings submittal, if required.

JOB CONDITIONS:

Do not deliver metal lockers until building is enclosed and ready for locker installation. Protect from damage during delivery, handling, storage, and installation.

PART 2 - PRODUCTS

ACCEPTABLE MANUFACTURERS:

Available Manufacturers: Subject to compliance with requirements, manufacturers offering products which may be incorporated in the work include, but are not limited to, the following:

> RETAIN ABOVE OR BELOW, FOR NONPROPRIETARY OR SEMIPROPRIETARY SPECIFICATION.

Manufacturer: Subject to compliance with requirements, provide products of one of the following:

All American Locker Div.; De Bourgh Mfg. Co.

> ABOVE PROVIDES ONLY ATHLETIC LOCKERS.

Art Metal Products Co
Interior Steel Equipment Co.
~~List Industries Inc.~~
Medart Inc.
~~Penco Products Inc.~~
Republic Storage Systems

BELOW ONLY PROVIDES WARDROBE LOCKERS.

Tennsco Corp.

ABOVE ARE PRIMARILY K-D LOCKERS. HEAVY DUTY, ALL-WELD LOCKERS AVAILABLE FROM SELECTED MFRS. (ART METAL, DE BROUGH AND LIST INDUSTRIES).

MATERIALS:

Sheet Steel: ~~Mild cold-rolled~~ and leveled steel, free from buckle, scale, and surface imperfections.

Expanded Metal: 3/4" mesh flattened carbon steel, 13 gage minimum.

Fasteners: Cadmium, zinc, or nickle plated steel; exposed bolt heads, slotless type; self-locking nuts or locker washers for nuts on moving parts.

Equipment: Hooks and hang rods of cadmium-plated or zinc-plated steel or cast aluminum.

FABRICATION, GENERAL:

Construction: Fabricate lockers square, rigid, and without warp, with metal faces flat and free of dents or distortion. Make all exposed metal edges safe to touch. Weld frame members together to form rigid, one-piece structure. Weld, bolt, or rivet other joints and connections as standard with manufacturer. Grind exposed welds flush. Do not expose bolts or rivet heads on fronts of locker doors or frames.

Frames: Fabricate of 16-gage channels or 12-gage angles, minimum, with continuous stop/strike formed on vertical members.

Finishing: Chemically pretreat metal with degreasing and phosphatizing process. Apply baked-on enamel finish to all surfaces, exposed and concealed, except plates and non-ferrous metal.

CUSTOM COLORS ALSO AVAILABLE FROM MOST MFRS.

Color: Provide locker units in color(s) as shown on drawings, or if not shown, as selected by Architect from manufacturer's standards. Unless otherwise indicated, concealed parts may be manufacturer's standard neutral color.

WARDROBE LOCKERS:

Body: Fabricate back and sides of minimum 24-gage steel, with double-flanged connections extending full height. Form top and bottom of not less than 24-gage steel, with flanged edges.

Provide 24-gage steel sheet hat shelf in single-tier units.

DELETE BELOW IF ALL LOCKERS RECESSED. NARROW (9"-12") DOORS MAY BE FABRICATED OF 18GA. MATERIAL

Form exposed ends of non-recessed lockers of minimum 16-gage steel.

Door: One-piece, minimum 16-gage sheet steel, flanged at all edges, constructed to prevent springing when opening or closing. Fabricate to swing 180°.

Reinforcing: Provide extra bracing or reinforcing on inside of doors over 15" wide.

DELETE OR REVISE BELOW IF REQUIREMENT FOR ACOUSTICAL TREATMENT IS RETAINED BELOW. SOME MFRS. OFFER CONCEALED VENTILATION SYSTEM.

Ventilation: Provide stamped, louvered vents in door face, as follows:

Single-tier lockers: Not less than 6 louver openings top and bottom.

Double-tier lockers: Not less than 3 louver openings top and bottom.

Multi-tier lockers: Not less than 2 louver openings top and bottom, or 3 louver openings top or bottom.

Hinges: Heavy-duty, not less than 0.050" thick steel, full-loop, 5-knuckle, tight pin, 2" high. Weld to inside of frame and secure to door with not less than 2 factory-installed fasteners which are completely concealed and tamperproof when door is closed.

Provide at least 3 hinges for each door over 42" high, at least 2 hinges for each door 42" high or less.

Projecting Handle and Latch: Positive automatic, prelocking, pry-resistant latch and pull with rubber silencers; chromium-plated, heavy-duty, vandalproof lift-up handle, containing strike and eye for padlock; and with latching action as follows:

DELETE ABOVE OR BELOW.

Recessed Handle and Latch: Manufacturer's standard design consisting of housing to form recess for latch lifter and locking devices; non-protruding latch lifter containing strike and eye for padlock; and automatic, prelocking, pry-resistant latch mechanism with latching action as follows:

RETAIN APPLICABLE LATCHING ACTION(S) BELOW WITH EITHER PROJECTING OR RECESSED HANDLE ABOVE.

Single-tier lockers: Not less than 3-point latching.

Double-tier lockers: Not less than 2-point latching.

Multi-tier lockers: Not less than one-point gravity or spring latch with padlock lugs.

DELETE BELOW IF NOT REQUIRED.

Acoustical Treatment: Provide construction treatment designed to significantly reduce noise of locker operation, including protected sound-absorbing material within door, nylon or plastic coatings on operating components to prevent metal-to-metal contact, and latching mechanism designed to operate without rattling.

IF ABOVE FEATURE RETAINED, DELETE REQUIREMENT FOR DOOR VENTS.

ATHLETIC LOCKERS:

Body: Fabricate top and bottom of not less than 16-gage steel sheet, and fabricate back of not less than 18-gage steel sheet. Construct sides and intermediate partitions of expanded metal welded to steel hemming.

Provide 16-gage perforated steel shelf in single-tier lockers.

Door: Manufacturer's standard of either expanded metal in steel frame or perforated steel sheet with flanged edges, not less than 14 gage, except 16 gage for multi-tier units.

Reinforcing: Provide extra bracing or reinforcing on inside of doors over 15" wide.

Hinges: Heavy-duty, not less than 0.050" thick steel, full-loop, 5-knuckle, tight pin, 2" high. Weld to inside of frame and secure to door with not less than 2 factory-installed fasteners which are completely concealed and tamperproof when door is closed.

Provide at least 3 hinges for each door over 42" high, at least 2 hinges for each door 42" high or less, or continuous piano hinge at top for multi-tier units.

Latching: Provide mechanism as follows for each locker type required:

REVISE BELOW IF RECESSED LOCKING/LATCHING REQUIRED. VERIFY AVAILABLITY FROM LISTED MFRS.

Single-, Double-, and Triple-Tier Units: Three-point latching device, engaging frame at top, bottom, and jamb, with chromium plated turn handle having provisions for padlock.

Multi-Tier Units: One-point latching device with lock clip for locking with padlock, built-in key, or combination lock.

LOCKER ACCESSORIES:

Locking: Fabricate lockers to receive the following locking devices:

SELECT TYPE OF LOCKING DEVICE. IF MORE THAN ONE, INDICATE TYPES ON DRAWINGS OR ADD DESCRIPTIVE LOCATIONS BELOW.

Key Lock: 5-pin tumbler, grooved-key flush lock, keyed separately and masterkeyed. Furnish 2 keys for each lock and 5 masterkeys. Provide bolt operation as follows:

SELECT TYPE OF BOLT OPERATION, OR INDICATE IF OPTIONAL.

Dead-bolt action.

Spring-bolt action.

Built-In Combination Lock: Key-controlled, 3-number dialing combination lock, with combination change made automatically by use of control key. Provide bolt operation as follows:

SELECT TYPE OF BOLT OPERATION, OR INDICATE IF OPTIONAL.

Automatic dead-bolt action.

~~Spring-bolt action.~~

~~Padlock: Provided by Owner.~~

REVISE BELOW TO SUIT PROJECT AND LOCKER
TYPES.

Equipment: Furnish each locker with the following items, unless
otherwise shown:

Single-Tier Units: Hat shelf, one double-prong hook and not
less than 2 single-prong wall hooks.

Double-Tier Units: One double-prong hook and not less than 2
single-prong wall hooks.

Lockers 18" Deep: Provide hang rod in lieu of hook.

Number Plates: Manufacturer's standard etched, embossed, or
stamped, non-ferrous metal number plates with numerals not less
than 3/8" high. Number lockers in sequence as directed by
Architect. Attach plates to each locker door, near top,
centered, with at least 2 fasteners of same finish as number
plate.

DELETE BELOW IF CONCRETE BASE OR METAL
BASE TO BE PROVIDED. REVISE IF INTEGRAL
LEGS/BENCH REQUIRED FOR "FOOD INDUSTRY"
TYPE LOCKERS. VERIFY AVAILABILITY FROM
LISTED MFRS.

Legs: Provide nominal 6" legs by extending vertical frame
members or by attaching gusset type legs made of not less than
16-gage steel sheet, with provision for fastening to floor.

DELETE BELOW IF CLOSED BASE NOT REQUIRED.

Continuous Metal Base: Minimum 20-gage cold-rolled steel,
fabricated in lengths as long as practicable to enclose base of
lockers without additional fastening devices. Flange bottoms
inward 3/4" for stiffening. Factory-finish metal base to match
lockers.

DELETE BELOW IF NONE. SLOPING TOPS
REQUIRE ADDITIONAL HEAD ROOM.

Continuous Sloping Tops: Not less than 20-gage sheet steel,
approximately 25° pitch, in lengths as long as practicable but
not less than 4 lockers. Provide closures at ends. Finish to
match lockers.

←— INSERT ①

DELETE BELOW IF ONLY SINGLE-TIER LOCKERS,
OR OTHERWISE NOT REQUIRED.

Separators: Provide horizontal dividers of not less than 16-gage sheet steel between doors of multiple-tier lockers, to ensure rigidity.

Provide perforated separators for athletic lockers.

DELETE BELOW IF NONE RECESSED.

Trim: Provide trim at jambs and head of recessed lockers, consisting of not less than 18-gage cold-rolled steel, 2" or 3" wide as necessary. Factory-finish trim to match lockers. Secure trim to lockers with concealed fastening clips.

DELETE BELOW UNLESS KNOWN TO BE NEEDED.

Filler Panels: Provide filler panels where indicated, of not less than 18-gage steel sheet, factory-fabricated and finished to match locker units.

DELETE BELOW IF NONE.

LOCKER ROOM BENCHES:

Manufacturer's standard units with laminated hardwood tops approximately 9½" wide by 1¼" thick, in lengths as indicated. Furnish steel pedestal supports not more than 6'-0" o.c., with provisions for fastening to floor and securing to bench. Furnish all anchorages. Apply manufacturer's standard clear coating to bench tops and baked enamel finish to pedestals.

PART 3 - EXECUTION

NORMALLY DELETE BELOW, EXCEPT FOR RECESSED LOCKERS IN UNUSUAL CONFIGURATIONS. SEE EVALUATION SHEETS.

PREPARATION:

Field Measurements: Take field measurements prior to preparation of shop drawings and fabrication of special components, when possible, to ensure proper fitting of work. However, allow for adjustment and fitting of trim and filler panels wherever taking of field measurements before fabrication might delay work.

INSTALLATION:

Install metal lockers at locations shown in accordance with manufacturer's instructions for plumb, level, rigid, and flush installation.

Space fastenings about 48" o.c., unless otherwise recommended by manufacturer, and apply through back-up reinforcing plates where necessary to avoid metal distortion; conceal fasteners insofar as possible.

Install ~~trim, metal base,~~ sloping top units, ~~and metal filler panels~~ where indicated, using concealed fasteners to provide flush, hairline joints against adjacent surfaces.

DELETE BELOW IF NONE

Install benches in compliance with manufacturer's instructions.

ADJUST AND CLEAN:

Adjust doors and latches to operate easily without binding. Verify that integral locking devices are operating properly.

Touch-up marred finishes, but replace units which cannot be restored to factory-finished appearance. Use only materials and procedures recommended or furnished by locker manufacturer.

END OF SECTION 10500

INSERT ①

→ EXPOSED ENDS : FORM HIPS IN EXPOSED ENDS

AT SLOPING TOPS.

A/S/C Section Cover Sheet

Explaining scope and basis of this issue

New

Updated ●

BASIC - 10500 - METAL LOCKERS

8/85

<u>This</u> <u>section</u> <u>specifies</u> standard, factory-fabricated metal lockers of both the wardrobe type and perforated athletic type. Commonly specified accessories and optional features are also included.

<u>Not</u> <u>included</u> in this section are coin-operated lockers, plastic laminate finished wood lockers, open basket systems, security storage units and other special types. If required they should be specified in separate, narrowscope sections in Division 10.

<u>Updating</u> <u>this</u> <u>section</u> can be summarized as follows:

• Addition of items under Description of Work.

• Revisions to manufacturer's listing and identification of products produced.

• Minor revisions to text and notes to reflect industry standards.

The foregoing explanations are not intended to facilitate rekeyboarding of updates; contact AIA/SC for availability of special keyboarding mark-up copy.

Green sheet evaluations were revised to include comments about accessibility for physically handicapped, for ventilation, and energy considerations. Gray sheet drawing coordination notes remain unchanged.

METAL LOCKERS

PRODUCT EVALUATION:

Manufacturers listed in this section produce products which are essentially similar, although not identical. In most cases, the text of this section has been written in such a way that the standard products of all the manufacturers included will comply with the materials and fabrication requirements specified. In other cases, optional features included herein may not be available exactly as specified from all manufacturers listed. Whenever customized features or specialty items are required for a project, it may be necessary or desirable to alter the list of manufacturers.

In any case, it should be understood that any special features such as customized colors or unusual installation methods, will affect both costs and availability.

In addition to "stock" metal units, there are also specialty systems which include vinyl faced, plastic laminate, wood faced, and units of tempered glass. Needless to say, they are not included in the section.

Standard installations include both free-standing units and recessed lockers. The lockers may have legs, which should be fastened to the floor, or they may be installed on factory-fabricated metal bases or concrete pads formed on the site by others. If recessed installations are required, openings should be carefully dimensioned to permit some flexibility, because final dimensions of assembled units may vary for different manufacturers, in spite of common nominal dimensions.

The products specified in this section are not intended for exterior applications, although they may perform adequately in some climates when protected from direct exposure to the weather.

Accessibility of lockers for the physically handicapped is not a subject specifically addressed in locker manufacturer's product literature nor are lockers, per se covered in ANSI A117.1, "Specifications for Making Buildings and Facilities Accessible to and Usable by Physically Handicapped People". Storage requirements, however, are included and these would be applicable to lockers. Factors which must be considered in selecting lockers to comply with these requirements are reach ranges of shelves, hooks and hang rods; and hardware. There also may be other requirements imposed by local and state governments.

Ventilation of lockers is another subject which requires careful attention. In the ASHRAE Systems Handbook chapter on "Ventilation of the Industrial Environment" there is a section which discusses ventilation of locker rooms as well as toilet and shower spaces. Details are included showing methods of providing locker exhaust by either an exhaust plenum formed by sloping top or in a raised base. For lockers used by personnel performing heavy or hot tasks, a recommendation is made that air be exhausted directly from lockers. This air would not be in addition to locker exhaust air but would be a part of it. If locker units are to be integrally ventilated by a mechanical system, it will be necessary to coordinate the specification and drawings with related mechanical and electrical work. Responsibility for connections and closures will have to be determined, and specifications and drawings prepared accordingly.

ENERGY CONSIDERATIONS:

There are no direct energy considerations related to work of this section. Indirectly, energy expended in the production process is saved by selecting lockers which will not require early replacement due to wear or corrosion. Selecting more corrosion-resistant materials or finishes, heavier duty hardware, or better ventilation will not only reduce maintenance costs but also reduce future expenditures of scarce energy resources.

REFERENCE MATERIALS:

Manufacturer's literature represents the major source of reference materials for the lockers themselves. Other references to accessibility for the physically handicapped and for ventilation are mentioned in the paragraphs on these subjects.

There is a Federal Specification AA-L-00486H(1) for steel lockers which might be some help if you need a qualitative analysis for government work.

* * * * *

METAL LOCKERS

In addition to general AIA/SC MASTERSPEC Instructions for coordinating drawings with specifications, it is suggested that drawings indicate the following information related to metal locker units:

Location, depth, and number of units.

Type, arrangement, and size of units by elevations.

Color of each locker or group of lockers. If only one color required for entire project, it could be added to the specifications instead.

Size of any recessed openings, with detail sections of jamb, base, and head showing trim conditions.

Locker numbering sequence.

Typical interior layout of equipment, if other than standard specified.

Metal filler or closure panels.

Coordination with mechanical and electrical drawings for forced ventilation systems.

* * * * *

SECTION 10500 - METAL LOCKERS

PART 1 - GENERAL

RELATED DOCUMENTS:

Drawings and general provisions of Contract, including General and Supplementary Conditions and Division-1 Specification sections, apply to work of this section.

DESCRIPTION OF WORK:

Extent of metal lockers is shown on drawings.

Types of products in this section include the following:

    Standard wardrobe lockers.
        Single-tier lockers.
    Locker room benches.
Concrete base for lockers is specified in Division 3.

QUALITY ASSURANCE:

Uniformity: Provide each type of metal locker as produced by a single manufacturer, including necessary mounting accessories, fittings, and fastenings.

SUBMITTALS:

Product Data: Submit manufacturer's technical data and installation instructions for metal locker units.

Samples: Submit color samples on squares of same metal to be used for fabrication of lockers.

TYPICAL MANUFACTURING CO.   METAL LOCKERS
INDUSTRIAL PLANT & OFFICES   10500-1

Shop Drawings: Submit shop drawings for metal lockers, verifying dimensions affecting locker installations. Show lockers in detail, method of installation, fillers, trim, base, and accessories. Include locker numbering sequence information.

Combination Listing: Submit listings for combination locks and their respective locker numbers. Coordinate with shop drawings submittal, if required.

JOB CONDITIONS:

Do not deliver metal lockers until building is enclosed and ready for locker installation. Protect from damage during delivery, handling, storage, and installation.

PART 2 - PRODUCTS

ACCEPTABLE MANUFACTURERS:

Manufacturer: Subject to compliance with requirements, provide products of one of the following:

Art Metal Products Co
Interior Steel Equipment Co.
Medart Inc.
Republic Storage Systems
Tennsco Corp.

MATERIALS:

Expanded Metal: 3/4" mesh flattened carbon steel, 13 gage minimum.

Fasteners: Cadmium, zinc, or nickel plated steel; exposed bolt heads, slotless type; self-locking nuts or locker washers for nuts on moving parts.

Equipment: Hooks and hang rods of cadmium-plated or zinc-plated steel or cast aluminum.

FABRICATION, GENERAL:

Construction: Fabricate lockers square, rigid, and without warp, with metal faces flat and free of dents or distortion. Make all exposed metal edges safe to touch. Weld frame members together to form rigid, one-piece structure. Weld, bolt, or rivet other joints and connections as standard with manufacturer. Grind exposed welds flush. Do not expose bolts or rivet heads on fronts of locker doors or frames.

Frames: Fabricate of 16-gage channels or 12-gage angles, minimum, with continuous stop/strike formed on vertical members.

Finishing: Chemically pretreat metal with degreasing and phoshatizing process. Apply baked-on enamel finish to all surfaces, exposed and concealed, except plates and non-ferrous metal.

Color: Provide locker units in color(s) as shown on drawings, or if not shown, as selected by Architect from manufacturer's standards. Unless otherwise indicated, concealed parts may be manufacturer's standard neutral color.

WARDROBE LOCKERS:

Body: Fabricate back and sides of minimum 24-gauge steel, with double-flanged connections extending full height. Form top and bottom of not less than 24-gauge steel, with flanged edges.

Provide 24-gauge steel sheet hat shelf in single-tier units.
Form exposed ends of non-recessed lockers of minimum 16-gauge
steel.

Door: One-piece, minimum 16-gauge sheet steel, flanged at all
edges, constructed to prevent springing when opening or closing.
Fabricate to swing 180 degrees.

Reinforcing: Provide extra bracing or reinforcing on inside
of doors over 15" wide.

Ventilation: Provide stamped, louvered vents in door face, as
follows:

Single-tier_lockers: Not less than 6 louver openings top
and bottom.

Hinges: Heavy-duty, not less than 0.050" thick steel, full-loop,
5-knuckle, tight pin, 2" high. Weld to inside of frame and
secure to door with not less than 2 factory-installed fasteners
which are completely concealed and tamperproof when door is
closed.

Recessed Handle and Latch: Manufacturer's standard design
consisting of housing to form recess for latch lifter and locking
devices; non-protruding latch lifter containing strike and eye
for padlock; and automatic, prelocking, pry-resistant latch
mechanism with latching action as follows:

Single-tier lockers: No less than 3-point latching.

LOCKER ACCESSORIES:

Locking: Fabricate lockers to receive the following locking devices.

Built-In Combination Lock: Key-controlled, 3-number dialing combination lock, with combination change made automatically by use of control key. Provide bolt operation as follows:

Automatic dead-bolt action.

Equipment: Furnish each locker with the following items, unless otherwise shown:

Single-Tier Units: Hat shelf, one double-prong hook and not less than 2 single-prong wall hooks.

Number Plates: Manufacturer's standard etched, embossed, or stamped, non-ferrous metal number plates with numerals not less than 3/8" high. Number lockers in sequence as directed by Architect. Attach plates to each locker door, near top, centered, with at least 2 fasteners of same finish as number plate.

Continuous Sloping Tops: Not less than 20-gauge sheet steel, approximately 25 degrees pitch, in lengths as long as practicable but not less than 4 lockers. Provide closures at ends. Finish to match lockers.

Exposed Ends: Form hips in exposed ends at sloping tops.

LOCKER ROOM BENCHES:
Manufacturer's standard units with laminated hardwood tops approximatey 9-1/2" wide by 1-1/4" thick, in lengths as indicated. Furnish steel pedestal supports not more than 6'-0" o.c., with provisions for fastening to floor and securing to

bench.   Furnish all anchorages. Apply manufacturer's standard
clear coating to bench tops and baked enamel finish to pedestals.

PART 3 - EXECUTION

PREPARATION:

Field Measurements: Take field measurements prior to preparation
of shop drawings and fabrication of special components, when
possible, to ensure proper fitting of work.   However, allow for
adjustment and fitting of trim and filler panels wherever taking
of field measurements before fabrication might delay work.

INSTALLATION:

Install metal lockers at locations shown in accordance with
manufacturer's instructions for plumb, level, rigid, and flush
installation.

Space fastenings about 48" o.c., unless otherwise recommended by
manufacturer, and apply through back-up reinforcing plates where
necessary to avoid metal distortion; conceal fasteners insofar as
possible.

Install sloping top units, where indicated, using concealed
fasteners to provide flush, hairline joints against   adjacent
surfaces.

Install benches in compliance with manufacturer's instructions.

ADJUST AND CLEAN:

Adjust doors and latches to operate easily without binding.
Verify that integral locking devices are operating properly.

Touch-up marred finishes, but replace units which cannot be restored to factory-finished appearance. Use only materials and procedures recommended or furnished by locker manufacturer.

END OF SECTION 10500

General Conditions, Supplementary Conditions

The General Conditions of the Contract for Construction serve to set forth the rights, duties, obligations, and relationships of the parties involved in a building construction contract. The architect is not a party to the Owner-Contractor Agreement and the General Conditions of the Contract. However, he does assist in the preparation of these documents and is responsible for performance of the duties assigned to him in these documents.

The AIA General Conditions of the Contract for Construction is a standard preprinted form which sets forth in detail the conditions most common to a typical construction project. Any additions of articles, if required, should be added in the Supplementary Conditions. The Supplementary Conditions modify the General Conditions to meet the requirements of each particular locality, type of project, and owner.

The most widely used document in the industry is the American Institute of Architects General Conditions of the Contract for Construction, Document A201. This form consists of fourteen articles which are in essence as follows:

"Article 1—General Provisions"—defines the following: the Contract Documents; the contract; the work; the project; the drawings; the specifications; the project manual; the execution, correlation and intent; the ownership and use of the documents; the capitalization of terms and titles; and the interpretation of statements.

"Article 2—The Owner"—defines the owner, information and

services required of the owner, the owner's right to stop the work, and the owner's right to carry out the work.

"Article 3—The Contractor"—defines the contractor and his responsibilities in the review of the Contract Documents and field conditions, supervision and construction procedures, provision of labor and materials, the warranty, taxes, permits, fees and notices, cash allowances, employment of a competent superintendent, responsibility for those performing the work, the construction schedule, the documents and samples required at the site, submittals, use of the site, cutting and patching, access to the work, clean up, royalties, patents, and indemnification of the owner and architect against actions resulting from the contractor's operations.

"Article 4—Administration of the Contract"—defines the architect and his function in administration of the contract, lists the architect's responsibilities in acting as the owner's representative in administration of the construction contracts, outlines procedures for communications among owner, contractor and architect, outlines procedures for the filing and resolution of claims and disputes, and outlines provisions for arbitration.

"Article 5—Subcontractors"—defines the subcontractor, limiting the term to those having a direct contract with the contractor to perform work at the site; and outlines provisions related to the award of subcontracts for portions of the work. Also included is a definition of the owner and architect's position with regard to approval of subcontractors, vendors and suppliers, a provision on subcontractual relations, and the contingent assignment of subcontracts in the event of termination of the contract by the owner for cause.

"Article 6—Construction by Owner or by Separate Contractors"— defines the owner's right to perform work and to award separate contracts, the mutual responsibility of contractors, cutting and patching under separate contracts, and the owner's right to clean up.

"Article 7—Changes In the Work"—defines procedures for Change Orders, Construction Change Directives, and minor changes in the work.

"Article 8—Time"—defines the contract time, progress and completion, delays and extensions of time.

"Article 9—Payments and Completion"—defines the contract sum, the Schedule of Values, the procedures for Applications and Certificates for Payment, defines reasons for withholding certification, requires the contractor to make progress payments to subcontractors, outlines provision to be followed in the event of failure of payment, defines procedures to be followed upon substantial completion, final completion and final payment.

"Article 10—Protection of Persons and Property"—defines the contractor's responsibilities in regard to safety precautions and programs, asbestos and PCB, safety of persons and property, and emergencies.

"Article 11—Insurance and Bonds"—defines the requirements of the contractor's liability insurance, the owner's liability insurance and property insurance, boiler and machinery insurance, loss of use insurance, and the owner's right to require a Performance Bond and a Payment Bond.

"Article 12—Uncovering and Correction of the Work"—defines procedures for uncovering of the work, correction of the work, and acceptance of non-conforming work.

"Article 13—Miscellaneous Provisions"—defines the governing law of the contract, successors and assigns, written notice, rights and remedies, tests and inspections, interest and the commencement of the statutory limitation period.

"Article 14—Termination or Suspension of the Contract"—defines conditions and procedures for termination of the contract by the contractor and by the owner. Also outlines procedures for suspension of the work by the owner for convenience.

The Supplementary Conditions modify the articles of the General Conditions to satisfy the specific requirements of the particular project as to governmental regulations of the locality, type of project and owner's special needs. In addition, if articles of a legal nature relating to the contract for the project are required, they should be included in the Supplementary Conditions.

Nontechnical work requirements are placed in Division 1, General Requirements, of the specifications rather than in the Supplementary Conditions. For example, temporary facilities and procedural matters such as number of copies of shop drawings to be submitted are placed in the specifications under General Requirements. Matters of a contractual-legal nature such as the owner's insurance requirements are placed in the Supplementary Conditions.

The AIA Guide for Supplementary Conditions, Document A511, has been prepared to describe the types of additional information most frequently required in the Supplementary Conditions. However, it should be noted that there are variations in needs from project to project and locality to locality. Therefore, when the project is governed by laws and local building practices unfamiliar to the architect, competent professional advice should be obtained from those familiar with the requirements of the project area.

Care must always be exercised when making modifications or deletions to the standard AIA General Conditions. The owner's attorney should be consulted since this document contains contractual and legal stipulations not covered in other contract forms. Furthermore, portions of the AIA General Conditions are interrelated with other AIA forms such as the Owner-Contractor Agreement, the Instructions to Bidders and the bond forms. In addition, the architect's assistance must not be construed to be legal advice. Therefore, all proposed modifications and deletions should be approved in writing by the owner and his attorney both before issuance for bidding and prior to execution of the construction contract.

THE AMERICAN INSTITUTE OF ARCHITECTS

AIA Document A201

General Conditions of the Contract for Construction

THIS DOCUMENT HAS IMPORTANT LEGAL CONSEQUENCES; CONSULTATION WITH AN ATTORNEY IS ENCOURAGED WITH RESPECT TO ITS MODIFICATION

1987 EDITION
TABLE OF ARTICLES

This document has been approved and endorsed by the Associated General Contractors of America.

INDEX

AIA DOCUMENT A201 • GENERAL CONDITIONS OF THE CONTRACT FOR CONSTRUCTION • FOURTEENTH EDITION
AIA® • ©1987 THE AMERICAN INSTITUTE OF ARCHITECTS, 1735 NEW YORK AVENUE, N.W., WASHINGTON, D.C. 20006

AIA DOCUMENT A201 • GENERAL CONDITIONS OF THE CONTRACT FOR CONSTRUCTION • FOURTEENTH EDITION
AIA® • ©1987 THE AMERICAN INSTITUTE OF ARCHITECTS, 1735 NEW YORK AVENUE, N.W., WASHINGTON, D.C. 20006

ARTICLE 1

GENERAL PROVISIONS

1.1 BASIC DEFINITIONS

1.1.1 THE CONTRACT DOCUMENTS

The Contract Documents consist of the Agreement between Owner and Contractor (hereinafter the Agreement), Conditions of the Contract (General, Supplementary and other Conditions), Drawings, Specifications, addenda issued prior to execution of the Contract, other documents listed in the Agreement and Modifications issued after execution of the Contract. A Modification is (1) a written amendment to the Contract signed by both parties, (2) a Change Order, (3) a Construction Change Directive or (4) a written order for a minor change in the Work issued by the Architect. Unless specifically enumerated in the Agreement, the Contract Documents do not include other documents such as bidding requirements (advertisement or invitation to bid, Instructions to Bidders, sample forms, the Contractor's bid or portions of addenda relating to bidding requirements).

1.1.2 THE CONTRACT

The Contract Documents form the Contract for Construction. The Contract represents the entire and integrated agreement between the parties hereto and supersedes prior negotiations, representations or agreements, either written or oral. The Contract may be amended or modified only by a Modification. The Contract Documents shall not be construed to create a contractual relationship of any kind (1) between the Architect and Contractor, (2) between the Owner and a Subcontractor or Sub-subcontractor or (3) between any persons or entities other than the Owner and Contractor. The Architect shall, however, be entitled to performance and enforcement of obligations under the Contract intended to facilitate performance of the Architect's duties.

1.1.3 THE WORK

The term "Work" means the construction and services required by the Contract Documents, whether completed or partially completed, and includes all other labor, materials, equipment and services provided or to be provided by the Contractor to fulfill the Contractor's obligations. The Work may constitute the whole or a part of the Project.

1.1.4 THE PROJECT

The Project is the total construction of which the Work performed under the Contract Documents may be the whole or a part and which may include construction by the Owner or by separate contractors.

1.1.5 THE DRAWINGS

The Drawings are the graphic and pictorial portions of the Contract Documents, wherever located and whenever issued, showing the design, location and dimensions of the Work, generally including plans, elevations, sections, details, schedules and diagrams.

1.1.6 THE SPECIFICATIONS

The Specifications are that portion of the Contract Documents consisting of the written requirements for materials, equip-ment, construction systems, standards and workmanship for the Work, and performance of related services.

1.1.7 THE PROJECT MANUAL

The Project Manual is the volume usually assembled for the Work which may include the bidding requirements, sample forms, Conditions of the Contract and Specifications.

1.2 EXECUTION, CORRELATION AND INTENT

1.2.1 The Contract Documents shall be signed by the Owner and Contractor as provided in the Agreement. If either the Owner or Contractor or both do not sign all the Contract Documents, the Architect shall identify such unsigned Documents upon request.

1.2.2 Execution of the Contract by the Contractor is a representation that the Contractor has visited the site, become familiar with local conditions under which the Work is to be performed and correlated personal observations with requirements of the Contract Documents.

1.2.3 The intent of the Contract Documents is to include all items necessary for the proper execution and completion of the Work by the Contractor. The Contract Documents are complementary, and what is required by one shall be as binding as if required by all; performance by the Contractor shall be required only to the extent consistent with the Contract Documents and reasonably inferable from them as being necessary to produce the intended results.

1.2.4 Organization of the Specifications into divisions, sections and articles, and arrangement of Drawings shall not control the Contractor in dividing the Work among Subcontractors or in establishing the extent of Work to be performed by any trade.

1.2.5 Unless otherwise stated in the Contract Documents, words which have well-known technical or construction industry meanings are used in the Contract Documents in accordance with such recognized meanings.

1.3 OWNERSHIP AND USE OF ARCHITECT'S DRAWINGS, SPECIFICATIONS AND OTHER DOCUMENTS

1.3.1 The Drawings, Specifications and other documents prepared by the Architect are instruments of the Architect's service through which the Work to be executed by the Contractor is described. The Contractor may retain one contract record set. Neither the Contractor nor any Subcontractor, Sub-subcontractor or material or equipment supplier shall own or claim a copyright in the Drawings, Specifications and other documents prepared by the Architect, and unless otherwise indicated the Architect shall be deemed the author of them and will retain all common law, statutory and other reserved rights, in addition to the copyright. All copies of them, except the Contractor's record set, shall be returned or suitably accounted for to the Architect, on request, upon completion of the Work. The Drawings, Specifications and other documents prepared by the Architect, and copies thereof furnished to the Contractor, are for use solely with respect to this Project. They are not to be used by the Contractor or any Subcontractor, Sub-subcontractor or material or equipment supplier on other projects or for additions to this Project outside the scope of the

Work without the specific written consent of the Owner and Architect. The Contractor, Subcontractors, Sub-subcontractors and material or equipment suppliers are granted a limited license to use and reproduce applicable portions of the Drawings, Specifications and other documents prepared by the Architect appropriate to and for use in the execution of their Work under the Contract Documents. All copies made under this license shall bear the statutory copyright notice, if any, shown on the Drawings, Specifications and other documents prepared by the Architect. Submittal or distribution to meet official regulatory requirements or for other purposes in connection with this Project is not to be construed as publication in derogation of the Architect's copyright or other reserved rights.

1.4 CAPITALIZATION

1.4.1 Terms capitalized in these General Conditions include those which are (1) specifically defined, (2) the titles of numbered articles and identified references to Paragraphs, Subparagraphs and Clauses in the document or (3) the titles of other documents published by the American Institute of Architects.

1.5 INTERPRETATION

1.5.1 In the interest of brevity the Contract Documents frequently omit modifying words such as "all" and "any" and articles such as "the" and "an," but the fact that a modifier or an article is absent from one statement and appears in another is not intended to affect the interpretation of either statement.

ARTICLE 2

OWNER

2.1 DEFINITION

2.1.1 The Owner is the person or entity identified as such in the Agreement and is referred to throughout the Contract Documents as if singular in number. The term "Owner" means the Owner or the Owner's authorized representative.

2.1.2 The Owner upon reasonable written request shall furnish to the Contractor in writing information which is necessary and relevant for the Contractor to evaluate, give notice of or enforce mechanic's lien rights. Such information shall include a correct statement of the record legal title to the property on which the Project is located, usually referred to as the site, and the Owner's interest therein at the time of execution of the Agreement and, within five days after any change, information of such change in title, recorded or unrecorded.

2.2 INFORMATION AND SERVICES REQUIRED OF THE OWNER

2.2.1 The Owner shall, at the request of the Contractor, prior to execution of the Agreement and promptly from time to time thereafter, furnish to the Contractor reasonable evidence that financial arrangements have been made to fulfill the Owner's obligations under the Contract. *[Note: Unless such reasonable evidence were furnished on request prior to the execution of the Agreement, the prospective contractor would not be required to execute the Agreement or to commence the Work.]*

2.2.2 The Owner shall furnish surveys describing physical characteristics, legal limitations and utility locations for the site of the Project, and a legal description of the site.

2.2.3 Except for permits and fees which are the responsibility of the Contractor under the Contract Documents, the Owner shall secure and pay for necessary approvals, easements, assess-

ments and charges required for construction, use or occupancy of permanent structures or for permanent changes in existing facilities.

2.2.4 Information or services under the Owner's control shall be furnished by the Owner with reasonable promptness to avoid delay in orderly progress of the Work.

2.2.5 Unless otherwise provided in the Contract Documents, the Contractor will be furnished, free of charge, such copies of Drawings and Project Manuals as are reasonably necessary for execution of the Work.

2.2.6 The foregoing are in addition to other duties and responsibilities of the Owner enumerated herein and especially those in respect to Article 6 (Construction by Owner or by Separate Contractors), Article 9 (Payments and Completion) and Article 11 (Insurance and Bonds).

2.3 OWNER'S RIGHT TO STOP THE WORK

2.3.1 If the Contractor fails to correct Work which is not in accordance with the requirements of the Contract Documents as required by Paragraph 12.2 or persistently fails to carry out Work in accordance with the Contract Documents, the Owner, by written order signed personally or by an agent specifically so empowered by the Owner in writing, may order the Contractor to stop the Work, or any portion thereof, until the cause for such order has been eliminated; however, the right of the Owner to stop the Work shall not give rise to a duty on the part of the Owner to exercise this right for the benefit of the Contractor or any other person or entity, except to the extent required by Subparagraph 6.1.3.

2.4 OWNER'S RIGHT TO CARRY OUT THE WORK

2.4.1 If the Contractor defaults or neglects to carry out the Work in accordance with the Contract Documents and fails within a seven-day period after receipt of written notice from the Owner to commence and continue correction of such default or neglect with diligence and promptness, the Owner may after such seven-day period give the Contractor a second written notice to correct such deficiencies within a second seven-day period. If the Contractor within such second seven-day period after receipt of such second notice fails to commence and continue to correct any deficiencies, the Owner may, without prejudice to other remedies the Owner may have, correct such deficiencies. In such case an appropriate Change Order shall be issued deducting from payments then or thereafter due the Contractor the cost of correcting such deficiencies, including compensation for the Architect's additional services and expenses made necessary by such default, neglect or failure. Such action by the Owner and amounts charged to the Contractor are both subject to prior approval of the Architect. If payments then or thereafter due the Contractor are not sufficient to cover such amounts, the Contractor shall pay the difference to the Owner.

ARTICLE 3

CONTRACTOR

3.1 DEFINITION

3.1.1 The Contractor is the person or entity identified as such in the Agreement and is referred to throughout the Contract Documents as if singular in number. The term "Contractor" means the Contractor or the Contractor's authorized representative.

3.2 REVIEW OF CONTRACT DOCUMENTS AND FIELD CONDITIONS BY CONTRACTOR

3.2.1 The Contractor shall carefully study and compare the Contract Documents with each other and with information furnished by the Owner pursuant to Subparagraph 2.2.2 and shall at once report to the Architect errors, inconsistencies or omissions discovered. The Contractor shall not be liable to the Owner or Architect for damage resulting from errors, inconsistencies or omissions in the Contract Documents unless the Contractor recognized such error, inconsistency or omission and knowingly failed to report it to the Architect. If the Contractor performs any construction activity knowing it involves a recognized error, inconsistency or omission in the Contract Documents without such notice to the Architect, the Contractor shall assume appropriate responsibility for such performance and shall bear an appropriate amount of the attributable costs for correction.

3.2.2 The Contractor shall take field measurements and verify field conditions and shall carefully compare such field measurements and conditions and other information known to the Contractor with the Contract Documents before commencing activities. Errors, inconsistencies or omissions discovered shall be reported to the Architect at once.

3.2.3 The Contractor shall perform the Work in accordance with the Contract Documents and submittals approved pursuant to Paragraph 3.12.

3.3 SUPERVISION AND CONSTRUCTION PROCEDURES

3.3.1 The Contractor shall supervise and direct the Work, using the Contractor's best skill and attention. The Contractor shall be solely responsible for and have control over construction means, methods, techniques, sequences and procedures and for coordinating all portions of the Work under the Contract, unless Contract Documents give other specific instructions concerning these matters.

3.3.2 The Contractor shall be responsible to the Owner for acts and omissions of the Contractor's employees, Subcontractors and their agents and employees, and other persons performing portions of the Work under a contract with the Contractor.

3.3.3 The Contractor shall not be relieved of obligations to perform the Work in accordance with the Contract Documents either by activities or duties of the Architect in the Architect's administration of the Contract, or by tests, inspections or approvals required or performed by persons other than the Contractor.

3.3.4 The Contractor shall be responsible for inspection of portions of Work already performed under this Contract to determine that such portions are in proper condition to receive subsequent Work.

3.4 LABOR AND MATERIALS

3.4.1 Unless otherwise provided in the Contract Documents, the Contractor shall provide and pay for labor, materials, equipment, tools, construction equipment and machinery, water, heat, utilities, transportation, and other facilities and services necessary for proper execution and completion of the Work, whether temporary or permanent and whether or not incorporated or to be incorporated in the Work.

3.4.2 The Contractor shall enforce strict discipline and good order among the Contractor's employees and other persons carrying out the Contract. The Contractor shall not permit employment of unfit persons or persons not skilled in tasks assigned to them.

3.5 WARRANTY

3.5.1 The Contractor warrants to the Owner and Architect that materials and equipment furnished under the Contract will be of good quality and new unless otherwise required or permitted by the Contract Documents, that the Work will be free from defects not inherent in the quality required or permitted, and that the Work will conform with the requirements of the Contract Documents. Work not conforming to these requirements, including substitutions not properly approved and authorized, may be considered defective. The Contractor's warranty excludes remedy for damage or defect caused by abuse, modifications not executed by the Contractor, improper or insufficient maintenance, improper operation, or normal wear and tear under normal usage. If required by the Architect, the Contractor shall furnish satisfactory evidence as to the kind and quality of materials and equipment.

3.6 TAXES

3.6.1 The Contractor shall pay sales, consumer, use and similar taxes for the Work or portions thereof provided by the Contractor which are legally enacted when bids are received or negotiations concluded, whether or not yet effective or merely scheduled to go into effect.

3.7 PERMITS, FEES AND NOTICES

3.7.1 Unless otherwise provided in the Contract Documents, the Contractor shall secure and pay for the building permit and other permits and governmental fees, licenses and inspections necessary for proper execution and completion of the Work which are customarily secured after execution of the Contract and which are legally required when bids are received or negotiations concluded.

3.7.2 The Contractor shall comply with and give notices required by laws, ordinances, rules, regulations and lawful orders of public authorities bearing on performance of the Work.

3.7.3 It is not the Contractor's responsibility to ascertain that the Contract Documents are in accordance with applicable laws, statutes, ordinances, building codes, and rules and regulations. However, if the Contractor observes that portions of the Contract Documents are at variance therewith, the Contractor shall promptly notify the Architect and Owner in writing, and necessary changes shall be accomplished by appropriate Modification.

3.7.4 If the Contractor performs Work knowing it to be contrary to laws, statutes, ordinances, building codes, and rules and regulations without such notice to the Architect and Owner, the Contractor shall assume full responsibility for such Work and shall bear the attributable costs.

3.8 ALLOWANCES

3.8.1 The Contractor shall include in the Contract Sum all allowances stated in the Contract Documents. Items covered by allowances shall be supplied for such amounts and by such persons or entities as the Owner may direct, but the Contractor shall not be required to employ persons or entities against which the Contractor makes reasonable objection.

3.8.2 Unless otherwise provided in the Contract Documents:

    .1 materials and equipment under an allowance shall be selected promptly by the Owner to avoid delay in the Work;

    .2 allowances shall cover the cost to the Contractor of materials and equipment delivered at the site and all required taxes, less applicable trade discounts;

.3 Contractor's costs for unloading and handling at the site, labor, installation costs, overhead, profit and other expenses contemplated for stated allowance amounts shall be included in the Contract Sum and not in the allowances;

.4 whenever costs are more than or less than allowances, the Contract Sum shall be adjusted accordingly by Change Order. The amount of the Change Order shall reflect (1) the difference between actual costs and the allowances under Clause 3.8.2.2 and (2) changes in Contractor's costs under Clause 3.8.2.3.

3.9 SUPERINTENDENT

3.9.1 The Contractor shall employ a competent superintendent and necessary assistants who shall be in attendance at the Project site during performance of the Work. The superintendent shall represent the Contractor, and communications given to the superintendent shall be as binding as if given to the Contractor. Important communications shall be confirmed in writing. Other communications shall be similarly confirmed on written request in each case.

3.10 CONTRACTOR'S CONSTRUCTION SCHEDULES

3.10.1 The Contractor, promptly after being awarded the Contract, shall prepare and submit for the Owner's and Architect's information a Contractor's construction schedule for the Work. The schedule shall not exceed time limits current under the Contract Documents, shall be revised at appropriate intervals as required by the conditions of the Work and Project, shall be related to the entire Project to the extent required by the Contract Documents, and shall provide for expeditious and practicable execution of the Work.

3.10.2 The Contractor shall prepare and keep current, for the Architect's approval, a schedule of submittals which is coordinated with the Contractor's construction schedule and allows the Architect reasonable time to review submittals.

3.10.3 The Contractor shall conform to the most recent schedules.

3.11 DOCUMENTS AND SAMPLES AT THE SITE

3.11.1 The Contractor shall maintain at the site for the Owner one record copy of the Drawings, Specifications, addenda, Change Orders and other Modifications, in good order and marked currently to record changes and selections made during construction, and in addition approved Shop Drawings, Product Data, Samples and similar required submittals. These shall be available to the Architect and shall be delivered to the Architect for submittal to the Owner upon completion of the Work.

3.12 SHOP DRAWINGS, PRODUCT DATA AND SAMPLES

3.12.1 Shop Drawings are drawings, diagrams, schedules and other data specially prepared for the Work by the Contractor or a Subcontractor, Sub-subcontractor, manufacturer, supplier or distributor to illustrate some portion of the Work.

3.12.2 Product Data are illustrations, standard schedules, performance charts, instructions, brochures, diagrams and other information furnished by the Contractor to illustrate materials or equipment for some portion of the Work.

3.12.3 Samples are physical examples which illustrate materials, equipment or workmanship and establish standards by which the Work will be judged.

3.12.4 Shop Drawings, Product Data, Samples and similar submittals are not Contract Documents. The purpose of their submittal is to demonstrate for those portions of the Work for which submittals are required the way the Contractor proposes to conform to the information given and the design concept expressed in the Contract Documents. Review by the Architect is subject to the limitations of Subparagraph 4.2.7.

3.12.5 The Contractor shall review, approve and submit to the Architect Shop Drawings, Product Data, Samples and similar submittals required by the Contract Documents with reasonable promptness and in such sequence as to cause no delay in the Work or in the activities of the Owner or of separate contractors. Submittals made by the Contractor which are not required by the Contract Documents may be returned without action.

3.12.6 The Contractor shall perform no portion of the Work requiring submittal and review of Shop Drawings, Product Data, Samples or similar submittals until the respective submittal has been approved by the Architect. Such Work shall be in accordance with approved submittals.

3.12.7 By approving and submitting Shop Drawings, Product Data, Samples and similar submittals, the Contractor represents that the Contractor has determined and verified materials, field measurements and field construction criteria related thereto, or will do so, and has checked and coordinated the information contained within such submittals with the requirements of the Work and of the Contract Documents.

3.12.8 The Contractor shall not be relieved of responsibility for deviations from requirements of the Contract Documents by the Architect's approval of Shop Drawings, Product Data, Samples or similar submittals unless the Contractor has specifically informed the Architect in writing of such deviation at the time of submittal and the Architect has given written approval to the specific deviation. The Contractor shall not be relieved of responsibility for errors or omissions in Shop Drawings, Product Data, Samples or similar submittals by the Architect's approval thereof.

3.12.9 The Contractor shall direct specific attention, in writing or on resubmitted Shop Drawings, Product Data, Samples or similar submittals, to revisions other than those requested by the Architect on previous submittals.

3.12.10 Informational submittals upon which the Architect is not expected to take responsive action may be so identified in the Contract Documents.

3.12.11 When professional certification of performance criteria of materials, systems or equipment is required by the Contract Documents, the Architect shall be entitled to rely upon the accuracy and completeness of such calculations and certifications.

3.13 USE OF SITE

3.13.1 The Contractor shall confine operations at the site to areas permitted by law, ordinances, permits and the Contract Documents and shall not unreasonably encumber the site with materials or equipment.

3.14 CUTTING AND PATCHING

3.14.1 The Contractor shall be responsible for cutting, fitting or patching required to complete the Work or to make its parts fit together properly.

3.14.2 The Contractor shall not damage or endanger a portion of the Work or fully or partially completed construction of the Owner or separate contractors by cutting, patching or otherwise altering such construction, or by excavation. The Contractor shall not cut or otherwise alter such construction by the

Owner or a separate contractor except with written consent of the Owner and of such separate contractor; such consent shall not be unreasonably withheld. The Contractor shall not unreasonably withhold from the Owner or a separate contractor the Contractor's consent to cutting or otherwise altering the Work.

3.15 CLEANING UP

3.15.1 The Contractor shall keep the premises and surrounding area free from accumulation of waste materials or rubbish caused by operations under the Contract. At completion of the Work the Contractor shall remove from and about the Project waste materials, rubbish, the Contractor's tools, construction equipment, machinery and surplus materials.

3.15.2 If the Contractor fails to clean up as provided in the Contract Documents, the Owner may do so and the cost thereof shall be charged to the Contractor.

3.16 ACCESS TO WORK

3.16.1 The Contractor shall provide the Owner and Architect access to the Work in preparation and progress wherever located.

3.17 ROYALTIES AND PATENTS

3.17.1 The Contractor shall pay all royalties and license fees. The Contractor shall defend suits or claims for infringement of patent rights and shall hold the Owner and Architect harmless from loss on account thereof, but shall not be responsible for such defense or loss when a particular design, process or product of a particular manufacturer or manufacturers is required by the Contract Documents. However, if the Contractor has reason to believe that the required design, process or product is an infringement of a patent, the Contractor shall be responsible for such loss unless such information is promptly furnished to the Architect.

3.18 INDEMNIFICATION

3.18.1 To the fullest extent permitted by law, the Contractor shall indemnify and hold harmless the Owner, Architect, Architect's consultants, and agents and employees of any of them from and against claims, damages, losses and expenses, including but not limited to attorneys' fees, arising out of or resulting from performance of the Work, provided that such claim, damage, loss or expense is attributable to bodily injury, sickness, disease or death, or to injury to or destruction of tangible property (other than the Work itself) including loss of use resulting therefrom, but only to the extent caused in whole or in part by negligent acts or omissions of the Contractor, a Subcontractor, anyone directly or indirectly employed by them or anyone for whose acts they may be liable, regardless of whether or not such claim, damage, loss or expense is caused in part by a party indemnified hereunder. Such obligation shall not be construed to negate, abridge, or reduce other rights or obligations of indemnity which would otherwise exist as to a party or person described in this Paragraph 3.18.

3.18.2 In claims against any person or entity indemnified under this Paragraph 3.18 by an employee of the Contractor, a Subcontractor, anyone directly or indirectly employed by them or anyone for whose acts they may be liable, the indemnification obligation under this Paragraph 3.18 shall not be limited by a limitation on amount or type of damages, compensation or benefits payable by or for the Contractor or a Subcontractor under workers' or workmen's compensation acts, disability benefit acts or other employee benefit acts.

3.18.3 The obligations of the Contractor under this Paragraph 3.18 shall not extend to the liability of the Architect, the Architect's consultants, and agents and employees of any of them arising out of (1) the preparation or approval of maps, drawings, opinions, reports, surveys, Change Orders, designs or specifications, or (2) the giving of or the failure to give directions or instructions by the Architect, the Architect's consultants, and agents and employees of any of them provided such giving or failure to give is the primary cause of the injury or damage.

ARTICLE 4

ADMINISTRATION OF THE CONTRACT

4.1 ARCHITECT

4.1.1 The Architect is the person lawfully licensed to practice architecture or an entity lawfully practicing architecture identified as such in the Agreement and is referred to throughout the Contract Documents as if singular in number. The term "Architect" means the Architect or the Architect's authorized representative.

4.1.2 Duties, responsibilities and limitations of authority of the Architect as set forth in the Contract Documents shall not be restricted, modified or extended without written consent of the Owner, Contractor and Architect. Consent shall not be unreasonably withheld.

4.1.3 In case of termination of employment of the Architect, the Owner shall appoint an architect against whom the Contractor makes no reasonable objection and whose status under the Contract Documents shall be that of the former architect.

4.1.4 Disputes arising under Subparagraphs 4.1.2 and 4.1.3 shall be subject to arbitration.

4.2 ARCHITECT'S ADMINISTRATION OF THE CONTRACT

4.2.1 The Architect will provide administration of the Contract as described in the Contract Documents, and will be the Owner's representative (1) during construction, (2) until final payment is due and (3) with the Owner's concurrence, from time to time during the correction period described in Paragraph 12.2. The Architect will advise and consult with the Owner. The Architect will have authority to act on behalf of the Owner only to the extent provided in the Contract Documents, unless otherwise modified by written instrument in accordance with other provisions of the Contract.

4.2.2 The Architect will visit the site at intervals appropriate to the stage of construction to become generally familiar with the progress and quality of the completed Work and to determine in general if the Work is being performed in a manner indicating that the Work, when completed, will be in accordance with the Contract Documents. However, the Architect will not be required to make exhaustive or continuous on-site inspections to check quality or quantity of the Work. On the basis of on-site observations as an architect, the Architect will keep the Owner informed of progress of the Work, and will endeavor to guard the Owner against defects and deficiencies in the Work.

4.2.3 The Architect will not have control over or charge of and will not be responsible for construction means, methods, techniques, sequences or procedures, or for safety precautions and programs in connection with the Work, since these are solely the Contractor's responsibility as provided in Paragraph 3.3. The Architect will not be responsible for the Contractor's failure to carry out the Work in accordance with the Contract Documents. The Architect will not have control over or charge of and will not be responsible for acts or omissions of the Con-

AIA DOCUMENT A201 • GENERAL CONDITIONS OF THE CONTRACT FOR CONSTRUCTION • FOURTEENTH EDITION
AIA® • ©1987 THE AMERICAN INSTITUTE OF ARCHITECTS, 1735 NEW YORK AVENUE, N.W., WASHINGTON, D.C. 20006

tractor, Subcontractors, or their agents or employees, or of any other persons performing portions of the Work.

4.2.4 Communications Facilitating Contract Administration. Except as otherwise provided in the Contract Documents or when direct communications have been specially authorized, the Owner and Contractor shall endeavor to communicate through the Architect. Communications by and with the Architect's consultants shall be through the Architect. Communications by and with Subcontractors and material suppliers shall be through the Contractor. Communications by and with separate contractors shall be through the Owner.

4.2.5 Based on the Architect's observations and evaluations of the Contractor's Applications for Payment, the Architect will review and certify the amounts due the Contractor and will issue Certificates for Payment in such amounts.

4.2.6 The Architect will have authority to reject Work which does not conform to the Contract Documents. Whenever the Architect considers it necessary or advisable for implementation of the intent of the Contract Documents, the Architect will have authority to require additional inspection or testing of the Work in accordance with Subparagraphs 13.5.2 and 13.5.3, whether or not such Work is fabricated, installed or completed. However, neither this authority of the Architect nor a decision made in good faith either to exercise or not to exercise such authority shall give rise to a duty or responsibility of the Architect to the Contractor, Subcontractors, material and equipment suppliers, their agents or employees, or other persons performing portions of the Work.

4.2.7 The Architect will review and approve or take other appropriate action upon the Contractor's submittals such as Shop Drawings, Product Data and Samples, but only for the limited purpose of checking for conformance with information given and the design concept expressed in the Contract Documents. The Architect's action will be taken with such reasonable promptness as to cause no delay in the Work or in the activities of the Owner, Contractor or separate contractors, while allowing sufficient time in the Architect's professional judgment to permit adequate review. Review of such submittals is not conducted for the purpose of determining the accuracy and completeness of other details such as dimensions and quantities, or for substantiating instructions for installation or performance of equipment or systems, all of which remain the responsibility of the Contractor as required by the Contract Documents. The Architect's review of the Contractor's submittals shall not relieve the Contractor of the obligations under Paragraphs 3.3, 3.5 and 3.12. The Architect's review shall not constitute approval of safety precautions or, unless otherwise specifically stated by the Architect, of any construction means, methods, techniques, sequences or procedures. The Architect's approval of a specific item shall not indicate approval of an assembly of which the item is a component.

4.2.8 The Architect will prepare Change Orders and Construction Change Directives, and may authorize minor changes in the Work as provided in Paragraph 7.4.

4.2.9 The Architect will conduct inspections to determine the date or dates of Substantial Completion and the date of final completion, will receive and forward to the Owner for the Owner's review and records written warranties and related documents required by the Contract and assembled by the Contractor, and will issue a final Certificate for Payment upon compliance with the requirements of the Contract Documents.

4.2.10 If the Owner and Architect agree, the Architect will provide one or more project representatives to assist in carrying out the Architect's responsibilities at the site. The duties, responsibilities and limitations of authority of such project representatives shall be as set forth in an exhibit to be incorporated in the Contract Documents.

4.2.11 The Architect will interpret and decide matters concerning performance under and requirements of the Contract Documents on written request of either the Owner or Contractor. The Architect's response to such requests will be made with reasonable promptness and within any time limits agreed upon. If no agreement is made concerning the time within which interpretations required of the Architect shall be furnished in compliance with this Paragraph 4.2, then delay shall not be recognized on account of failure by the Architect to furnish such interpretations until 15 days after written request is made for them.

4.2.12 Interpretations and decisions of the Architect will be consistent with the intent of and reasonably inferable from the Contract Documents and will be in writing or in the form of drawings. When making such interpretations and decisions, the Architect will endeavor to secure faithful performance by both Owner and Contractor, will not show partiality to either and will not be liable for results of interpretations or decisions so rendered in good faith.

4.2.13 The Architect's decisions on matters relating to aesthetic effect will be final if consistent with the intent expressed in the Contract Documents.

4.3 CLAIMS AND DISPUTES

4.3.1 Definition. A Claim is a demand or assertion by one of the parties seeking, as a matter of right, adjustment or interpretation of Contract terms, payment of money, extension of time or other relief with respect to the terms of the Contract. The term "Claim" also includes other disputes and matters in question between the Owner and Contractor arising out of or relating to the Contract. Claims must be made by written notice. The responsibility to substantiate Claims shall rest with the party making the Claim.

4.3.2 Decision of Architect. Claims, including those alleging an error or omission by the Architect, shall be referred initially to the Architect for action as provided in Paragraph 4.4. A decision by the Architect, as provided in Subparagraph 4.4.4, shall be required as a condition precedent to arbitration or litigation of a Claim between the Contractor and Owner as to all such matters arising prior to the date final payment is due, regardless of (1) whether such matters relate to execution and progress of the Work or (2) the extent to which the Work has been completed. The decision by the Architect in response to a Claim shall not be a condition precedent to arbitration or litigation in the event (1) the position of Architect is vacant, (2) the Architect has not received evidence or has failed to render a decision within agreed time limits, (3) the Architect has failed to take action required under Subparagraph 4.4.4 within 30 days after the Claim is made, (4) 45 days have passed after the Claim has been referred to the Architect or (5) the Claim relates to a mechanic's lien.

4.3.3 Time Limits on Claims. Claims by either party must be made within 21 days after occurrence of the event giving rise to such Claim or within 21 days after the claimant first recognizes the condition giving rise to the Claim, whichever is later. Claims must be made by written notice. An additional Claim made after the initial Claim has been implemented by Change Order will not be considered unless submitted in a timely manner.

4.3.4 Continuing Contract Performance. Pending final resolution of a Claim including arbitration, unless otherwise agreed in writing the Contractor shall proceed diligently with performance of the Contract and the Owner shall continue to make payments in accordance with the Contract Documents.

4.3.5 Waiver of Claims: Final Payment. The making of final payment shall constitute a waiver of Claims by the Owner except those arising from:

   .1 liens, Claims, security interests or encumbrances arising out of the Contract and unsettled;

   .2 failure of the Work to comply with the requirements of the Contract Documents; or

   .3 terms of special warranties required by the Contract Documents.

4.3.6 Claims for Concealed or Unknown Conditions. If conditions are encountered at the site which are (1) subsurface or otherwise concealed physical conditions which differ materially from those indicated in the Contract Documents or (2) unknown physical conditions of an unusual nature, which differ materially from those ordinarily found to exist and generally recognized as inherent in construction activities of the character provided for in the Contract Documents, then notice by the observing party shall be given to the other party promptly before conditions are disturbed and in no event later than 21 days after first observance of the conditions. The Architect will promptly investigate such conditions and, if they differ materially and cause an increase or decrease in the Contractor's cost of, or time required for, performance of any part of the Work, will recommend an equitable adjustment in the Contract Sum or Contract Time, or both. If the Architect determines that the conditions at the site are not materially different from those indicated in the Contract Documents and that no change in the terms of the Contract is justified, the Architect shall so notify the Owner and Contractor in writing, stating the reasons. Claims by either party in opposition to such determination must be made within 21 days after the Architect has given notice of the decision. If the Owner and Contractor cannot agree on an adjustment in the Contract Sum or Contract Time, the adjustment shall be referred to the Architect for initial determination, subject to further proceedings pursuant to Paragraph 4.4.

4.3.7 Claims for Additional Cost. If the Contractor wishes to make Claim for an increase in the Contract Sum, written notice as provided herein shall be given before proceeding to execute the Work. Prior notice is not required for Claims relating to an emergency endangering life or property arising under Paragraph 10.3. If the Contractor believes additional cost is involved for reasons including but not limited to (1) a written interpretation from the Architect, (2) an order by the Owner to stop the Work where the Contractor was not at fault, (3) a written order for a minor change in the Work issued by the Architect, (4) failure of payment by the Owner, (5) termination of the Contract by the Owner, (6) Owner's suspension or (7) other reasonable grounds, Claim shall be filed in accordance with the procedure established herein.

4.3.8 Claims for Additional Time

4.3.8.1 If the Contractor wishes to make Claim for an increase in the Contract Time, written notice as provided herein shall be given. The Contractor's Claim shall include an estimate of cost and of probable effect of delay on progress of the Work. In the case of a continuing delay only one Claim is necessary.

4.3.8.2 If adverse weather conditions are the basis for a Claim for additional time, such Claim shall be documented by data substantiating that weather conditions were abnormal for the period of time and could not have been reasonably anticipated, and that weather conditions had an adverse effect on the scheduled construction.

4.3.9 Injury or Damage to Person or Property. If either party to the Contract suffers injury or damage to person or property because of an act or omission of the other party, of any of the other party's employees or agents, or of others for whose acts such party is legally liable, written notice of such injury or damage, whether or not insured, shall be given to the other party within a reasonable time not exceeding 21 days after first observance. The notice shall provide sufficient detail to enable the other party to investigate the matter. If a Claim for additional cost or time related to this Claim is to be asserted, it shall be filed as provided in Subparagraphs 4.3.7 or 4.3.8.

4.4   RESOLUTION OF CLAIMS AND DISPUTES

4.4.1 The Architect will review Claims and take one or more of the following preliminary actions within ten days of receipt of a Claim: (1) request additional supporting data from the claimant, (2) submit a schedule to the parties indicating when the Architect expects to take action, (3) reject the Claim in whole or in part, stating reasons for rejection, (4) recommend approval of the Claim by the other party or (5) suggest a compromise. The Architect may also, but is not obligated to, notify the surety, if any, of the nature and amount of the Claim.

4.4.2 If a Claim has been resolved, the Architect will prepare or obtain appropriate documentation.

4.4.3 If a Claim has not been resolved, the party making the Claim shall, within ten days after the Architect's preliminary response, take one or more of the following actions: (1) submit additional supporting data requested by the Architect, (2) modify the initial Claim or (3) notify the Architect that the initial Claim stands.

4.4.4 If a Claim has not been resolved after consideration of the foregoing and of further evidence presented by the parties or requested by the Architect, the Architect will notify the parties in writing that the Architect's decision will be made within seven days, which decision shall be final and binding on the parties but subject to arbitration. Upon expiration of such time period, the Architect will render to the parties the Architect's written decision relative to the Claim, including any change in the Contract Sum or Contract Time or both. If there is a surety and there appears to be a possibility of a Contractor's default, the Architect may, but is not obligated to, notify the surety and request the surety's assistance in resolving the controversy.

4.5   ARBITRATION

4.5.1 Controversies and Claims Subject to Arbitration. Any controversy or Claim arising out of or related to the Contract, or the breach thereof, shall be settled by arbitration in accordance with the Construction Industry Arbitration Rules of the American Arbitration Association, and judgment upon the award rendered by the arbitrator or arbitrators may be entered in any court having jurisdiction thereof, except controversies or Claims relating to aesthetic effect and except those waived as provided for in Subparagraph 4.3.5. Such controversies or Claims upon which the Architect has given notice and rendered a decision as provided in Subparagraph 4.4.4 shall be subject to arbitration upon written demand of either party. Arbitration may be commenced when 45 days have passed after a Claim has been referred to the Architect as provided in Paragraph 4.3 and no decision has been rendered.

AIA DOCUMENT A201 • GENERAL CONDITIONS OF THE CONTRACT FOR CONSTRUCTION • FOURTEENTH EDITION
AIA® • ©1987 THE AMERICAN INSTITUTE OF ARCHITECTS, 1735 NEW YORK AVENUE, N.W., WASHINGTON, D.C. 20006

4.5.2 Rules and Notices for Arbitration. Claims between the Owner and Contractor not resolved under Paragraph 4.4 shall, if subject to arbitration under Subparagraph 4.5.1, be decided by arbitration in accordance with the Construction Industry Arbitration Rules of the American Arbitration Association currently in effect, unless the parties mutually agree otherwise. Notice of demand for arbitration shall be filed in writing with the other party to the Agreement between the Owner and Contractor and with the American Arbitration Association, and a copy shall be filed with the Architect.

4.5.3 Contract Performance During Arbitration. During arbitration proceedings, the Owner and Contractor shall comply with Subparagraph 4.3.4.

4.5.4 When Arbitration May Be Demanded. Demand for arbitration of any Claim may not be made until the earlier of (1) the date on which the Architect has rendered a final written decision on the Claim, (2) the tenth day after the parties have presented evidence to the Architect or have been given reasonable opportunity to do so, if the Architect has not rendered a final written decision by that date, or (3) any of the five events described in Subparagraph 4.3.2.

4.5.4.1 When a written decision of the Architect states that (1) the decision is final but subject to arbitration and (2) a demand for arbitration of a Claim covered by such decision must be made within 30 days after the date on which the party making the demand receives the final written decision, then failure to demand arbitration within said 30 days' period shall result in the Architect's decision becoming final and binding upon the Owner and Contractor. If the Architect renders a decision after arbitration proceedings have been initiated, such decision may be entered as evidence, but shall not supersede arbitration proceedings unless the decision is acceptable to all parties concerned.

4.5.4.2 A demand for arbitration shall be made within the time limits specified in Subparagraphs 4.5.1 and 4.5.4 and Clause 4.5.4.1 as applicable, and in other cases within a reasonable time after the Claim has arisen, and in no event shall it be made after the date when institution of legal or equitable proceedings based on such Claim would be barred by the applicable statute of limitations as determined pursuant to Paragraph 13.7.

4.5.5 Limitation on Consolidation or Joinder. No arbitration arising out of or relating to the Contract Documents shall include, by consolidation or joinder or in any other manner, the Architect, the Architect's employees or consultants, except by written consent containing specific reference to the Agreement and signed by the Architect, Owner, Contractor and any other person or entity sought to be joined. No arbitration shall include, by consolidation or joinder or in any other manner, parties other than the Owner, Contractor, a separate contractor as described in Article 6 and other persons substantially involved in a common question of fact or law whose presence is required if complete relief is to be accorded in arbitration. No person or entity other than the Owner, Contractor or a separate contractor as described in Article 6 shall be included as an original third party or additional third party to an arbitration whose interest or responsibility is insubstantial. Consent to arbitration involving an additional person or entity shall not constitute consent to arbitration of a dispute not described therein or with a person or entity not named or described therein. The foregoing agreement to arbitrate and other agreements to arbitrate with an additional person or entity duly consented to by parties to the Agreement shall be specifically enforceable under applicable law in any court having jurisdiction thereof.

4.5.6 Claims and Timely Assertion of Claims. A party who files a notice of demand for arbitration must assert in the demand all Claims then known to that party on which arbitration is permitted to be demanded. When a party fails to include a Claim through oversight, inadvertence or excusable neglect, or when a Claim has matured or been acquired subsequently, the arbitrator or arbitrators may permit amendment.

4.5.7 Judgment on Final Award. The award rendered by the arbitrator or arbitrators shall be final, and judgment may be entered upon it in accordance with applicable law in any court having jurisdiction thereof.

ARTICLE 5

SUBCONTRACTORS

5.1 DEFINITIONS

5.1.1 A Subcontractor is a person or entity who has a direct contract with the Contractor to perform a portion of the Work at the site. The term "Subcontractor" is referred to throughout the Contract Documents as if singular in number and means a Subcontractor or an authorized representative of the Subcontractor. The term "Subcontractor" does not include a separate contractor or subcontractors of a separate contractor.

5.1.2 A Sub-subcontractor is a person or entity who has a direct or indirect contract with a Subcontractor to perform a portion of the Work at the site. The term "Sub-subcontractor" is referred to throughout the Contract Documents as if singular in number and means a Sub-subcontractor or an authorized representative of the Sub-subcontractor.

5.2 AWARD OF SUBCONTRACTS AND OTHER CONTRACTS FOR PORTIONS OF THE WORK

5.2.1 Unless otherwise stated in the Contract Documents or the bidding requirements, the Contractor, as soon as practicable after award of the Contract, shall furnish in writing to the Owner through the Architect the names of persons or entities (including those who are to furnish materials or equipment fabricated to a special design) proposed for each principal portion of the Work. The Architect will promptly reply to the Contractor in writing stating whether or not the Owner or the Architect, after due investigation, has reasonable objection to any such proposed person or entity. Failure of the Owner or Architect to reply promptly shall constitute notice of no reasonable objection.

5.2.2 The Contractor shall not contract with a proposed person or entity to whom the Owner or Architect has made reasonable and timely objection. The Contractor shall not be required to contract with anyone to whom the Contractor has made reasonable objection.

5.2.3 If the Owner or Architect has reasonable objection to a person or entity proposed by the Contractor, the Contractor shall propose another to whom the Owner or Architect has no reasonable objection. The Contract Sum shall be increased or decreased by the difference in cost occasioned by such change and an appropriate Change Order shall be issued. However, no increase in the Contract Sum shall be allowed for such change unless the Contractor has acted promptly and responsively in submitting names as required.

5.2.4 The Contractor shall not change a Subcontractor, person or entity previously selected if the Owner or Architect makes reasonable objection to such change.

5.3 SUBCONTRACTUAL RELATIONS

5.3.1 By appropriate agreement, written where legally required for validity, the Contractor shall require each Subcontractor, to the extent of the Work to be performed by the Subcontractor, to be bound to the Contractor by terms of the Contract Documents, and to assume toward the Contractor all the obligations and responsibilities which the Contractor, by these Documents, assumes toward the Owner and Architect. Each subcontract agreement shall preserve and protect the rights of the Owner and Architect under the Contract Documents with respect to the Work to be performed by the Subcontractor so that subcontracting thereof will not prejudice such rights, and shall allow to the Subcontractor, unless specifically provided otherwise in the subcontract agreement, the benefit of all rights, remedies and redress against the Contractor that the Contractor, by the Contract Documents, has against the Owner. Where appropriate, the Contractor shall require each Subcontractor to enter into similar agreements with Sub-sub-contractors. The Contractor shall make available to each proposed Subcontractor, prior to the execution of the subcontract agreement, copies of the Contract Documents to which the Subcontractor will be bound, and, upon written request of the Subcontractor, identify to the Subcontractor terms and conditions of the proposed subcontract agreement which may be at variance with the Contract Documents. Subcontractors shall similarly make copies of applicable portions of such documents available to their respective proposed Sub-subcontractors.

5.4 CONTINGENT ASSIGNMENT OF SUBCONTRACTS

5.4.1 Each subcontract agreement for a portion of the Work is assigned by the Contractor to the Owner provided that:

.1 assignment is effective only after termination of the Contract by the Owner for cause pursuant to Paragraph 14.2 and only for those subcontract agreements which the Owner accepts by notifying the Subcontractor in writing; and

.2 assignment is subject to the prior rights of the surety, if any, obligated under bond relating to the Contract.

5.4.2 If the Work has been suspended for more than 30 days, the Subcontractor's compensation shall be equitably adjusted.

ARTICLE 6

CONSTRUCTION BY OWNER OR BY SEPARATE CONTRACTORS

6.1 OWNER'S RIGHT TO PERFORM CONSTRUCTION AND TO AWARD SEPARATE CONTRACTS

6.1.1 The Owner reserves the right to perform construction or operations related to the Project with the Owner's own forces, and to award separate contracts in connection with other portions of the Project or other construction or operations on the site under Conditions of the Contract identical or substantially similar to these including those portions related to insurance and waiver of subrogation. If the Contractor claims that delay or additional cost is involved because of such action by the Owner, the Contractor shall make such Claim as provided elsewhere in the Contract Documents.

6.1.2 When separate contracts are awarded for different portions of the Project or other construction or operations on the site, the term "Contractor" in the Contract Documents in each case shall mean the Contractor who executes each separate Owner-Contractor Agreement.

6.1.3 The Owner shall provide for coordination of the activities of the Owner's own forces and of each separate contractor with the Work of the Contractor, who shall cooperate with them. The Contractor shall participate with other separate contractors and the Owner in reviewing their construction schedules when directed to do so. The Contractor shall make any revisions to the construction schedule and Contract Sum deemed necessary after a joint review and mutual agreement. The construction schedules shall then constitute the schedules to be used by the Contractor, separate contractors and the Owner until subsequently revised.

6.1.4 Unless otherwise provided in the Contract Documents, when the Owner performs construction or operations related to the Project with the Owner's own forces, the Owner shall be deemed to be subject to the same obligations and to have the same rights which apply to the Contractor under the Conditions of the Contract, including, without excluding others, those stated in Article 3, this Article 6 and Articles 10, 11 and 12.

6.2 MUTUAL RESPONSIBILITY

6.2.1 The Contractor shall afford the Owner and separate contractors reasonable opportunity for introduction and storage of their materials and equipment and performance of their activities and shall connect and coordinate the Contractor's construction and operations with theirs as required by the Contract Documents.

6.2.2 If part of the Contractor's Work depends for proper execution or results upon construction or operations by the Owner or a separate contractor, the Contractor shall, prior to proceeding with that portion of the Work, promptly report to the Architect apparent discrepancies or defects in such other construction that would render it unsuitable for such proper execution and results. Failure of the Contractor so to report shall constitute an acknowledgment that the Owner's or separate contractors' completed or partially completed construction is fit and proper to receive the Contractor's Work, except as to defects not then reasonably discoverable.

6.2.3 Costs caused by delays or by improperly timed activities or defective construction shall be borne by the party responsible therefor.

6.2.4 The Contractor shall promptly remedy damage wrongfully caused by the Contractor to completed or partially completed construction or to property of the Owner or separate contractors as provided in Subparagraph 10.2.5.

6.2.5 Claims and other disputes and matters in question between the Contractor and a separate contractor shall be subject to the provisions of Paragraph 4.3 provided the separate contractor has reciprocal obligations.

6.2.6 The Owner and each separate contractor shall have the same responsibilities for cutting and patching as are described for the Contractor in Paragraph 3.14.

6.3 OWNER'S RIGHT TO CLEAN UP

6.3.1 If a dispute arises among the Contractor, separate contractors and the Owner as to the responsibility under their respective contracts for maintaining the premises and surrounding area free from waste materials and rubbish as described in Paragraph 3.15, the Owner may clean up and allocate the cost among those responsible as the Architect determines to be just.

AIA DOCUMENT A201 • GENERAL CONDITIONS OF THE CONTRACT FOR CONSTRUCTION • FOURTEENTH EDITION
AIA® • ©1987 THE AMERICAN INSTITUTE OF ARCHITECTS, 1735 NEW YORK AVENUE, N.W., WASHINGTON, D.C. 20006

ARTICLE 7

CHANGES IN THE WORK

7.1 CHANGES

7.1.1 Changes in the Work may be accomplished after execution of the Contract, and without invalidating the Contract, by Change Order, Construction Change Directive or order for a minor change in the Work, subject to the limitations stated in this Article 7 and elsewhere in the Contract Documents.

7.1.2 A Change Order shall be based upon agreement among the Owner, Contractor and Architect; a Construction Change Directive requires agreement by the Owner and Architect and may or may not be agreed to by the Contractor; an order for a minor change in the Work may be issued by the Architect alone.

7.1.3 Changes in the Work shall be performed under applicable provisions of the Contract Documents, and the Contractor shall proceed promptly, unless otherwise provided in the Change Order, Construction Change Directive or order for a minor change in the Work.

7.1.4 If unit prices are stated in the Contract Documents or subsequently agreed upon, and if quantities originally contemplated are so changed in a proposed Change Order or Construction Change Directive that application of such unit prices to quantities of Work proposed will cause substantial inequity to the Owner or Contractor, the applicable unit prices shall be equitably adjusted.

7.2 CHANGE ORDERS

7.2.1 A Change Order is a written instrument prepared by the Architect and signed by the Owner, Contractor and Architect, stating their agreement upon all of the following:

.1 a change in the Work;

.2 the amount of the adjustment in the Contract Sum, if any; and

.3 the extent of the adjustment in the Contract Time, if any.

7.2.2 Methods used in determining adjustments to the Contract Sum may include those listed in Subparagraph 7.3.3.

7.3 CONSTRUCTION CHANGE DIRECTIVES

7.3.1 A Construction Change Directive is a written order prepared by the Architect and signed by the Owner and Architect, directing a change in the Work and stating a proposed basis for adjustment, if any, in the Contract Sum or Contract Time, or both. The Owner may by Construction Change Directive, without invalidating the Contract, order changes in the Work within the general scope of the Contract consisting of additions, deletions or other revisions, the Contract Sum and Contract Time being adjusted accordingly.

7.3.2 A Construction Change Directive shall be used in the absence of total agreement on the terms of a Change Order.

7.3.3 If the Construction Change Directive provides for an adjustment to the Contract Sum, the adjustment shall be based on one of the following methods:

.1 mutual acceptance of a lump sum properly itemized and supported by sufficient substantiating data to permit evaluation;

.2 unit prices stated in the Contract Documents or subsequently agreed upon;

.3 cost to be determined in a manner agreed upon by the parties and a mutually acceptable fixed or percentage fee; or

.4 as provided in Subparagraph 7.3.6.

7.3.4 Upon receipt of a Construction Change Directive, the Contractor shall promptly proceed with the change in the Work involved and advise the Architect of the Contractor's agreement or disagreement with the method, if any, provided in the Construction Change Directive for determining the proposed adjustment in the Contract Sum or Contract Time.

7.3.5 A Construction Change Directive signed by the Contractor indicates the agreement of the Contractor therewith, including adjustment in Contract Sum and Contract Time or the method for determining them. Such agreement shall be effective immediately and shall be recorded as a Change Order.

7.3.6 If the Contractor does not respond promptly or disagrees with the method for adjustment in the Contract Sum, the method and the adjustment shall be determined by the Architect on the basis of reasonable expenditures and savings of those performing the Work attributable to the change, including, in case of an increase in the Contract Sum, a reasonable allowance for overhead and profit. In such case, and also under Clause 7.3.3.3, the Contractor shall keep and present, in such form as the Architect may prescribe, an itemized accounting together with appropriate supporting data. Unless otherwise provided in the Contract Documents, costs for the purposes of this Subparagraph 7.3.6 shall be limited to the following:

.1 costs of labor, including social security, old age and unemployment insurance, fringe benefits required by agreement or custom, and workers' or workmen's compensation insurance;

.2 costs of materials, supplies and equipment, including cost of transportation, whether incorporated or consumed;

.3 rental costs of machinery and equipment, exclusive of hand tools, whether rented from the Contractor or others;

.4 costs of premiums for all bonds and insurance, permit fees, and sales, use or similar taxes related to the Work; and

.5 additional costs of supervision and field office personnel directly attributable to the change.

7.3.7 Pending final determination of cost to the Owner, amounts not in dispute may be included in Applications for Payment. The amount of credit to be allowed by the Contractor to the Owner for a deletion or change which results in a net decrease in the Contract Sum shall be actual net cost as confirmed by the Architect. When both additions and credits covering related Work or substitutions are involved in a change, the allowance for overhead and profit shall be figured on the basis of net increase, if any, with respect to that change.

7.3.8 If the Owner and Contractor do not agree with the adjustment in Contract Time or the method for determining it, the adjustment or the method shall be referred to the Architect for determination.

7.3.9 When the Owner and Contractor agree with the determination made by the Architect concerning the adjustments in the Contract Sum and Contract Time, or otherwise reach agreement upon the adjustments, such agreement shall be effective immediately and shall be recorded by preparation and execution of an appropriate Change Order.

7.4 MINOR CHANGES IN THE WORK

7.4.1 The Architect will have authority to order minor changes in the Work not involving adjustment in the Contract Sum or extension of the Contract Time and not inconsistent with the intent of the Contract Documents. Such changes shall be effected by written order and shall be binding on the Owner and Contractor. The Contractor shall carry out such written orders promptly.

ARTICLE 8

TIME

8.1 DEFINITIONS

8.1.1 Unless otherwise provided, Contract Time is the period of time, including authorized adjustments, allotted in the Contract Documents for Substantial Completion of the Work.

8.1.2 The date of commencement of the Work is the date established in the Agreement. The date shall not be postponed by the failure to act of the Contractor or of persons or entities for whom the Contractor is responsible.

8.1.3 The date of Substantial Completion is the date certified by the Architect in accordance with Paragraph 9.8.

8.1.4 The term "day" as used in the Contract Documents shall mean calendar day unless otherwise specifically defined.

8.2 PROGRESS AND COMPLETION

8.2.1 Time limits stated in the Contract Documents are of the essence of the Contract. By executing the Agreement the Contractor confirms that the Contract Time is a reasonable period for performing the Work.

8.2.2 The Contractor shall not knowingly, except by agreement or instruction of the Owner in writing, prematurely commence operations on the site or elsewhere prior to the effective date of insurance required by Article 11 to be furnished by the Contractor. The date of commencement of the Work shall not be changed by the effective date of such insurance. Unless the date of commencement is established by a notice to proceed given by the Owner, the Contractor shall notify the Owner in writing not less than five days or other agreed period before commencing the Work to permit the timely filing of mortgages, mechanic's liens and other security interests.

8.2.3 The Contractor shall proceed expeditiously with adequate forces and shall achieve Substantial Completion within the Contract Time.

8.3 DELAYS AND EXTENSIONS OF TIME

8.3.1 If the Contractor is delayed at any time in progress of the Work by an act or neglect of the Owner or Architect, or of an employee of either, or of a separate contractor employed by the Owner, or by changes ordered in the Work, or by labor disputes, fire, unusual delay in deliveries, unavoidable casualties or other causes beyond the Contractor's control, or by delay authorized by the Owner pending arbitration, or by other causes which the Architect determines may justify delay, then the Contract Time shall be extended by Change Order for such reasonable time as the Architect may determine.

8.3.2 Claims relating to time shall be made in accordance with applicable provisions of Paragraph 4.3.

8.3.3 This Paragraph 8.3 does not preclude recovery of damages for delay by either party under other provisions of the Contract Documents.

ARTICLE 9

PAYMENTS AND COMPLETION

9.1 CONTRACT SUM

9.1.1 The Contract Sum is stated in the Agreement and, including authorized adjustments, is the total amount payable by the Owner to the Contractor for performance of the Work under the Contract Documents.

9.2 SCHEDULE OF VALUES

9.2.1 Before the first Application for Payment, the Contractor shall submit to the Architect a schedule of values allocated to various portions of the Work, prepared in such form and supported by such data to substantiate its accuracy as the Architect may require. This schedule, unless objected to by the Architect, shall be used as a basis for reviewing the Contractor's Applications for Payment.

9.3 APPLICATIONS FOR PAYMENT

9.3.1 At least ten days before the date established for each progress payment, the Contractor shall submit to the Architect an itemized Application for Payment for operations completed in accordance with the schedule of values. Such application shall be notarized, if required, and supported by such data substantiating the Contractor's right to payment as the Owner or Architect may require, such as copies of requisitions from Subcontractors and material suppliers, and reflecting retainage if provided for elsewhere in the Contract Documents.

9.3.1.1 Such applications may include requests for payment on account of changes in the Work which have been properly authorized by Construction Change Directives but not yet included in Change Orders.

9.3.1.2 Such applications may not include requests for payment of amounts the Contractor does not intend to pay to a Subcontractor or material supplier because of a dispute or other reason.

9.3.2 Unless otherwise provided in the Contract Documents, payments shall be made on account of materials and equipment delivered and suitably stored at the site for subsequent incorporation in the Work. If approved in advance by the Owner, payment may similarly be made for materials and equipment suitably stored off the site at a location agreed upon in writing. Payment for materials and equipment stored on or off the site shall be conditioned upon compliance by the Contractor with procedures satisfactory to the Owner to establish the Owner's title to such materials and equipment or otherwise protect the Owner's interest, and shall include applicable insurance, storage and transportation to the site for such materials and equipment stored off the site.

9.3.3 The Contractor warrants that title to all Work covered by an Application for Payment will pass to the Owner no later than the time of payment. The Contractor further warrants that upon submittal of an Application for Payment all Work for which Certificates for Payment have been previously issued and payments received from the Owner shall, to the best of the Contractor's knowledge, information and belief, be free and clear of liens, claims, security interests or encumbrances in favor of the Contractor, Subcontractors, material suppliers, or other persons or entities making a claim by reason of having provided labor, materials and equipment relating to the Work.

9.4 CERTIFICATES FOR PAYMENT

9.4.1 The Architect will, within seven days after receipt of the Contractor's Application for Payment, either issue to the

AIA DOCUMENT A201 • GENERAL CONDITIONS OF THE CONTRACT FOR CONSTRUCTION • FOURTEENTH EDITION
AIA® • ©1987 THE AMERICAN INSTITUTE OF ARCHITECTS, 1735 NEW YORK AVENUE, N.W., WASHINGTON, D.C. 20006

Owner a Certificate for Payment, with a copy to the Contractor, for such amount as the Architect determines is properly due, or notify the Contractor and Owner in writing of the Architect's reasons for withholding certification in whole or in part as provided in Subparagraph 9.5.1.

9.4.2 The issuance of a Certificate for Payment will constitute a representation by the Architect to the Owner, based on the Architect's observations at the site and the data comprising the Application for Payment, that the Work has progressed to the point indicated and that, to the best of the Architect's knowledge, information and belief, quality of the Work is in accordance with the Contract Documents. The foregoing representations are subject to an evaluation of the Work for conformance with the Contract Documents upon Substantial Completion, to results of subsequent tests and inspections, to minor deviations from the Contract Documents correctable prior to completion and to specific qualifications expressed by the Architect. The issuance of a Certificate for Payment will further constitute a representation that the Contractor is entitled to payment in the amount certified. However, the issuance of a Certificate for Payment will not be a representation that the Architect has (1) made exhaustive or continuous on-site inspections to check the quality or quantity of the Work, (2) reviewed construction means, methods, techniques, sequences or procedures, (3) reviewed copies of requisitions received from Subcontractors and material suppliers and other data requested by the Owner to substantiate the Contractor's right to payment or (4) made examination to ascertain how or for what purpose the Contractor has used money previously paid on account of the Contract Sum.

9.5   DECISIONS TO WITHHOLD CERTIFICATION

9.5.1 The Architect may decide not to certify payment and may withhold a Certificate for Payment in whole or in part, to the extent reasonably necessary to protect the Owner, if in the Architect's opinion the representations to the Owner required by Subparagraph 9.4.2 cannot be made. If the Architect is unable to certify payment in the amount of the Application, the Architect will notify the Contractor and Owner as provided in Subparagraph 9.4.1. If the Contractor and Architect cannot agree on a revised amount, the Architect will promptly issue a Certificate for Payment for the amount for which the Architect is able to make such representations to the Owner. The Architect may also decide not to certify payment or, because of subsequently discovered evidence or subsequent observations, may nullify the whole or a part of a Certificate for Payment previously issued, to such extent as may be necessary in the Architect's opinion to protect the Owner from loss because of:

   .1 defective Work not remedied;

   .2 third party claims filed or reasonable evidence indicating probable filing of such claims;

   .3 failure of the Contractor to make payments properly to Subcontractors or for labor, materials or equipment;

   .4 reasonable evidence that the Work cannot be completed for the unpaid balance of the Contract Sum;

   .5 damage to the Owner or another contractor;

   .6 reasonable evidence that the Work will not be completed within the Contract Time, and that the unpaid balance would not be adequate to cover actual or liquidated damages for the anticipated delay; or

   .7 persistent failure to carry out the Work in accordance with the Contract Documents.

9.5.2 When the above reasons for withholding certification are removed, certification will be made for amounts previously withheld.

9.6   PROGRESS PAYMENTS

9.6.1 After the Architect has issued a Certificate for Payment, the Owner shall make payment in the manner and within the time provided in the Contract Documents, and shall so notify the Architect.

9.6.2 The Contractor shall promptly pay each Subcontractor, upon receipt of payment from the Owner, out of the amount paid to the Contractor on account of such Subcontractor's portion of the Work, the amount to which said Subcontractor is entitled, reflecting percentages actually retained from payments to the Contractor on account of such Subcontractor's portion of the Work. The Contractor shall, by appropriate agreement with each Subcontractor, require each Subcontractor to make payments to Sub-subcontractors in similar manner.

9.6.3 The Architect will, on request, furnish to a Subcontractor, if practicable, information regarding percentages of completion of amounts applied for by the Contractor and action taken thereon by the Architect and Owner on account of portions of the Work done by such Subcontractor.

9.6.4 Neither the Owner nor Architect shall have an obligation to pay or to see to the payment of money to a Subcontractor except as may otherwise be required by law.

9.6.5 Payment to material suppliers shall be treated in a manner similar to that provided in Subparagraphs 9.6.2, 9.6.3 and 9.6.4.

9.6.6 A Certificate for Payment, a progress payment, or partial or entire use or occupancy of the Project by the Owner shall not constitute acceptance of Work not in accordance with the Contract Documents.

9.7   FAILURE OF PAYMENT

9.7.1 If the Architect does not issue a Certificate for Payment, through no fault of the Contractor, within seven days after receipt of the Contractor's Application for Payment, or if the Owner does not pay the Contractor within seven days after the date established in the Contract Documents the amount certified by the Architect or awarded by arbitration, then the Contractor may, upon seven additional days' written notice to the Owner and Architect, stop the Work until payment of the amount owing has been received. The Contract Time shall be extended appropriately and the Contract Sum shall be increased by the amount of the Contractor's reasonable costs of shut-down, delay and start-up, which shall be accomplished as provided in Article 7.

9.8   SUBSTANTIAL COMPLETION

9.8.1 Substantial Completion is the stage in the progress of the Work when the Work or designated portion thereof is sufficiently complete in accordance with the Contract Documents so the Owner can occupy or utilize the Work for its intended use.

9.8.2 When the Contractor considers that the Work, or a portion thereof which the Owner agrees to accept separately, is substantially complete, the Contractor shall prepare and submit to the Architect a comprehensive list of items to be completed or corrected. The Contractor shall proceed promptly to complete and correct items on the list. Failure to include an item on such list does not alter the responsibility of the Contractor to complete all Work in accordance with the Contract Documents. Upon receipt of the Contractor's list, the Architect will make an inspection to determine whether the Work or designated portion thereof is substantially complete. If the Architect's inspection discloses any item, whether or not included on the Contractor's list, which is not in accordance with the requirements of the Contract Documents, the Contractor shall, before issuance of the Certificate of Substantial Completion, complete or correct such item upon notification by the Architect. The Contractor shall then submit a request for another inspection by the Architect to determine Substantial Completion. When the Work or designated portion thereof is substantially complete, the Architect will prepare a Certificate of Substantial Completion which shall establish the date of Substantial Completion, shall establish responsibilities of the Owner and Contractor for security, maintenance, heat, utilities, damage to the Work and insurance, and shall fix the time within which the Contractor shall finish all items on the list accompanying the Certificate. Warranties required by the Contract Documents shall commence on the date of Substantial Completion of the Work or designated portion thereof unless otherwise provided in the Certificate of Substantial Completion. The Certificate of Substantial Completion shall be submitted to the Owner and Contractor for their written acceptance of responsibilities assigned to them in such Certificate.

9.8.3 Upon Substantial Completion of the Work or designated portion thereof and upon application by the Contractor and certification by the Architect, the Owner shall make payment, reflecting adjustment in retainage, if any, for such Work or portion thereof as provided in the Contract Documents.

9.9 PARTIAL OCCUPANCY OR USE

9.9.1 The Owner may occupy or use any completed or partially completed portion of the Work at any stage when such portion is designated by separate agreement with the Contractor, provided such occupancy or use is consented to by the insurer as required under Subparagraph 11.3.11 and authorized by public authorities having jurisdiction over the Work. Such partial occupancy or use may commence whether or not the portion is substantially complete, provided the Owner and Contractor have accepted in writing the responsibilities assigned to each of them for payments, retainage if any, security, maintenance, heat, utilities, damage to the Work and insurance, and have agreed in writing concerning the period for correction of the Work and commencement of warranties required by the Contract Documents. When the Contractor considers a portion substantially complete, the Contractor shall prepare and submit a list to the Architect as provided under Subparagraph 9.8.2. Consent of the Contractor to partial occupancy or use shall not be unreasonably withheld. The stage of the progress of the Work shall be determined by written agreement between the Owner and Contractor or, if no agreement is reached, by decision of the Architect.

9.9.2 Immediately prior to such partial occupancy or use, the Owner, Contractor and Architect shall jointly inspect the area to be occupied or portion of the Work to be used in order to determine and record the condition of the Work.

9.9.3 Unless otherwise agreed upon, partial occupancy or use of a portion or portions of the Work shall not constitute acceptance of Work not complying with the requirements of the Contract Documents.

9.10 FINAL COMPLETION AND FINAL PAYMENT

9.10.1 Upon receipt of written notice that the Work is ready for final inspection and acceptance and upon receipt of a final Application for Payment, the Architect will promptly make such inspection and, when the Architect finds the Work acceptable under the Contract Documents and the Contract fully performed, the Architect will promptly issue a final Certificate for Payment stating that to the best of the Architect's knowledge, information and belief, and on the basis of the Architect's observations and inspections, the Work has been completed in accordance with terms and conditions of the Contract Documents and that the entire balance found to be due the Contractor and noted in said final Certificate is due and payable. The Architect's final Certificate for Payment will constitute a further representation that conditions listed in Subparagraph 9.10.2 as precedent to the Contractor's being entitled to final payment have been fulfilled.

9.10.2 Neither final payment nor any remaining retained percentage shall become due until the Contractor submits to the Architect (1) an affidavit that payrolls, bills for materials and equipment, and other indebtedness connected with the Work for which the Owner or the Owner's property might be responsible or encumbered (less amounts withheld by Owner) have been paid or otherwise satisfied, (2) a certificate evidencing that insurance required by the Contract Documents to remain in force after final payment is currently in effect and will not be cancelled or allowed to expire until at least 30 days' prior written notice has been given to the Owner, (3) a written statement that the Contractor knows of no substantial reason that the insurance will not be renewable to cover the period required by the Contract Documents, (4) consent of surety, if any, to final payment and (5), if required by the Owner, other data establishing payment or satisfaction of obligations, such as receipts, releases and waivers of liens, claims, security interests or encumbrances arising out of the Contract, to the extent and in such form as may be designated by the Owner. If a Subcontractor refuses to furnish a release or waiver required by the Owner, the Contractor may furnish a bond satisfactory to the Owner to indemnify the Owner against such lien. If such lien remains unsatisfied after payments are made, the Contractor shall refund to the Owner all money that the Owner may be compelled to pay in discharging such lien, including all costs and reasonable attorneys' fees.

9.10.3 If, after Substantial Completion of the Work, final completion thereof is materially delayed through no fault of the Contractor or by issuance of Change Orders affecting final completion, and the Architect so confirms, the Owner shall, upon application by the Contractor and certification by the Architect, and without terminating the Contract, make payment of the balance due for that portion of the Work fully completed and accepted. If the remaining balance for Work not fully completed or corrected is less than retainage stipulated in the Contract Documents, and if bonds have been furnished, the written consent of surety to payment of the balance due for that portion of the Work fully completed and accepted shall be submitted by the Contractor to the Architect prior to certification of such payment. Such payment shall be made under terms and conditions governing final payment, except that it shall not constitute a waiver of claims. The making of final payment shall constitute a waiver of claims by the Owner as provided in Subparagraph 4.3.5.

9.10.4 Acceptance of final payment by the Contractor, a Subcontractor or material supplier shall constitute a waiver of claims by that payee except those previously made in writing and identified by that payee as unsettled at the time of final Application for Payment. Such waivers shall be in addition to the waiver described in Subparagraph 4.3.5.

ARTICLE 10

PROTECTION OF PERSONS AND PROPERTY

10.1 SAFETY PRECAUTIONS AND PROGRAMS

10.1.1 The Contractor shall be responsible for initiating, maintaining and supervising all safety precautions and programs in connection with the performance of the Contract.

10.1.2 In the event the Contractor encounters on the site material reasonably believed to be asbestos or polychlorinated biphenyl (PCB) which has not been rendered harmless, the Contractor shall immediately stop Work in the area affected and report the condition to the Owner and Architect in writing. The Work in the affected area shall not thereafter be resumed except by written agreement of the Owner and Contractor if in fact the material is asbestos or polychlorinated biphenyl (PCB) and has not been rendered harmless. The Work in the affected area shall be resumed in the absence of asbestos or polychlorinated biphenyl (PCB), or when it has been rendered harmless, by written agreement of the Owner and Contractor, or in accordance with final determination by the Architect on which arbitration has not been demanded, or by arbitration under Article 4.

10.1.3 The Contractor shall not be required pursuant to Article 7 to perform without consent any Work relating to asbestos or polychlorinated biphenyl (PCB).

10.1.4 To the fullest extent permitted by law, the Owner shall indemnify and hold harmless the Contractor, Architect, Architect's consultants and agents and employees of any of them from and against claims, damages, losses and expenses, including but not limited to attorneys' fees, arising out of or resulting from performance of the Work in the affected area if in fact the material is asbestos or polychlorinated biphenyl (PCB) and has not been rendered harmless, provided that such claim, damage, loss or expense is attributable to bodily injury, sickness, disease or death, or to injury to or destruction of tangible property (other than the Work itself) including loss of use resulting therefrom, but only to the extent caused in whole or in part by negligent acts or omissions of the Owner, anyone directly or indirectly employed by the Owner or anyone for whose acts the Owner may be liable, regardless of whether or not such claim, damage, loss or expense is caused in part by a party indemnified hereunder. Such obligation shall not be construed to negate, abridge, or reduce other rights or obligations of indemnity which would otherwise exist as to a party or person described in this Subparagraph 10.1.4.

10.2 SAFETY OF PERSONS AND PROPERTY

10.2.1 The Contractor shall take reasonable precautions for safety of, and shall provide reasonable protection to prevent damage, injury or loss to:

    .1 employees on the Work and other persons who may be affected thereby;

    .2 the Work and materials and equipment to be incorporated therein, whether in storage on or off the site, under care, custody or control of the Contractor or the Contractor's Subcontractors or Sub-subcontractors; and

    .3 other property at the site or adjacent thereto, such as trees, shrubs, lawns, walks, pavements, roadways, structures and utilities not designated for removal, relocation or replacement in the course of construction.

10.2.2 The Contractor shall give notices and comply with applicable laws, ordinances, rules, regulations and lawful orders of public authorities bearing on safety of persons or property or their protection from damage, injury or loss.

10.2.3 The Contractor shall erect and maintain, as required by existing conditions and performance of the Contract, reasonable safeguards for safety and protection, including posting danger signs and other warnings against hazards, promulgating safety regulations and notifying owners and users of adjacent sites and utilities.

10.2.4 When use or storage of explosives or other hazardous materials or equipment or unusual methods are necessary for execution of the Work, the Contractor shall exercise utmost care and carry on such activities under supervision of properly qualified personnel.

10.2.5 The Contractor shall promptly remedy damage and loss (other than damage or loss insured under property insurance required by the Contract Documents) to property referred to in Clauses 10.2.1.2 and 10.2.1.3 caused in whole or in part by the Contractor, a Subcontractor, a Sub-subcontractor, or anyone directly or indirectly employed by any of them, or by anyone for whose acts they may be liable and for which the Contractor is responsible under Clauses 10.2.1.2 and 10.2.1.3, except damage or loss attributable to acts or omissions of the Owner or Architect or anyone directly or indirectly employed by either of them, or by anyone for whose acts either of them may be liable, and not attributable to the fault or negligence of the Contractor. The foregoing obligations of the Contractor are in addition to the Contractor's obligations under Paragraph 3.18.

10.2.6 The Contractor shall designate a responsible member of the Contractor's organization at the site whose duty shall be the prevention of accidents. This person shall be the Contractor's superintendent unless otherwise designated by the Contractor in writing to the Owner and Architect.

10.2.7 The Contractor shall not load or permit any part of the construction or site to be loaded so as to endanger its safety.

10.3 EMERGENCIES

10.3.1 In an emergency affecting safety of persons or property, the Contractor shall act, at the Contractor's discretion, to prevent threatened damage, injury or loss. Additional compensation or extension of time claimed by the Contractor on account of an emergency shall be determined as provided in Paragraph 4.3 and Article 7.

ARTICLE 11

INSURANCE AND BONDS

11.1 CONTRACTOR'S LIABILITY INSURANCE

11.1.1 The Contractor shall purchase from and maintain in a company or companies lawfully authorized to do business in the jurisdiction in which the Project is located such insurance as will protect the Contractor from claims set forth below which may arise out of or result from the Contractor's operations under the Contract and for which the Contractor may be legally liable, whether such operations be by the Contractor or by a Subcontractor or by anyone directly or indirectly employed by any of them, or by anyone for whose acts any of them may be liable:

    .1 claims under workers' or workmen's compensation, disability benefit and other similar employee benefit acts which are applicable to the Work to be performed;

.2 claims for damages because of bodily injury, occupational sickness or disease, or death of the Contractor's employees;

.3 claims for damages because of bodily injury, sickness or disease, or death of any person other than the Contractor's employees;

.4 claims for damages insured by usual personal injury liability coverage which are sustained (1) by a person as a result of an offense directly or indirectly related to employment of such person by the Contractor, or (2) by another person;

.5 claims for damages, other than to the Work itself, because of injury to or destruction of tangible property, including loss of use resulting therefrom;

.6 claims for damages because of bodily injury, death of a person or property damage arising out of ownership, maintenance or use of a motor vehicle; and

.7 claims involving contractual liability insurance applicable to the Contractor's obligations under Paragraph 3.18.

11.1.2 The insurance required by Subparagraph 11.1.1 shall be written for not less than limits of liability specified in the Contract Documents or required by law, whichever coverage is greater. Coverages, whether written on an occurrence or claims-made basis, shall be maintained without interruption from date of commencement of the Work until date of final payment and termination of any coverage required to be maintained after final payment.

11.1.3 Certificates of Insurance acceptable to the Owner shall be filed with the Owner prior to commencement of the Work. These Certificates and the insurance policies required by this Paragraph 11.1 shall contain a provision that coverages afforded under the policies will not be cancelled or allowed to expire until at least 30 days' prior written notice has been given to the Owner. If any of the foregoing insurance coverages are required to remain in force after final payment and are reasonably available, an additional certificate evidencing continuation of such coverage shall be submitted with the final Application for Payment as required by Subparagraph 9.10.2. Information concerning reduction of coverage shall be furnished by the Contractor with reasonable promptness in accordance with the Contractor's information and belief.

11.2 OWNER'S LIABILITY INSURANCE

11.2.1 The Owner shall be responsible for purchasing and maintaining the Owner's usual liability insurance. Optionally, the Owner may purchase and maintain other insurance for self-protection against claims which may arise from operations under the Contract. The Contractor shall not be responsible for purchasing and maintaining this optional Owner's liability insurance unless specifically required by the Contract Documents.

11.3 PROPERTY INSURANCE

11.3.1 Unless otherwise provided, the Owner shall purchase and maintain, in a company or companies lawfully authorized to do business in the jurisdiction in which the Project is located, property insurance in the amount of the initial Contract Sum as well as subsequent modifications thereto for the entire Work at the site on a replacement cost basis without voluntary deductibles. Such property insurance shall be maintained, unless otherwise provided in the Contract Documents or otherwise agreed in writing by all persons and entities who are beneficiaries of such insurance, until final payment has been made as provided in Paragraph 9.10 or until no person or entity

other than the Owner has an insurable interest in the property required by this Paragraph 11.3 to be covered, whichever is earlier. This insurance shall include interests of the Owner, the Contractor, Subcontractors and Sub-subcontractors in the Work.

11.3.1.1 Property insurance shall be on an all-risk policy form and shall insure against the perils of fire and extended coverage and physical loss or damage including, without duplication of coverage, theft, vandalism, malicious mischief, collapse, falsework, temporary buildings and debris removal including demolition occasioned by enforcement of any applicable legal requirements, and shall cover reasonable compensation for Architect's services and expenses required as a result of such insured loss. Coverage for other perils shall not be required unless otherwise provided in the Contract Documents.

11.3.1.2 If the Owner does not intend to purchase such property insurance required by the Contract and with all of the coverages in the amount described above, the Owner shall so inform the Contractor in writing prior to commencement of the Work. The Contractor may then effect insurance which will protect the interests of the Contractor, Subcontractors and Sub-subcontractors in the Work, and by appropriate Change Order the cost thereof shall be charged to the Owner. If the Contractor is damaged by the failure or neglect of the Owner to purchase or maintain insurance as described above, without so notifying the Contractor, then the Owner shall bear all reasonable costs properly attributable thereto.

11.3.1.3 If the property insurance requires minimum deductibles and such deductibles are identified in the Contract Documents, the Contractor shall pay costs not covered because of such deductibles. If the Owner or insurer increases the required minimum deductibles above the amounts so identified or if the Owner elects to purchase this insurance with voluntary deductible amounts, the Owner shall be responsible for payment of the additional costs not covered because of such increased or voluntary deductibles. If deductibles are not identified in the Contract Documents, the Owner shall pay costs not covered because of deductibles.

11.3.1.4 Unless otherwise provided in the Contract Documents, this property insurance shall cover portions of the Work stored off the site after written approval of the Owner at the value established in the approval, and also portions of the Work in transit.

11.3.2 Boiler and Machinery Insurance. The Owner shall purchase and maintain boiler and machinery insurance required by the Contract Documents or by law, which shall specifically cover such insured objects during installation and until final acceptance by the Owner; this insurance shall include interests of the Owner, Contractor, Subcontractors and Sub-subcontractors in the Work, and the Owner and Contractor shall be named insureds.

11.3.3 Loss of Use Insurance. The Owner, at the Owner's option, may purchase and maintain such insurance as will insure the Owner against loss of use of the Owner's property due to fire or other hazards, however caused. The Owner waives all rights of action against the Contractor for loss of use of the Owner's property, including consequential losses due to fire or other hazards however caused.

11.3.4 If the Contractor requests in writing that insurance for risks other than those described herein or for other special hazards be included in the property insurance policy, the Owner shall, if possible, include such insurance, and the cost thereof shall be charged to the Contractor by appropriate Change Order.

11.3.5 If during the Project construction period the Owner insures properties, real or personal or both, adjoining or adjacent to the site by property insurance under policies separate from those insuring the Project, or if after final payment property insurance is to be provided on the completed Project through a policy or policies other than those insuring the Project during the construction period, the Owner shall waive all rights in accordance with the terms of Subparagraph 11.3.7 for damages caused by fire or other perils covered by this separate property insurance. All separate policies shall provide this waiver of subrogation by endorsement or otherwise.

11.3.6 Before an exposure to loss may occur, the Owner shall file with the Contractor a copy of each policy that includes insurance coverages required by this Paragraph 11.3. Each policy shall contain all generally applicable conditions, definitions, exclusions and endorsements related to this Project. Each policy shall contain a provision that the policy will not be cancelled or allowed to expire until at least 30 days' prior written notice has been given to the Contractor.

11.3.7 Waivers of Subrogation. The Owner and Contractor waive all rights against (1) each other and any of their subcontractors, sub-subcontractors, agents and employees, each of the other, and (2) the Architect, Architect's consultants, separate contractors described in Article 6, if any, and any of their subcontractors, sub-subcontractors, agents and employees, for damages caused by fire or other perils to the extent covered by property insurance obtained pursuant to this Paragraph 11.3 or other property insurance applicable to the Work, except such rights as they have to proceeds of such insurance held by the Owner as fiduciary. The Owner or Contractor, as appropriate, shall require of the Architect, Architect's consultants, separate contractors described in Article 6, if any, and the subcontractors, sub-subcontractors, agents and employees of any of them, by appropriate agreements, written where legally required for validity, similar waivers each in favor of other parties enumerated herein. The policies shall provide such waivers of subrogation by endorsement or otherwise. A waiver of subrogation shall be effective as to a person or entity even though that person or entity would otherwise have a duty of indemnification, contractual or otherwise, did not pay the insurance premium directly or indirectly, and whether or not the person or entity had an insurable interest in the property damaged.

11.3.8 A loss insured under Owner's property insurance shall be adjusted by the Owner as fiduciary and made payable to the Owner as fiduciary for the insureds, as their interests may appear, subject to requirements of any applicable mortgagee clause and of Subparagraph 11.3.10. The Contractor shall pay Subcontractors their just shares of insurance proceeds received by the Contractor, and by appropriate agreements, written where legally required for validity, shall require Subcontractors to make payments to their Sub-subcontractors in similar manner.

11.3.9 If required in writing by a party in interest, the Owner as fiduciary shall, upon occurrence of an insured loss, give bond for proper performance of the Owner's duties. The cost of required bonds shall be charged against proceeds received as fiduciary. The Owner shall deposit in a separate account proceeds so received, which the Owner shall distribute in accordance with such agreement as the parties in interest may reach, or in accordance with an arbitration award in which case the procedure shall be as provided in Paragraph 4.5. If after such loss no other special agreement is made, replacement of damaged property shall be covered by appropriate Change Order.

11.3.10 The Owner as fiduciary shall have power to adjust and settle a loss with insurers unless one of the parties in interest shall object in writing within five days after occurrence of loss to the Owner's exercise of this power; if such objection be made, arbitrators shall be chosen as provided in Paragraph 4.5. The Owner as fiduciary shall, in that case, make settlement with insurers in accordance with directions of such arbitrators. If distribution of insurance proceeds by arbitration is required, the arbitrators will direct such distribution.

11.3.11 Partial occupancy or use in accordance with Paragraph 9.9 shall not commence until the insurance company or companies providing property insurance have consented to such partial occupancy or use by endorsement or otherwise. The Owner and the Contractor shall take reasonable steps to obtain consent of the insurance company or companies and shall, without mutual written consent, take no action with respect to partial occupancy or use that would cause cancellation, lapse or reduction of insurance.

11.4 PERFORMANCE BOND AND PAYMENT BOND

11.4.1 The Owner shall have the right to require the Contractor to furnish bonds covering faithful performance of the Contract and payment of obligations arising thereunder as stipulated in bidding requirements or specifically required in the Contract Documents on the date of execution of the Contract.

11.4.2 Upon the request of any person or entity appearing to be a potential beneficiary of bonds covering payment of obligations arising under the Contract, the Contractor shall promptly furnish a copy of the bonds or shall permit a copy to be made.

ARTICLE 12

UNCOVERING AND CORRECTION OF WORK

12.1 UNCOVERING OF WORK

12.1.1 If a portion of the Work is covered contrary to the Architect's request or to requirements specifically expressed in the Contract Documents, it must, if required in writing by the Architect, be uncovered for the Architect's observation and be replaced at the Contractor's expense without change in the Contract Time.

12.1.2 If a portion of the Work has been covered which the Architect has not specifically requested to observe prior to its being covered, the Architect may request to see such Work and it shall be uncovered by the Contractor. If such Work is in accordance with the Contract Documents, costs of uncovering and replacement shall, by appropriate Change Order, be charged to the Owner. If such Work is not in accordance with the Contract Documents, the Contractor shall pay such costs unless the condition was caused by the Owner or a separate contractor in which event the Owner shall be responsible for payment of such costs.

12.2 CORRECTION OF WORK

12.2.1 The Contractor shall promptly correct Work rejected by the Architect or failing to conform to the requirements of the Contract Documents, whether observed before or after Substantial Completion and whether or not fabricated, installed or completed. The Contractor shall bear costs of correcting such rejected Work, including additional testing and inspections and compensation for the Architect's services and expenses made necessary thereby.

12.2.2 If, within one year after the date of Substantial Completion of the Work or designated portion thereof, or after the date for commencement of warranties established under Subparagraph 9.9.1, or by terms of an applicable special warranty required by the Contract Documents, any of the Work is found to be not in accordance with the requirements of the Contract Documents, the Contractor shall correct it promptly after receipt of written notice from the Owner to do so unless the Owner has previously given the Contractor a written acceptance of such condition. This period of one year shall be extended with respect to portions of Work first performed after Substantial Completion by the period of time between Substantial Completion and the actual performance of the Work. This obligation under this Subparagraph 12.2.2 shall survive acceptance of the Work under the Contract and termination of the Contract. The Owner shall give such notice promptly after discovery of the condition.

12.2.3 The Contractor shall remove from the site portions of the Work which are not in accordance with the requirements of the Contract Documents and are neither corrected by the Contractor nor accepted by the Owner.

12.2.4 If the Contractor fails to correct nonconforming Work within a reasonable time, the Owner may correct it in accordance with Paragraph 2.4. If the Contractor does not proceed with correction of such nonconforming Work within a reasonable time fixed by written notice from the Architect, the Owner may remove it and store the salvable materials or equipment at the Contractor's expense. If the Contractor does not pay costs of such removal and storage within ten days after written notice, the Owner may upon ten additional days' written notice sell such materials and equipment at auction or at private sale and shall account for the proceeds thereof, after deducting costs and damages that should have been borne by the Contractor, including compensation for the Architect's services and expenses made necessary thereby. If such proceeds of sale do not cover costs which the Contractor should have borne, the Contract Sum shall be reduced by the deficiency. If payments then or thereafter due the Contractor are not sufficient to cover such amount, the Contractor shall pay the difference to the Owner.

12.2.5 The Contractor shall bear the cost of correcting destroyed or damaged construction, whether completed or partially completed, of the Owner or separate contractors caused by the Contractor's correction or removal of Work which is not in accordance with the requirements of the Contract Documents.

12.2.6 Nothing contained in this Paragraph 12.2 shall be construed to establish a period of limitation with respect to other obligations which the Contractor might have under the Contract Documents. Establishment of the time period of one year as described in Subparagraph 12.2.2 relates only to the specific obligation of the Contractor to correct the Work, and has no relationship to the time within which the obligation to comply with the Contract Documents may be sought to be enforced, nor to the time within which proceedings may be commenced to establish the Contractor's liability with respect to the Contractor's obligations other than specifically to correct the Work.

12.3 ACCEPTANCE OF NONCONFORMING WORK

12.3.1 If the Owner prefers to accept Work which is not in accordance with the requirements of the Contract Documents, the Owner may do so instead of requiring its removal and correction, in which case the Contract Sum will be reduced as appropriate and equitable. Such adjustment shall be effected whether or not final payment has been made.

ARTICLE 13

MISCELLANEOUS PROVISIONS

13.1 GOVERNING LAW

13.1.1 The Contract shall be governed by the law of the place where the Project is located.

13.2 SUCCESSORS AND ASSIGNS

13.2.1 The Owner and Contractor respectively bind themselves, their partners, successors, assigns and legal representatives to the other party hereto and to partners, successors, assigns and legal representatives of such other party in respect to covenants, agreements and obligations contained in the Contract Documents. Neither party to the Contract shall assign the Contract as a whole without written consent of the other. If either party attempts to make such an assignment without such consent, that party shall nevertheless remain legally responsible for all obligations under the Contract.

13.3 WRITTEN NOTICE

13.3.1 Written notice shall be deemed to have been duly served if delivered in person to the individual or a member of the firm or entity or to an officer of the corporation for which it was intended, or if delivered at or sent by registered or certified mail to the last business address known to the party giving notice.

13.4 RIGHTS AND REMEDIES

13.4.1 Duties and obligations imposed by the Contract Documents and rights and remedies available thereunder shall be in addition to and not a limitation of duties, obligations, rights and remedies otherwise imposed or available by law.

13.4.2 No action or failure to act by the Owner, Architect or Contractor shall constitute a waiver of a right or duty afforded them under the Contract, nor shall such action or failure to act constitute approval of or acquiescence in a breach thereunder, except as may be specifically agreed in writing.

13.5 TESTS AND INSPECTIONS

13.5.1 Tests, inspections and approvals of portions of the Work required by the Contract Documents or by laws, ordinances, rules, regulations or orders of public authorities having jurisdiction shall be made at an appropriate time. Unless otherwise provided, the Contractor shall make arrangements for such tests, inspections and approvals with an independent testing laboratory or entity acceptable to the Owner, or with the appropriate public authority, and shall bear all related costs of tests, inspections and approvals. The Contractor shall give the Architect timely notice of when and where tests and inspections are to be made so the Architect may observe such procedures. The Owner shall bear costs of tests, inspections or approvals which do not become requirements until after bids are received or negotiations concluded.

13.5.2 If the Architect, Owner or public authorities having jurisdiction determine that portions of the Work require additional testing, inspection or approval not included under Subparagraph 13.5.1, the Architect will, upon written authorization from the Owner, instruct the Contractor to make arrangements for such additional testing, inspection or approval by an entity acceptable to the Owner, and the Contractor shall give timely notice to the Architect of when and where tests and inspections are to be made so the Architect may observe such procedures.

The Owner shall bear such costs except as provided in Sub-paragraph 13.5.3.

13.5.3 If such procedures for testing, inspection or approval under Subparagraphs 13.5.1 and 13.5.2 reveal failure of the portions of the Work to comply with requirements established by the Contract Documents, the Contractor shall bear all costs made necessary by such failure including those of repeated procedures and compensation for the Architect's services and expenses.

13.5.4 Required certificates of testing, inspection or approval shall, unless otherwise required by the Contract Documents, be secured by the Contractor and promptly delivered to the Architect.

13.5.5 If the Architect is to observe tests, inspections or approvals required by the Contract Documents, the Architect will do so promptly and, where practicable, at the normal place of testing.

13.5.6 Tests or inspections conducted pursuant to the Contract Documents shall be made promptly to avoid unreasonable delay in the Work.

13.6   INTEREST

13.6.1 Payments due and unpaid under the Contract Documents shall bear interest from the date payment is due at such rate as the parties may agree upon in writing or, in the absence thereof, at the legal rate prevailing from time to time at the place where the Project is located.

13.7   COMMENCEMENT OF STATUTORY LIMITATION PERIOD

13.7.1 As between the Owner and Contractor:

 .1 Before Substantial Completion. As to acts or failures to act occurring prior to the relevant date of Substantial Completion, any applicable statute of limitations shall commence to run and any alleged cause of action shall be deemed to have accrued in any and all events not later than such date of Substantial Completion;

 .2 Between Substantial Completion and Final Certificate for Payment. As to acts or failures to act occurring subsequent to the relevant date of Substantial Completion and prior to issuance of the final Certificate for Payment, any applicable statute of limitations shall commence to run and any alleged cause of action shall be deemed to have accrued in any and all events not later than the date of issuance of the final Certificate for Payment; and

 .3 After Final Certificate for Payment. As to acts or failures to act occurring after the relevant date of issuance of the final Certificate for Payment, any applicable statute of limitations shall commence to run and any alleged cause of action shall be deemed to have accrued in any and all events not later than the date of any act or failure to act by the Contractor pursuant to any warranty provided under Paragraph 3.5, the date of any correction of the Work or failure to correct the Work by the Contractor under Paragraph 12.2, or the date of actual commission of any other act or failure to perform any duty or obligation by the Contractor or Owner, whichever occurs last.

ARTICLE 14

TERMINATION OR SUSPENSION OF THE CONTRACT

14.1   TERMINATION BY THE CONTRACTOR

14.1.1 The Contractor may terminate the Contract if the Work is stopped for a period of 30 days through no act or fault of the Contractor or a Subcontractor, Sub-subcontractor or their agents or employees or any other persons performing portions of the Work under contract with the Contractor, for any of the following reasons:

 .1 issuance of an order of a court or other public authority having jurisdiction;

 .2 an act of government, such as a declaration of national emergency, making material unavailable;

 .3 because the Architect has not issued a Certificate for Payment and has not notified the Contractor of the reason for withholding certification as provided in Subparagraph 9.4.1, or because the Owner has not made payment on a Certificate for Payment within the time stated in the Contract Documents;

 .4 if repeated suspensions, delays or interruptions by the Owner as described in Paragraph 14.3 constitute in the aggregate more than 100 percent of the total number of days scheduled for completion, or 120 days in any 365-day period, whichever is less; or

 .5 the Owner has failed to furnish to the Contractor promptly, upon the Contractor's request, reasonable evidence as required by Subparagraph 2.2.1.

14.1.2 If one of the above reasons exists, the Contractor may, upon seven additional days' written notice to the Owner and Architect, terminate the Contract and recover from the Owner payment for Work executed and for proven loss with respect to materials, equipment, tools, and construction equipment and machinery, including reasonable overhead, profit and damages.

14.1.3 If the Work is stopped for a period of 60 days through no act or fault of the Contractor or a Subcontractor or their agents or employees or any other persons performing portions of the Work under contract with the Contractor because the Owner has persistently failed to fulfill the Owner's obligations under the Contract Documents with respect to matters important to the progress of the Work, the Contractor may, upon seven additional days' written notice to the Owner and the Architect, terminate the Contract and recover from the Owner as provided in Subparagraph 14.1.2.

14.2   TERMINATION BY THE OWNER FOR CAUSE

14.2.1 The Owner may terminate the Contract if the Contractor:

 .1 persistently or repeatedly refuses or fails to supply enough properly skilled workers or proper materials;

 .2 fails to make payment to Subcontractors for materials or labor in accordance with the respective agreements between the Contractor and the Subcontractors;

 .3 persistently disregards laws, ordinances, or rules, regulations or orders of a public authority having jurisdiction; or

 .4 otherwise is guilty of substantial breach of a provision of the Contract Documents.

14.2.2 When any of the above reasons exist, the Owner, upon certification by the Architect that sufficient cause exists to justify such action, may without prejudice to any other rights or remedies of the Owner and after giving the Contractor and the Contractor's surety, if any, seven days' written notice, terminate employment of the Contractor and may, subject to any prior rights of the surety:

.1 take possession of the site and of all materials, equipment, tools, and construction equipment and machinery thereon owned by the Contractor;

.2 accept assignment of subcontracts pursuant to Paragraph 5.4; and

.3 finish the Work by whatever reasonable method the Owner may deem expedient.

14.2.3 When the Owner terminates the Contract for one of the reasons stated in Subparagraph 14.2.1, the Contractor shall not be entitled to receive further payment until the Work is finished.

14.2.4 If the unpaid balance of the Contract Sum exceeds costs of finishing the Work, including compensation for the Architect's services and expenses made necessary thereby, such excess shall be paid to the Contractor. If such costs exceed the unpaid balance, the Contractor shall pay the difference to the Owner. The amount to be paid to the Contractor or Owner, as the case may be, shall be certified by the Architect, upon application, and this obligation for payment shall survive termination of the Contract.

14.3 SUSPENSION BY THE OWNER FOR CONVENIENCE

14.3.1 The Owner may, without cause, order the Contractor in writing to suspend, delay or interrupt the Work in whole or in part for such period of time as the Owner may determine.

14.3.2 An adjustment shall be made for increases in the cost of performance of the Contract, including profit on the increased cost of performance, caused by suspension, delay or interruption. No adjustment shall be made to the extent:

.1 that performance is, was or would have been so suspended, delayed or interrupted by another cause for which the Contractor is responsible; or

.2 that an equitable adjustment is made or denied under another provision of this Contract.

14.3.3 Adjustments made in the cost of performance may have a mutually agreed fixed or percentage fee.

TYPICAL MANUFACTURING CO.   ABC ARCHITECTS
INDUSTRIAL PLANT & OFFICES   600 MAIN ST.
HAYWARD, CALIFORNIA   SAN FRANCISCO

SUPPLEMENTARY CONDITIONS

THE FOLLOWING SUPPLEMENTARY CONDITIONS SHALL MODIFY, DELETE FROM
AND/OR ADD TO THE "GENERAL CONDITIONS OF THE CONTRACT FOR
CONSTRUCTION," AIA DOCUMENT A201, FOURTEENTH EDITION, 1987. WHERE
ANY ARTICLE, PARAGRAPH, SUBPARAGRAPH OR CLAUSE OF THE GENERAL
CONDITIONS IS MODIFIED OR DELETED BY ONE OF THE FOLLOWING
SUPPLEMENTS, THE UNALTERED PROVISIONS OF THAT ARTICLE, PARAGRAPH,
SUBPARAGRAPH OR CLAUSE SHALL REMAIN IN EFFECT.

ARTICLE 1 - GENERAL PROVISIONS

ADD TO SUBPARAGRAPH:

"1.2.3 IN THE EVENT OF CONFLICTS OR DISCREPANCIES AMONG THE
CONTRACT DOCUMENTS, INTERPRETATIONS WILL BE BASED ON THE
FOLLOWING PRIORITIES.

    1. THE AGREEMENT

    2. ADDENDA, WITH THOSE OF LATER DATE HAVING PRECEDENCE OVER
    THOSE OF EARLIER DATE.

    3. THE SUPPLEMENTARY CONDITIONS

    4. THE GENERAL CONDITIONS OF THE CONTRACT FOR CONSTRUCTION.

    5. DRAWINGS AND SPECIFICATIONS.

IN THE CASE OF INCONSISTENCY BETWEEN DRAWINGS AND SPECIFICATIONS
OR WITHIN EITHER DOCUMENT NOT CLARIFIED BY ADDENDUM, THE BETTER
QUALITY OR GREATER QUANTITY OF WORK SHALL BE PROVIDED IN
ACCORDANCE WITH THE ARCHITECT'S INTERPRETATION."

ARTICLE 2 - OWNER

DELETE SUBPARAGRAPH 2.2.5 AND SUBSTITUTE THE FOLLOWING:

"2.2.5 THE CONTRACTOR WILL BE FURNISHED FREE OF CHARGE
TWENTY-FIVE COPIES OF DRAWINGS AND PROJECT MANUALS. ADDITIONAL
SETS WILL BE FURNISHED AT THE COST OF REPRODUCTION, POSTAGE AND
HANDLING."

ARTICLE 3 – CONTRACTOR

3.4 LABOR AND MATERIALS

ADD THE FOLLOWING SUBPARAGRAPHS 3.4.3 AND 3.4.4 TO 3.4:

"3.4.3   AFTER THE CONTRACT HAS BEEN EXECUTED, THE OWNER AND ARCHITECT WILL CONSIDER A FORMAL REQUEST FOR THE SUBSTITUTION OF PRODUCTS IN PLACE OF THOSE SPECIFIED ONLY UNDER THE CONDITIONS SET FORTH IN THE GENERAL REQUIREMENTS (DIVISION 1 OF THE SPECIFICATIONS).

3.4.4   BY MAKING REQUESTS FOR SUBSTITUTIONS BASED ON SUBPARAGRAPH 3.4.3 ABOVE, THE CONTRACTOR:

.1 REPRESENTS THAT THE CONTRACTOR HAS PERSONALLY INVESTIGATED THE PROPOSED SUBSTITUTE PRODUCT AND DETERMINED THAT IT IS EQUAL OR SUPERIOR IN ALL RESPECTS TO THAT SPECIFIED.

.2 REPRESENTS THAT THE CONTRACTOR WILL PROVIDE THE SAME WARRANTY FOR THE SUBSTITUTION THAT THE CONTRACTOR WOULD FOR THAT SPECIFIED.

.3 CERTIFIES THAT THE COST DATA PRESENTED IS COMPLETE AND INCLUDES ALL RELATED COSTS UNDER THIS CONTRACT EXCEPT THE ARCHITECT'S REDESIGN COSTS, AND WAIVES ALL CLAIMS FOR ADDITIONAL COSTS RELATED TO THE SUBSTITUTION WHICH SUBSEQUENTLY BECOME APPARENT; AND

.4 WILL COORDINATE THE INSTALLATION OF THE ACCEPTED SUBSTITUTE, MAKING SUCH CHANGES AS MAY BE REQUIRED FOR THE WORK TO BE COMPLETE IN ALL RESPECTS."

ARTICLE 9 – PAYMENTS AND COMPLETION

9.3.1   ADD THE FOLLOWING SENTENCE TO SUBPARAGRAPH 9.3.1:

"THE FORM OF APPLICATION FOR PAYMENT SHALL BE A NOTARIZED AIA DOCUMENT G702, APPLICATION AND CERTIFICATION FOR PAYMENT, SUPPORTED BY AIA DOCUMENT G703, CONTINUATION SHEET."

ADD THE FOLLOWING CLAUSE 9.3.1.3 TO 9.3.1:

"9.3.1.3   UNTIL SUBSTANTIAL COMPLETION, THE OWNER SHALL PAY 90 PERCENT OF THE AMOUNT DUE THE CONTRACTOR ON ACCOUNT OF PROGRESS PAYMENTS."

9.8.3   ADD THE FOLLOWING SENTENCE:

"THE PAYMENT SHALL BE SUFFICIENT TO INCREASE THE TOTAL PAYMENTS
TO 90 PERCENT OF THE CONTRACT SUM, LESS SUCH AMOUNTS AS THE
ARCHITECT SHALL DETERMINE FOR INCOMPLETE WORK AND UNSETTLED
CLAIMS."

9.11   ADD THE FOLLOWING PARAGRAPH 9.11 TO ARTICLE 9:

"9.11.1   THE CONTRACTOR AND THE CONTRACTOR'S SURETY, IF ANY,
SHALL BE LIABLE FOR AND SHALL PAY THE OWNER THE SUMS HEREINAFTER
STIPULATED AS LIQUIDATED DAMAGES FOR EACH CALENDAR DAY OF DELAY
UNTIL THE WORK IS SUBSTANTIALLY COMPLETE: FOUR HUNDRED AND FIFTY
DOLLARS ($450.00)."

(AUTHOR'S NOTE: THE ABOVE SUPPLEMENTARY CONDITIONS ARE FROM THE
"GUIDE FOR SUPPLEMENTARY CONDITIONS", AIA DOCUMENT A511, 1987,
AND ARE FOR STUDY MATERIAL ONLY. THE ARCHITECT'S ASSISTANCE MUST
NOT BE CONSTRUED TO BE LEGAL ADVICE. ALL PROPOSED MODIFICATIONS
AND DELETIONS TO THE STANDARD AIA GENERAL CONDITIONS MUST BE
APPROVED BY THE THE OWNER AND HIS ATTORNEY BOTH BEFORE ISSUANCE
FOR BIDDING AND PRIOR TO EXECUTION OF THE CONSTRUCTION CONTRACT.
THE AMERICAN INSTITUTE OF ARCHITECT'S DOCUMENT 511, "GUIDE FOR
SUPPLEMENTARY CONDITIONS, CONTAINS BOTH EXPLANATORY NOTES AND
MATERIAL INTENDED AS MODEL LANGUAGE FOR THE SUPPLEMENTARY
CONDITIONS OF SPECIFIC PROJECTS. NOT ALL THE MODIFICATIONS LISTED
ARE NECESSARY FOR EACH PROJECT. IN ADDITION, SOME CLAUSES MAY
HAVE TO BE ADDED TO, DELETED OR REVISED TO MEET THE NEEDS OF A
PARTICULAR PROJECT.)

Bidding Documents

The Bidding Documents provide a description of the project to prospective bidders. These documents are prepared, assembled and distributed to bidders so that they may prepare proposals for the construction of the project.

In addition to the drawings and specifications which provide technical information and describe the scope and quality of the project, several other documents are needed on a typical architectural project. These are written documents which are used to describe the requirements for bidding, obtain the bids, award the construction contract and assure completion of the project.

In order to notify contractors who might be interested in obtaining Bidding Documents and preparing a proposal for the proposed project, advertisements for bids are published in local newspapers or trade journals. The advertisements are often placed three or four times per week for three or four weeks depending on the type of coverage the owner desires.

In private work, as an alternative to advertising for bids, the owner may wish to mail bid invitations directly to prospective bidders. In this case, only selected contractors are invited to bid. This "Invitation to Bid" is a brief description of the scope of the project together with the following information:

A. Project name, location, owner's name and architect's name.

B. Brief description of the work, stating in simple terms the type of structure, function of building and approximate size.

C. Description of the type of proposal required, stating whether the bid is to be lump sum, segregated, or based on unit cost.

D. Time and place for bid delivery and opening of bids.

E. Place where plans and specifications may be examined and obtained and what document deposit charges are required.

F. Type of bid security required.

The architect's professional responsibilities regarding Bidding Documents include assisting the owner and his attorney in the preparation of construction contracts for the project and the awarding of the contract for performing the work to the successful bidder. This assistance involves the administration of the bidding process, the review of the proposed contractor's qualifications, the analysis of bids or negotiated proposals, and the provision of recommendations on the selection of contractors. It should be noted that the architect does not give legal advice.

The architect should obtain the participation of the owner and his attorney in stipulating specific requirements for the project such as the form of Owner-Contractor Agreement desired, bidding procedures, the date of substantial completion, requirements for liquidated damages, the amount of the retained percentage, and any special modifications to standard documents. The architect should be prepared to explain the need for the information and provide the owner and his attorney with copies of standard documents, such as the AIA General Conditions, for their review. A form expressly designed for the purpose of obtaining this type of information from the owner is AIA Document G611, Owner's Instructions Regarding Bidding Documents and Procedures. This document should be utilized as early as possible in the project delivery process to give the architect advance notice of any special services or requirements the owner may require of the architect and to allow the architect ample time to incorporate the owner's instructions into the Contract Documents. All forms, contracts, agreements and conditions should be carefully reviewed by the owner's attorney to assure the owner that his needs will be met.

The Bidding Documents are generally bound in a volume referred to as the Project Manual. This provides prospective bidders with an orderly and systematic arrangement of project requirements. The contents of the Project Manual are divided into two parts: (1) Bidding Requirements, which provide a description of requirements governing the activities prior to execution of the Owner-Contractor Agreement and (2) Contract Documents (except drawings) which form the contract for construction between owner and contractor. The drawings, of course, are too large to be bound within the 8 1/2 x 11 format of the manual. However, in some cases, 8-1/2 x 11 sheets of details are also included in the Project Manual.

The principal documents on a typical construction project include the following:

Invitation to Bid or Advertisement to Bid

BIDDING REQUIREMENTS

Instructions to Bidders
Information Available to Bidders
    Geotechnical Data
    Existing Conditions
Bid Forms
Supplements to Bid Forms
    Bid Bond Form
    List of Proposed Subcontractors Form

CONTRACT DOCUMENTS

Form of Owner-Contractor Agreement
Bonds and Certificates
      Performance Bond
      Payment Bond Form
General Conditions of the Contract
Supplementary Conditions
      Specifications
      Drawings and Schedules
      Addenda issued prior to receipt of bids

It should be noted that the Instructions to Bidders, the General Conditions and the Supplementary Conditions call for several other important documents. These documents which are submitted at various stages in the project delivery process include the following:

Contractor's Qualification Statement Form
Contractor's Schedule of Values Form
Contractor's Construction Schedule
Contractor's Schedule of Submittals
Certificate of Insurance Form
Application and Certificate for Payment Form
Certificate of Substantial Completion
Contractor's Affidavit of Payment of Debts and Claims
Contractor's Affidavit of Release of Liens
Consent of Surety to Final Payment

Sample - Invitation to Bid

Project: Typical Manufacturing Co.   ABC Architects
Industrial Plant & Offices   600 Main Street
100 Industrial Blvd.   San Francisco, California
Hayward, California

March 1, 1988

You are invited to bid on a General Contract, including mechanical and electrical work, for a one story, reinforced concrete industrial plant and offices, of approximately 100,000 square feet. All bids shall be on a lump sum basis; segregated bids will not be accepted.

Typical Manufacturing Co. will accept sealed bids until 4 p.m. Pacific Standard Time on April 15, 1988 at Typical Manufacturing Co. Corporate Offices, 950 Broadway Blvd., Oakland, California. Bids received after this time will not be accepted. Bids will be opened publicly at 4:01 p.m. on April 15, 1988 and read aloud. All bidders are invited to attend.

The contract documents are on file and may be examined at the offices of the owner or architect or at the West Coast Builder's Center, 1900 State St., Oakland, California.

Copies of the documents will be issued at the office of the architect upon deposit of $100 per set. Deposit is refundable upon return of documents in good condition within 10 days after receipt of bids.

Bid Security in the amount of 10% of the bid must accompany each bid in accordance with the Instructions to Bidders.

In order to receive consideration, all bids shall be made and submitted in accordance with the requirements and conditions of the Instructions to Bidders. Typical Manufacturing Co. reserves the right to waive irregularities and to reject bids.

    Typical Manufacturing Co.
    950 Broadway Blvd.
    Oakland, California

    William Jones, President

Instructions to Bidders

The Instructions to Bidders contains detailed information concerning legal requirements which pertain to the preparation, submission and consideration of proposals. Included in the American Institute of Architects Instructions to Bidders, Document A701, are definitions, information, and requirements relating to: the bidder's representation by making his bid, examination of Bidding Documents by bidders, interpretation or correction of Bidding Documents, substitutions, addenda, bidding procedures, form and style of bids, bid security required of bidders, submission of bids, modification or withdrawal of bids, consideration of bids, opening of bids, rejection of bids, acceptance of bid (award), submission of the Contractor's Qualification Statement, submission of post-bid information by the bidder, the owner's right to require the contractor to furnish a Performance Bond and a Payment Bond, the time of delivery and form of the bonds, and the form to be used in the agreement between owner and contractor.

The architect should fully familiarize himself with the AIA Instructions to Bidders, Document A701. This form consists of nine articles. Important aspects of this document include the following:

"ARTICLE 1—DEFINITIONS"—define the Bidding Documents, addenda, a bid, a base bid, an alternate bid, a unit price, a bidder and a sub-bidder.

"ARTICLE 2—BIDDER'S REPRESENTATIONS"—Every bidder, by making his bid represents that: A) He has examined and understands the drawings and all other Contract Documents. B) He has visited the project site and has familiarized himself with the actual and proposed conditions and the work to be performed. C) His bid is based upon materials and equipment described in the Bidding Documents.

"ARTICLE 3—BIDDING DOCUMENTS"—AVAILABILITY OF DOCUMENTS —Bidders may obtain complete sets of Bidding Documents from the places indicated in the Invitation or Advertisement to Bid. (These are usually the offices of the owner and the architect.) Bidding Documents are not issued to sub-bidders directly. Complete sets of documents must be used in preparing bids.

INTERPRETATION OR CORRECTION OF BIDDING DOCU-MENTS—Bidders shall notify the architect of any discrepancies, errors or omissions that they discover in the Bidding Documents. Requests for clarification or interpretations shall be made in writing not later than seven (7) days before bids will be opened. Correction of Bidding Documents will be made only by addendum which will be mailed or delivered to each bidder.

SUBSTITUTIONS—The materials and equipment described in the Bidding Documents establish a standard of quality, size and function to be met by any proposed substitution. No substitutions are considered unless submitted in writing ten (10) days before bids will be opened. The burden of proof of the proposed substitution is on the bidder. If the architect approves any proposed substitution, such approval will be made only in an addendum. No substitutions are permitted after award of contract.

ADDENDA—Addenda will be sent to all who are known to have received Bidding Documents. Each bidder shall acknowledge in his bid that he has received all addenda issued. (This acknowledgement is usually made on the Bid Form.)

"ARTICLE 4, BIDDING PROCEDURE"—FORM AND STYLE OF

BIDS—Bids shall be submitted on the Bid Form provided by the architect which is included in the Bidding Documents. Bidders must fill in all blanks on the Bid Form. (Bids are generally submitted in duplicate.) Sums are expressed in both words and figures. In the case of discrepancies between the two, the written amount governs.

BID SECURITY—If stipulated in the Invitation or Advertisement to Bid, each bid shall be accompanied by a bid security in the form required by Paragraph 4.2.2. (This can be a certified check but is generally a Bid Bond written on AIA Document A310. The requirement of bid security and amount is a decision of the owner and his legal counsel.)

SUBMISSION OF BIDS—All copies of the bid, the bid security, if any, and all other documents required to be submitted with the bid shall be enclosed in a sealed envelope. Bids are deposited at the location designated in the Invitation or Advertisement to Bid. Bids shall be delivered prior to time and date designated in the Invitation or Advertisement to Bid. Oral bids, bids by telephone or bids by telegraph will not be considered.

MODIFICATION OR WITHDRAWAL OF BID—No bid may be modified, withdrawn or canceled by the bidder for a stipulated period of time after the time and date designated for receipt of bids. (This period of time is often thirty to sixty days.) Bids submitted early may be modified or withdrawn prior to time and date designated for receipt of bids. Such notice shall be in writing and delivered to the place designated for receipt of bids. Withdrawn bids may be resubmitted up to the time designated for receipt of bids. The resubmitted bid must be in full conformance with the Instructions to Bidders.

"ARTICLE 5—CONSIDERATION OF BIDS"—OPENING OF BIDS—Unless the Invitation or Advertisement for Bids indicates otherwise, properly identified bids received on time will be opened publicly and read aloud. (The bids, after opening, should be analyzed by the owner and architect to determine the successful bidder. The analysis should include the overall bid price, total time proposed to complete the work and the subcontractors proposed to perform the work.)

REJECTION OF BIDS—The owner shall have the right to reject any or all bids. (Particular care should be used to reject bids not accompanied by required bid security or data required by the Bidding Documents. Furthermore, the owner has the right to reject bids that are irregular or incomplete.)

ACCEPTANCE OF BID (AWARD)—It is the intent of the owner to award the contract to the lowest responsible bidder provided the bid has been submitted in accordance with the Bidding Document's requirements and does not exceed funds available for the project. The owner shall have the right to waive any informality or irregularity in any bid received. The owner also has the right to accept alternates and determine the low bidder on the basis of such alternates accepted.

"ARTICLE 6—POST BID INFORMATION"—CONTRACTOR'S QUALIFICATION STATEMENT— Bidders shall submit a Contractor's Qualification Statement, AIA Document A305, upon request, unless previously submitted prior to issuance of the Bidding Documents.

OWNER'S FINANCIAL CAPABILITY—The owner shall furnish, at the successful bidder's request, reasonable evidence that the owner has made financial arrangements to fulfill the contract obligations. Unless such evidence is furnished, the bidder is not required to execute the agreement.

SUBMITTALS—Within seven (7) days of notification of award of contract, the bidder shall submit the following to the architect:

Instructions to Bidders

1. Work to be performed by bidder's own forces.

2. Suppliers of principal materials and equipment.

3. List of proposed subcontractors. (It is often required that the bidder submit his list of proposed subcontractors with his bid proposal.)

The bidder will be required to establish to the satisfaction of the architect and owner the reliability and responsibility of the proposed subcontractors.

Prior to the award of contract, the architect will notify the bidder in writing if either the owner or architect, after due investigation, has reasonable objection to any organization on such list. If the owner or architect has a reasonable objection and refuses in writing to accept such organization, the bidder may:

1. Withdraw his bid.

2. Submit an acceptable substitute subcontractor with an increase in bid price to cover the differences in cost occasioned by such substitution.

The owner may, at his discretion, accept the increased bid price or he may disqualify the bidder. In this event, the bid security is not forfeited.

Subcontractors and other organizations proposed by the bidders and accepted by the owner and architect must be used on the work for which they were proposed and shall not be changed except with written approval of the owner and architect.

"ARTICLE 7—PERFORMANCE BOND AND PAYMENT BOND"—BOND REQUIREMENTS—Prior to signing the agreement, if required in the Supplementary Conditions, the bidder shall furnish bonds covering faithful performance of the contract and payment of all obligations in the amount the owner may prescribe.

TIME OF DELIVERY AND FORM OF BONDS—The bidder shall deliver the required bonds to the owner not later than three days following the date of execution of the agreement. The bonds shall be written on AIA Document A312, Performance Bond and Payment Bond. (Blank bond forms should be included in the Project Manual.)

"ARTICLE 8—FORM OF AGREEMENT BETWEEN OWNER AND CONTRACTOR"—The form of agreement the contractor will be required to execute is AIA Document A101, Standard Form of Agreement Between Owner and Contractor. (This form should be included in the Project Manual.)

Note that paragraph 1.1.1 of the AIA General conditions excludes the bidding requirements such as the Invitation to Bid, the Instructions to Bidders, sample forms and the contractor's Bid Form from the Contract Documents. This is further emphasized in paragraph 9.1.7 of the AIA Owner-Contractor Agreement which states that the bidding requirements are not Contract Documents unless enumerated in the Owner-Contractor Agreement and are to be listed only if they are intended to be included in the Contract Documents. While the Instructions to Bidders is not a Contract Document, it does have important legal consequences. Therefore, like the Contract Documents, it should be reviewed and approved by the owner and his attorney.

AIA Document A701

Instructions to Bidders

1987 EDITION

TABLE OF ARTICLES

1. DEFINITIONS

2. BIDDER'S REPRESENTATIONS

3. BIDDING DOCUMENTS

4. BIDDING PROCEDURES

5. CONSIDERATION OF BIDS

6. POST-BID INFORMATION

7. PERFORMANCE BOND AND PAYMENT BOND

8. FORM OF AGREEMENT BETWEEN OWNER AND CONTRACTOR

ARTICLE 1
DEFINITIONS

1.1 Bidding Documents include the Bidding Requirements and the proposed Contract Documents. The Bidding Requirements consist of the Advertisement or Invitation to Bid, Instructions to Bidders, Supplementary Instructions to Bidders, the bid form, and other sample bidding and contract forms. The proposed Contract Documents consist of the form of Agreement between the Owner and Contractor, Conditions of the Contract (General, Supplementary and other Conditions), Drawings, Specifications and all Addenda issued prior to execution of the Contract.

1.2 Definitions set forth in the General Conditions of the Contract for Construction, AIA Document A201, or in other Contract Documents are applicable to the Bidding Documents.

1.3 Addenda are written or graphic instruments issued by the Architect prior to the execution of the Contract which modify or interpret the Bidding Documents by additions, deletions, clarifications or corrections.

1.4 A Bid is a complete and properly signed proposal to do the Work for the sums stipulated therein, submitted in accordance with the Bidding Documents.

1.5 The Base Bid is the sum stated in the Bid for which the Bidder offers to perform the Work described in the Bidding Documents as the base, to which Work may be added or from which Work may be deleted for sums stated in Alternate Bids.

1.6 An Alternate Bid (or Alternate) is an amount stated in the Bid to be added to or deducted from the amount of the Base Bid if the corresponding change in the Work, as described in the Bidding Documents, is accepted.

1.7 A Unit Price is an amount stated in the Bid as a price per unit of measurement for materials, equipment or services or a portion of the Work as described in the Bidding Documents.

1.8 A Bidder is a person or entity who submits a Bid.

1.9 A Sub-bidder is a person or entity who submits a bid to a Bidder for materials, equipment or labor for a portion of the Work.

ARTICLE 2
BIDDER'S REPRESENTATIONS

2.1 The Bidder by making a Bid represents that:

2.1.1 The Bidder has read and understands the Bidding Documents and the Bid is made in accordance therewith.

2.1.2 The Bidder has read and understands the Bidding Documents or contract documents, to the extent that such documentation relates to the Work for which the Bid is submitted, for other portions of the Project, if any, being bid concurrently or presently under construction.

2.1.3 The Bidder has visited the site, become familiar with local conditions under which the Work is to be performed and

has correlated the Bidder's personal observations with the requirements of the proposed Contract Documents.

2.1.4 The Bid is based upon the materials, equipment and systems required by the Bidding Documents without exception.

ARTICLE 3
BIDDING DOCUMENTS

3.1 COPIES

3.1.1 Bidders may obtain complete sets of the Bidding Documents from the issuing office designated in the Advertisement or Invitation to Bid in the number and for the deposit sum, if any, stated therein. The deposit will be refunded to Bidders who submit a bona fide Bid and return the Bidding Documents in good condition within ten days after receipt of Bids. The cost of replacement of missing or damaged documents will be deducted from the deposit. A Bidder receiving a Contract award may retain the Bidding Documents and the Bidder's deposit will be refunded.

3.1.2 Bidding Documents will not be issued directly to Subbidders or others unless specifically offered in the Advertisement or Invitation to Bid, or in supplementary instructions to bidders.

3.1.3 Bidders shall use complete sets of Bidding Documents in preparing Bids; neither the Owner nor Architect assumes responsibility for errors or misinterpretations resulting from the use of incomplete sets of Bidding Documents.

3.1.4 In making copies of the Bidding Documents available on the above terms, the Owner and the Architect do so only for the purpose of obtaining Bids on the Work and do not confer a license or grant permission for any other use of the Bidding Documents.

3.2 INTERPRETATION OR CORRECTION OF BIDDING DOCUMENTS

3.2.1 The Bidder shall carefully study and compare the Bidding Documents with each other, and with other work being bid concurrently or presently under construction to the extent that it relates to the Work for which the Bid is submitted, shall examine the site and local conditions, and shall at once report to the Architect errors, inconsistencies or ambiguities discovered.

3.2.2 Bidders and Sub-bidders requiring clarification or interpretation of the Bidding Documents shall make a written request which shall reach the Architect at least seven days prior to the date for receipt of Bids.

3.2.3 Interpretations, corrections and changes of the Bidding Documents will be made by Addendum. Interpretations, corrections and changes of the Bidding Documents made in any other manner will not be binding, and Bidders shall not rely upon them.

3.3 SUBSTITUTIONS

3.3.1 The materials, products and equipment described in the Bidding Documents establish a standard of required function, dimension, appearance and quality to be met by any proposed substitution.

3.3.2 No substitution will be considered prior to receipt of Bids unless written request for approval has been received by the Architect at least ten days prior to the date for receipt of Bids. Such requests shall include the name of the material or equipment for which it is to be substituted and a complete description of the proposed substitution including drawings, performance and test data, and other information necessary for an evaluation. A statement setting forth changes in other materials, equipment or other portions of the Work including changes in the work of other contracts that incorporation of the proposed substitution would require shall be included. The burden of proof of the merit of the proposed substitution is upon the proposer. The Architect's decision of approval or disapproval of a proposed substitution shall be final.

3.3.3 If the Architect approves a proposed substitution prior to receipt of Bids, such approval will be set forth in an Addendum. Bidders shall not rely upon approvals made in any other manner.

3.3.4 No substitutions will be considered after the Contract award unless specifically provided in the Contract Documents.

3.4 ADDENDA

3.4.1 Addenda will be mailed or delivered to all who are known by the issuing office to have received a complete set of Bidding Documents.

3.4.2 Copies of Addenda will be made available for inspection wherever Bidding Documents are on file for that purpose.

3.4.3 No Addenda will be issued later than four days prior to the date for receipt of Bids except an Addendum withdrawing the request for Bids or one which includes postponement of the date for receipt of Bids.

3.4.4 Each Bidder shall ascertain prior to submitting a Bid that the Bidder has received all Addenda issued, and the Bidder shall acknowledge their receipt in the Bid.

ARTICLE 4

BIDDING PROCEDURES

4.1 FORM AND STYLE OF BIDS

4.1.1 Bids shall be submitted on forms identical to the form included with the Bidding Documents.

4.1.2 All blanks on the bid form shall be filled in by typewriter or manually in ink.

4.1.3 Where so indicated by the makeup of the bid form, sums shall be expressed in both words and figures, and in case of discrepancy between the two, the amount written in words shall govern.

4.1.4 Interlineations, alterations and erasures must be initialed by the signer of the Bid.

4.1.5 All requested Alternates shall be bid. If no change in the Base Bid is required, enter "No Change."

4.1.6 Where two or more Bids for designated portions of the Work have been requested, the Bidder may, without forfeiture

of the bid security, state the Bidder's refusal to accept award of less than the combination of Bids stipulated by the Bidder. The Bidder shall make no additional stipulations on the bid form nor qualify the Bid in any other manner.

4.1.7 Each copy of the Bid shall include the legal name of the Bidder and a statement that the Bidder is a sole proprietor, partnership, corporation or other legal entity. Each copy shall be signed by the person or persons legally authorized to bind the Bidder to a contract. A Bid by a corporation shall further give the state of incorporation and have the corporate seal affixed. A Bid submitted by an agent shall have a current power of attorney attached certifying the agent's authority to bind the Bidder.

4.2 BID SECURITY

4.2.1 If so stipulated in the Advertisement or Invitation to Bid, or supplementary instructions to bidders, each Bid shall be accompanied by a bid security in the form and amount required, pledging that the Bidder will enter into a Contract with the Owner on the terms stated in the Bid and will, if required, furnish bonds covering the faithful performance of the Contract and payment of all obligations arising thereunder. Should the Bidder refuse to enter into such Contract or fail to furnish such bonds if required, the amount of the bid security shall be forfeited to the Owner as liquidated damages, not as a penalty. The amount of the bid security shall not be forfeited to the Owner in the event the Owner fails to comply with Subparagraph 6.2.1.

4.2.2 If a surety bond is required, it shall be written on AIA Document A310, Bid Bond, unless otherwise provided in the Bidding Documents, and the attorney-in-fact who executes the bond on behalf of the surety shall affix to the bond a certified and current copy of the power of attorney.

4.2.3 The Owner will have the right to retain the bid security of Bidders to whom an award is being considered until either (a) the Contract has been executed and bonds, if required, have been furnished, or (b) the specified time has elapsed so that Bids may be withdrawn, or (c) all Bids have been rejected.

4.3 SUBMISSION OF BIDS

4.3.1 All copies of the Bid, the bid security, if any, and other documents required to be submitted with the Bid shall be enclosed in a sealed opaque envelope. The envelope shall be addressed to the party receiving the Bids and shall be identified with the Project name, the Bidder's name and address and, if applicable, the designated portion of the Work for which the Bid is submitted. If the Bid is sent by mail, the sealed envelope shall be enclosed in a separate mailing envelope with the notation "SEALED BID ENCLOSED" on the face thereof.

4.3.2 Bids shall be deposited at the designated location prior to the time and date for receipt of Bids. Bids received after the time and date for receipt of Bids will be returned unopened.

4.3.3 The Bidder shall assume full responsibility for timely delivery at the location designated for receipt of Bids.

4.3.4 Oral, telephonic or telegraphic Bids are invalid and will not receive consideration.

4.4 MODIFICATION OR WITHDRAWAL OF BID

4.4.1 A Bid may not be modified, withdrawn or canceled by the Bidder during the stipulated time period following the time

AIA DOCUMENT A701 • INSTRUCTIONS TO BIDDERS • FOURTH EDITION • AIA® • ©1987 • THE
AMERICAN INSTITUTE OF ARCHITECTS, 1735 NEW YORK AVENUE, N.W., WASHINGTON, D.C. 20006

and date designated for the receipt of Bids, and each Bidder so agrees in submitting a Bid.

4.4.2 Prior to the time and date designated for receipt of Bids, a Bid submitted may be modified or withdrawn by notice to the party receiving Bids at the place designated for receipt of Bids. Such notice shall be in writing over the signature of the Bidder or by telegram; if by telegram, written confirmation over the signature of the Bidder shall be mailed and postmarked on or before the date and time set for receipt of Bids. A change shall be so worded as not to reveal the amount of the original Bid.

4.4.3 Withdrawn Bids may be resubmitted up to the date and time designated for the receipt of Bids provided that they are then fully in conformance with these Instructions to Bidders.

4.4.4 Bid security, if required, shall be in an amount sufficient for the Bid as modified or resubmitted.

ARTICLE 5
CONSIDERATION OF BIDS

5.1 OPENING OF BIDS

5.1.1 Unless stated otherwise in the Advertisement or Invitation to Bid, the properly identified Bids received on time will be opened publicly and will be read aloud. An abstract of the Bids will be made available to Bidders. When it has been stated that Bids will be opened privately, an abstract of the same information may, at the discretion of the Owner, be made available to the Bidders within a reasonable time.

5.2 REJECTION OF BIDS

5.2.1 The Owner shall have the right to reject any or all Bids, reject a Bid not accompanied by a required bid security or by other data required by the Bidding Documents, or reject a Bid which is in any way incomplete or irregular.

5.3 ACCEPTANCE OF BID (AWARD)

5.3.1 It is the intent of the Owner to award a Contract to the lowest responsible Bidder provided the Bid has been submitted in accordance with the requirements of the Bidding Documents and does not exceed the funds available. The Owner shall have the right to waive informalities or irregularities in a Bid received and to accept the Bid which, in the Owner's judgment, is in the Owner's own best interests.

5.3.2 The Owner shall have the right to accept Alternates in any order or combination, unless otherwise specifically provided in the Bidding Documents, and to determine the low Bidder on the basis of the sum of the Base Bid and Alternates accepted.

ARTICLE 6
POST-BID INFORMATION

6.1 CONTRACTOR'S QUALIFICATION STATEMENT

6.1.1 Bidders to whom award of a Contract is under consideration shall submit to the Architect, upon request, a properly executed AIA Document A305, Contractor's Qualification Statement, unless such a Statement has been previously required and submitted as a prerequisite to the issuance of Bidding Documents.

6.2 OWNER'S FINANCIAL CAPABILITY

6.2.1 The Owner shall, at the request of the Bidder to whom award of a Contract is under consideration and no later than seven days prior to the expiration of the time for withdrawal of Bids, furnish to the Bidder reasonable evidence that financial arrangements have been made to fulfill the Owner's obligations under the Contract. Unless such reasonable evidence is furnished, the Bidder will not be required to execute the Agreement between the Owner and Contractor.

6.3 SUBMITTALS

6.3.1 The Bidder shall, as soon as practicable after notification of selection for the award of a Contract, furnish to the Owner through the Architect in writing:

.1 a designation of the Work to be performed with the Bidder's own forces;

.2 names of the manufacturers, products and the suppliers of principal items or systems of materials and equipment proposed for the Work; and

.3 names of persons or entities (including those who are to furnish materials or equipment fabricated to a special design) proposed for the principal portions of the Work.

6.3.2 The Bidder will be required to establish to the satisfaction of the Architect and Owner the reliability and responsibility of the persons or entities proposed to furnish and perform the Work described in the Bidding Documents.

6.3.3 Prior to the award of the Contract, the Architect will notify the Bidder in writing if either the Owner or Architect, after due investigation, has reasonable objection to a person or entity proposed by the Bidder. If the Owner or Architect has reasonable objection to a proposed person or entity, the Bidder may, at the Bidder's option, (1) withdraw the Bid, or (2) submit an acceptable substitute person or entity with an adjustment in the Base Bid or Alternate Bid to cover the difference in cost occasioned by such substitution. The Owner may accept the adjusted bid price or disqualify the Bidder. In the event of either withdrawal or disqualification, bid security will not be forfeited.

6.3.4 Persons and entities proposed by the Bidder and to whom the Owner and Architect have made no reasonable objection must be used on the Work for which they were proposed and shall not be changed except with the written consent of the Owner and Architect.

ARTICLE 7
PERFORMANCE BOND AND PAYMENT BOND

7.1 BOND REQUIREMENTS

7.1.1 If stipulated in the Bidding Documents, the Bidder shall furnish bonds covering the faithful performance of the Contract and payment of all obligations arising thereunder. Bonds may be secured through the Bidder's usual sources.

7.1.2 If the furnishing of such bonds is stipulated in the Bidding Documents, the cost shall be included in the Bid. If the furnishing of such bonds is required after receipt of bids and before execution of the Contract, the cost of such bonds shall be added to the Bid in determining the Contract Sum.

7.1.3 If the Owner requires that bonds be secured from other than the Bidder's usual sources, changes in cost will be adjusted as provided in the Contract Documents.

7.2   TIME OF DELIVERY AND FORM OF BONDS

7.2.1 The Bidder shall deliver the required bonds to the Owner not later than three days following the date of execution of the Contract. If the Work is to be commenced prior thereto in response to a letter of intent, the Bidder shall, prior to commencement of the Work, submit evidence satisfactory to the Owner that such bonds will be furnished and delivered in accordance with this Subparagraph 7.2.1.

7.2.2 Unless otherwise provided, the bonds shall be written on AIA Document A312, Performance Bond and Payment Bond. Both bonds shall be written in the amount of the Contract Sum.

7.2.3 The bonds shall be dated on or after the date of the Contract.

7.2.4 The Bidder shall require the attorney-in-fact who executes the required bonds on behalf of the surety to affix thereto a certified and current copy of the power of attorney.

ARTICLE 8

FORM OF AGREEMENT BETWEEN OWNER AND CONTRACTOR

8.1   FORM TO BE USED

8.1.1 Unless otherwise required in the Bidding Documents, the Agreement for the Work will be written on AIA Document A101, Standard Form of Agreement Between Owner and Contractor Where the Basis of Payment Is a Stipulated Sum.

AIA DOCUMENT A701 • INSTRUCTIONS TO BIDDERS • FOURTH EDITION • AIA® • ©1987 • THE AMERICAN INSTITUTE OF ARCHITECTS, 1735 NEW YORK AVENUE, N.W., WASHINGTON, D.C. 20006

Bonds

The owner's rights to require the contractor to furnish a Performance Bond and Payment Bond are contained in paragraph 11.4.1 of the General Conditions, AIA Document A201. The provision requiring the furnishing of these bonds is contained in paragraph 7.1.1 of the Instructions to Bidders, AIA Document A701. The requirements of these paragraphs should be fully understood in order to provide adequate protection for the owner during construction. Whether a contractor should be required to submit bonds in any particular instance is, however, a subject for decision by the owner and his legal counsel. Paragraph 7.2.2 of the AIA Instructions to Bidders stipulates that the bonds, if required, are to be written on AIA Document 312, Performance Bond and Payment Bond, unless otherwise stated in the Contract Documents.

Surety bonds are a form of assurance to the owner that the contractor will perform the work according to the Contract Documents including payment of debts for labor and materials. A surety bond is an agreement under which one party, called a surety, agrees to answer to another party, called an obligee, for the debt, default, or failure of a third party, called the principal, to carry out his contract obligations. The surety is ordinarily a corporation that underwrites bonds, the obligee is usually the owner, and the principal is usually the contractor.

The type of surety bonding which should be utilized is that furnished by a reputable surety possessing sufficient financial resources and experience; known for expedient and prudent action; and operating under state license. Note that if substantial changes are made during the course of of the contract, the surety's consent to such changes is required to guarantee continued coverage of the bond.

There are several types of bonds having various functions:

The Bid Bond is used to assure the owner that, if the contractor is awarded the contract within a certain number of days from the date of his bid (usually 30 to 60 days), he will enter into the contract to construct the project for the bid price and furnish the Performance Bond and the Payment Bond as required. In the event of default by the low bidder without justification, the difference between his proposal and the next highest bid is forfeited to the owner up to the maximum amount of the bond penalty. The standard form of a Bid Bond is the American Institute of Architects Document A310.

The bidder may refuse to enter into the contract on the grounds of changes in conditions of the contract, or a mistake in the bid. If such a mistake is the result of a clerical error, the contractor and the surety company are generally excused from any penalty. For instance, if a contractor submits a bid and then discovers that an error in addition resulted in his bid being low, he may notify the owner of such error and ask that his bid be withdrawn. If the owner is notified before the bid is accepted, the bidder and surety are generally relieved of liability on the bond. However, if the bidder fails to execute the contract or fails to provide Performance or Payment Bonds as required after notification of award of contract, then the bidder's obligations have not been fulfilled and the surety is liable for the difference between the bid amount and the amount of the bid selected, up to the maximum amount of the bond penalty.

In private work, the deposit of a certified check may be used instead of the Bid Bond. This is at the discretion of the owner. The bid deposit or face amount of the Bid Bond is usually 10% of the amount of the bid.

Bonds

The function of the Performance Bond is to guarantee the owner that the contractor will complete the project in accordance with the terms and conditions of the construction contract. In the event of default, the surety will protect the owner against loss up to the amount of the bond. The bond amount for both the Performance Bond and the Payment Bond is often 100% of the contract price.

Paragraph 14.2.1 of the AIA General Conditions defines the reasons the owner may terminate the contract, in other words, declare the contractor in default: failure to furnish enough labor and materials, failure to pay subcontractors, disregard of laws or regulations, or substantial violation of provisions of the Contract Documents. Further, as outlined in paragraph 14.2.2, the owner may terminate the contract, upon seven days' notice to the contractor and the surety, when any of the above conditions exist. However, as stated in paragraph 14.2.2, these conditions must be certified by the architect as being sufficient cause to justify termination.

If the owner, as certified by the architect, does declare the contractor in default, the surety should be notified promptly. Such notification should request remedy from the surety in completing the contract. Recognize that notification to the surety is not a condition of the surety's liability. Except in the case where the contractor is bankrupt, the surety often claims it is not actually in default of the contract and that the owner's termination of the contract was incorrect. Also, the surety may claim that the default was a result of errors or omissions in the Contract Documents, problems caused by the owner, or problems caused by the architect in the administration of the Contract Documents. For instance, the surety might claim that improper reductions by the architect in the amounts requested by the contractor in his Applications for Payment resulted in a reduction of operating funds available to the contractor and therefore a loss to the surety.

Another defense that the surety may claim against possible liability is that the owner breached his part of the contract first by failing to make timely payments to the contractor. Further, the surety may claim that the owner made major changes in the contractor's scope of work or other obligations without approval of the surety and therefore invalidated the bond. In addition, the surety may assert that the owner failed to make a claim within the proper time limits established in the bond.

Furthermore, the Performance Bond provides the option to the surety of either physically completing the contract, or arranging for a contract between the owner and another contractor and furnishing adequate funds for completion of the work up to the amount of the bond penalty. In the latter case, the owner assumes the responsibility for having the work finished. In general, the surety will not elect to complete the work physically, that is, take over completion of the contract. In this case, the surety takes over all the contractor's obligations. Therefore, the surety must assume all costs involved in completion of the project. These costs are not limited to the amount of the bond penalty.

The Payment Bond is issued to assure the owner that the surety will pay the contractor's debts for labor and material if the contractor defaults. For example, if a contractor defaults during the course of a project, there may be numerous laborers, material suppliers and subcontractors that have provided labor or materials for the project and have not been paid. In addition, the contractor may have been paid for such labor and materials, but failed to make payments to the laborers, suppliers or subcontractors. The Payment Bond ensures that such laborers, suppliers or subcontractors will be paid in full. This protects the owner from losses resulting from the filing of mechanic's liens on the owner's property by those who have furnished labor and materials and have not been paid. The Performance Bond and the Payment Bond should not be combined. This may create legal problems in the handling of any claims against the Bond because of competing interests of the owner and laborers and material suppliers.

While the architect is not a party to the Owner-Contractor Agreement or the bonds for the project, the architect can be affected by both. In addition, the architect affects the interactions of the owner and contractor that are direct parties to the agreement and bonds. For this reason, the architect must perform to the reasonable standard of care customarily employed by other architects in the community in regard to his duties related to areas that may affect bonds. For example, the architect prepares the drawings and specifications that the bids are based on and subsequently form a major portion of the contract. Further, he assists the owner during the Bidding Phase and acts as the owner's representative by assuming certain responsibilities in performing Construction Administration services for the project.

As outlined in the AIA General Conditions, the architect's responsibilities during the Construction Administration Phase include items as follows: the interpretation of matters concerning performance of the Contract Documents upon written request of the owner or contractor; the resolution of claims and disputes between the owner and contractor; and the review of the amounts requested by the contractor in his Application for Payment. In addition, the architect determines whether sufficient cause exists to justify termination of the contract by the owner. In this case, if it is necessary,the owner informs the surety of the contractor's default and notifies the surety to perform under the bond.

In some cases, a performing surety may make claims against the architect for negligent breach of duty to perform in accordance with the reasonable standard of care. Such allegations may involve claims of negligent certification of the amounts due the contractor, negligent release of the retained percentage, negligent interpretation of the Contract Documents or negligent observation of the work. Further, a surety may claim negligence on the part of the architect for failure to make notification of default in a timely manner, that is, at the earliest time the architect should have known that the contractor was in default. Recognize that paragraph 14.2.2 of the AIA General Conditions requires the owner to notify the surety in writing of termination of the contract for cause. However, paragraph 2.6.5 requires the architect to keep the owner informed of the progress and quality of the work.

There are other types of bonds in addition to those mentioned above which are used on some construction contracts.

The Lien Bond is sometimes used to protect the owner against loss from any liens that may be attached against his property resulting from unpaid labor or material bills.

The No Lien Bond is sometimes issued as a type of Performance Bond. In some states where the Owner-Contractor Agreement has been filed as a no lien contract, it is a statutory requirement. This bond has the effect of denying the right to file a lien in connection with the contract.

Maintenance Bonds guarantee the quality of construction and the maintenance of certain elements of the building for a given period after project completion. It is not common for bonds to be issued for maintenance only. These obligations are contained in the Owner-Contractor Agreement and are covered by the Performance Bond. Roofing guarantees are an exception. They are often furnished separately by manufacturers or roofing contractors for terms of up to twenty years from the date of completion.

A Release of Retained Percentage Bond is sometimes issued to protect the owner against loss resulting from situations where more of the project funds have been paid out than progress of the work justifies. Under this bond the owner is assured of faithful completion of the work even if the retained percentage is not sufficient to cover the cost of the work remaining. In addition, some statutory requirements prevent the release of the retained percentage unless the contractor furnishes such a bond.

A Statutory Bond is required by certain public bodies to comply with the terms of a statute or regulation. The main difference between this bond and the Performance Bond or Payment Bond is that it must be worded exactly in accordance with the wording of the law in order to comply with the statute.

Subcontract Bonds are Performance and Payment Bonds required by the contractor from his subcontractors which assure him of the faithful execution of the subcontractor's portion of the work.

Street Maintenance Bonds are often required of the contractor by municipal governments. These assure the municipality that a contractor who uses a city street for storage of materials or tears up a street for installation of utilities will repair the street, curbs, and sidewalk.

While the architect's duties do not include legal or insurance advice, the architect should bring to the owner's attention his right to require bonds under the terms of the contract. A form used to obtain the owner's requirements for bonds is AIA Document G610, "Owners Instructions for Bonds and Insurance." The bonds perform a very useful function in the project delivery process. They form a protection for the owner against possible default of the contractor. In many cases where a contractor has defaulted, the project would never have been successfully completed without the owner's requirement of bonds for the project.

THE AMERICAN INSTITUTE OF ARCHITECTS

AIA Document A310

Bid Bond

KNOW ALL MEN BY THESE PRESENTS, that we Quality Construction Co.
300 First Ave., Oakland, California   *(Here insert full name and address or legal title of Contractor)*

as Principal, hereinafter called the Principal, and Standard Surety Co.
120 Commercial Drive, San Francisco, California *(Here insert full name and address or legal title of Surety)*

a corporation duly organized under the laws of the State of California
as Surety, hereinafter called the Surety, are held and firmly bound unto Typical Manufacturing Co.
950 Broadway Blvd., Oakland, California   *(Here insert full name and address or legal title of Owner)*

as Obligee, hereinafter called the Obligee, in the sum of one million

Dollars ($1,000,000.00),
for the payment of which sum well and truly to be made, the said Principal and the said Surety, bind ourselves, our heirs, executors, administrators, successors and assigns, jointly and severally, firmly by these presents.

WHEREAS, the Principal has submitted a bid for Ten million dollars ($10,000,000)
for the Construction of Typical Manufacturing Co. *(Here insert full name, address and description of project)*
Industrial Plant and Offices
100 Industrial Blvd., Hayward, California

NOW, THEREFORE, if the Obligee shall accept the bid of the Principal and the Principal shall enter into a Contract with the Obligee in accordance with the terms of such bid, and give such bond or bonds as may be specified in the bidding or Contract Documents with good and sufficient surety for the faithful performance of such Contract and for the prompt payment of labor and material furnished in the prosecution thereof, or in the event of the failure of the Principal to enter such Contract and give such bond or bonds, if the Principal shall pay to the Obligee the difference not to exceed the penalty hereof between the amount specified in said bid and such larger amount for which the Obligee may in good faith contract with another party to perform the Work covered by said bid, then this obligation shall be null and void, otherwise to remain in full force and effect.

Signed and sealed this   Fifteenth   **day of**   April   19 88

	Quality Construction Co.
	_____ _____
	(Principal) *(Seal)*
_____	President of Company
(Witness)	_____
Robert Brown	*(Title)*
	Standard Surety Co.
	_____ _____
	(Surety) *(Seal)*
_____	Bonding Officer
(Witness)	_____
John Doe	*(Title)*

THE AMERICAN INSTITUTE OF ARCHITECTS

AIA Document A312

Performance Bond

Any singular reference to Contractor, Surety, Owner or other party shall be considered plural where applicable.

CONTRACTOR (Name and Address):

Robert Brown, President
Quality Construction Co.
300 First Ave.
Oakland, California

SURETY (Name and Principal Place of Business):

John Doe, Bonding Officer
Standard Surety Co.
120 Commercial Drive
San Francisco, California

OWNER (Name and Address):
William Jones, President
Typical Manufacturing Co.
950 Broadway Blvd.
Oakland, California

CONSTRUCTION CONTRACT
Date: May 1, 1988
Amount: Ten Million Dollars ($10,000,000.00)
Description (Name and Location): Construction of Typical Manufacturing Co. Industrial
Plant & Offices, 100 Industrial Blvd., Hayward, California

BOND
Date (Not earlier than Construction Contract Date): May 3, 1988
Amount: Ten Million Dollars ($10,000,000.00)
Modifications to this Bond: ☒ None   ☐ See Page 3

CONTRACTOR AS PRINCIPAL
Company: (Corporate Seal)
  Quality Construction Co.

Signature: _____
Name and Title:
  Robert Brown, President
(Any additional signatures appear on page 3)

SURETY
Company: (Corporate Seal)
  Standard Surety Co.

Signature: _____
Name and Title:
  John Doe, Bonding Officer

(FOR INFORMATION ONLY—Name, Address and Telephone)
AGENT or BROKER:

**OWNER'S REPRESENTATIVE (Architect, Engineer or
other party):** A B C Architects
                600 Main St.
                San Francisco, California

AIA DOCUMENT A312 · PERFORMANCE BOND AND PAYMENT BOND · DECEMBER 1984 ED. · AIA ®
THE AMERICAN INSTITUTE OF ARCHITECTS, 1735 NEW YORK AVE., N.W., WASHINGTON, D.C. 20006
THIRD PRINTING · MARCH 1987

A312-1984 1

1 The Contractor and the Surety, jointly and severally, bind themselves, their heirs, executors, administrators, successors and assigns to the Owner for the performance of the Construction Contract, which is incorporated herein by reference.

2 If the Contractor performs the Construction Contract, the Surety and the Contractor shall have no obligation under this Bond, except to participate in conferences as provided in Subparagraph 3.1.

3 If there is no Owner Default, the Surety's obligation under this Bond shall arise after:

3.1 The Owner has notified the Contractor and the Surety at its address described in Paragraph 10 below that the Owner is considering declaring a Contractor Default and has requested and attempted to arrange a conference with the Contractor and the Surety to be held not later than fifteen days after receipt of such notice to discuss methods of performing the Construction Contract. If the Owner, the Contractor and the Surety agree, the Contractor shall be allowed a reasonable time to perform the Construction Contract, but such an agreement shall not waive the Owner's right, if any, subsequently to declare a Contractor Default; and

3.2 The Owner has declared a Contractor Default and formally terminated the Contractor's right to complete the contract. Such Contractor Default shall not be declared earlier than twenty days after the Contractor and the Surety have received notice as provided in Subparagraph 3.1; and

3.3 The Owner has agreed to pay the Balance of the Contract Price to the Surety in accordance with the terms of the Construction Contract or to a contractor selected to perform the Construction Contract in accordance with the terms of the contract with the Owner.

4 When the Owner has satisfied the conditions of Paragraph 3, the Surety shall promptly and at the Surety's expense take one of the following actions:

4.1 Arrange for the Contractor, with consent of the Owner, to perform and complete the Construction Contract; or

4.2 Undertake to perform and complete the Construction Contract itself, through its agents or through independent contractors; or

4.3 Obtain bids or negotiated proposals from qualified contractors acceptable to the Owner for a contract for performance and completion of the Construction Contract, arrange for a contract to be prepared for execution by the Owner and the contractor selected with the Owner's concurrence, to be secured with performance and payment bonds executed by a qualified surety equivalent to the bonds issued on the Construction Contract, and pay to the Owner the amount of damages as described in Paragraph 6 in excess of the Balance of the Contract Price incurred by the Owner resulting from the Contractor's default; or

4.4 Waive its right to perform and complete, arrange for completion, or obtain a new contractor and with reasonable promptness under the circumstances:

.1 After investigation, determine the amount for

which it may be liable to the Owner and, as soon as practicable after the amount is determined, tender payment therefor to the Owner; or

.2 Deny liability in whole or in part and notify the Owner citing reasons therefor.

5 If the Surety does not proceed as provided in Paragraph 4 with reasonable promptness, the Surety shall be deemed to be in default on this Bond fifteen days after receipt of an additional written notice from the Owner to the Surety demanding that the Surety perform its obligations under this Bond, and the Owner shall be entitled to enforce any remedy available to the Owner. If the Surety proceeds as provided in Subparagraph 4.4, and the Owner refuses the payment tendered or the Surety has denied liability, in whole or in part, without further notice the Owner shall be entitled to enforce any remedy available to the Owner.

6 After the Owner has terminated the Contractor's right to complete the Construction Contract, and if the Surety elects to act under Subparagraph 4.1, 4.2, or 4.3 above, then the responsibilities of the Surety to the Owner shall not be greater than those of the Contractor under the Construction Contract, and the responsibilities of the Owner to the Surety shall not be greater than those of the Owner under the Construction Contract. To the limit of the amount of this Bond, but subject to commitment by the Owner of the Balance of the Contract Price to mitigation of costs and damages on the Construction Contract, the Surety is obligated without duplication for:

6.1 The responsibilities of the Contractor for correction of defective work and completion of the Construction Contract;

6.2 Additional legal, design professional and delay costs resulting from the Contractor's Default, and resulting from the actions or failure to act of the Surety under Paragraph 4; and

6.3 Liquidated damages, or if no liquidated damages are specified in the Construction Contract, actual damages caused by delayed performance or non-performance of the Contractor.

7 The Surety shall not be liable to the Owner or others for obligations of the Contractor that are unrelated to the Construction Contract, and the Balance of the Contract Price shall not be reduced or set off on account of any such unrelated obligations. No right of action shall accrue on this Bond to any person or entity other than the Owner or its heirs, executors, administrators or successors.

8 The Surety hereby waives notice of any change, including changes of time, to the Construction Contract or to related subcontracts, purchase orders and other obligations.

9 Any proceeding, legal or equitable, under this Bond may be instituted in any court of competent jurisdiction in the location in which the work or part of the work is located and shall be instituted within two years after Contractor Default or within two years after the Contractor ceased working or within two years after the Surety refuses or fails to perform its obligations under this Bond, whichever occurs first. If the provisions of this Paragraph are void or prohibited by law, the minimum period of limitation avail-

AIA DOCUMENT A312 • PERFORMANCE BOND AND PAYMENT BOND • DECEMBER 1984 ED. • AIA ®
THE AMERICAN INSTITUTE OF ARCHITECTS, 1735 NEW YORK AVE., N.W., WASHINGTON, D.C. 20006
THIRD PRINTING • MARCH 1987

A312-1984   2

able to sureties as a defense in the jurisdiction of the suit shall be applicable.

10 Notice to the Surety, the Owner or the Contractor shall be mailed or delivered to the address shown on the signature page.

11 When this Bond has been furnished to comply with a statutory or other legal requirement in the location where the construction was to be performed, any provision in this Bond conflicting with said statutory or legal requirement shall be deemed deleted herefrom and provisions conforming to such statutory or other legal requirement shall be deemed incorporated herein. The intent is that this Bond shall be construed as a statutory bond and not as a common law bond.

12 DEFINITIONS

12.1 Balance of the Contract Price: The total amount payable by the Owner to the Contractor under the Construction Contract after all proper adjustments have been made, including allowance to the Con-

tractor of any amounts received or to be received by the Owner in settlement of insurance or other claims for damages to which the Contractor is entitled, reduced by all valid and proper payments made to or on behalf of the Contractor under the Construction Contract.

12.2 Construction Contract: The agreement between the Owner and the Contractor identified on the signature page, including all Contract Documents and changes thereto.

12.3 Contractor Default: Failure of the Contractor, which has neither been remedied nor waived, to perform or otherwise to comply with the terms of the Construction Contract.

12.4 Owner Default: Failure of the Owner, which has neither been remedied nor waived, to pay the Contractor as required by the Construction Contract or to perform and complete or comply with the other terms thereof.

MODIFICATIONS TO THIS BOND ARE AS FOLLOWS:

(Space is provided below for additional signatures of added parties, other than those appearing on the cover page.)

CONTRACTOR AS PRINCIPAL		SURETY	
Company:	(Corporate Seal)	Company:	(Corporate Seal)

Signature: _____ Signature: _____
Name and Title: Name and Title:
Address: Address:

AIA DOCUMENT A312 • PERFORMANCE BOND AND PAYMENT BOND • DECEMBER 1984 ED. • AIA ®
THE AMERICAN INSTITUTE OF ARCHITECTS, 1735 NEW YORK AVE., N.W., WASHINGTON, D.C. 20006
THIRD PRINTING • MARCH 1987

A312-1984 3

THE AMERICAN INSTITUTE OF ARCHITECTS

AIA Document A312

Payment Bond

Any singular reference to Contractor, Surety, Owner or other party shall be considered plural where applicable.

CONTRACTOR (Name and Address):

Robert Brown, President
Quality Construction Co.
300 First Ave.
Oakland, California

OWNER (Name and Address):

William Jones, President
Typical Manufacturing Co.
950 Broadway Blvd.
Oakland, California

SURETY (Name and Principal Place of Business):

John Doe, Bonding Officer
Standard Surety Co.
120 Commercial Drive
San Francisco, California

CONSTRUCTION CONTRACT

Date: May 1, 1988
Amount: Ten Million Dollars ($10,000,000.00)
Description (Name and Location): Construction of Typical Manufacturing Co. Industrial
Plant & Offices, 100 Industrial Blvd., Hayward, California

BOND

Date (Not earlier than Construction Contract Date): May 3, 1988
Amount: Ten Million Dollars ($10,000,000.00)
Modifications to this Bond: ☒ None   ☐ See Page 6

CONTRACTOR AS PRINCIPAL		SURETY	
Company:	(Corporate Seal)	Company:	(Corporate Seal)
Quality Construction Co.		Standard Surety Co.	

Signature: _____   Signature: _____
Name and Title: Name and Title:
Robert Brown, President   John Doe, Bonding Officer
(Any additional signatures appear on page 6)

(FOR INFORMATION ONLY—Name, Address and Telephone)

AGENT or BROKER:

OWNER'S REPRESENTATIVE (Architect, Engineer or other party):

A B C Architects
600 Main St.
San Francisco, California

AIA DOCUMENT A312 • PERFORMANCE BOND AND PAYMENT BOND • DECEMBER 1984 ED. • AIA ®
THE AMERICAN INSTITUTE OF ARCHITECTS, 1735 NEW YORK AVE., N.W., WASHINGTON, D.C. 20006
THIRD PRINTING • MARCH 1987

A312-1984 4

1 The Contractor and the Surety, jointly and severally, bind themselves, their heirs, executors, administrators, successors and assigns to the Owner to pay for labor, materials and equipment furnished for use in the performance of the Construction Contract, which is incorporated herein by reference.

2 With respect to the Owner, this obligation shall be null and void if the Contractor:

2.1 Promptly makes payment, directly or indirectly, for all sums due Claimants, and

2.2 Defends, indemnifies and holds harmless the Owner from claims, demands, liens or suits by any person or entity whose claim, demand, lien or suit is for the payment for labor, materials or equipment furnished for use in the performance of the Construction Contract, provided the Owner has promptly notified the Contractor and the Surety (at the address described in Paragraph 12) of any claims, demands, liens or suits and tendered defense of such claims, demands, liens or suits to the Contractor and the Surety, and provided there is no Owner Default.

3 With respect to Claimants, this obligation shall be null and void if the Contractor promptly makes payment, directly or indirectly, for all sums due.

4 The Surety shall have no obligation to Claimants under this Bond until:

4.1 Claimants who are employed by or have a direct contract with the Contractor have given notice to the Surety (at the address described in Paragraph 12) and sent a copy, or notice thereof, to the Owner, stating that a claim is being made under this Bond and, with substantial accuracy, the amount of the claim.

4.2 Claimants who do not have a direct contract with the Contractor:

    .1 Have furnished written notice to the Contractor and sent a copy, or notice thereof, to the Owner, within 90 days after having last performed labor or last furnished materials or equipment included in the claim stating, with substantial accuracy, the amount of the claim and the name of the party to whom the materials were furnished or supplied or for whom the labor was done or performed; and

    .2 Have either received a rejection in whole or in part from the Contractor, or not received within 30 days of furnishing the above notice any communication from the Contractor by which the Contractor has indicated the claim will be paid directly or indirectly; and

    .3 Not having been paid within the above 30 days, have sent a written notice to the Surety (at the address described in Paragraph 12) and sent a copy, or notice thereof, to the Owner, stating that a claim is being made under this Bond and enclosing a copy of the previous written notice furnished to the Contractor.

5 If a notice required by Paragraph 4 is given by the Owner to the Contractor or to the Surety, that is sufficient compliance.

6 When the Claimant has satisfied the conditions of Paragraph 4, the Surety shall promptly and at the Surety's expense take the following actions:

6.1 Send an answer to the Claimant, with a copy to the Owner, within 45 days after receipt of the claim, stating the amounts that are undisputed and the basis for challenging any amounts that are disputed.

6.2 Pay or arrange for payment of any undisputed amounts.

7 The Surety's total obligation shall not exceed the amount of this Bond, and the amount of this Bond shall be credited for any payments made in good faith by the Surety.

8 Amounts owed by the Owner to the Contractor under the Construction Contract shall be used for the performance of the Construction Contract and to satisfy claims, if any, under any Construction Performance Bond. By the Contractor furnishing and the Owner accepting this Bond, they agree that all funds earned by the Contractor in the performance of the Construction Contract are dedicated to satisfy obligations of the Contractor and the Surety under this Bond, subject to the Owner's priority to use the funds for the completion of the work.

9 The Surety shall not be liable to the Owner, Claimants or others for obligations of the Contractor that are unrelated to the Construction Contract. The Owner shall not be liable for payment of any costs or expenses of any Claimant under this Bond, and shall have under this Bond no obligations to make payments to, give notices on behalf of, or otherwise have obligations to Claimants under this Bond.

10 The Surety hereby waives notice of any change, including changes of time, to the Construction Contract or to related subcontracts, purchase orders and other obligations.

11 No suit or action shall be commenced by a Claimant under this Bond other than in a court of competent jurisdiction in the location in which the work or part of the work is located or after the expiration of one year from the date (1) on which the Claimant gave the notice required by Subparagraph 4.1 or Clause 4.2.3, or (2) on which the last labor or service was performed by anyone or the last materials or equipment were furnished by anyone under the Construction Contract, whichever of (1) or (2) first occurs. If the provisions of this Paragraph are void or prohibited by law, the minimum period of limitation available to sureties as a defense in the jurisdiction of the suit shall be applicable.

12 Notice to the Surety, the Owner or the Contractor shall be mailed or delivered to the address shown on the signature page. Actual receipt of notice by Surety, the Owner or the Contractor, however accomplished, shall be sufficient compliance as of the date received at the address shown on the signature page.

13 When this Bond has been furnished to comply with a statutory or other legal requirement in the location where the construction was to be performed, any provision in this Bond conflicting with said statutory or legal requirement shall be deemed deleted herefrom and provisions conforming to such statutory or other legal requirement shall be deemed incorporated herein. The intent is that this

AIA DOCUMENT A312 • PERFORMANCE BOND AND PAYMENT BOND • DECEMBER 1984 ED. • AIA®
THE AMERICAN INSTITUTE OF ARCHITECTS, 1735 NEW YORK AVE., N.W., WASHINGTON, D.C. 20006
THIRD PRINTING • MARCH 1987

A312-1984 **5**

Bond shall be construed as a statutory bond and not as a common law bond.

14 Upon request by any person or entity appearing to be a potential beneficiary of this Bond, the Contractor shall promptly furnish a copy of this Bond or shall permit a copy to be made.

15 DEFINITIONS

15.1 Claimant: An individual or entity having a direct contract with the Contractor or with a subcontractor of the Contractor to furnish labor, materials or equipment for use in the performance of the Contract. The intent of this Bond shall be to include without limitation in the terms "labor, materials or equipment" that part of water, gas, power, light, heat, oil, gasoline, telephone service or rental equipment used in the Construction Contract, architectural and engineering services required for performance of the work of the Contractor and the Contractor's subcontractors, and all other items for which a mechanic's lien may be asserted in the jurisdiction where the labor, materials or equipment were furnished.

15.2 Construction Contract: The agreement between the Owner and the Contractor identified on the signature page, including all Contract Documents and changes thereto.

15.3 Owner Default: Failure of the Owner, which has neither been remedied nor waived, to pay the Contractor as required by the Construction Contract or to perform and complete or comply with the other terms thereof.

MODIFICATIONS TO THIS BOND ARE AS FOLLOWS:

(Space is provided below for additional signatures of added parties, other than those appearing on the cover page.)

CONTRACTOR AS PRINCIPAL		SURETY	
Company:	(Corporate Seal)	Company:	(Corporate Seal)

Signature: _____   Signature: _____
Name and Title: Name and Title:
Address: Address:

AIA DOCUMENT A312 • PERFORMANCE BOND AND PAYMENT BOND • DECEMBER 1984 ED. • AIA ®
THE AMERICAN INSTITUTE OF ARCHITECTS, 1735 NEW YORK AVE., N.W., WASHINGTON, D.C. 20006
THIRD PRINTING • MARCH 1987

A312-1984 6

Insurance

Provisions for general insurance requirements for the project are outlined in Article 11 of the American Institute of Architects Document A201, General Conditions of the Contract for Construction. The owner should transmit written instructions to the architect regarding modifications to Article 11, if any. Modifications, including special insurance requirements, should be outlined in the Supplementary Conditions of the Contract Documents.

It is important to recognize that the architect's responsibilities do not include insurance advice. In addition, architect's professional liability insurance does not include coverage on providing insurance advice. This is not the architect's area of professional expertise. It is the responsibility of the owner and his insurance counselor to determine proper amounts of insurance coverage for the project. Therefore, the architect should not make recommendations about insurance or approve policies or certificates under any circumstances.

In addition, the owner should be advised to obtain legal and insurance counsel not only on his insurance requirements, but also on that insurance to be carried by the contractor for the protection of the owner's interests in the project. In both the contractor's insurance and the owner's insurance, minimum amounts of coverage should be determined in advance by the owner and stated in the Supplementary Conditions of the Contract Documents. In addition, the contractor should be required to submit certificates of coverage for the owner's review.

Article 11 calls for appropriate basic insurance requirements.

Provisions under this section call for (1) contractor's liability insurance; (2) owner's liability insurance; (3) property insurance which is purchased and maintained by the owner; (4) boiler and machinery insurance; and (5) at the owner's option, loss of use insurance. Upon written request by the contractor, other special coverages may be included in the owner's property insurance. In this case, the cost of the special coverage is charged to the contractor by change order. The contractor's liability insurance provisions include requirements for the contractor to purchase and maintain liability insurance required by statute in the state in which the work is performed, and comprehensive general liability insurance. Under provisions of the statutory liability insurance requirements, the contractor must provide and maintain workmen's compensation insurance and disability benefits in amounts as required by employee benefit acts.

Under provisions of the contractor's liability insurance requirements, the contractor is required to purchase and maintain liability insurance that will protect him against claims which include not only bodily injury, as a result of accidents, occupational disease or death; but also, personal injury claims such as those alleging false arrest, libel, slander, defamation of character, wrongful eviction, and so on. The insurance must also include protection against claims for property damage resulting from execution of the work or acts of negligence of the contractor, subcontractors or any employees. In addition, automobile liability insurance must be provided for both bodily injury and property damage.

The contractor's liability insurance for property damage generally excludes claims arising from explosion; collapse due to excavation, moving and shoring; and damage to underground property. Therefore, careful consideration must be given by the owner and his insurance counselor for the possible need to include X-C-U coverage (explosion—collapse—underground) as a requirement for special insurance provisions to be designated in the Supplementary Conditions.

Notice that paragraph 8.2.2 of the AIA General Conditions states that the contractor shall not, except by the owner's written agreement, commence operations prior to the effective date of insurance. Further, the date of commencement of the work is not to be changed by the effective date of such insurance. Also, as outlined by paragraph 11.1.2, the insurance coverage limits shall not be less than those specified in the Contract Documents. In addition, insurance coverages shall be maintained without interruption from the date of commencement of the work until the date of final payment and termination of any coverage required to be maintained after final payment.

The contractor's liability insurance certificates should be filed with the owner prior to the commencement of the work. All certificates should be reviewed and approved by the owner. Further, the owner should notify the architect in writing when the contractor has provided satisfactory evidence of insurance. The architect should not issue any certificate for payment until he has received such notification.

The American Institute of Architects Document G705, Certificate of Insurance, is a form designed to provide the owner with a summary of the contractor's insurance coverages. This form expedites confirmation of compliance with the insurance requirements specified in the Contract Documents. Its use standardizes the reporting of coverage and prevents errors and omissions.

In addition, all the contractor's insurance policies should contain a clause stating that their coverages cannot be canceled without thirty days prior written notice to the owner. The insurance policies should be issued by an insurance company licensed to do business in the state in which the work is being executed.

Additional portions of Article 11 discuss the owner's liability insurance. The owner is responsible for obtaining and maintaining his own liability insurance and for securing coverage that will protect him against claims which could arise from operations under the contract. In this case, as in all other instances, the owner should be advised to seek insurance counsel for advice regarding this coverage. The owner should obtain this insurance prior to the commencement of the work. The architect should receive confirmation of the insurance coverage and the limits of liability established by the owner.

Further provisions of Article 11 outline requirements for property insurance which is secured and maintained by the owner. This insurance protects the owner against losses resulting from fire, theft, vandalism and other hazards during the course of construction. In essence, the property insurance protects that portion of the work that is owned by the owner. Note that title to all work covered by an Application for Payment passes to the owner no later than the time of payment as outlined in the AIA General Conditions, paragraph 9.3.3. The coverage should be for the full insurable value of the work including material and equipment stored on the site. The insurance must include coverage on the contractor and all subcontractors in addition to the owner.

As outlined in paragraph 11.3.1.4 of the AIA General Conditions, the owner's property insurance must cover portions of the work stored off the site after written approval of the owner. Further, portions of the work in transit must also be covered unless otherwise provided in the Contract Documents. Paragraph 9.3.2 states that the owner shall make payment for material stored off the site if it is approved in advance by the owner. Such payment, however, is made upon the condition that the contractor establishes the owner's title to these materials and includes applicable insurance. This insurance requirement of paragraph 9.3.2 is a check upon the possibility that the owner may not have actually purchased the insurance required by paragraph 11.3.1.4. If such coverage has not been obtained, may request the contractor to purchase and maintain it. In this case, the contractor is reimbursed by a Change Order since this insurance is the owner's responsibility as outlined in paragraph 11.3.1.4.

In addition, the owner must file copies of the policies with the contractor prior to commencement of the work. Additional and extended coverages may be requested by the contractor. If possible, the owner includes such coverage, and the cost of such additional coverage is paid by the contractor. If the owner does not obtain property insurance, he must notify the contractor. In this case, the contractor may obtain the required insurance and charge the costs to the owner through a Change Order.

The owner is also required to carry boiler and machinery insurance. This coverage is not provided in normal fire and extended coverage property insurance. This coverage must include the interests of the owner, contractor and all sub-contractors.

Final portions of Article 11 state the owner's right, at his option, to obtain loss of use insurance. This coverage insures the owner against loss of use of his property due to fire or other hazards which delay occupancy of the building. This coverage is particularly important where the work is an addition or alteration to an existing building. In this case, damages an the existing structure constitute a major loss. It is the responsibility of the owner to carry insurance against such loss.

It is the architect's responsibility to transmit written notice to the owner bringing to his attention the requirements under Article 11 of the General Conditions concerning insurance. At this time, the architect should request the owner's instructions regarding insurance provisions to be incorporated in the Supplementary Conditions. Further, this notice should advise the owner to obtain recommendations from his insurance counselor in regard to coverage required.

The American Institute of Architects Handbook of Professional Practice, Volume 4, provides a form for use in requesting the owner's insurance instructions. The form provides the owner with a means of indicating his instructions regarding the contractor's insurance and owner's insurance to be incorporated in the Supplementary Conditions. The form for this purpose is AIA Document G610, "Owner's Instructions for Bonds and Insurance."

The architect may wish to carry professional liability insurance to cover claims for errors, omissions, or negligence arising out of the performance of his professional services. The architect may be liable not only to the owner but also to others with whom he held no contractual obligations. This may involve injuries or damages to users of the building resulting from the architect's negligence in the design of the building or administration of the contract.

As an alternative to year round coverage, the architect may wish to consider professional liability insurance on a project basis. In this case, a specific project is covered through its various phases and up to several years after completion. There are several advantages to this type of coverage. Claims on this policy are not charged against an annual policy that may have a fixed maximum limit of coverage. Also, premiums are lower than those for annual coverage. In addition, the architect may be able to charge this cost to the owner as a reimbursable expense item. However, this must be agreed upon in advance since the AIA Owner-Architect Agreement does not include professional liability insurance as a reimbursable item.

Written agreements cannot be relied upon to protect the architect against claims arising from negligent acts or the failure to exercise a reasonable standard of care in providing professional services, since the rights of a third party are often involved. In addition, the architect must pay the cost of legal defense of claims, even if cleared of all allegations. In many cases, injured parties file claims against all persons even remotely connected with the occurrence.

Necessary legal defense of claims is generally covered by professional liability insurance. In addition, it covers the liability for errors, omissions or negligent acts. The policy not only insures the architect but also any partner or employee acting within the scope of his duties. Retroactive coverage is also available to cover errors, omissions or negligent acts discovered during the policy period, even though they occurred in the past. Extended coverage for retired or inactive architects is available at reduced rates. Further, there is optional design phase coverage at reduced rates to protect the architect for the design phase of the work only.

The architect's choice of insurance companies is very important. This is because each annual renewal of the policy generally includes coverage of the architect's projects completed in prior years while continuously covered with that company. Therefore, if the architect changes companies, a serious situation develops if a claim is made on a prior project after the change is made. Now, neither the original carrier or the new company may cover the claim. For this reason, it is important to obtain retroactive coverage from any new company. Note that such coverage must be clearly indicated. Also recognize that it could have different limits and terms from the original policy.

The architect must fully familiarize himself with the terms and conditions of the policy. Particular care must be used to ascertain what professional activities are covered and what is excluded under the policy. While each policy is different, typical exclusions include the following: delays in the delivery of Contract Documents, business errors, errors in the preliminary estimate of construction cost, services related to dams, tunnels or bridges that exceed 150 feet in length, consultant's services, the cost of arbitration hearings and arbitration awards. Recognize that any professional service beyond those normally required in an architect's work may be excluded from a policy. Further, any warranty given by the architect may be excluded since the assumption of most claims is only that a reasonable standard of care must have been adhered to by the architect.

Other services generally excluded from policies are geotechnical testing, laboratory testing of materials and site surveys. These services are normally provided by consultants under direct contract with the owner rather than by the architect or by consultants under contract with the architect. In this way, the architect is not liable for their services. Further, any work related to pollution or hazardous materials is excluded from coverage. This generally includes not only the cleanup activities involving hazardous materials, but also the design of sewage treatment plants and even in some cases, HVAC systems that circulate air within the project. The architect should review policies with his attorney to determine if specific activities performed by his firm are covered. In some cases, endorsements to the policy can be added to cover excluded activities.

There are two important limits of coverage on any professional liability insurance policy: the deductible amount and the limit of coverage. The architect must pay for any claim below the deductible amount or above the limit of coverage. The architect should review these limits prior to any project and add additional coverage as the size or risks of the project may warrant. Recognize that the maximum limit of coverage is somewhat deceptive. This is generally defined as the maximum aggregate amount of claims against the architect that will be paid by the insurance company in one year and not the maximum amount per claim. Many problems have developed over this misunderstanding. For example, if several large claims are filed in one year, the maximum limit on the policy may be exceeded. Other problems may develop over the lower limit, that is, the deductible amount. Note that the deductible is generally applied to each claim.

Therefore, if the deductible is high, numerous small claims may add up to a large amount of liability that is not insured.

The architect has certain duties under most professional liability insurance policies in the event that a claim is made. The architect should carefully review such duties to avoid allegations by the insurance company that time limits, or terms and conditions of the policy were not adhered to. Each company's policy is different and must be reviewed. In general, such duties include the prompt reporting of any claims to the company, providing written statements and depositions upon request, prompt forwarding to the company of any summons or written notices served on the architect, and appearing in court for hearings and testimony. It is important to respond to these matters in a timely manner since the insurance company will want to take immediate action to document facts in any claim. Such procedures may entail obtaining written statements of witnesses; taking photographs of a portion of the work where a claim is involved; or preserving physical portions of the work if such evidence is necessary.

In addition, it is good professional practice for the architect to require his consultants to carry professional liability insurance protection as outlined in paragraph 10.6.1 of the Architect-Consultant Agreement. Submission of evidence of coverage should be required as outlined in paragraph 10.6.4 of the Architect-Consultant Agreement. If the consultant's coverages are not adequate, the liability extends to the architect. Note that certificates should contain provisions requiring that the architect be given 30 days' written notice prior to any cancellation of such coverage.

CERTIFICATE OF INSURANCE

AIA DOCUMENT G705

This certificate is issued as a matter of information only and confers no rights upon the addressee. It does not amend, extend or alter the coverage afforded by the policies listed below.

Name and Address of Insured

Quality Construction Company

Covering (Project Name and Location)

Typical Mfg. Co. Plant & Offices

100 Industrial Blvd., Hayward, California

Addressee:
(Owner)

William Jones, President
Typical Manufacturing Company
950 Broadway Blvd.
Oakland, California

COMPANIES AFFORDING COVERAGE

A	Reputable Insurance Company
B	
C	
D	
E	
F	

This is to certify that the following described policies, subject to their terms, conditions and exclusions, have been issued to the above named insured and are in force at this time.

TYPE OF INSURANCE	CO. CODE	POLICY NUMBER	EXPIRATION DATE	LIMITS OF LIABILITY IN THOUSANDS	EACH OCCURRENCE	AGGREGATE
1. (a) Workers' Compensation		1000	8/1/89	Statutory		
(b) Employer's Liability		2000	8/1/89		$	Each Accident
2. Comprehensive General Liability including:		3000	8/1/89	Bodily Injury	$	$
☒ Premises - Operations				Property Damage	$	$
☒ Independent Contractors						
☒ Products and Completed Operations						
☒ Broad Form Property Damage				Bodily Injury and Property Damage Combined	$	$
☒ Contractual Liability						
☒ Explosion and Collapse Hazard						
☒ Underground Hazard				*Applies to Products and Completed Operations Hazard		$
☒ Personal Injury with Employment Exclusion Deleted						(Personal Injury)
3. Comprehensive Automobile Liability		4000	8/1/89	Bodily Injury (Each Person)	$	
☒ Owned				Bodily Injury (Each Accident)	$	
☒ Hired				Property Damage	$	
☒ Non-Owned				Bodily Injury and Property Damage Combined	$	
4. Excess Liability		5000	8/1/89	Bodily Injury and Property Damage Combined	$	$
☒ Umbrella Form						
☐ Other than Umbrella						
5. Other (Specify) **Comprehensive Mat'l. stored off site**		6000	8/1/89			

1. Products and Completed Operations coverage will be maintained for a minimum period of ☐ 1 ☒ 2 year(s) after final payment.

2. Has each of the above listed policies been endorsed to reflect the company's obligation to notify the addressee in the event of cancellation or non-renewal? ☒ Yes ☐ No

CERTIFICATION

I hereby certify that I am an authorized representative of each of the insurance companies listed above, and that the coverages afforded under the policies listed above will not be cancelled or allowed to expire unless thirty (30) days written notice has been given to the addressee of this certificate.

Johnson Insurance Agency

Name of Issuing Agency

3400 North Av., Oakland, California

Address

Corporate Officer

Signature of Authorized Representative   Fred Johnson

May 1, 1988

Date of Issue

Bid Forms-Alternates-Addenda

Unless a special form is furnished to the architect by the owner, the architect should prepare the Bid Form. Thus, the architect is able to include all provisions and insure that all proposals will be identical in form and all bidders will compete for the same work. The form of the proposal is usually bound in the project manual as a part of the bidding requirements for the project. Much of the information placed on the Bid Form is furnished by the owner. A form used to obtain this information is AIA Document G611, Owner's Instructions Regarding Bidding Documents and Procedures.

The format of the Bid Form is generally that of a letter from the bidder to the owner. It contains blanks to be filled in and a space for the bidder's signature to indicate agreement with all provisions of the form. Each bidder must fill in all blank spaces and submit the form as a formal Bid Document. The Bid Form is not a part of the Contract Documents unless it is specifically listed under paragraph 9.1.7 of the AIA Owner-Contractor Agreement or is specifically enumerated in the Supplementary Conditions as a part of the Contract Documents. The Bid Form should contain all information necessary to select the bidder. The Bid Form includes the following:

A) Project description, which should identify the project and concisely describe the scope of work.

B) Acknowledgment of the documents on which the bid is based; that include the following: the list of drawings, the specifications, the project manual, and any addenda issued. (The addenda are interpretations, clarifications or modifications of the documents made after their initial issuance but prior to opening of the bids.)

C) Statements that the bidder will hold his bid open for a stated period of time (often thirty to sixty days) and that the bidder accepts specific agreements as outlined in the Instructions to Bidders.

D) Proposed cost of the project. (The base bid price should be given in both figures and writing.)

E) The Performance Bond and the Payment Bond if required by the owner.

F) The amount and type of bid security and the conditions regarding its forfeiture or return.

G) Statement that information required by the Instructions to Bidders, such as the List of Subcontractors, the Contractor's Qualification Statement and Bid Security, is attached.

H) Signatures, addresses and corporate seals of the bidder.

I) When alternates or unit prices are called for, these should be made a part of the bid proposal. Furthermore, alternates must be carefully defined in the Construction Documents.

ALTERNATES

An alternate is an amount stated in the bid to be added to or deducted from the amount of the base bid if the corresponding change in project scope or alternate material is accepted. Alternates are utilized as a means of ensuring that a proposal is within the construction budget. Furthermore, they provide an opportunity to make important decisions in the selection of materials or methods of construction. Alternates should be approved by the owner, acting on the architect's recommendations, in order to bring the cost of the project in line with budget limitations. The alternates chosen should be used in establishing the amount of the low bid. Alternates should not be selected to favor any one bidder over another. Those alternates accepted should be set forth in the Owner-Contractor Agreement. An example of an alternate for a project is as follows: Install vinyl tile as an alternate to carpeting on floors in corridors.

The bidder is generally required to submit a stipulated sum, that is, lump-sum price, for each alternate listed. Such alternates should be fully described in the Contract Documents in the same detail and format as the other materials and systems on the project. Further, price quotations on such alternates should be complete so that the owner can ascertain the true cost of the alternate material or equipment, and so on. Therefore, each quotation should include all applicable direct material and labor costs, job overhead costs, markup, bonds, insurance and taxes for the complete installation. Recognize that alternates make the bidding process somewhat more complicated. A large number of alternates should be avoided as it can affect the accuracy of the bids.

In addition to using alternate bids as a means of keeping the cost of the project within the budget, alternates are often used as a means of keeping prices in line when there are no other materials or equipment of a certain type available. The bid is often higher if there are no allowable substitutes. An example of an alternate when there are no allowable or available substitutes is as follows: Eliminate pneumatic tube system in manufacturing area. In this case, the entire system would be eliminated if the alternate bid is not reasonably in line with available funds. Obviously, this approach is valid only if a product or system can be eliminated without affecting the safe and proper functioning of the owner's project.

ADDENDA

An addendum is used to modify or clarify the original Bidding Documents prior to the award of the construction contract. The information which is listed in addenda is often the result of questions from bidders concerning the drawings, specifications and other Bidding Documents. Therefore, additional information which was not listed or shown in the original Bidding Documents may often be required. These clarifications or modifications should be incorporated into the Contract Documents in a formal addendum.

Another use of an addendum is to notify bidders of additional products or manufacturers to be incorporated into the specifications as acceptable manufacturers or materials. Article 3.3 of the AIA Instructions to Bidders outlines the process for proposed substitutions by bidders. The materials and products specified in the Bidding Documents establish a required standard of appearance and quality that must be met by any substitution proposed by a bidder. No substitutions are considered unless they are requested in writing and received at least ten days prior to the date for receipt of bids. Further, the proof of the merit of the proposed substitution is on the bidder. Therefore, such proposals should be accompanied by supporting materials that include performance and test data, drawings and any other information required for the architect's evaluation. In addition, a statement describing changes in other materials or equipment required by the incorporation of the proposed substitution must also be submitted. If the architect approves the proposed substitution, he issues an addendum to all bidders of record. No substitutions are considered after the contract award.

Additional information listed in addenda may take several forms as appropriate to the particular situation. This additional information is made a part of the Contract Documents as a result of the addendum which is issued to all bidders of record. The architect should keep an accurate record of each bidder's name and address every time a set of documents is issued to a bidder. These parties are the bidders of record. A form used for maintaining a record of recipients of Bid Documents is AIA Document G804, Register of Bid Documents. The addendum is issued by sending each bidder of record a copy by certified mail with a return receipt postcard. The postcard with the bidder's signature is confirmation that he received the addendum. Therefore, the return receipt should be kept in the project files. A copy of the addendum should also be sent to the owner for his information. Information typically listed includes the following: clarifica-tion of discrepancies; interpretation of questions; correction of errors, omissions and conflicts in the documents; changes in the quality or scope of work; changes regarding time or place of receipt of bids; and listing of additional products or manufacturers to be incorporated into the specifications as acceptable manufacturers or materials.

All addenda should be prepared and issued in a precise written format so there is no misinterpretation of verbal instructions. Necessary graphic information should be attached and listed. Modifications or clarifications to the working drawings are generally accomplished by the submittal of revised drawing sheets to the bidders. Changed areas are indicated by "clouds" that call the bidders attention to the revision. The addendum should contain information on the name and address of the project and the architect, addendum number, date, and an introductory statement. The addendum changes should then be listed in a logical sequence which is arranged in a definite order. The order should follow the same sequence of listing as the table of contents of the Project Manual. Addendum changes are often listed in an order which is as follows:

1) Previously issued Addenda

2) Table of Contents of Project Manual

3) Invitation to Bid

4) Instructions to Bidders

5) Bid Forms:

Form of Proposal (Reissue entirely if changes required)

Bid Bond Form

List of Subcontractors Form

6) Owner-Contractor Agreement Form

7) Bond Forms

8) General and Supplementary Conditions

9) Specification Sections-in order listed

10) Drawings-in order listed

All addenda issued should be formally acknowledged by each bidder on the Bid Form. (See chapter entitled "Changes in the Work" for a description of documents used to correct or change the Construction Documents after execution of the contract.)

From seemingly basic responsibilities involved with the bidding process, such as evaluating proposed substitutions and issuing addenda, the architect has the risk of potential liability from either the owner or the contractor. For example, as a result of pressure to keep the bidding process on schedule and the bid opening on time, the architect may give verbal instructions to bidders without written confirmation in an addendum. In spite of the fact that such changes or instructions may seem insignificant, they may not be. Such verbal instructions often lead to disputes and claims for construction cost overruns. Even if the architect is cleared of such allegations, these claims may lead to substantial legal fees and costs.

Further, the architect may be held accountable to the owner for exceeding authority if the owner has not approved the changes or substitutions listed in addenda. Therefore, the architect should always keep the owner informed and insist on written approval of any changes in products, systems, equipment or manufacturers, even if the owner approves of the changes verbally.

In order to control the process of bidding, evaluating substitutions, and issuing of addenda more effectively, the architect may wish to designate one individual, preferably the specification writer or project manager, to take care of all questions from contractors, subcontractors, manufacturers or material suppliers concerning substitutions or clarifications. Further, the architect should require that all questions be submitted in writing and all communications to bidders be in writing. In addition, the architect may wish to include protective language in the Bidding Documents that excludes the bidder from relying upon verbal communications from any source in preparing his bid.

Also, the architect may wish to include information in the Bidding Documents that defines exactly what is to be submitted with a substitution request. The architect may also include a special statement that is to be signed by the contractor and included with each proposed substitution. This statement would require the contractor to indicate how the contract time will be affected if the substitution is accepted.

Finish materials, such as flooring material in the entrance lobby, should be closely controlled against unwanted substitutions. Good specifications are the best way of controlling this problem. The basic element in a specification is that it should be well researched and appropriate to a specific project. The architect should accept the bidder's proposed substitution only when such materials or systems are consistent with the specifications and architect's knowledge of acceptable alternatives. Recognize that the architect should always maintain control over design interpretations.

A complex addendum that requires considerable effort by the bidders in preparing their bids should not be issued if there is insufficient time for the bidders to account for such a change. In this case, the architect should issue an addendum altering the date for receipt of bids. Further, in private work, changes could be negotiated with the low bidder before the award of contract. These changes should be set forth appropriately and incorporated into the contract by addendum prior to execution of the agreement.

The architect's consultants should not issue addenda directly to bidders. All addenda involving structural, mechanical, or electrical consultants, or any other consultant retained by the architect, should be issued through the architect to all bidders of record. In this way the architect can check and coordinate the consultant's addenda with other portions of the Bidding Documents to avoid possible conflicts. Further, a copy of all addenda issued should be sent to the architect's consultants.

SAMPLE ADDENDUM

Project: Date: March 21, 1988
Typical Manufacturing Co.
New Industrial Plant & Offices   A B C Architects
100 Industrial Blvd.   600 Main St.
Hayward, California   San Francisco, California

To: All prime contract bidders of record.

Addendum #1

Prime contract bidders of record for the subject project are
hereby informed that this Addendum forms a part of the Contract
Documents and modifies the original drawings and specifications
dated March 1, 1988 as noted below. Receipt of this Addendum
shall be acknowledged in the space provided on the Bid Form.

This addendum consists of this sheet. Attachments: none.
(Indicate number of sheets and any attachments or drawings
comprising the addendum.)

    1. Sheet A5.1, Detail 6/A5.1

        All steel beams in Mechanical Equipment Room, (Room 179),
        to receive two-hour rated sprayed-on fireproofing in
        lieu of two-hour gypsum board fireproofing.

    2. Sheet M-1.2:

        At Conference Room, (Room 113), change 12x6
        H.V.A.C. duct to 12x16.

<u>SAMPLE - BID FORM</u>

To: Mr. William Jones, President
     Typical Manufacturing Co.
     950 Broadway Blvd.
     Oakland, California

Re: Proposal for Typical Manufacturing Company's
     New Industrial Plant and Offices
     100 Industrial Blvd.
     Hayward, California

I have received the Documents titled "Typical Manufacturing

Co. Project Manual, New Industrial Plant and Offices, Hayward,

California," and the working drawings consisting of sheets

A0.1 through A9.3, S0.1 through S7.2, M0.1 through M6.3,

P0.1 through P5.1, E0.1 through E7.2, C0.1 through C3.2,

D0.1 through D2.1, L0.1 through L2.1, Q0.1 through Q3.2 all

dated March 1, 1988.

   I also acknowledge receiving addenda nos:

   #1

_____

and have included their provisions in my bid price.

   I have examined the documents and the site and attended the

Pre-Bid conference. In submitting this bid, I agree:

1. To hold my bid open for 60 days from the date of the
    bid opening.

2. To accept the provisions of the Instructions to Bidders
    regarding disposition of the Bid Security.

3. To enter into and execute a contract if awarded on the
    basis of this bid, and to furnish Guarantee Bonds in
    accordance with the Instructions to Bidders and the
    General Conditions of this contract.

4. To accomplish the Work in accordance with the Contract
    Documents.

5. To complete the Work in the time stated in this bid as
    modified by agreement with the Owner before execution
    of the Agreement.

SAMPLE - BID FORM

I will construct this Project for the lump sum price of

_____

_____Ten Million_____Dollars ($ _10,000,000.00_____),

including fees and taxes.

I will construct changes to the work for the cost of the changes

plus a fee of ___15___ % of the said cost.

ALTERNATES:

I will include the following alternates as specified for

the costs listed:

  1. Vinyl tile as an alternate
      to carpeting in corridors   deduct $ _15,000_

  2. Cold mixed bituminous surfacing as
      an alternate to concrete surfacing
      on sidewalls and service areas   deduct $ _35,000_

  3. Eliminate pneumatic tube system in
      manufacturing plant   deduct $ _200,000_

UNIT PRICES

The Unit Prices for the following items are the complete in-place
prices and include all items of cost, overhead and profit for
the Contractor and any Subcontractor involved. It is understood
and agreed that these Unit Prices will be used throughout
without modification in determining equitable adjustment to the
Contract Price for changes authorized by the Owner for work under
the Contract. It is also understood and agreed that the Owner
reserves the right to reject any or all of these Unit Prices.

	ADD
Excavation per cubic yard-earth	$ 4.50
Excavation per cubic yard-rock	$ 15.00
Engineered fill per cubic yard	$ 9.50

SAMPLE - BID FORM

I have reviewed the Drawings, Specifications and other Contract Documents, of the Project Manual, agree to construct the Project in accordance with them, and propose

_____*July 1, 1989*_____ as the final completion date.

I have attached the required Bid Security and List of Subcontractors to this bid.

FIRM: _____*Quality Construction Co.*_____

Address: _____*300 First Ave., Oakland, CA.*_____

Signed: _____

Name: _____*Robert Brown*_____

Title: _____*President*_____

Date: _____*April 15, 1988*_____

Contractor's License #: _____*G-1000*_____

SAMPLE - ONE PAGE OF LIST OF SUBCONTRACTORS FORM

Project: Typical Manufacturing Co.   ABC Architects
Industrial Plant & Offices   600 Main St.
100 Industrial Blvd.   San Francisco, Ca.
Hayward, California

Contractor: _Quality Construction Co._   DATE: _April 15, 1988_

Address: _300 First Ave._

          Oakland, California   Sheet _1_ of _3_

In accordance with the contract documents, each Bidder shall
list the subcontractors and material suppliers proposed for
each of the principal portions of the work for the above noted
project. Submit this list with the Bid Proposal.

Item of Work	Subcontractor or Supplier	Address	Phone
1. Site Clearing, Excavation & Grading	AAA Excavators, Inc.	100 First St. Oakland, California	111-1000
2. Landscaping	BBB Landscaping Co.	200 Second St. Oakland, California	222-2000
3. Asphalt Paving	CCC Surfacing Co.	300 Third St. Hayward, California	333-3000
4. Concrete	DDD Concrete Co.	400 Fourth St. Hayward, California	444-4000
5. Reinforcing Steel	EEE Steel Corp.	500 Fifth St. San Jose, California	555-5000
6. Metal Decking	FFF Metals, Inc.	600 Sixth St. Oakland, California	666-6000

Acceptance of Bids

Subsequent to the receipt of all necessary approvals from governing authorities, the owner's written approval of the Construction Documents, and his written authorization to proceed to the Bidding or Negotiation Phase, the architect assists the owner in selecting a contractor for construction of the project.

For the direct selection system of construction award, the architect obtains and reviews qualification statements from interested bidders and assists the owner in selecting a single contractor for negotiation. When all terms are acceptable to both owner and contractor, the owner awards the contract. The primary disadvantage of this system is that there is no incentive for the contractor to limit the cost of the work.

In competitive bidding conducted by private owners, bidders should be limited to pre-qualified contractors of established skill and proven competence. The bidders should be required to conform to performance or experience standards established by the owner prior to receiving bids. The architect should make recommendations for or against the bidder with the final selection by the owner. This is the preferable method unless prohibited by legal requirements. Note that the architect should not make recommendations against a contractor except in an objective and factual way in order to avoid possible claims of defamation of the contractor.

The assumption in competitive bidding is that this process will achieve the lowest project cost for the owner. Further, the competitive bidding process is simple and easy to administer in comparison to other methods. However, without careful scrutiny, the owner has no assurance that the low bidder and his subcontractors have the expertise, reliability and financial resources to complete the work correctly. For instance, after careful review of the architect's Contract Documents for errors and omissions, an unscrupulous contractor may intentionally underestimate costs in his bid. Then, after obtaining the contract with the owner, such contractors will attempt to make large profits on Change Orders for the errors and omissions.

In accordance with paragraph 6.1.1 of the AIA Instructions to Bidders, the contractor must submit a Qualification Statement upon the architect's request. A form specifically prepared for this purpose is AIA Document A305, Contractor's Qualification Statement. A careful review of this statement along with a careful analysis of bids submitted will help protect the owner against inexperienced, unreliable or financially weak contractors. The architect frequently extends the review of qualification statements to the contractor's subcontractors. Generally, the architect should make written recommendations to the owner that both the contractor's and his subcontractors' qualifications be reviewed. This is due to the fact that many contractors perform only a small portion of the work with their own personnel and the remainder of the work is subcontracted. Even if the owner rejects such recommendations, they will serve the architect well in the event of a claim for damages due to improper construction. The architect can then demonstrate that he proposed pre-qualification safeguards to help assure quality work by competent contractors.

For the open bidding method, the owner, usually a public agency, publishes an advertisement for bids. Then the architect obtains and reviews qualification statements from interested bidders.

The objective of pre-qualifying bidders is to insure that the contractor is financially sound and has maintained a high quality of construction on previous jobs. The architect should advise the owner to disqualify those who do not meet these standards. Methods which can be used to establish qualifications are: requiring bid security in the form of a certified check for 10% of the bid amount, rather than a Bid Bond, to screen out financially weak bidders; requiring a statement from an approved surety certifying that a Performance Bond and a Payment Bond will be provided if the bidder is awarded the contract; and requiring a statement listing all heavy equipment and tools owned by the bidder. The architect also checks the Contractor's Qualification Statement to verify the contractor's general reputation; demonstrated ability with respect to performance of work of the character and size involved; construction experience of his personnel; and general responsibility.

The architect distributes Bidding Documents to bidders and obtains document deposits and bid security. The distribution of Bidding Documents appears to be quite simple. However, claims and delays can result from this area of the architect's services. Like other services, the determination of potential liability is based primarily on his ability to prove that his actions have met the reasonable standard of care used by other architects, given the same time, place and circumstances.

Some important matters related to the distribution of Bidding Documents include the following items. The architect should keep an accurate Register of Bid Documents. The AIA Document, G804, Register of Bid Documents, is expressly designed for this purpose. This preprinted form should be filled in each time a set of documents is issued to a bidder. Included on the form are such items as the name, address and phone number of the bidder, the date the documents were received, the amount of document deposit or document fee received and the number of sets picked up. Generally, the architect numbers each set and records the numbers of the sets distributed to each bidder.

As noted in previous chapters, addenda are often issued to make modifications to the documents prior to receipt of bids. The architect must also exercise care in this area to ensure that a copy of the addendum is issued to each bidder of record. The AIA Register of Bid Documents contains a check box for recording the issue of each addendum. Further, each addendum should be sent by certified mail, with a return receipt postcard, to each bidder. The return receipt should be kept in the architect's records. Also, the bidder must acknowledge receipt of all addenda on his bid form. A copy of the addendum is sent to a bidder for each set of documents the bidder originally obtained. In addition, a copy of each addendum should be included with any document sets that may be distributed to bidders after the addendum was issued.

The architect should recognize that if all bidders do not receive identical sets of documents upon which to base their bids, claims of bidding irregularity could be made. For example, suppose that after issuing several sets of Bidding Documents the architect detects an error and issues an addendum to all bidders of record. Further, he corrects the error on the original documents and distributes subsequent sets of documents to bidders with the error corrected. Note that the addendum was subject to the bidder's interpretation. The documents distributed later with the correction made were subject to the architect's interpretation. The corrected set of documents are not the same as the original set with its addendum. Such irregularities can influence each bidder's determination of the cost of the work and therefore create cause for litigation, delays or possible rebidding of the project.

The architect may wish to estimate the total number of sets of documents required for bidding and then have this number of sets reproduced at the outset of the Bidding Phase. Also, reproducible copies such as sepias are generally made of all drawings at this time. Therefore, not only is a record set established for the architect's project files, but additional sets can be made from the reproducibles if more sets are needed in the future. In this way identical sets of documents can always be distributed even if changes are made to the original documents.

A further issue pertains to the clarity and accuracy of the Bidding Documents. If the documents are unclear to the point where more than one interpretation is possible, the bids will come in with wide discrepancies which could force the rejection of all bids. Further, the owner's specific methods concerning the evaluation of bids should be added as a supplement to the Instructions to Bidders. In this way, the procedure will be fair, objective and can be applied equally to all bidders.

Prior to receiving bids, the pre-bid conference is held. The purpose of the pre-bid conference is to answer questions and clarify any matters relating to the Contract Documents and the submitting of bids. In addition to the architect, client and general contractors submitting bids, principal subcontractors and the architect's consultants should be present.

The pre-bid conference should include a tour of the job site, a description of the proposed work and discussion of any questions raised by the participants. Attendance at the pre-bid conference should be a prerequisite for submitting a bid for the work. Therefore, a record of those in attendance should be taken. In addition, all interpretations and corrections of the Contract Documents resulting from questions posed at this conference should be delivered to each bidder of record.

As outlined in paragraphs 4.4.2 and 4.4.3 of the AIA Instructions to Bidders, bids may be either modified or withdrawn on or before the time and date for the receipt of bids. Also, withdrawn bids may be resubmitted up to the time and date designated for bid receipt. Further, as outlined in paragraph 4.4.1, bids may not be modified or withdrawn for a stipulated period of time after the time and date designated for bid receipt. The stipulated time period is generally designated on the Bid Form.

Bids are received up until the time and date stipulated in the Invitation or Advertisement to Bid. At this time, the bids are usually opened publicly and read aloud. The successful bidder is not selected until the bids are tabulated and analyzed.

Note that paragraph 5.2.1 of the AIA Instructions to Bidders gives the owner the right to reject bids that are not accompanied by a required bid security or by any other data required by the Bidding Documents. In addition, the owner may reject bids that are incomplete or irregular. However, it should also be recognized that paragraph 5.3.1 states that the owner has the right to waive informalities and irregularities in a bid and accept the bid which, in the owner's opinion, is in his best interest. These statements apply to private projects. Recognize that public projects have far less flexible rules for opening, rejection, acceptance, and documentation of bids.

Furthermore, paragraph 5.3.1 states that it is the owner's intention to award the contract to the lowest responsible bidder, provided the bid has been submitted in conformance with the Bidding Document requirements and does not exceed funds available. The requirement for a "responsible" bidder entails the ability of the bidder to perform the work. Methods used to establish such qualifications were discussed previously in this chapter. A bid submitted in conformance with Bidding Document requirements establishes that the bid is "responsive." A responsive bid contains all required documents completely and properly filled out without conditions or exceptions at the time of bid opening.

Several important items regarding the analysis of bids include the following: the sealed bid was received by the designated time on the designated day; the bid was submitted on the Bid Form included in the project manual; the Bid Form acknowledged all addenda issued; other forms and schedules required by the Bidding Documents were included; all forms were dated and signed where required by an officer of the company making the bid; the bidder clearly stated the dollar amount in both figures and writing; unit prices were indicated where required; the contractor's license number and any specialized licensing requirements were clearly indicated; the List of Subcontractors and the List of Material Suppliers were included; the Bid Bond was included, properly executed on the prescribed form, if it was required by the owner; all line items were properly filled out; no changes or modifications of any documents were made; and no conditions or exceptions were attached to the bid.

The contractor's bid should not contain conditions or exceptions regarding cost, quality, quantity or time for performing the work. Further, the bidder should not be allowed to correct such deficiencies after the bids are opened. Ambiguities related to these items give the bidder an unfair advantage over other bidders. For example, the low bidder qualifies his bid by placing a condition on the quality of materials furnished for the project. Upon consideration, the owner insists that the original quality of materials specified for the project be maintained and requests a price based on those items. The bidder then modifies his bid to be just slightly lower than the next highest bid which was already disclosed at the bid opening.

Note that there is a difference between a bid being responsive and a bid that contains irregularities. An "irregularity" is a discrepancy or variance from the requirements of the bidding requirements that can be waived by the owner because it does not affect the cost, quality or quantity of time for performing the work. Therefore, such a deviation does not give the bidder an unfair advantage over other bidders. For example, assume on a private sector project a bidder submits all information required but omits a signature on a minor form. Such an omission could be corrected after bid opening and would generally not disqualify a bidder unless the Bidding Documents make such an item a condition of responsiveness.

It is often difficult to ascertain whether the omission of information, signatures on forms, etc., required by the Bidding Documents is sufficient cause to reject the bid, or, if the deviation is simply an irregularity that can be corrected after the bid opening. For this reason, the architect may wish to define the terms and conditions for submitting a bid very explicitly in the Bidding Documents. For example, such conditions may make the submittal of certain forms or the signatures required on documents a condition of responsiveness. Without such clearly defined conditions, the omission of such information may only be considered a bid irregularity. Naturally, such terms and conditions should be placed in the Bidding Documents only with the approval of the owner and his legal counsel.

At the time of the bid opening, each bid is carefully checked to determine if it is responsive as defined by the Bidding Documents. The architect may wish to prepare a checklist in advance to facilitate the checking of all items that must be submitted, signed, and so on, before a bid is considered responsive and therefore accepted. Next the bidder's name and bid amount are read aloud and recorded on a bid tabulation sheet. Generally, the low bidder is not announced at the time of bid opening since the final selection is subject to confirmation only after careful evaluation of the bid and other information submitted. Further, determination of the low bid is a calculation based on the bid amount and any alternatives that may be accepted by the owner.

Upon tabulating and analyzing the bids, the architect recommends for or against acceptance by the owner and obtains the owner's acceptance or rejection in writing. Note that selection of the contractor is a decision of the owner. The decision is made with the architect's assistance but the architect does not actually approve or reject the bidders or bids received himself. The architect should emphasize to the owner that his greatest protection against poor construction and defective work is in the trustworthiness, expertise, and capacity to perform the work of the contractor he selects. If bids are received only from pre-qualified and invited bidders, the contract generally is awarded to the lowest bidder. If the owner accepts the low bid, the architect notifies the successful bidder of the award. He then assists the owner and contractor in the execution of the construction contract.

Owner-Contractor Agreement

The Owner-Contractor Agreement, when completed and signed, becomes the basic contract. It defines the relationships and obligations between owner and contractor and incorporates by reference all the other Contract Documents and makes them a part of the contract. It also states the contract sum, describes the work, names the architect, specifies the time of commencement and completion, and the method of payment to the contractor.

The architect's responsibility in the preparation of the Owner-Contractor Agreement should be confined to advice on technical matters relating to the practice of architecture. His advice must not be such that it can be construed to be legal or insurance advice.

The American Institute of Architects publishes three standard forms of Owner-Contractor Agreements:

The Stipulated Sum Agreement, Document A101. This lump-sum or fixed-price type of agreement is used more commonly than any other form. It is almost always used on competitively bid contracts. The advantage of this method is that it gives the owner advance knowledge of the cost of the work. In addition, it provides flexibility in determining the contract sum through the use of alternates, it can be modified to effect changes in the work, and the accounting for payments to the contractor is relatively straightforward.

While the competitively bid lump sum agreement often obtains lower bids for the owner, the disadvantage is that price, rather than ability, is the primary basis for the selection of the contractor. Further, it is the responsibility of the contractor to complete the work in accordance with the Contract Documents for the amount of the bid. This is in spite of the fact that the contractor's expenses could exceed the amount of the bid. For example, due to labor problems, unanticipated construction difficulties, or excessive costs for materials and equipment, the total cost of the work could be greater than the total contract sum. Or, the contractor could have underestimated the cost of the work.

In the event of such problems, the contractor may seek financial relief in the provisions of the Contract Documents that allow for the extra costs for changed conditions, or the contractor may try to decrease the quality of the work. Therefore, work under this agreement requires increased responsibility on the part of the architect to assure contract compliance since the contractor may attempt to perform the work for maximum profit with secondary consideration to the quality of construction. Pre-qualification of bidders can greatly improve the quality of the work, especially when the bidders selected are of comparable reliability and competence.

The American Institute of Architects Owner-Contractor Agreement-Stipulated Sum, Document A 101, consists of nine articles which are in essence as follows:

"Article 1—The Contract Documents"—defines the Contract Documents and incorporates them by reference in the Contract. The Contract Documents are defined as the Owner-Contractor Agreement, General Conditions, Supplementary Conditions, Drawings, Specifications and any Addenda issued. If other documents are to be included in the contract, they are enumerated in Article 9 of the Owner-Contractor Agreement.

"Article 2—The Work of This Contract"—The scope of the work is defined as that described in the Contract Documents with the exception of items listed to specifically be the responsibility of others. Space is provided to list exceptions.

"Article 3—Date of Commencement and Substantial Completion"—defines the date of commencement and substantial completion of the work and gives provisions for liquidated damages if any. The date of substantial completion is usually considered to be the date on which the owner may occupy the project for the use for which it is intended.

Liquidated damages, if required by the owner, should be based on actual costs the owner will incur if the work is not finished by the date of substantial completion. The amount per day the contractor is to be assessed for this loss must be clearly stated in the Agreement. It must be clear that a penalty is not to be imposed on the contractor and the loss must be provable. For example, the cost per day of renting commercial space to house a business if the owner's building cannot be occupied when needed is a tangible, provable value.

Penalty clauses alone have been found to be legally invalid. Penalty for delay must be considered along with a bonus for early completion. These should also be determined on the basis of a tangible value.

"Article 4—Contract Sum"—defines the contract sum as the accepted bid or negotiated price, adjusted by alternates. This article also gives the owner the right to adjust the contract amount through the use of Change Orders, while the work is in progress, without invalidating the contract. Alternates accepted by the owner are identified and listed. Unit prices are described here as being those prices negotiated at the time of award of the contract to determine the cost of later changes. These may also apply to items bid on estimated quantities. The use of unit prices for items which are indeterminate at the time of execution of the contract, or subject to change, expedites administration of the contract and prevents disputes while the work is in progress.

"Article 5—Progress Payments"—defines due dates for progress payments; defines the Schedule of Values; states the amount of the retained percentage which is often ten percent; and provides for payment for work in place and for materials and equipment stored on the site. Payment for work in place is to be based on the Schedule of Values. The contractor is required by the General Conditions to submit this schedule before the first Application for Payment. This schedule is approved by the architect and used in all subsequent Applications for Payment. Payments for stored materials and equipment should be based on invoices only. This payment is usually for only seventy-five percent of the invoice amount. The architect should check that all stored materials and equipment are adequately protected against weather and vandalism, secure from removal, and properly insured.

It should be noted that AIA General Conditions paragraph 9.3.3 states that the contractor warrants that title to all work covered by an Application for Payment will pass to the owner. Further, to the best of the contractor's information and belief, such work is free and clear of all liens and encumbrances.

The article also defines the date upon which the contractor evaluates the work for payment. This should be not less than fourteen days before the payment date. This allows the architect seven days for assessment of the contractor's Application for Payment and to issue a Certificate for Payment to the owner. In addition, this allows seven days for the owner to make payment.

Payment at the Date of Substantial Completion is also described. A percentage of the contract sum is due to the contractor upon substantial completion of the project. Often, this amount is ninety percent; however, this amount should be determined by the owner and his legal counsel.

The contract sum as defined here is the total amount payable by the owner to the contractor for performance of the work. This includes all Change Orders issued up to the date of the Application for Payment. All payments must therefore be based on the current contract sum.

"Article 6—Final Payment"—defines the due date for final payment which is widely accepted as five days after the period for filing liens has elapsed. (It is desirable to withhold final payment to the contractor until the period for filing mechanics liens has elapsed. Check with local regulations for the exact time period allowed for filing of mechanics liens. These laws vary from state to state.) This normally allows adequate time for final completion of the work. It should be noted that this time is binding only if the work is totally completed and the contract fully performed. Certification of completion, acceptance of the work, final inspection, and the issuance of a final Certificate for Payment are a critical part of the architect's responsibilities. These processes are described in detail in the following sections of this manual.

"Article 7—Miscellaneous Provisions"—defines by reference terms used in the agreement as those used in the General Conditions; the interest rate on unpaid amounts is listed.

"Article 8—Termination or Suspension"—states that the contract may be terminated or suspended as provided in Article 14 of the General Conditions.

"Article 9—Enumeration of Contract Documents"—the specific Contract Documents are enumerated here in terms of document number, title and number of pages; and the specifications, drawings and addenda are also enumerated. If space for the list of specification sections and drawings is not adequate, as it usually is not, they may be listed in an exhibit and attached to the Agreement. (See Exhibit A, Specifications and Exhibit B, Drawings.) The last part of Article 9 provides space for other documents such as the Invitation to Bid, the Instructions to Bidders, sample forms and the Bid Form. These forms and documents are not a part of the Contract Documents unless they are specifically listed here. They should be listed only if they are intended to be a part of the Contract Documents.

Other American Institute of Architects standard forms of Owner-Contractor Agreements are: The Short Form Stipulated Sum Agreement for Small Construction Contracts, Document A107, and The Cost of the Work Plus a Fee Agreement, Document A111.

The Short Form Stipulated Sum Agreement combines the same fundamental provisions as the AIA Owner-Contractor Agreement Stipulated Sum, Document A101, and the AIA General Conditions, Document A201. The entire contract is often comprised of this document, the drawings and the specifications.

Certain portions of Document A201 are omitted from the Short Form Agreement. Thus, the rights and responsibilities of the owner, architect and contractor are less specifically defined. For this reason, misunderstandings could arise concerning the exact duties, rights and relationships of the parties to the contract. Therefore, this form should be used only for small projects of limited scope and short duration where a simplified contract is appropriate for the scope of the project.

Under the Cost-Plus Fee Agreement, the contractor is paid for the actual cost of the work and a fee for his services. These agreements are often negotiated between the owner and contractor. Provisions related to compensation of the contractor for his services are the main variables among the types of Cost-Plus Fee Agreements. Recognize that, as opposed to the Stipulated Sum Agreement, the owner has no financial certainty under this type of agreement. The cost of the project is not known to the owner until the construction is completed. However, a guaranteed maximum cost provision can be included as a part of this agreement. In this case, the contractor guarantees the owner that the project will be built in accordance with the Contract Documents and will not exceed a guaranteed maximum cost. If the cost of the project exceeds the guaranteed maximum, the contractor must pay any amount over the assured maximum.

One way of determining the contractor's compensation for his services on a Cost-Plus Fee Agreement is as a percentage of the construction cost. However, there is little incentive for the contractor to limit the cost of construction unless the agreement contains a provision for a guaranteed maximum cost. Another way of determining the cost of contractor's compensation is as a fixed fee. Here the Contract Documents must provide a well defined scope of work in order that the contractor can make an accurate estimate for the cost of his services. In the fixed fee type of arrangement it is to the contractor's advantage to perform the work in a manner that will minimize cost and time. In this way, the contractor's overhead expenses are reduced and labor and equipment may be utilized on other projects more quickly. Further, as an incentive for the contractor to limit the cost of construction, the contractor is often given a percentage of any savings below the guaranteed maximum. The percent of the savings allocated to the contractor is generally in the range of 25 to 35 percent.

A major advantage of the Cost-Plus Fee Agreement is that construction work can often be started before the Construction Documents are completed. It also permits pre-selection of a qualified contractor, avoiding competitive bidding among contractors of possible varying abilities. Furthermore, the contractor's financial interest is limited to the fee, thus his role is more professional. His skill in purchasing materials and equipment is carried out on behalf of the owner and may be rewarded by incentives to minimize costs. Such incentives should be stated in writing and incorporated in the agreement.

The reasons for utilizing a Cost-Plus Fee type of contract include the following: The work is of an emergency nature and must be started before drawings and specifications are completed. Many changes and alterations are anticipated during the course of the project. The cost of labor and materials is subject to wide variation. Superior quality of work is desired.

In the above noted examples, construction risks are unusually high. Contractors will usually submit proposals with large contingencies on lump sum contracts to cover these important risks. In these situations, the cost plus fee contract is usually less costly than the lump sum contract. Furthermore, in projects where many changes are likely to occur during the course of construction, such as remodeling jobs, the cost plus fee contract is often preferable to the contractor submitting costly change orders.

The disadvantage of this system is that it does not have the financial certainty of the lump sum agreement. In addition, extensive record keeping is required which is often undertaken by the owner's staff or a public accounting firm. The architect's responsibility for record keeping and the accuracy of the contractor's cost estimate must be limited and clearly defined. Most disagreements in this area can be avoided by defining in the Owner-Contractor Agreement the details of accounting procedures, record keeping requirements, procedures for purchasing materials and equipment, and the process for awarding subcontracts. Items that constitute reimbursable expenses to the contractor should also be carefully defined and incorporated in the Owner-Contractor Agreement. For example, the cost of construction equipment should be defined on a per day, per hour, per week or per month basis. Further, it should be stated in writing what these rates include.

AIA Document A101

Standard Form of Agreement Between Owner and Contractor

where the basis of payment is a

STIPULATED SUM

1987 EDITION

THIS DOCUMENT HAS IMPORTANT LEGAL CONSEQUENCES; CONSULTATION WITH AN ATTORNEY IS ENCOURAGED WITH RESPECT TO ITS COMPLETION OR MODIFICATION.

The 1987 Edition of AIA Document A201, General Conditions of the Contract for Construction, is adopted in this document by reference. Do not use with other general conditions unless this document is modified.

This document has been approved and endorsed by The Associated General Contractors of America.

AGREEMENT

made as of the   First   day of   May   in the year of
Nineteen Hundred and Eighty-eight.

BETWEEN the Owner: Typical Manufacturing Co.
(Name and address)   950 Broadway Blvd.
                              Oakland, California

and the Contractor: Quality Construction Co.
(Name and address)   300 First Ave.
                              Oakland, California

The Project is: Typical Manufacturing Co. Industrial Plant and Offices
(Name and location)   100 Industrial Blvd.
                              Hayward, California

The Architect is: A B C Architects
(Name and address)   600 Main St.
                              San Francisco, California

The Owner and Contractor agree as set forth below.

ARTICLE 1
THE CONTRACT DOCUMENTS

The Contract Documents consist of this Agreement, Conditions of the Contract (General, Supplementary and other Conditions). Drawings, Specifications, Addenda issued prior to execution of this Agreement, other documents listed in this Agreement and Modifications issued after execution of this Agreement; these form the Contract, and are as fully a part of the Contract as if attached to this Agreement or repeated herein. The Contract represents the entire and integrated agreement between the parties hereto and supersedes prior negotiations, representations or agreements, either written or oral. An enumeration of the Contract Documents, other than Modifications, appears in Article 9.

ARTICLE 2
THE WORK OF THIS CONTRACT

The Contractor shall execute the entire Work described in the Contract Documents, except to the extent specifically indicated in the Contract Documents to be the responsibility of others, or as follows:

```
Construction of Typical Manufacturing Co. Industrial Plant and Offices
100 Industrial Blvd., Hayward, California
```

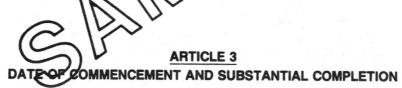

ARTICLE 3
DATE OF COMMENCEMENT AND SUBSTANTIAL COMPLETION

3.1 The date of commencement is the date from which the Contract Time of Paragraph 3.2 is measured, and shall be the date of this Agreement, as first written above, unless a different date is stated below or provision is made for the date to be fixed in a notice to proceed issued by the Owner.

(Insert the date of commencement, if it differs from the date of this Agreement or, if applicable, state that the date will be fixed in a notice to proceed.)

```
The work to be performed under this contract shall be commenced on the date
stipulated in the Owner's written Notice to Proceed.
```

Unless the date of commencement is established by a notice to proceed issued by the Owner, the Contractor shall notify the Owner in writing not less than five days before commencing the Work to permit the timely filing of mortgages, mechanic's liens and other security interests.

3.2 The Contractor shall achieve Substantial Completion of the entire Work not later than

(Insert the calendar date or number of calendar days after the date of commencement. Also insert any requirements for earlier Substantial Completion of certain portions of the Work, if not stated elsewhere in the Contract Documents.)

```
four hundred (400) calendar days after the date stipulated in the Owner's
written Notice to Proceed.
```

, subject to adjustments of this Contract Time as provided in the Contract Documents.

(Insert provisions, if any, for liquidated damages relating to failure to complete on time.)

```
The Contractor and the Contractor's surety, if any, shall be liable for and
shall pay the Owner the sums hereinafter stipulated as liquidated damages
for each calendar day of delay until the Work is substantially complete:
Four Hundred and Fifty Dollars  ($450.00)
```

ARTICLE 4
CONTRACT SUM

4.1 The Owner shall pay the Contractor in current funds for the Contractor's performance of the Contract the Contract Sum of
Ten Million   Dollars
($ 10,000,000.00   ), subject to additions and deductions as provided in the Contract Documents.

4.2 The Contract Sum is based upon the following alternates, if any, which are described in the Contract Documents and are hereby accepted by the Owner:

(State the numbers or other identification of accepted alternates. If decisions on other alternates are to be made by the Owner subsequent to the execution of this Agreement, attach a schedule of such other alternates showing the amount for each and the date until which that amount is valid.)

4.3 Unit prices, if any, are as follows:

The unit prices as listed below shall determine the value of extra work or changes, as applicable. They shall be considered complete including all material and equipment, labor, installation costs, overhead and profit and shall be used uniformly for either additions or deductions.

Excavation – earth	$4.50/Cubic yard
Excavation – rock	$15.00/Cubic yard
Engineered Fill	$9.50/Cubic yard

ARTICLE 5
PROGRESS PAYMENTS

5.1 Based upon Applications for Payment submitted to the Architect by the Contractor and Certificates for Payment issued by the Architect, the Owner shall make progress payments on account of the Contract Sum to the Contractor as provided below and elsewhere in the Contract Documents.

5.2 The period covered by each Application for Payment shall be one calendar month ending on the last day of the month, or as follows:

5.3 Provided an Application for Payment is received by the Architect not later than the **tenth (10th)** day of a month, the Owner shall make payment to the Contractor not later than the **twenty-fourth (24th)** day of the **same** month. If an Application for Payment is received by the Architect after the application date fixed above, payment shall be made by the Owner not later than **fourteen (14)** days after the Architect receives the Application for Payment.

5.4 Each Application for Payment shall be based upon the Schedule of Values submitted by the Contractor in accordance with the Contract Documents. The Schedule of Values shall allocate the entire Contract Sum among the various portions of the Work and be prepared in such form and supported by such data to substantiate its accuracy as the Architect may require. This Schedule, unless objected to by the Architect, shall be used as a basis for reviewing the Contractor's Applications for Payment.

5.5 Applications for Payment shall indicate the percentage of completion of each portion of the Work as of the end of the period covered by the Application for Payment.

5.6 Subject to the provisions of the Contract Documents, the amount of each progress payment shall be computed as follows:

5.6.1 Take that portion of the Contract Sum properly allocable to completed Work as determined by multiplying the percentage completion of each portion of the Work by the share of the total Contract Sum allocated to that portion of the Work in the Schedule of Values, less retainage of **ten** percent (**10** %). Pending final determination of cost to the Owner of changes in the Work, amounts not in dispute may be included as provided in Subparagraph 7.3.7 of the General Conditions even though the Contract Sum has not yet been adjusted by Change Order;

5.6.2 Add that portion of the Contract Sum properly allocable to materials and equipment delivered and suitably stored at the site for subsequent incorporation in the completed construction (or, if approved in advance by the Owner, suitably stored off the site at a location agreed upon in writing), less retainage of **twenty-five** percent (**25** %);

5.6.3 Subtract the aggregate of previous payments made by the Owner; and

5.6.4 Subtract amounts, if any, for which the Architect has withheld or nullified a Certificate for Payment as provided in Paragraph 9.5 of the General Conditions.

5.7 The progress payment amount determined in accordance with Paragraph 5.6 shall be further modified under the following circumstances:

5.7.1 Add, upon Substantial Completion of the Work, a sum sufficient to increase the total payments to **ninety** percent (**90** %) of the Contract Sum, less such amounts as the Architect shall determine for incomplete Work and unsettled claims; and

5.7.2 Add, if final completion of the Work is thereafter materially delayed through no fault of the Contractor, any additional amounts payable in accordance with Subparagraph 9.10.3 of the General Conditions.

5.8 Reduction or limitation of retainage, if any, shall be as follows: **none**

(If it is intended, prior to Substantial Completion of the entire Work, to reduce or limit the retainage resulting from the percentages inserted in Subparagraphs 5.6.1 and 5.6.2 above, and this is not explained elsewhere in the Contract Documents, insert here provisions for such reduction or limitation.)

ARTICLE 6
FINAL PAYMENT

Final payment, constituting the entire unpaid balance of the Contract Sum, shall be made by the Owner to the Contractor when (1) the Contract has been fully performed by the Contractor except for the Contractor's responsibility to correct nonconforming Work as provided in Subparagraph 12.2.2 of the General Conditions and to satisfy other requirements, if any, which necessarily survive final payment; and (2) a final Certificate for Payment has been issued by the Architect; such final payment shall be made by the Owner not more than 30 days after the issuance of the Architect's final Certificate for Payment, or as follows:

ARTICLE 7
MISCELLANEOUS PROVISIONS

7.1 Where reference is made in this Agreement to a provision of the General Conditions or another Contract Document, the reference refers to that provision as amended or supplemented by other provisions of the Contract Documents.

7.2 Payments due and unpaid under the Contract shall bear interest from the date payment is due at the rate stated below, or in the absence thereof, at the legal rate prevailing from time to time at the place where the Project is located.
(Insert rate of interest agreed upon, if any.)

Eight percent (8%) annually for amounts not paid 30 days after date payment is due.

(Usury laws and requirements under the Federal Truth in Lending Act, similar state and local consumer credit laws and other regulations at the Owner's and Contractor's principal places of business, the location of the Project and elsewhere may affect the validity of this provision. Legal advice should be obtained with respect to deletions or modifications, and also regarding requirements such as written disclosures or waivers.)

7.3 Other provisions:

ARTICLE 8
TERMINATION OR SUSPENSION

8.1 The Contract may be terminated by the Owner or the Contractor as provided in Article 14 of the General Conditions.

8.2 The Work may be suspended by the Owner as provided in Article 14 of the General Conditions.

ARTICLE 9
ENUMERATION OF CONTRACT DOCUMENTS

9.1 The Contract Documents, except for Modifications issued after execution of this Agreement, are enumerated as follows:

9.1.1 The Agreement is this executed Standard Form of Agreement Between Owner and Contractor, AIA Document A101, 1987 Edition.

9.1.2 The General Conditions are the General Conditions of the Contract for Construction, AIA Document A201, 1987 Edition.

9.1.3 The Supplementary and other Conditions of the Contract are those contained in the Project Manual dated March 1, 1988 , and are as follows:

Document	Title	Pages
00610	Performance Bond Form (AIA Document 312)	1 – 3
00620	Payment Bond Form (AIA Document 312)	4 – 6
00650	Certificate of Insurance Form (AIA Document G705)	1
00660	Certificates of Compliance with Applicable Laws and Regulations	4
00800	Supplementary Conditions	22

9.1.4 The Specifications are those contained in the Project Manual dated as in Subparagraph 9.1.3, and are as follows:
(Either list the Specifications here or refer to an exhibit attached to this Agreement.)

Section	Title	Pages
(See Exhibit A)		

9.1.5 The Drawings are as follows, and are dated March 1, 1988   unless a different date is shown below:

(Either list the Drawings here or refer to an exhibit attached to this Agreement.)

Number   **Title**   **Date**

(See Exhibit B)

9.1.6 The Addenda, if any, are as follows:

Number   **Date**   **Pages**

1   March 21, 1988   1

Portions of Addenda relating to bidding requirements are not part of the Contract Documents unless the bidding requirements are also enumerated in this Article 9.

9.1.7 Other documents, if any, forming part of the Contract Documents are as follows:

(List here any additional documents which are intended to form part of the Contract Documents. The General Conditions provide that bidding requirements such as advertisement or invitation to bid, Instructions to Bidders, sample forms and the Contractor's bid are not part of the Contract Documents unless enumerated in this Agreement. They should be listed here only if intended to be part of the Contract Documents.)

This Agreement is entered into as of the day and year first written above and is executed in at least three original copies of which one is to be delivered to the Contractor, one to the Architect for use in the administration of the Contract, and the remainder to the Owner.

OWNER
Typical Manufacturing Co.
950 Broadway Blvd.
Oakland, California

CONTRACTOR
Quality Construction Co.
300 First Ave.
Oakland, California

_____
(Signature)
William Jones
President
_____
(Printed name and title)

_____
(Signature)
Robert Brown
President
_____
(Printed name and title)

EXHIBIT A — SPECIFICATIONS

SECTION   TITLE   PAGES
                    DATED MARCH 1, 1988

DIVISION 1 — GENERAL REQUIREMENTS

01010   SUMMARY OF THE WORK   6 PP.
01030   ALTERNATES   2 PP.
01040   COORDINATION   3 PP.
01200   PROJECT MEETINGS   2 PP.
01300   SUBMITTALS   4 PP.
01400   QUALITY CONTROL   4 PP.
01500   CONSTRUCTION FACILITIES & TEMP. CONTROLS   3 PP.
01630   PRODUCT OPTIONS & SUBSTITUTIONS   5 PP.
01650   STARTING OF SYSTEMS/COMMISSIONING   7 PP.
01700   CONTRACT CLOSEOUT   6 PP.
01710   FINAL CLEANING   4 PP.
01720   PROJECT RECORD DOCUMENTS   3 PP.
01740   WARRANTIES & BONDS   4 PP.

DIVISION 2 — SITEWORK

02050   DEMOLITION   5 PP.
02110   SITE CLEARING   2 PP.
02200   EARTHWORK   8 PP.
02500   PAVING & SURFACING   5 PP.
02825   FOUNTAIN & POOL   7 PP.
02900   LANDSCAPING   9 PP.

DIVISION 3 — CONCRETE

03100   CONCRETE FORMWORK   8 PP.
03200   CONCRETE REINFORCEMENT   6 PP.
03300   CAST-IN-PLACE CONCRETE   9 PP.
03345   CONCRETE FINISHING   5 PP.
03400   PRECAST CONCRETE   7 PP.

DIVISION 4 — MASONRY

(NOT IN USE.)

DIVISION 5 — METALS

05120   STRUCTURAL STEEL   7 PP.
05300   METAL DECKING   5 PP.
05400   COLD-FORMED METAL FRAMING   5 PP.
05500   METAL FABRICATIONS   6 PP.

DIVISION 6 - WOOD & PLASTICS

06100	CARPENTRY, ROUGH	8 PP.
06240	PLASTIC LAMINATE	4 PP.

DIVISION 7 - THERMAL & MOISTURE PROTECTION

07265	MINERAL FIBER FIREPROOFING	6 PP.
07510	BUILT-UP BITUMINOUS ROOFING	9 PP.
07600	FLASHING & SHEET METAL	5 PP.
07900	JOINT SEALERS	4 PP.

DIVISION 8 - DOORS & WINDOWS

08100	METAL DOORS & FRAMES	7 PP.
08210	WOOD DOORS	4 PP.
08305	ACCESS DOORS	3 PP.
08330	COILING DOORS	3 PP.
08410	ALUMINUM ENTRANCES & STOREFRONT	6 PP.
08710	FINISH HARDWARE	9 PP.
08800	GLAZING	4 PP.

DIVISION 9 - FINISHES

09250	GYPSUM BOARD	5 PP.
09650	RESILIENT FLOORING	3 PP.
09680	CARPET	4 PP.
09900	PAINTING	9 PP.
09960	VINYL WALL COVERING	4 PP.

DIVISION 10 - SPECIALITIES

10500	METAL LOCKERS	6 PP.

DIVISION 11 - EQUIPMENT

11160	LOADING DOCK EQUIPMENT	7 PP.

DIVISION 12 - FURNISHINGS

12300	MANUFACTURED CASEWORK	6 PP.

DIVISION 13 — SPECIAL CONSTRUCTION

13400   INDUSTRIAL & PROCESS CONTROL SYSTEMS   9 PP.

DIVISION 14 — CONVEYING SYSTEMS

14200   ELEVATORS   7 PP.
14585   PNEUMATIC TUBE SYSTEM   9 PP.

DIVISION 15 — MECHANICAL

15010   BASIC MECHANICAL REQUIREMENTS   7 PP.
15055   BASIC PIPING MATERIALS & METHODS   8 PP.
15125   EXPANSION COMPENSATION   4 PP.
15140   SUPPORTS & ANCHORS   5 PP.
15190   MECHANICAL IDENTIFICATION   3 PP.
15250   MECHANICAL INSULATION   4 PP.
15420   DRAINAGE & VENT SYSTEM   5 PP.
15500   HEATING, VENTILATING & AIR CONDITIONING   9 PP.
15990   TESTING, ADJUSTING & BALANCING   3 PP.

DIVISION 16 — ELECTRICAL

16010   BASIC ELECTRICAL REQUIREMENTS   4 PP.
16050   BASIC ELECTRICAL MATERIALS & METHODS   9 PP.
16500   LIGHTING   5 PP.
16720   ALARM & DETECTION EQUIPMENT   7 PP.
16740   TELEPHONE SYSTEMS   6 PP.

EXHIBIT B

ALL DRAWINGS DATED MARCH 1, 1988

NUMBER   TITLE

ARCHITECTURAL DRAWINGS

A0.1   TITLE SHEET, INDEX, LOCATION MAP
A0.2   SYMBOLS, ABBREVIATIONS
A1.1   DEMOLITION PLAN
A1.2   SITE PLAN
A2.1   OFFICE AREA FLOOR PLANS
          1ST FLOOR PLAN
          2ND FLOOR PLAN
A2.2   MANUFACTURING AREA FLOOR PLAN
A2.3   SCHEDULES
          DOORS
          WINDOWS
          ROOM FINISHES
A2.4   ROOF PLAN
A3.1   SECTIONS
A3.2   ELEVATIONS - EXTERIOR
A4.1   TOILET ROOM PLANS & DETAILS
          COUNTERS
          INTERIOR ELEVATIONS
          ACCESSORIES/MIRRORS
A4.2   LOCKER ROOM PLANS & DETAILS
          LOCKER ELEVATIONS
A5.1   INTERIOR ELEVATIONS
A6.1   REFLECTED CEILING PLANS
          1ST FLOOR - OFFICE AREA
          2ND FLOOR - OFFICE AREA
A6.2   REFLECTED CEILING PLAN
          MANUFACTURING AREA
A7.1   STAIR PLANS & DETAILS
        ELEVATOR PLANS & DETAILS
A8.1   DETAILS - EXTERIOR
          WALL SECTIONS
A8.2   DETAILS - EXTERIOR
          WINDOWS
          ARCHES
A8.3   DETAILS - EXTERIOR
          EXTERIOR DOORS & FRAMES
          STORE FRONT
A9.1   DETAILS - INTERIOR
          INTERIOR DOORS & FRAMES
          PARTITIONS
A9.2   DETAILS - INTERIOR
          CASEWORK
          HANDRAILS
          BUILDING DIRECTORY
A9.3   DETAILS - MISCELLANEOUS
          FLAGPOLE
          FOUNTAIN

STRUCTURAL DRAWINGS

S0.1	GENERAL NOTES, SYMBOLS & ABBREVIATIONS
S1.1	STRUCTURAL SITE PLAN
S2.1	FOUNDATION PLAN
	OFFICE AREA
S2.2	FOUNDATION PLAN
	MANUFACTURING AREA
S2.3	FRAMING PLANS
	1ST FLOOR – OFFICE AREA
	2ND FLOOR – OFFICE AREA
S2.4	FRAMING PLAN
	MANUFACTURING AREA
S3.1	FRAMING ELEVATIONS & WALL SECTIONS
S4.1	COLUMN SCHEDULE, BEAM SCHEDULE, FOOTING SCHEDULE
S5.1	COLUMN & BEAM DETAILS
S6.1	FOOTING DETAILS
S7.1	MISCELLANEOUS STRUCTURAL DETAILS
S7.2	STAIR PLANS & DETAILS

MECHANICAL DRAWINGS

M0.1	GENERAL NOTES, SYMBOLS & ABBREVIATIONS
M1.1	MECHANICAL SITE PLAN
M1.2	MECHANICAL ROOF PLAN
M2.1	HEATING, VENTILATING & AIR CONDITIONING PLANS
	1ST FLOOR – OFFICE AREA
	2ND FLOOR – OFFICE AREA
M2.2	HEATING, VENTILATING & AIR CONDITIONING PLAN
	MANUFACTURING AREA
M3.1	MECHANICAL EQUIPMENT ROOM PLAN
M4.1	EQUIPMENT DRAIN LINE PLAN
M5.1	MECHANICAL DETAILS
M6.1	DUCT RISER DIAGRAMS
M6.2	AIR FLOW DIAGRAMS
M6.3	CONTROL DIAGRAMS

PLUMBING DRAWINGS

P0.1	GENERAL NOTES, SYMBOLS & ABBREVIATIONS
P1.1	PLUMBING SITE PLAN
P2.1	PLUMBING PLAN
	1ST FLOOR – OFFICE AREA
	2ND FLOOR – OFFICE AREA
P2.1	PLUMBING PLAN
	MANUFACTURING AREA
P3.1	RISER DIAGRAMS
P4.1	PIPING FLOW DIAGRAMS
P5.1	PLUMBING DETAILS

ELECTRICAL DRAWINGS

EO.1   GENERAL NOTES, SYMBOLS & ABBREVIATIONS
E1.1   ELECTRICAL SITE PLAN
E2.1   LIGHTING PLANS
             1ST FLOOR - OFFICE AREA
             2ND FLOOR - OFFICE AREA
E2.2   LIGHTING PLAN
             MANUFACTURING AREA
E3.1   POWER/COMMUNICATION PLAN
             1ST FLOOR - OFFICE AREA
             2ND FLOOR - OFFICE AREA
E3.2   POWER/COMMUNICATION PLAN
             MANUFACTURING AREA
E4.1   DETAILED PLANS - ELECTRICAL ROOMS
E5.1   RISER DIAGRAMS
E6.1   LIGHTING FIXTURE SCHEDULE, PANEL SCHEDULE
E7.1   ELECTRICAL DETAILS
E7.2   LIGHTING FIXTURE DETAILS & WIRING DIAGRAMS

CIVIL DRAWINGS

CO.1   GENERAL NOTES, SYMBOLS & ABBREVIATIONS
C1.1   GRADING & DRAINAGE SITE PLAN
C2.1   DETAILED GRADING PLANS & SECTIONS
C3.1   DRAINAGE DETAILS
C3.2   ROADWAY, CURB & GUTTER DETAILS

DEMOLITION DRAWINGS

DO.1   GENERAL NOTES, SYMBOLS & ABBREVIATIONS
D1.1   DEMOLITION SITE PLAN
D2.1   DEMOLITION PLAN - EXISTING WAREHOUSE

LANDSCAPE DRAWINGS

LO.1   GENERAL NOTES, SYMBOLS & ABBREVIATIONS
L1.1   LANDSCAPE SITE PLAN
L1.2   DETAILED LANDSCAPE PLANS
L2.1   LANDSCAPE DETAILS

SPECIAL EQUIPMENT DRAWINGS

QO.1   GENERAL NOTES, SYMBOLS & ABBREVIATIONS
Q1.1   EQUIPMENT LAYOUT PLAN
             MANUFACTURING AREA
Q2.1   SPECIAL EQUIPMENT SCHEDULE
Q3.1   DETAILED PLANS - SPECIAL EQUIPMENT
Q3.2   EQUIPMENT INSTALLATION DETAILS

Administration of Construction Contract

As defined by paragraph 2.6.1 of the AIA Owner-Architect Agreement, the Construction Administration Phase begins when the owner awards the contract to the selected contractor and ends either when the Final Certificate for Payment is issued to the owner or 60 days after the date of substantial completion of the project, whichever is earlier. The architect provides Administration of the Construction Contract as outlined in the Owner-Architect Agreement and the General Conditions of the Contract for Construction.

The main reason for construction administration is to ensure that the provisions of the Contract Documents are adhered to. In this way, a quality project is delivered by the contractor to the owner. The reduction of the architect's potential liability is another factor. The concern in both cases is basically the same. There are basic architectural services required during the Construction Phase in order to ensure that the contractor interprets and implements the Contract Documents correctly.

Article 4 of the AIA General Conditions describes the architect's duties in the administration of the contract. The reasonable standard of care to which the architect must conform in the performance of construction administration is the same as that required in the design phases. He must exercise reasonable care, skill and diligence equivalent to what is reasonably required of another architect in the same community, given the same time and similar circumstances. He may be held liable to the owner for any damages resulting from a breach of these duties. The duties outlined in the AIA General Conditions include the following:

The architect will visit the site at intervals appropriate to the stage of construction to make field observations and evaluations. He will familiarize himself with the progress and quality of the work and determine in general if the work, when completed, will be in accordance with the Contract Documents. He will keep the owner informed of the progress of the work. He will not be required to make exhaustive or continuous on-site inspections. Further, he will not be held responsible for supervision of construction or the contractor's failure to carry out the work. Nor is the architect responsible for construction means, methods or techniques, or safety programs or precautions.

The architect's authority is limited to the provisions of the Owner-Architect Agreement and the General Conditions:

The architect shall have access to the work at all times.

The architect determines the payment amounts based on his observations and the contractor's Application for Payment and issues Certificates for Payment.

The architect is the interpreter of the Contract Documents upon written request of the owner or contractor. Matters are initially referred to the architect. Decisions are to be impartial, made in a reasonable period of time, and consistent with the intent of the Contract Documents. Any claim or dispute is subject to arbitration upon the written request of the owner or contractor. Exceptions are matters of aesthetic effect. In this case, the architect's decision is final.

The architect has the authority to reject work which does not conform to the Contract Documents. Further, he may require inspection or testing at any point during the construction process to determine if the work is in accordance with the Contract Documents. If the contractor fails to correct defective work or persistently fails to construct the project in conformance with the Contract Documents, the owner may order the contractor to stop the work or any portion of the work until the problem is corrected or eliminated. Such an order must be in writing and signed by the owner or his specifically designated agent.

The architect must review shop drawings and samples, but only for conformance with the design concept of the work and information in the Contract Documents. The contractor is responsible for dimensions, assembly, components, etc.

The architect prepares change orders and construction change directives as required to modify the work while it is in progress.

The architect conducts inspections to determine the dates of substantial completion and final completion.

Further sections of this manual describe the above noted duties in greater detail.

Furthermore, prior to the start of the project, the architect obtains, reviews and forwards to the owner the contractor's Performance Bond and Payment Bond, if such bonds are required by the owner. He requires the contractor to file with the owner his Certificate of Insurance and to secure and pay for all building permits for the project. He reviews the contractor's list of subcontractors, notifies the contractor of any rejections and requires substitutes if necessary. He obtains and reviews the contractor's construction schedule and schedule of submittals. Prior to the first Application for Payment by the contractor, the architect reviews and approves the contractor's Schedule of Values for the costs of labor and materials.

In addition, the architect schedules the pre-construction conference and weekly job conferences during this phase of the project delivery process. After the general contractor has been selected, the pre-construction conference is held prior to start of construction. All participants in the project should be present: the architect and his consultants, the owner, the general contractor, principle subcontractors, principle material suppliers and the contractor's safety representative and superintendent.

The purpose of the pre-construction conference is to discuss the expectations of all parties and establish the methods of communication. Recognize that all the architect's communications should be through the general contractor and not directly with subcontractors or material suppliers, etc. The owner and contractor should communicate through the architect. Exceptions, such as direct communication in emergency situations, should be noted in the Contract Documents. Other items of importance are: reviewing the General Conditions; designating of responsible personnel by all parties; discussing the construction schedule and a means of monitoring the progress of the work; establishing a filing system and the procedure for maintaining record documents; submitting shop drawings and samples and the number of copies required; processing of Change Orders, Architect's Supplemental Instructions and Construction Change Directives; and discussing procedures for safety, first-aid and security.

Weekly job conferences are held throughout the construction period for the purpose of review of the progress of the work and to provide for systematic discussion of problems that may arise regarding the construction of the project. It is important to identify problems which impede the planned progress of the work and develop corrective measures to regain the planned schedule. Field observations should be reviewed in regard to maintaining proper quality of construction and standards of workmanship. The minutes of previous meetings should be reviewed and approved. In addition, the minutes of all meetings should be taken, signed by the owner, contractor and architect and distributed to all parties attending.

Establishing a filing system is an important responsibility of the architect during this phase of the project delivery process. All correspondence, phone conversation, minutes of meetings and other documents should be carefully filed in case disputes should arise at a later date and the need for documentation develop. On small jobs a chronological file is often sufficient. However, on large jobs, where huge amounts of documents and correspondence are generated, both a chronological file and a well organized filing/information retrieval system must be developed. A sample filing/information retrieval system for a large job follows on the last page of this section.

Most importantly, careful documentation and concise record keeping are a part of risk management. Needless to say, this must be carefully considered in advance. The architect should develop project management record forms and checklists to make such documentation systematic. Many architects furnish staff members with a bound diary and a manual outlining the firm's project management system. The manual sets down guidelines that are to be followed by each member of the design and construction administration team. Included in the manual are standard forms on which to record decisions, actions and communications. Routing directions for various forms are included. Transmittal forms are used for important communications to the owner or contractor. Note that such communications may require the use of registered mail or courier service with the recipient's signature for documentation that the communication was actually received.

Recognize that each project is unique and no standard forms and guidelines can be developed that will apply for every project. Therefore, the architect and his staff should be thoroughly familiar with the rights, duties and responsibilities assigned to the architect under the standard Owner-

Architect Agreement and General Conditions of the contract between the owner and the contractor. Further, if any modifications are made to the standard documents, the architect should familiarize his staff with the terms of the actual agreement. Once the mechanics of the construction administration process and documentation system are established for a particular project, it is important to see that the entire firm works consistently with it. Any member of the firm may be considered an agent of the firm. Their actions can create legal duties through their conduct.

The architect should consider his duties in the Construction Administration Phase prior to the start of construction. In fact, the architect must consider this issue when the owner-architect agreement is negotiated. Often, the architect seeks compensation for the Construction Administration Phase on a lump sum, that is, fixed fee basis. The major problem with this method is that the architect has little assurance he will be compensated fairly. For example, the contractor may take far longer to construct the project than originally anticipated, the owner could stop the project for convenience, or poor quality construction and other problems may cause the architect's duties to be very time consuming.

A well negotiated Owner-Architect Agreement should anticipate this problem and provide compensation for the architect if he has to spend more than a pre-determined amount of time on Construction Administration. For example, if compensation for this phase is on a fixed fee basis, every hour required over the initially estimated quantity reduces the architect's profit. Also, the architect's consultants will often have to be closely involved in problem projects. Note that the cost of the consultant's services can also greatly reduce the architect's profit if his compensation is based on a fixed fee and the consultants are billing the architect on an hourly basis.

As outlined in paragraph 3.3.6 of the AIA Owner-Architect Agreement, providing services made necessary by the contractor's default, major defects or deficiencies, or the failure of either the owner or contractor to perform are Contingent Additional Services. If such services are required, the architect notifies the owner in writing. Further, as outlined in paragraph 3.1.1, if the owner considers that the services are not required, he notifies the architect and the architect has no obligation to perform the services. Therefore, the architect may wish to define the number of hours of Construction Administration Phase services included in a fixed fee and require that the owner pay for additional services beyond the maximum number of hours.

In spite of the architect's concern over the means of compensation, Construction Administration Phase services should always be included as a part of the basic services provided. If the owner refuses to include Construction Administration as a part of the architect's services, such projects should be avoided. In projects where the architect provides Construction Documents and no Construction Administration services, the architect's potential liability is increased considerably. This is because the architect is excluded from involvement in observing construction to see that the Contract Documents are followed; preparing clarifications, interpretations or Change Orders that may be related to allegations of the architect's own errors and omissions; and approving payments to contractors for such Change Orders.

Typical Construction Administration Files

1. Chronological File
2. Correspondence to/from Owner
3. Correspondence to/from Contractor
4. Correspondence to/from Consultants
5. Correspondence to/from Government Review Agencies
6. Correspondence-Inter-Office
7. Telephone Conversation Verification/Notes
8. Field Observation Reports/Notes
9. Minutes of Meetings   Communication
10. Contingent Additional Services
11. Optional Additional Services   Additional Services
12. Bidding/Addendum Files
13. Applications/Certificates for Payment   Bidding/Payments
14. Proposal Requests Pending/Issued
15. Change Orders Executed/Pending
16. Construction Change Directives
17. Clarifications
18. Change Authorizations
19. Architect's Supplemental Instructions   Changes in the Work
20. Consultant Observations/Test Reports
21. Transmittals to/from Contractor
22. Transmittals to/from Consultants
23. Shop Drawing Index
24. Finish & Color Submittals   Project Technical Information
25. Punch Lists
26. Certificates of Inspection
27. Certificate of Completion   Project Close Out

Note: It is often convenient to color-code the labels of the various sections of the file folders to expedite filing and retrieval of information and documents. In addition, each file folder label should have the dates of the information contained within.

Architect, Owner, Contractor Relationship

In essence, the relationship that exists among the parties of a construction contract is as follows: The architect designs the work; prepares the Contract Documents; and administers the construction contract. The contractor prepares the bid proposals for the cost of the work and upon award of the contract, supervises the construction and builds the project in accordance with the Contract Documents. The owner furnishes relevant information concerning program requirements and the site, pays for the cost of professional services, and pays for the cost of the work associated with the development of the project.

Throughout the project, the architect is the owner's professional adviser. During the design phase, the architect serves as an objective professional endeavoring to carry out the owner's wishes. During the construction phase the architect administers the contract between the owner and contractor. During this phase the architect acts in a dual capacity. He serves as the owner's professional advisor and agent, and he also serves as an impartial interpreter of the Contract Documents upon written request of the owner or contractor. He must perform these duties without partiality to either owner or contractor and enforce faithful performance of the contract by both owner and contractor.

It is important to understand that the architect signs a contract with the owner, The Owner-Architect Agreement. In addition, the contractor signs a contract with the owner, the Owner-Contractor Agreement. These contracts are entirely separate. There is no contractual obligation between the architect and contractor. The architect is responsible for the administration of the contract between the owner and contractor as a result of his contractual agreement with the owner which outlines his duties in this area. Secondly, the General Conditions, which are a part of the contract between the owner and contractor, outline the architect's duties in regard to administration of the construction contract.

Therefore, the architect performs his duties in administering the contract as a limited agent of the owner. His authority is limited to that defined in the Owner-Architect Agreement and the General Conditions.

An agent is a person or firm empowered to act for another and transact business with third parties. The architect is a limited agent with authority to conduct transactions on behalf of the owner as expressed or implied by the Contract Documents.

It is the architect's responsibility to interpret and enforce the provisions of the Contract Documents upon the written request of either the owner or contractor. In addition, the architect determines if the contractor's work is in accordance with the Contract Documents. Furthermore, the architect rejects defective work. However, this authority does not extend to directing construction techniques, the time in which the work is done, safety procedures or sequences of construction.

Most decisions of the architect to reject work are subject to arbitration. Exceptions are matters of aesthetic effect.

The architect has no authority to alter the terms and conditions of the contract. However, provisions in the contract allow for changes in the work. This is accomplished by transmitting written Change Orders and Construction Change Directives to the contractor signed by the owner and architect.

All parties to the construction contract should have a clear understanding of the division of responsibilities. A recognition of these relationships often expedites the performance of the various duties of the parties required by the Contract Documents.

Note the relationship intended to exist as outlined in paragraph 4.2.3 of the AIA General Conditions. The architect is not responsible for construction means, methods, techniques or safety precautions for the project. Nor is the architect responsible for acts or omissions of the contractor. This represents the traditional legal relationship between the contractor and the architect. Further, it is restated in paragraph 3.3.1 that the contractor is responsible for construction means, methods, and techniques unless the Contract Documents give other instructions concerning these matters.

Recognize that such instructions may be given by the architect for the purpose of protecting the public health, safety, and welfare or the interests of the owner. For example, the architect might give the contractor the following instructions regarding the removal of concrete formwork: Remove forms only after concrete has developed sufficient strength to safely sustain its own weight and superimposed loads, but not sooner than specified in the American Concrete Institute Standard 347, "Recommended Practice for Concrete Formwork," paragraph 3.6.2.3.

The language in the AIA General Conditions, paragraph 3.3.1, gives proper power to the architect related to technical matters. Furthermore, it negates the possible objections of the contractor on giving specific instructions on how to perform the work in these cases.

It should be noted that the AIA General Conditions virtually restate the architect's responsibilities regarding administration of the construction contract which are stipulated in the AIA Owner-Architect Agreement. The General Conditions are in turn incorporated by reference into the AIA

Owner-Contractor Agreement. Therefore, by executing the AIA Owner-Contractor Agreement, the contractor agrees to the architect's role in administration of the construction contract as stipulated in the AIA General Conditions.

Architectural Field Observations

As outlined in the AIA Owner-Architect Agreement, Document B141, the architect visits the site at intervals appropriate to the stage of construction or as otherwise agreed in writing to make field observations and evaluations. He familiarizes himself with the progress and quality of the work and determines in general if the work, when completed, will be in accordance with the Contract Documents. He endeavors to guard the owner against defects and deficiencies in the work of the contractor. The architect is not required to make extensive or continuous on-site inspections to check the quality or quantity of the work. He should periodically inform the owner of the progress of the work.

The main purpose of the architect's field observations at intervals appropriate to the stage of construction is to give the owner a higher degree of assurance that the design intent of the Contract Documents will be implemented as the construction proceeds. Further, the end result of such a process provides the owner with higher quality construction. For example, during periodic field observations the architect compares the work illustrated in the drawings and the provisions of the specifications to the completed work in place. (Note that the work illustrated in drawings would include details that have been reviewed and approved through the shop drawing submittal procedure outlined in the General Conditions.)

Not only is field observation of the work required, but also the architect's observation of testing required by law or by the specifications is a part of the field observation process. For example, the architect observes the sample taking and testing at the site of various items as the work is in progress. This is of particular importance for items that are site fabricated such as concrete poured on the jobsite or hot mopped, built-up tar and gravel roofing. Obviously, the architect's observation of finished work does not necessarily mean that the material, system or equipment was installed in accordance with the Contract Documents. The work should be observed at intervals appropriate to the stage of construction as the construction proceeds.

Also, the architect makes field observations in order to ascertain the percentage of work completed and determine the amounts due the contractor since it is the architect that certifies the contractor's application for payment. For example, upon receiving the contractor's application for payment, the architect makes a field observation to determine if the percentage of work claimed to have been completed has progressed to the point indicated. In addition, the architect determines if the quality of such work is in accordance with the Contract Documents.

The architect does not supervise the construction and is not responsible for construction methods, techniques, sequences or procedures, or for safety precautions or programs in connection with the work. These duties are the responsibility of the contractor. Further, the architect is not responsible for the contractor's default, failure to carry out the work, errors or omissions. In addition, the architect may visit the site and has access to the work at all times in accordance with the AIA General Conditions.

The words "supervision" and "inspection" should not be used in relation to the architect's field observations. The term "inspection" implies an extensive and detailed on-site examination of the construction and an approval that such work has been done correctly. This term unduly widens the architects potential liability for undiscovered errors or omissions in the construction. For example, if the architect agreed to "inspect" the construction and an undetected error or omission on the part of the contractor caused an eventual building failure, the architect could be held liable. However, as outlined in the AIA General Conditions, the architect "observes" the work to determine if it is proceeding in accordance with the Contract Documents. The contractor "supervises" and directs the construction and is responsible for completing the work in accordance with the Contract Documents. Furthermore, as outlined in paragraph 3.3.4 of the AIA General Conditions, the contractor is responsible for inspecting portions of the work already in place to determine if these portions are in proper condition to receive subsequent work.

This type of detailed inspection cannot be performed by the architect who visits the site only at intervals. Nor is this type of inspection performed by the building department inspector who visits the site intermittently. The building inspector's main concern is compliance with the building code requirements. In most cases, the building code requirements are simply minimum standards. Therefore, the building inspector checks for compliance with the minimum standards required by the code. Recognize that the building inspector makes necessary checks for compliance with life-safety, fire protection, handicapped regulations, and so on, but does not attempt to control other items related to the quality of the building such as the joining of woodwork, quality of the installation of finish materials, etc. However, the architect is concerned with these items and observes the construction for compliance with the quality of materials and workmanship along with any other items outlined in the specifications.

The architect makes field observations of various items as the work progresses. Such items include the following: bench marks; building layouts; excavations; soil under footings; public utility connections; foundations and reinforcing; pile driving; concrete quality, placing, forms, and tests; structural frame; fireproofing; floor openings; weather protection; masonry; partition layout; mechanical and electrical work; setting of frames; closing in; roofing and flashing; windows and doors; tile work; cabinet work; elevators; plaster; gypsum board; finishing; painting; hardware; plumbing; equipment; and various other items as required.

Such observations should be recorded in writing, dated, and kept in a project file. The standard form for field observations is the American Institute of Architects Document G711, Architect's Field Report. Such field reports contain important information that includes the following: an estimated percent of completion of work that has taken place; the work in progress at the time of the observation; trades on the site and the number of workers of each trade; weather, temperature and site conditions; general observations on the progress of the work and the location and type of materials being placed; observation on the contractor's overall conformance to the construction schedule; items to verify; and notes on action required on any item. Further, the architect may wish to use photographs to document the progress of the work. To provide meaningful documentation, such photographs must be taken and developed with a processing date stamp on a regular basis. In addition, photographs should be utilized to document problems, especially those involving additional cost, building failures or injuries.

As outlined in paragraph 2.6.5 of the AIA Owner-Architect Agreement, the architect is specifically required to keep the owner informed of the progress and quality of the work. Therefore, the architect may wish to send a letter each week to both the owner and the contractor that summarizes the developments recorded in the architect's field observation reports. Those problems that are particularly critical should be emphasized. Other important information may be included in the letter as appropriate. For example, the status of a contractor's claim pending changes in the work, or communications received may be included. Further, the architect may wish to document the timeliness of the contractor's response to requests for additional information related to claims and the timeliness of the contractor's submittal of shop drawings. In this way, the architect may reduce the possibility of liability from claims for damages by either the owner or the contractor for delay of the project.

Another area of potential liability for the architect may result from the failure to point out hazards, or discrepancies between the contractor's work and the Contract Documents which were observed during a site visit. In this case, the architect should promptly inform the contractor's superintendent on the jobsite in writing. The architect should carry extra field report forms and carbon paper on site visits so that a written memo with a carbon copy can be made at the site should the need arise. Further, the owner should be notified in writing. (See "Sample Notification to Owner of Unsafe Condition.") Copies of such notices should be kept in the architect's files in case a problem related to this matter arises at a later date and the need for documentation develops. In this way, the architect will have kept the owner informed of the progress and quality of the work and put the owner on notice in regard to the problem.

For example, on a site visit an architect observes that no shoring has been installed around a deep excavation where workers are pouring concrete. The architect also notices that the sides of the excavation indicate that there is a danger of collapse. Should litigation develop, it will be asked if the architect acted within the reasonable standard of care of other architects in the community.

The architect may wish to consider various courses of action in cases of this nature that would include the following: prompt written notification of the unsafe condition to the contractor's superintendent, the owner, and if it is necessary, notification of local safety officials who have jurisdiction over the project. The architect should not direct correction measures since construction means, methods and techniques are the responsibility of the contractor. Also, if the contractor does not take corrective action, the architect may wish to contact the owner and advise the owner to stop the construction until the contractor corrects the problem. Notice that it is possible that the owner may not respond in a timely manner. Recognize that if the unsafe condition is a substantial one, the architect may not be able to eliminate the possibility of liability by pointing to the owner's failure to act. Also, if an architect ascertains that the contractor's procedures are seriously unsafe and in complete disregard of health or safety regulations, the architect may wish to consider a temporary suspension of work in the part of the project affected, until the problem is corrected, instead of stopping the entire project. However, it should be recognized that suspending or stopping the work is an extreme measure that can have a major effect on the project in terms of both cost and time. Such action should be taken only after giving careful consideration to the significant effects of the suspension or stoppage.

Note that the AIA documents do not state that the architect has the right to stop the work. In some cases the owner may wish to modify the standard provisions and give the architect the right to stop the work. However, in many cases when the architect has ordered the contractor to stop the work, the contractor has instigated litigation against the architect for alleged losses because of the delay. Therefore, the architect may wish to avoid contract provisions that grant the architect the right to stop the work since they broaden the architect's responsibilities and potential liability.

Architectural field observations are an important responsibility which improves the overall quality of the project. However, the field observations are not intended to be a substitution for the adequate fulfillment of the contractor's obligation, which is to construct the project in accordance with the Contract Documents and to guarantee the completed project. For this reason, the architect may wish to exercise caution if asked by the contractor to interpret drawings or specifications during field observations. If possible, it is better to respond to questions with a written clarification. For example, during a site visit the contractor asks the architect for an interpretation on an alleged ambiguity in the drawings or specifications. The architect may clarify this matter by referring the contractor to other details or provisions in the contract documents. However, if the architect rules on the alleged ambiguity through an interpretation, he could imply negligence in the preparation of the Contract Documents and therefore be liable for changes required. Further, the architect may wish to state in the Contract Documents that all requests for interpretations or clarifications be made in writing and that all responses are in writing.

The nature of the contractual agreement by the architect to visit the site at intervals appropriate to the stage of construction should be fully understood by the owner to avoid unwarranted expectations that the architect will be making exhaustive or continuous on-site inspections or supervising the construction. The areas of the AIA Owner-Architect Agreement and the AIA General Conditions which establish that the architect is not responsible for construction means, methods, techniques, sequences or safety precautions and programs should be pointed out to the client at the outset of the project. This avoids the possibility of misunderstandings regarding architectural field observations during later stages of the project.

The contract language of the AIA documents leaves the definition of "intervals appropriate to the stage of construction" to the judgment of the architect. For instance, the scheduling of site visits for field observations to a complex manufacturing plant would be different from those to a warehouse of the same size. The frequency of site visits for field observation will depend upon the type and complexity of the project. For simple projects, field observations once a week and site visits as required to observe tests and specific items such as concrete pours are often sufficient. A complex project requires more frequent site visits to reduce unnecessary delays that may occur due to claims of changed conditions, defective work, and requests for interpretations or clarifications.

Furthermore, fees generally charged for the Administration of the Construction Phase do not adequately cover exhaustive or continuous on-site inspections. If such services are required by the client, governmental regulations or special conditions of the project, provisions should be made in the Owner-Architect Agreement for payments for these additional services. The size and cost of the project are not the only factors involved in deciding whether or not to have continuous on-site observations. The other factor is the end result desired by the owner. For example, work of a custom nature, such as the renovation of a historic building, may require full time construction observation. Also, when life safety is an important issue, such as in the construction of a hospital, continuous on-site observation is often required.

ARCHITECT'S FIELD REPORT

AIA DOCUMENT G711

OWNER	☒
ARCHITECT	☒
CONSULTANT	☒
FIELD	☒

PROJECT: Typical Mfg.Co. Plant and Offices
100 Industrial Blvd.
CONTRACT: Hayward, California

FIELD REPORT NO: 54

ARCHITECT'S PROJECT NO: 87-116

DATE June 15, 1989 **TIME** 10 AM **WEATHER** Hot, Sunny **TEMP. RANGE** 75-80° F

EST. % OF COMPLETION 95% **CONFORMANCE WITH SCHEDULE (+, −)** +

WORK IN PROGRESS	PRESENT AT SITE
Carpeting	4 Carpet Layers
Painting	3 Painters
Electrical	2 Electricians

OBSERVATIONS

1. Exterior work and site work 100% complete.
2. Interior Finish Work 95% complete.
3. Carpet is complete except for conference room.
4. All walls were inspected for damage prior to furniture move in. All locations of construction damage will be noted on final punch list.
5. All walls will be inspected after furniture installation and any damage will be noted on a separate punch list.
6. Painting Complete except for toilet rooms.
7. Electricians installing security alarm system. System complete except for rear entry door installation.

ITEMS TO VERIFY

1. Keying schedule and all keys
2. Removal of Temporary Field Office

INFORMATION OR ACTION REQUIRED

1. Owner's maintence crew to verify that all keys are properly tagged and all locks in proper working order.

ATTACHMENTS 2. Contractor states he will remove temporary field office by June 30, 1989.

REPORT BY: Tim Smith, Project Manager

A B C Architects
600 Main Street
San Francisco, California

William Jones, President
Typical Manufacturing Co.
950 Broadway Blvd.
Oakland, California

June 20, 1989

Dear Mr. Jones:

On today's date, the following unsafe condition was noted at Typical Manufacturing Company's Industrial Plant and Offices construction site at 100 Industrial Blvd., Hayward, California: An open pipe trench was not protected with barricades. We immediately brought this to the attention of Gerald Clark, jobsite superintendent, of Quality Construction Company.

To the best of our knowledge, the unsafe condition has not been corrected. It may represent a serious safety problem to workers or passer-bys in that area of the jobsite. The trench is located at the front of the building near the sidewalk.

Jobsite safety is the contractor's responsibility and is governed by the contractor's agreement with you. These responsibilities are outlined in paragraphs 10.1.1, 10.2.1, 10.2.2, 10.2.3 and 10.2.6 of the AIA General Conditions which is included by reference as a part of the Owner-Contractor Agreement. We recommend that you notify Quality Construction Company to correct the unsafe condition without delay.

As outlined in the supplementary provisions of our agreement concerning unsafe conditions, please communicate directly with the contractor in this matter.

Very truly yours,

Tim Smith
Project Representative
A B C Architects

Hand delivered by Joseph Harrison, A B C Architects, June 20, 1989

Received for Typical Manufacturing Co. by:-----------------------

Date:--------------------   Time:---------------------

Submittals

As noted in the AIA General Conditions, the architect receives and approves the contractor's submittals such as shop drawings, schedules and samples, but only for the limited purpose of checking for conformance with the design concept of the work and compliance with the information given in the Contract Documents. No deviations from the Contract Documents are included in the review process unless they are specifically called to the attention of the architect in writing and approved in writing. The contractor is responsible for dimensions and their confirmation at the jobsite; for determination and verification of materials; substantiation of instructions for installation or performance of equipment; coordination of the information in submittals with the requirements of the work and the Contract Documents; and for quantities.

Shop drawings are drawings, diagrams or schedules specially prepared to illustrate a specific portion of the work such as structural steel or cabinetwork. These are usually prepared by a subcontractor, manufacturer, supplier or distributor and show specific components in detail including exact dimensions.

Product literature and data are illustrations, charts, schedules, performance charts, pamphlets, booklets, photos, and so on, furnished by the contractor to give information on a particular product, material or system for a portion of the work.

Samples are physical portions of particular materials which illustrate colors, textures, workmanship, or pieces of equipment such as light fixtures.

These items establish standards of quality by which the architect can judge the work.

Informational submittals, those that are required for documentation but not intended to require a response by the architect, should be identified in the Contract Documents. Examples of such submittals are certificates of inspection, test reports, etc.

Professional certifications of performance criteria may also be required by the Contract Documents. In this case, the architect may rely upon the accuracy and completeness of these calculations. However, the architect must check to insure that these submittals have received the professional stamp of a licensed engineer. An example of such a certification would be the submittal of stamped engineering calculations certifying that a manufacturer's skylight meets the loading conditions required by the building code.

The contractor must prepare and submit to the architect a schedule of submittals that is coordinated with the construction schedule. Submittals must be made by the contractor giving sufficient time, in the architect's professional judgment, for an adequate review. The architect's review does not include approval of safety precautions or, unless stated specifically by the architect, review of construction means, methods, sequences or techniques.

Furthermore, the architect's approval of a specific item does not indicate approval of an assembly of which the item is a component. For example, if the architect approves a submittal for a single item such as an air conditioning unit, this does not indicate approval of ductwork or other items of the assembly that are components of the system.

Submittals are not Contract Documents. They show how the contractor proposes to conform with the information given and the design concept in the Contract Documents. The contractor must review, approve and submit all shop drawings, product data and samples required by the Contract Documents. Requests for these submittals are usually made in the specifications under the specific headings. By approving and submitting these items, the contractor represents that he has verified all materials, catalog numbers and field measurements, and he has checked and coordinated the information with the requirements of the work and the Contract Documents. The contractor is not relieved of responsibility for any deviation from the Contract Documents, errors or omissions by the architect's approval of submittals.

In addition, the contractor may not proceed with any part of the work requiring the submission of a shop drawing, product literature or sample until the submittal has been approved by the architect. Further, these parts of the work must be done in conformance with the approved shop drawings.

Shop drawings should be submitted to the architect in the form of sepias or other reproducible means. These transparencies may then be easily printed with notes, corrections, changes or approvals. All modifications required for approval are noted on the transparency and the required copies are printed and returned to the contractor. This avoids possible errors through failure to record notes and changes on all copies.

The contractor is required to make corrections and changes noted by the architect or his consultants and resubmit the corrected shop drawings until they are approved. In some instances, the architect may have to review the shop drawings several times before they are approved. For this reason, the architect may wish to add a supplement to the AIA Owner-Architect Agreement and AIA General Conditions which stipulates that the architect will review the contractor's submittals only twice without additional charges for architectural services. The contractor will be required to pay the owner for the cost of additional reviews. The owner will then pay the architect for the services required for the additional reviews.

The contractor must direct special attention to proposed deviations from the Contract Documents either in writing or by notes with heavy lines around the proposed changes. The architect's approval of a submittal does not relieve the contractor of the responsibility for deviations from the Contract Documents unless such deviation is called to the attention of the architect in writing and approved by the architect in writing.

Product literature should be submitted in multiple copies so that some may be returned to the contractor and some retained in the architect's office suitably marked for filing. This product literature should include dimensions, performance data, wiring diagrams, specifications of equipment, and other information as required by the architect and his consultants in the evaluation of the product. The contractor should clearly identify model numbers and items to be furnished.

Upon receipt of shop drawings in the architect's office, they must be date stamped and suitably marked for filing. All shop drawings should contain the following information: name of project, architect, contractor, originating subcontractor or distributor, and portion of the work for which the submittal is made. In addition, space for the architect's review stamp should be provided. Upon review, the architect returns prints of the shop drawings to the contractor stamped and with a check in one of the following boxes:

approved	( )
approved as corrected	( )
revise or resubmit	( )
not approved	( )

Some professional liability insurance companies and some lawyers have advised architects that the word "approved" places an unnecessary risk on the architect when used on the review stamp. On the other hand, others argue that regardless of the word substituted for "approve", the architect is afforded no more protection. Courts have held varying interpretations with no consistent decision on this issue. Some have contended that the architect's approval is implied even if not stated. For support of this contention, claimants have referred to paragraph 4.2.7 of the AIA General Conditions which states, "The Architect will review and approve or take other appropriate action as required on the Contractor's submittals....". the argument here is that this article makes the architect responsible for the contractor's shop drawings to a certain degree regardless of the word used on the stamp.

Note, however, that the "approval" is carefully defined by further language in paragraph 4.2.7 as "only for the limited purpose of checking for conformance with information given and the design concept expressed in the Contract Documents." Further, paragraph 3.12.5 of the AIA General Conditions requires the contractor to review and approve sub-mittals prior to submitting them to the architect. The architect's "approval" is used in this context. Therefore, submittals made by the contractor which do not have the contractor's prior approval may be returned to the contractor without action. In this case, a cover letter should be attached which calls the provision of paragraph 3.12.5 to the contractor's attention.

Other court decisions have made the distinction between the word "approved" and other words on a shop drawing stamp such as "reviewed" or "no exceptions taken." However, these words are not a guaranteed improvement of the architect's liability position. For this reason, the architect may wish to restate, or summarize the pertinent provisions of the AIA General Condition paragraphs 3.12.7, 3.12.8 and 4.2.7 on the shop drawing stamp.

Submittals

The architect should maintain a shop drawing and sample record indicating the date of receipt; shop drawing number and title; subcontractor or trade; consultant referred to, if any; action taken and where copies were sent. The architect sends submittals related to a consultant's portion of the work to the appropriate consultant for review and approval prior to the architect performing his review. Therefore, the consultant must review, approve or take other action before the architect places his review stamp on such submittals.

The architect should outline the submittal procedural requirements in the specifications under Division 1, General Requirements, Section 01300. These are generally placed in this location in the project manual in accordance with the Construction Specifications Institute's recommendations. Here the administrative procedural requirements for submittals are outlined. Specific requirements for submittals are included in the individual sections of specification Divisions 2-16 which describe the various materials, products and systems of the project. Items discussed in detail in Section 01300 include such items as the schedule of submittals; the number of copies of submittals required; transmittal forms required; the numbering system; information required on the submittal; requirements for shop drawings, product data, samples and calculations; the contractor's responsibilities; the architect's responsibilities; resubmission requirements; and the distribution of submittals after they are reviewed. These items should be discussed in detail by the architect in the pre-construction conference to insure that the contractor understands the procedures for processing submittals, review and approval sequence and methods of transmittal.

For example, assume the architect specified steel windows for the project under specification section 08510. Within this section the architect required the submittal of shop drawings as follows: Include typical unit elevations and full size section details of typical composite members. Show anchors, hardware, operators, and accessories not fully detailed in the manufacturer's standard product data. Include glazing details.

Based on information in the architect's Contract Documents, the steel window manufacturer would prepare shop drawings depicting the various components of the windows. Other items illustrated would include the type, thickness or gauge of materials, relationship of the components to other portions of the work, field dimensions and installation accessories. Naturally, the submittal should also be in accordance with the requirements of Section 01300. For instance, the submittal should conform to the schedule previously submitted by the contractor, have the correct number of copies, and so on.

The shop drawings would be sent by the manufacturer to the contractor first. The contractor checks the shop drawings against the requirements of the Contract Documents, field dimensions of window openings, verifies materials and coordinates the shop drawings with other components of the work. The contractor notes approval of the work as appropriate. The contractor numbers the drawing in accordance with Section 01300. In addition, if the contractor proposes a deviation in the thickness of the metal or glass from that shown in the Contract Documents, he brings this to the attention of the architect in writing at the time of submittal. This in turn must be approved by the architect in writing if it is acceptable. After the contractor has approved the submittal, it is transmitted to the architect for review.

Upon receiving the submittal, the architect checks first to see that it has received the contractor's prior approval. If not, he returns the submittal without action. If so, he checks for conformance with the design intent and information in the Contract Documents. If, for example, the architect's drawings show steel windows with operable awning type component members, the design intent is not met with casement windows. If the drawings are approved or approved as corrected, the architect stamps the drawings, checks the appropriate box and returns it to the contractor along with a print with any corrections. The title, number, subcontractor or manufacturer, related specification section, action taken and so on is recorded in the architect's shop drawing log. A form specifically prepared for this purpose is AIA Document G712, "Shop Drawing and Sample Record."

Upon receiving the documents, the contractor notes the status of the shop drawing and any corrections made by the architect. The shop drawings and corrections are then sent back to the manufacturer for any corrections. If the architect marked "revise or resubmit," or "not approved," then the process is repeated until approval is received. "Clouds" are generally placed around revisions on resubmittals to indicate the revised areas. Once the shop drawings are approved they are then distributed as appropriate to manufacturers, subcontractors and project site files.

Rejection of Work

The architect interprets the Contract Documents in an impartial manner. As outlined in paragraph 4.2.6 of the AIA General Conditions, the architect has the authority to reject work that does not conform to the Contract Documents and has the authority to require additional inspection or testing in accordance with provisions of the Contract Documents. However, this authority, or decisions made in good faith to exercise or not to exercise this authority, does not create a responsibility on the part of the architect to the contractor or others performing portions of the work.

If the architect requires additional testing, inspections or approvals not included in the usual project tests, inspections and approvals outlined in paragraph 13.5.1 of the AIA General Conditions, the owner bears the costs. If such tests prove failure of the work, equipment or material to meet requirements of the Contract Documents or applicable laws, the contractor must bear the cost of the testing as outlined in paragraph 13.5.3. In addition, he must remove or correct the defective work and pay for any additional services of the architect made necessary by such failure or defect.

In the event of a dispute over a construction problem, the authority to require additional testing, outlined in paragraph 13.5.2 of the AIA General Conditions, may assist the architect in reducing potential liability. For example, if the HVAC system does not provide cool air for the building, the architect may reduce his responsibilities to reject work, required by the Contract Documents, through advising the owner in writing to obtain additional testing with reports from an independent testing agency. The architect can then base his decision on how to handle the problem on the report prepared by the testing agency. Even if the owner refuses to secure such testing, the architect can now document the request for testing and the fact that the owner declined to obtain the tests. Recognize that there should be reasonable grounds for such tests. Furthermore, these reasons should also be conveyed to the owner in writing since the owner bears the cost of the testing if the work is found to be in conformance with the Contract Documents.

As outlined in paragraph 12.3.1 of the AIA General Conditions, the owner may elect to accept work which is not in accordance with the Contract Documents as an option to removing or correcting the defect. Therefore, when the architect rejects non-conforming work, he should not automatically order the contractor to correct the deficiency. The architect should notify the owner of such rejected work in order to give the owner the choice as to whether or not to have the defect corrected or to take a price reduction. Obviously, this option should be exercised only in certain situations where structural integrity, proper functioning of mechanical or electrical systems, or questions of safety are not at issue. An example is the acceptance of a lesser quality flooring material or wall covering. In this case, the architect should issue a change order to reflect a reduction in the contract sum.

It is important to recognize that under the AIA General Conditions, any rejections of materials, equipment or workmanship are subject to arbitration if requested in writing by either the contractor or owner. Exceptions to this are matters of aesthetic effect. In this case, the architect's decision is final. In addition, paragraph 2.3.1 of the AIA General Conditions state that if the contractor fails to correct defective work, or persistently fails to carry out the work in accordance with the Contract Documents, the owner, by a written order, may order the contractor to stop the work. The architect has the duty to exercise a reasonable standard of care and competence in observing the progress of the work and in determining whether it is proceeding in accordance with the Contract Documents. It is the architect's responsibility to establish standards of acceptability, judge the conformity and make written records of the way in which any of the contractor's work is not in accordance with the requirements of the Contract Documents. Any non-conforming work should be formally rejected in writing. As outlined in paragraph 9.5.1 of the AIA General Conditions, the architect may withhold funds from a certificate for payment to protect the owner from loss for defective work that has not been corrected by the contractor.

Also, to protect the owner from loss, the architect may request that portions of the work be left uncovered until observed by the architect. As outlined in paragraph 12.1.1 of the AIA General Conditions, if a portion of the work is covered contrary to the architect's request or provisions of the Contract Documents, such work must be uncovered for the architect's observation and replaced at the contractor's expense. This must be requested by the architect in writing. For example, if a portion of the roof leaks during construction, the architect may request that the suspended ceiling not be installed until after the roof is repaired and then tested for leaks. The architect can then be on the site during testing to observe the performance of the roof while it is tested, for instance, by flooding the surface.

Further, as outlined in paragraph 12.1.2, if a portion of the work has been covered which the architect did not request to observe prior to its being covered, the architect may request to see this work uncovered by the contractor. If such work is in accordance with the Contract Documents, the cost of uncovering and replacement are paid by the owner by change order. If the work is not in accordance with the Contract Documents, the contractor pays all necessary costs for correction of the work. For example, the architect visits the job site and notices that wiring currently being installed is not being placed in a conduit as required by the Contract Documents. The architect may then wish to have walls uncovered in other parts of the project already completed in order to ensure that wiring in those areas has been properly installed in conduits.

As outlined in paragraph 12.2.1 of the AIA General Conditions, the contractor must promptly correct work rejected by the architect whether observed before or after substantial completion of the project. The contractor must pay for all costs associated with the correction including testing and the services of the architect made necessary by the defect. Paragraph 12.2.3 requires the contractor to remove rejected work from the site. Further, the contractor is required by paragraph 12.2.5 to pay for damages to other work caused by removal of defects.

The contractor must promptly replace non-conforming work upon written request by the owner for a period of one year after the date of substantial completion. This period may be extended by special warranties. For instance, the roofing specification may require the contractor to furnish a five year guarantee. Also, the one year period is extended for work performed after substantial completion by the time between substantial completion and the time when the work was actually performed.

If the contractor fails to correct defective work, the owner may correct it in accordance with the condition stated in paragraph 2.4.1 of the AIA General Conditions. As outlined, the owner must give the contractor two seven-day notices to correct the defect. This notification is subject to prior approval of the architect. If the contractor fails to act after the second notice, the owner may correct the deficiencies and the cost of such corrections are then deducted from payments due the contractor by change order. Further, as outlined in paragraph 12.2.4, the owner may remove and store any salvageable materials and equipment at the contractor's expense. After a time fixed by the architect's written notice to the contractor, the owner may sell the material or equipment after sending two ten-day notices to the contractor.

The language of the AIA General Conditions attempts to reduce or eliminate the possibility of the architect incurring liability for defective work performed by the contractor. However, the language is not a complete protection. The architect could be faced with allegations that he has not met the reasonable standard of care if he fails to reject obviously defective portions of the contractor's work during regular field observations. This is particularly true if the failure to point out obvious defects is consistent and forms a pattern over the course of the construction phase.

The architect may avoid these problems through careful field observations that are thorough enough to identify defective work that is patent. (Patent defects are those that are visible and recognizable. Those that are concealed are considered latent.) Further, the architect should notify the contractor in writing of any problems he observes. In addition, a copy of such notification should be sent to the owner.

It is important to understand that while the architect endeavors to his utmost to insure compliance of the work with the Contract Documents, he does not guarantee the work. The contractor provides a warranty on materials, equipment and workmanship as outlined in paragraph 3.5.1 of the AIA General Conditions. Obviously, it is impossible for the architect to supervise construction workers in the field. This is the contractor's responsibility. In addition, as outlined in the AIA General Conditions, the safety precautions and programs, construction means, methods, techniques, sequences, procedures and coordination are the responsibility of the contractor. Further, it is the contractor's responsibility under the AIA Owner-Contractor Agreement to complete the work in accordance with the Contract Documents. It is not the architect's responsibility should the contractor fail to complete the terms of the contract. The architect makes observations of the progress of the work, records the degree of conformance of the project to the Contract Documents, and rejects work which is not within the standards of acceptability.

The acceptability of the work should be based on compliance with the requirements of the Contract Documents. For example, the specifications outline accepted standards of quality for materials, equipment, and installation of these items. Often, these are ASTM Standards, code requirements, or trade association standards for the items involved. The specifications can require a quality of material or workmanship that exceeds these standards. If so, additional requirements of acceptability should be clearly outlined in the specifications.

Changes in the Work

A Change Order is a written instruction to the contractor, issued after signing of the contract, authorizing a change in the scope of the work, or an adjustment in the contract sum or contract time. This document is based upon agreement among the owner, architect, and contractor. It is usually prepared by the architect and consists of drawings, sketches or written instructions regarding additions or deletions to the work. The Change Order must be signed by the owner, the contractor and the architect. Therefore, a Change Order that is signed by these three parties indicates that all terms, including the adjustment to contract sum and contract time, are acceptable.

However, the parties do not always agree on the amount of adjustment to be made. If the contractor's agreement cannot be obtained on contract sum or contract time, a Construction Change Directive, signed by both the owner and architect is issued. This is a written document, prepared by the architect that directs the contractor to proceed with the work described and states a proposed adjustment to contract sum or contract time or both. This document is used in the event that total agreement on the terms of a Change Order cannot be obtained, but the parties wish to proceed with a change. The purpose of this document is to make a clear distinction between changes that have been fully agreed upon (the Change Order) and those for which cost and/or time must be determined later (the Construction Change Directive.) A Construction Change Directive signed by the contractor indicates the contractor's agreement with the architect's proposed adjustment to contract sum and time and then is recorded as a Change Order.

In accordance with the AIA General Conditions, the owner may order changes in the work, including altering, adding to or deducting from the work, or canceling any previous order for change, without invalidating the contract. The architect issues Architect's Supplemental Instructions for minor changes not affecting the contract sum or time. Changes involving the contract sum or contract time must be authorized by a written Change Order or Construction Change Directive. The provisions of the contract apply to all changes with the same effect as if they were initially embodied in the contract.

For example, after the Owner-Contractor Agreement is signed, the owner may wish to incorporate a material or system in the work that would improve the completed project. If the owner wishes to have underground conduit installed below floor slabs, under the parking area and around the perimeter of the site for a future closed circuit T.V. security system, it would be advantageous to install the conduit before the slabs are poured and the parking lot completed. Therefore, the owner may have the conduit installed before the work is finished and presumably save money. In this case the architect would prepare a Bulletin and accompanying documents and request a quotation for the proposed change from the contractor. (See sample Bulletin.)

However, the owner could receive an unreasonably high estimate for the cost of the work. Further, it may not be possible to resolve the issue of cost or time through negotiation. Therefore, in accordance with the AIA General Conditions the owner has the right, subject to agreement of the architect, to require that the change be made through a Construction Change Directive. In this instance, the cost and time could now be determined after this work is completed on a time and materials plus overhead and profit basis.

The Change Order, AIA Document G701, is utilized to document the complete mutual agreement of the owner, contractor, and architect. Note that mutual agreement may be reached in at least two points as the change process proceeds. The intent of the process is to obtain the agreement of the parties at the outset. Since this is not always possible, a Construction Change Directive, which does not require the contractor's agreement, may be issued. This document requires the signatures of the owner and architect. The contractor may sign this document at various points in the process, thus indicating complete agreement with its terms. The first point for agreement is when the Construction Change Directive is initially sent to the contractor. At this point the contractor may sign it and return it to the architect. Another opportunity for agreement comes upon completion of the work, after the architect has evaluated the contractor's invoices for materials and equipment, labor, and so on, for the change. The signature of the contractor on a Construction Change Directive indicates agreement on cost and time. In this case, the agreement is effective immediately and is recorded as a Change Order as outlined in paragraph 7.3.5 of the AIA General Conditions.

A Change Order or a Construction Change Directive may adjust the contract price upward or downward in one or more of the following ways: acceptance of a lump sum, on the basis of unit prices named in the contract or subsequently agreed upon, or on the basis of cost plus a mutually accepted percentage fee.

For work performed under the cost plus percentage fee, the contractor is paid an amount equal to the direct costs of labor, materials, supplies and transportation plus a percentage, which is often fifteen percent, of the direct costs as an allowance for overhead and profit. In addition, he is reimbursed for payroll taxes, sales tax and insurance.

For work performed by a subcontractor, the contractor is allowed an amount equal to the cost that would have been applicable had the contractor performed the work, plus an additional percentage which is often five percent.

If the cost of a Change Order cannot be agreed upon in advance, the contractor is obligated to proceed with the work upon receiving a Construction Change Directive. In this case, the architect is required to determine the cost of the work involved. This determination may be subject to arbitration if so requested by the contractor. The cost of the work is based upon any of the methods of payment described above or, if the contractor does not respond promptly or disagrees with the method for adjustment, the architect determines the cost of the Construction Change Directive based on reasonable expenditures for materials, labor, and equipment, bonds, insurance, taxes, permits and supervision plus an allowance for overhead and profit. The contractor must keep an itemized accounting together with supporting data such as payrolls and receipts. A decrease in the contract sum is the actual net cost of any deletion as confirmed by the architect.

Extra costs or credits due to unforeseen conditions below the surface of the ground are determined by the facts as they are encountered at the site. If conditions are encountered below grade which differ from the conditions indicated by the Contract Documents or if conditions are found to be of an unusual nature materially different from those normally encountered, the contractor may initiate a claim for additional costs or time. An example would be the discovery of an abandoned sewer line not shown on the drawings. The cost of removal would result in additional costs to the contract. In this case, the contractor prepares a claim for extra time and cost in accordance with paragraphs 4.3.7 and 4.3.8 of the AIA General Conditions and submits it to the architect in the form of a Change Proposal. (See sample contractor's Change Proposal.) If the architect approves the Change Proposal, he forwards it to the owner with recommendation for approval. (Note that if the Change Proposal involves the work related to the architect's consultants such as structural, mechanical or electrical work, the architect should obtain the approval of the consultant before recommending approval of the Change Order to the owner.) If the owner approves the Change Proposal, the architect prepares a Change Order for execution with the contract sum and time adjusted accordingly. (See sample Change Order.)

If the owner and contractor cannot agree on the amount of the adjustment, the architect must utilize a Construction Change Directive. Any requests for changes in contract sum or time must be made by the contractor in writing within twenty-one days of the first observation of the unforeseen condition as stipulated in Article 4.3.6 of the AIA General Conditions.

In the event a change in the work is required or if the owner wishes to make a change in the original contract, the architect issues a request for a Change Proposal to the contractor describing the change and attaches any revised or new documents required. The method of obtaining a Change Proposal varies from office to office. A common procedure is by use of a Bulletin. The Bulletin is a request for a quotation for making the described change in the contract. Additional paragraphs are often added in the Supplementary Conditions to describe the procedure for changes in the work in greater detail than that outlined in Article 7 of the AIA General Conditions. This is because it is the architect's responsibility to manage the change process and develop further procedures when necessary. The General Conditions provide a fundamental basis for the change process. However, further details are often needed for specific projects.

Since contract time is an important consideration on most projects, Bulletins should be written to indicate one of the following: that the contractor should include requests for additional time in his change proposal, that contract time will not be extended due to the change, or that contract time will be extended a given number of days. In this way, the contractor is required to quote a price which will include overtime pay if any is necessary.

The contractor analyzes the change and submits a Change Proposal to the owner through the architect. The Change Proposal sets forth any requested adjustment in the contract sum or contract time. Included is an itemized cost breakdown for all quantities of material and labor and a quotation for total cost of the change. A substantiation of any claim for extension of the contract time should also be included. This Change Proposal is a quotation which the owner may accept or reject.

If the owner rejects the Change Proposal, the contractor is given written notice of the rejection and proceeds with the original contract as if no Bulletin had been issued. For example, if the owner wishes a more expensive wall finish material in the conference room, such as walnut paneling, but the price cannot be agreed upon, the Change Proposal may be rejected. However, if the changes required are necessary for safe or proper functioning of the owner's project, the changes must be made. If the price cannot be agreed upon or negotiated, the contractor must proceed with the work upon receiving a written Construction Change Directive from the owner. In this case, as briefly outlined in the earlier paragraphs of this chapter, the architect is required to determine the cost of the work involved. This process is described in detail in Article 7.3 of the AIA General Conditions.

If the owner elects to accept the contractor's Change Proposal, or if the Change Proposal quotation of time and cost is negotiated and subsequently agreed upon, the architect prepares a Change Order for execution. The contract sum and contract time are adjusted through the Change Order as agreed upon by the owner and contractor. The AIA Change Order form, Document G701, contains blank spaces for signatures and adjustments to the contract sum and the contract time. This reduces the possibility for errors or omissions and expedites processing.

The Architect's Supplemental Instructions, a standard AIA document, can be used by the architect to give interpretations of the Contract Documents which are minor in nature. It can also be utilized to order minor changes in the work not involving a change in contract sum or contract time. This form is utilized by the architect in performing his duties as the interpreter of the Contract Documents as required by the Owner-Architect Agreement and the General Conditions. This form is not used for changes involving contract sum or contract time. If the contractor believes that a change in contract sum or contract time is involved, the Change Order form or the Construction Change Authorization form is used.

The Construction Change Authorization form, AIA Document G713, is used instead of the Change Order form only for immediate changes in the work which, if not processed expeditiously, might delay the project. These changes are generally initiated in the field and involve changes which affect the contract sum or contract time. (See sample Construction Change Authorization.) This is not a Change Order, but an authorization to proceed with a change for subsequent inclusion in a Change Order. This form establishes a basis for the change in time or cost.

The architect should use caution in utilizing this form. Note that the AIA General Conditions do not give the architect the authority to make changes involving contract sum or contract time. Therefore, the owner's written authorization should be obtained before the architect utilizes this form. Otherwise, the owner could hold the architect liable for unauthorized changes. If this form is to be utilized, the owner should give the architect prior written authorization to issue the Construction Change Authorization. It is often to the owner's advantage to give the architect such authorization to issue a Construction Change Authorization up to a certain dollar amount. Without such authorization, relatively minor changes could delay the project's completion while the Change Order process is being facilitated.

<u>Sample - Bulletin</u>

Project: Bulletin No. 1
Typical Manufacturing Co.
Industrial Plant & Office   ABC Architects
100 Industrial Blvd.   600 Main St.
Hayward, California   San Francisco, California

To:
Mr. Robert Brown, President   May 10, 1988
Quality Construction Co.
300 First Ave.
Oakland, California

This is a request for a quotation. It is not a Change Order.

General

This Bulletin is issued to inform the contractor of the proposed changes to the Contract described below. All such work shall be executed under the terms of the original Contract unless expressly provided otherwise.

Contractor shall submit a Change Proposal and substantiate any requested increase in Contract Time for the work described below. Furnish a complete cost breakdown of both credits and extras for the change involved.

Do not proceed with this work until you receive a Change Order signed by both the Owner and the Architect.

Description of Proposed Work:

Provide underground conduit beneath floor slabs, under parking area and around perimeter of site for future closed circuit T.V. security system as indicated on the attached drawing.

(Contractor's Claim For Extra Time and Cost)

Sample - Change Proposal

Project: Change Proposal No. 2
Typical Manufacturing Co.
Industrial Plant & Offices   Quality Construction Co.
100 Industrial Blvd.   300 First Ave.
Hayward, California   Oakland, California

To:
Mr. Frank Smith, President   June 8, 1988
ABC Architects
600 Main St.
San Francisco, California

We submit our estimate in the amount of $20,000.00 for
performing the following extra work.

Furnishing and installing labor, material and equipment to
remove abandoned 10" diameter sewer line as required where
encountered in excavation for basement, foundation and other
new construction. This line runs the entire length of the
site and is located in conflict with excavations for the
project.

Attached find an itemized cost estimate, jobsite photos and
our drawing showing the location of the abandoned line.
This sewer line is not shown in the contract documents dated
March 1 , 1988, nor is it included in the Addenda.

This proposal is our request for a Change Order to reimburse us
for this work. Further, in accordance with the contract
documents, we request an extension of the Contract Time due
to this change. We estimate an additional three (3) days will
be required for completion of the project.

                              by_____
                                Robert Brown, President
                                Quality Construction Co.

cc: Mr. William Jones, President
    Typical Manufacturing Co.

CHANGE ORDER

AIA DOCUMENT G701

Distribution to:
OWNER ☒
ARCHITECT ☒
CONTRACTOR ☒
FIELD ☒
OTHER ☐

PROJECT: Typical Mfg. Co.Plant and Office
(name, address) 100 Industrial Blvd.
Hayward, California

TO (Contractor):

Mr. Robert Brown, President
Quality Construction Co.
300 First Ave.
Oakland, California

CHANGE ORDER NUMBER: 2

INITIATION DATE: June 7, 1988

ARCHITECT'S PROJECT NO: 87-116

CONTRACT FOR: The Construction of Industrial Plant and Offices

CONTRACT DATE: May 1, 1988

You are directed to make the following changes in this Contract:

Remove abandoned 10" diameter sewer line as required where encountered in excavation for basement, foundations, and other new construction. Sewer line was not shown on site plan and therefore not included in Contractor's base bid.

Reference: Quality Construction Co. Change Proposal #2
dated June 8, 1988........$20,000.00 TOTAL

Not valid until signed by both the Owner and Architect.
Signature of the Contractor indicates his agreement herewith, including any adjustment in the Contract Sum or Contract Time.

The original (Contract Sum) ~~(Guaranteed Maximum Cost)~~ was .... $ 10,000,000

Net change by previously authorized Change Orders .... $ 10,000

The (Contract Sum) ~~(Guaranteed Maximum Cost)~~ prior to this Change Order was .... $ 10,010,000

The (Contract Sum) ~~(Guaranteed Maximum Cost)~~ will be (increased) ~~(decreased) (unchanged)~~
by this Change Order .... $ 20,000

The new (Contract Sum) ~~(Guaranteed Maximum Cost)~~ including this Change Order will be ... $ 10,030,000

The Contract Time will be (increased) ~~(decreased) (unchanged)~~ by (2) Days.

The Date of Substantial Completion as of the date of this Change Order therefore is July 3, 1989

A B C Architects	Quality Construction Co.	Authorized: Typical Mfg. Co.
ARCHITECT	CONTRACTOR	OWNER
600 Main St.	300 First St.	950 Broadway Blvd.
Address	Address	Address
San Francisco, California	Oakland, California	Oakland, California
BY	BY	BY
Fank Smith, Principal	Robert Brown, President	William Jones, President
DATE June 10, 1988	DATE June 14, 1988	DATE June 17, 1988

AIA DOCUMENT G701 • CHANGE ORDER • APRIL 1978 EDITION • AIA® • © 1978
THE AMERICAN INSTITUTE OF ARCHITECTS, 1735 NEW YORK AVE., N.W., WASHINGTON, D.C. 20006

G701 — 1978

ARCHITECT'S SUPPLEMENTAL INSTRUCTIONS

Owner	☒
Architect	☒
Consultant	☐
Contractor	☒
Field	☒
Other	☐

AIA DOCUMENT G710 (Instructions on reverse side)

PROJECT: Typical Manufacturing Co.
(name, address) 100 Industrial Blvd.
Hayward, CA

OWNER: Typical Manufacturing Co.

TO: Mr. Robert Brown, President
(Contractor) Quality Construction Co.
300 First Ave.
Oakland, CA

CONTRACT FOR: Construction of
Industrial Plant and Offices

ARCHITECT'S SUPPLEMENTAL
INSTRUCTION NO: 8

DATE OF ISSUANCE: May 15, 1989

ARCHITECT: ABC Architects
600 Main St.
San Francisco, CA

ARCHITECT'S PROJECT NO: 87-116

The Work shall be carried out in accordance with the following supplemental instructions issued in accordance with the Contract Documents without change in Contract Sum or Contract Time. Prior to proceeding in accordance with these instructions, indicate your acceptance of these instructions for minor change to the Work as consistent with the Contract Documents and return a copy to the Architect.

Description:

As we discussed in our recent phone conversation, install Acme "Desert Beige" ceramic tile, mfg. #701, in lieu of Star "Chatum Tan" ceramic tile in the men's and women's toilet rooms.

You reported that Star Manufacturing Company's "Chatum Tan" ceramic tile is currently out of stock and unavailable for delivery.

Attachments: *(Here insert listing of documents that support description.)*

ISSUED:

BY

Architect Frank Smith, Principal
ABC Architects

ACCEPTED:

BY

Contractor Robert Brown, Pres.   Date May 16, 1989
Quality Construction Co.

CONSTRUCTION CHANGE
AUTHORIZATION

Owner	☒
Architect	☒
Consultant	☒
Contractor	☒
Field	☒
Other	☐

AIA DOCUMENT G713 (Instructions on reverse side)

PROJECT: (name, address) Typical Manufacturing Co. 100 Industrial Blvd. Hayward, CA

OWNER: Typical Manufacturing Co.

TO: (Contractor) Mr. Robert Brown, President Quality Construction Co. 300 First Ave. Oakland, CA

CONTRACT FOR: Construction of Industrial Plant and Offices

CONSTRUCTION CHANGE AUTHORIZATION NO: 4

DATE OF ISSUANCE: July 20, 1988

ARCHITECT: ABC Architects 600 Main St. San Francisco, CA

ARCHITECT'S PROJECT NO: 87-116

In order to expedite the Work and avoid or minimize delays in the Work which may affect Contract Sum or Contract Time, the Contract Documents are hereby amended as described below. Proceed with this Work promptly. Submit final costs for Work involved and change in Contract Time (if any), for inclusion in a subsequent Change Order.

Description: Remove silt encountered in excavation for foundation at column line B-3 and provide engineered fill. Contractor's estimate of silt to be removed: 100 cubic yards.

Attachments: *(Here insert listing of documents that support description.)*

The following is based on information provided by the Contractor:

Method of Determining Change in the Contract Sum: Excavation $4.50/C. Yd. Unit Price - Engineered fill $9.50/C.Yd.

(lump sum, unit prices, cost plus fee or other)

☐ Fixed
☒ Estimated } Change in Contract Sum of $ 1,400.00
☐ Maximum

☒ Fixed
☐ Estimated } Change in Contract Time of one (1)
☐ Maximum   days

ISSUED:	AUTHORIZED:	CONFIRMED:
BY	BY 7/20/88	BY 7/20/88
Architect	Owner Date	Contractor Date
Frank Smith, President	William Jones, President	Robert Brown, President
ABC Architects	Typical Manufacturing Co.	Quality Construction Co.

Testing

During the course of the project, the architect obtains and reviews required test reports and gets assistance from consultants as required. He and his consultants visit the site to observe specific tests as conditions warrant. He makes a field report of each test and keeps a record of the progress of the work.

When testing of the work or material is required by the Contract Documents, laws, ordinances, rules, regulations or orders of any public authority having jurisdiction over the project, the contractor must give the architect adequate notice so that he may observe such inspections or tests. The contractor must give notice in writing of the time, location and date of such tests. The contractor must pay for all testing required by local public agencies and the specifications.

When, in the opinion of the owner or architect, additional testing or inspections are required because of the manner in which the contractor executed the work, such tests and inspections are paid for by the owner. If the tests prove that the work fails to be in accordance with the requirements of the Contract Documents or local laws, the contractor must pay the cost of removal or correction and pay for any additional services required by the architect.

The contractor must secure required certificates of inspection, test reports or approvals and promptly deliver them to the architect. In addition, prompt observation of such required tests by the architect will avoid claims for delay by the contractor. Further, the contractor must make close visual inspection of all materials when delivered and promptly return all defective materials without waiting for their rejection by the architect.

Generally, the architect does not inspect and test materials. He should, however, observe the procedures used in tests specified or ordered by him. Tests are usually carried out by an independent testing laboratory selected by the owner. The specifications should indicate which materials are to be tested and give a detailed description of the testing required: how the results are reported, how material samples and specimens are to be obtained, how frequently the tests are to be made, and who will bear the costs of such tests and inspections.

On a typical project, areas of testing include: soil tests; concrete tests for compressive strength and workability; steel tests for yield strength; weld strength tests; masonry test walls for coursing and pattern; asphalt paving, roofing and sealants tests for proper weights and quantities of materials utilized; tests of windows for leakage; elevator load tests; and tests of mechanical and electrical equipment under actual working conditions.

Soil tests should be furnished by the owner and performed by an independent testing agency. Exploration methods consist of test pits, auger borings, wash borings, percussion drilling or rotary drilling. Samples are taken through means which include wash borings, representative samples (driven), undisturbed samples (forced), bailers and core samples. The soil is usually tested for standard penetration, moisture content, dry density, compression, and cohesion. A geotechnical engineer then determines the bearing capacity of the soil and develops a soil report. The architect and his structural engineering consultant base their designs on the contents and recommendations of the soil report.

HAZARDOUS MATERIALS

Note that testing may be required for hazardous materials that could be present on the project site. Such testing is particularly important in existing buildings to be renovated or for projects located on former industrial sites. The liability problems for architects that arise concerning hazardous materials are numerous. In general, architects have no specialized training in these areas. In addition, note that professional liability insurance policies do not include coverage in these areas. However, limited protection is offered under paragraph 9.8 of the AIA Owner-Architect Agreement which states that the architect and his consultants have no responsibility for the discovery, removal or exposure to persons to hazardous materials on the project site. Further, paragraphs 4.6 and 4.6.1 of the Owner-Architect Agreement state that the owner shall furnish the services of a geotechnical engineer and other consultants reasonably required, if they are requested by the architect. Therefore, where appropriate, the architect should go on record at the outset of the project recommending the retention of consultants and testing for hazardous materials. Even if the owner is unwilling to pay the expense for these services, such recommendations assist the architect's defense in the event of a claim for damages. Further, if the owner proceeds with such testing, the cost of removal or encapsulation can be estimated in advance and considered in the cost of the project.

Paragraph 10.1.2 of the AIA General Conditions outlines procedures to be followed if the contractor encounters either asbestos or PCB on the project site. Further, paragraph 10.1.3 provides that the contractor is not required to perform work in the presence of these two hazardous materials without consent. Recognize that the architect may become involved in this matter since paragraph 10.1.2 further states that work is resumed in the absence of asbestos or PCB, when it is rendered harmless, by written agreement of the owner and contractor, or, in accordance with final determination by the architect. If such determination is requested, the architect would in all likelihood request that the owner furnish the services of an independent consulting service for analysis, evaluation, recommendations and handling of any asbestos and/or PCB related problems that the contractor has encountered. Further, the architect may wish to consider this problem in advance and place supplemental provisions in the Owner-Architect Agreement stating specific procedures to be followed in the event that such a determination is requested of the architect.

To protect against potential claims, the architect may wish to consider including stronger statements disclaiming responsibility for hazardous materials in such supplemental provisions. For instance, the architect may state that the owner acknowledges that the architect's services do not include work related to detection, removal or disposal of hazardous materials. Furthermore, if the architect, owner, or contractor encounter hazardous materials on the project site or any adjacent areas that may affect the architect's services, the architect may temporarily suspend services. The architect's services may remain suspended until the site is certified to be free of hazardous materials. First, the owner provides the services of a special consultant to survey the site, verify the existence of hazardous materials and identify their location. The owner's special consultant will then prepare specifications and drawings for the removal of the hazardous materials discovered. Further, the special consultant will be required to make field observations in regard to the removal and disposal of such materials.

Also, the owner should be required to furnish a special contractor to remove the hazardous materials in accordance with the specifications and drawings prepared by the owner's special consultant. After completion of the work, the architect should not be required to visit the jobsite until the owner provides a certification, signed by the owner's special consultant, that the hazardous materials have been removed from the project site and the site does not contain concentrations of hazardous materials that exceed those allowed by local, state and federal regulations in force at the time of certification. In addition, since the architect is not performing services related to the discovery or removal of hazardous materials, the architect may wish to ask the owner to agree to indemnify, defend and hold the architect harmless from services performed by any special consultant or contractor hired by the owner to remove hazardous materials on the project.

It is important to understand that the testing laboratory and the geotechnical engineer are independent consultants to the owner. This is also true of the civil engineer who makes the topography and boundary survey for the site. In accordance with paragraph 4.9 of the AIA Owner-Architect Agreement, the architect may rely upon the accuracy and completeness of such information furnished by the owner. Therefore, the architect and his consultants may not be held liable for errors or held responsible for the correctness of the geotechnical report or site survey.

Certificates for Payment

Prior to submitting the first Application for Payment, the Contractor must submit a Schedule of Values which appropriates valuation to the various portions of the work. These values are then used as a basis for subsequent payments to the contractor as the work progresses and various portions are completed. A detailed Schedule of Values will greatly expedite the processing of Applications for Payment throughout the Construction Phase.

In order to reduce potential liability, the architect may only wish to certify documents for those to whom he owes this responsibility under contract. For example, the architect may be asked to certify progress payments by lending institutions. Also, the architect may be asked to certify that the construction has reached a certain percentage of completion by the owner's surety company. In spite of the fact that the architect has no contract with either the lending institution or the surety, he could incur liability if inaccurate or improper certification causes them financial loss. As outlined in paragraph 4.2.5 of the AIA General Conditions, it is the architect's responsibility to make field observations in order to evaluate the contractor's Application for Payment, certify the amounts due the contractor and issue Certificates for Payment to the owner. Therefore, the architect may wish to avoid providing Certificates for Payment to any party other than the owner under normal contract provisions.

At least fourteen days prior to the date upon which the owner is to make his progress payment, the contractor must submit an itemized Application for Payment. This application is usually made on the American Institute of Architects Application and Certificate for Payment, Document

G702. This form should be accompanied by supporting data to substantiate the contractor's claim, such as, payrolls, invoices, bills of sale, and so on. The form is convenient and complete and requires the contractor to list the original contract sum, the sum of the Change Orders to date, value of stored materials, the retained percentage, the total previous payments and the amount of current payment requested. By insisting on the submission of a detailed form and itemized supporting data, the architect is able to evaluate the form and ascertain the amount to be paid in an expeditious manner.

The amount due the contractor is based on the value of actual work performed, with the retained percentage deducted. For example, according to the contractor's Schedule of Values, the structural steel frame has a total value of $100,000. The contractor claims seventy-five percent completion for that portion of the work. Fifty percent completion had been claimed on previous applications. If the retained percentage is ten percent, his current payment due is twenty-five percent of $100,000 minus ten percent, which is $22,500. This valuation must be carefully determined. An inaccurate valuation may cause loss to either the owner or the contractor. In this case, the architect may be held liable for the loss.

The Application and Certificate for Payment form serves a dual purpose. It is both the contractor's Application for Payment and the architect's certification to the owner that to the best of the architect's knowledge, information and belief the work is in accordance with the Contract Documents, the work has progressed to the point indicated and the contractor is entitled to payment for that amount. The use of the combined form reduces the possibility for errors.

Evaluating the Application for Payment is one of the architect's most important responsibilities. In determining the amount to be paid the contractor on any Application for Payment, the architect should always verify that the value of the completed work has been calculated accurately by the contractor. In addition, the architect must verify that the retained percentage is deducted and the totals are correct and accurately computed.

Furthermore, it is the architect's responsibility to ascertain if there is any reason for withholding payment, such as non-conforming work which has not been corrected; evidence of the filing of third party claims; failure of the contractor to make payments to subcontractors, laborers, or to suppliers of materials and equipment; evidence that the work cannot be completed for the balance unpaid; notice of damage to the owner or another contractor; indication that the work cannot be completed within the contract time; or consistent failure to execute the work in conformance with the Contract Documents.

In addition, if payments are to be made for materials not incorporated in the work but delivered to and suitably stored on the site, the amounts should be carefully checked. Payments should be made only when applications are accompanied with bills of sale, receipts, invoices, etc. Payments are generally for seventy-five percent of the invoice amount.

Payments are sometimes made for materials suitably stored off the site if this arrangement is approved in advance by the owner. In this case, the stock should be checked periodically and the contractor must insure all materials against loss. This is important since title to all work, materials, supplies and equipment covered by an Application for Payment passes to the owner no later than receipt of payment by the contractor.

The architect must issue a Certificate for Payment to the owner within no more than seven days after the contractor's Application for Payment is received or notify the contractor he is withholding payment and state the reason in writing.

If the application is properly completed and deemed acceptable based on the architect's field observations and the contractor's supporting data, the architect certifies the application and transmits it to the owner. However, if the application contains amounts that cannot be verified by the architect or if there are errors or omissions in completion of the form, the architect must prepare a new form indicating the proper totals. This amended form is then transmitted to the owner and a copy transmitted to the contractor.

The architect does not represent that he has made extensive on-site inspections or reviewed construction means, methods, techniques or procedures in signing the Certificate. Further, the signing of a Certificate for Payment to the contractor does not indicate acceptance of work or materials that are not in conformance with the Contract Documents. In addition, the architect makes no representation that he has reviewed copies of invoices or other data received from subcontractors and material suppliers that were requested by the owner to substantiate the contractor's right to payment. Also, the architect is not required to determine how the contractor has used amounts previously paid on the contract sum.

The contractor must make payments to his subcontractors upon receiving payment from the owner. The payment must be an amount equal to the percentage of completion of the work less the retained percentage. In addition, should the architect withhold payment for a reason related to the general contractor but not to a subcontractor, the general contractor is still required to make payments to the subcontractor. For example, payment cannot be withheld from the electrical subcontractor because payment has been withheld from the general contractor for non-conforming partition construction.

As the project progresses, subcontractors or material suppliers may request information from the architect on the amounts the contractor has applied for and the percentage of completion claimed by the contractor for their portion of the work. The architect is required by paragraph 9.6.3 of the AIA General Conditions to provide this data to them if it is practicable. However, as indicated in paragraph 9.6.4, neither the architect nor the owner have any obligation to see that money is paid to subcontractors or material suppliers except as required by law.

If the architect fails to issue a Certificate for Payment, through no fault of the contractor, within seven days after receiving the Application for Payment; or if the owner does not pay the contractor within seven days after the date established in the Owner-Contractor Agreement, the contractor may stop the work seven days after submitting written notice to the owner. Further, the contractor may terminate the contract if the work is stopped for a 30 day period because the architect did not issue a Certificate for Payment and did not give notification to the contractor of the reason payment was withheld. Large projects may require longer processing periods. In this case, the time periods should be modified in the Supplementary Conditions.

There is one serious drawback to the progress payment process. Usually the contractor's Schedule of Values is divided up into a relatively small number of work categories. Since these categories are quite extensive, it is difficult to estimate the percentages of work completed. In addition, the contractor may inflate the value of work listed in the Schedule of Values which will be completed first, such as the foundations, in order to obtain a larger percentage of payout in the initial project stages. In addition, the contractor's estimate of the percentage of work completed tends to be overestimated.

Furthermore, it is difficult for the architect to verify these amounts. Actual field measurements of the work are very time consuming. Therefore, these percentages often must be rough estimates. It is the architect's responsibility to see that these estimates reasonably correspond to work completed. In cases where a defaulting contractor has received excessive progress payments, the surety often claims negligence on the part of the architect.

APPLICATION AND CERTIFICATE FOR PAYMENT *AIA DOCUMENT G702*

TO (OWNER): Typical Mfg. Co.
950 Broadway Blvd.
Oakland, California

PROJECT: Typical Mfg. Plant & Offices
100 Industrial Blvd.
Hayward, California

APPLICATION NO: 2

PERIOD TO: July 1, 1988

Distribution to:
[X] OWNER
[X] ARCHITECT
[X] CONTRACTOR
[ ]
[ ]

FROM (CONTRACTOR): Quality Construction Co.
300 First Ave.
Oakland, California

VIA (ARCHITECT): ABC Architects
600 Main Street
San Francisco, California

ARCHITECT'S
PROJECT NO: 87-116

CONTRACT FOR: Construction of Industrial Plant & Offices

CONTRACT DATE: May 1, 1988

Application is made for Payment, as shown below, in connection with the Contract. Continuation Sheet, AIA Document G703, is attached.

1. ORIGINAL CONTRACT SUM	$	10,000,000
2. Net change by Change Orders	$	30,000
3. CONTRACT SUM TO DATE (Line 1 ± 2)	$	10,030,000
4. TOTAL COMPLETED & STORED TO DATE	$	295,000

5. RETAINAGE:
a. 10 % of Completed Work $ 24,500 (Column D + E on G703)
b. 25 % of Stored Material $ 12,500 (Column F on G703)
Total Retainage (Line 5a + 5b or Total in Column I of G703)

6. TOTAL EARNED LESS RETAINAGE (Line 4 less Line 5 Total)	$	37,000
7. LESS PREVIOUS CERTIFICATES FOR PAYMENT (Line 6 from prior Certificate)		258,000
8. CURRENT PAYMENT DUE	$	108,000
9. BALANCE TO FINISH, PLUS RETAINAGE (Line 3 less Line 6)	$	150,000
		9,772,000

State of: California   County of: Alameda
Subscribed and sworn to before me this 1st day of July ,19 88
Notary Public: Susan Williams
My Commission expires: Jan. 1, 1990

CONTRACTOR'S APPLICATION FOR PAYMENT

CHANGE ORDER SUMMARY	ADDITIONS	DEDUCTIONS
Change Orders approved in previous months by Owner TOTAL One (1)	$10,000	0

Approved this Month

Number	Date Approved		
2	6/17/88	$20,000	
TOTALS		$30,000	0
Net change by Change Orders	+ $30,000	

The undersigned Contractor certifies that to the best of the Contractor's knowledge, information and belief the Work covered by this Application for Payment has been completed in accordance with the Contract Documents, that all amounts have been paid by the Contractor for Work for which previous Certificates for Payment were issued and payments received from the Owner, and that current payment shown herein is now due.

CONTRACTOR: Quality Construction Co.
Robert Brown, President

By: _____ Date: July 2, 1988

ARCHITECT'S CERTIFICATE FOR PAYMENT

AMOUNT CERTIFIED .... $ 150,000
(Attach explanation if amount certified differs from the amount applied for.)
ARCHITECT: ABC Architects, Frank Smith, Principal

By: _____ Date: July 5, 1988

In accordance with the Contract Documents, based on on-site observations and the data comprising the above application, the Architect certifies to the Owner that to the best of the Architect's knowledge, information and belief the Work has progressed as indicated, the quality of the Work is in accordance with the Contract Documents, and the Contractor is entitled to payment of the AMOUNT CERTIFIED.

This Certificate is not negotiable. The AMOUNT CERTIFIED is payable only to the Contractor named herein. Issuance, payment and acceptance of payment are without prejudice to any rights of the Owner or Contractor under this Contract.

CONTINUATION SHEET

AIA DOCUMENT G703

AIA Document G702, APPLICATION AND CERTIFICATE FOR PAYMENT, containing Contractor's signed Certification is attached.
In tabulations below, amounts are stated to the nearest dollar.
Use Column I on Contracts where variable retainage for line items may apply.

A	B	C	D	E	F	G	H	I
ITEM NO.	DESCRIPTION OF WORK	SCHEDULED VALUE	WORK COMPLETED FROM PREVIOUS APPLICATION (D+E)	THIS PERIOD	MATERIALS PRESENTLY STORED (NOT IN D OR E)	TOTAL COMPLETED AND STORED TO DATE (D+E+F)	% (G÷C)	BALANCE TO FINISH (C−G)	RETAINAGE
1.	Temporary Facilities Field Office Barricades Temp. Utilities	15,000	10,000	5,000	0	15,000	100	0	1,500
2.	Site Work Demolition Clearing of Site Excavation & Fill	300,000	100,000	100,000	0	200,000	67	100,000	20,000
3.	Change Order #1	10,000	10,000	0		10,000	100	0	1,000
4.	Change Order #2	20,000	0	20,000	0	20,000	100	0	2,000
5.	Concrete Reinforcing steel stored on site	500,000	0	0	50,000	50,000	10	450,000	12,500
	Sub Total or Total	845,000	120,000	125,000	50,000	295,000		550,000	37,000

Certificate of Substantial Completion

As outlined in paragraph 9.8.2 of the AIA General Conditions, when the project nears completion, the contractor prepares a statement claiming substantial completion along with a list of items to be completed or corrected and submits this to the architect. The architect verifies the list through field observations and adds items to the list as required. The omission of any item on this list does not alleviate the responsibility of the contractor to complete all work in accordance with the Contract Documents.

When the project is substantially completed in accordance with the Contract Documents so that the owner can utilize the project for the use for which it is intended, the architect prepares a Certificate of Substantial Completion for the written approval and acceptance of the contractor and the owner. Attached is a list of items to be completed or corrected. In addition, the architect makes a determination of a reasonable period of time necessary for the contractor to complete his work after the Date of Substantial Completion. Furthermore, the architect establishes the exact Date of Substantial Completion. In addition, the responsibilities of the owner and contractor in regard to security, maintenance, heat, utilities, damages and insurance are stated on the certificate. The form most widely used for this purpose is the American Institute of Architects Document G704, Certificate of Substantial Completion.

The Date of Substantial Completion has legal significance. It is the date upon which the guarantee period starts. Therefore, the architect must use caution before issuing such a certificate to ascertain that the work is in conformance with the definition of substantial completion contained in the Contract Documents. Paragraph 9.8.2 of the AIA General Conditions states that upon receipt of the contractor's list of items to be corrected, the architect "will make an inspection." Recognize that the word "inspection" denotes a more extensive process than what the architect does during field observations when he determines the progress of the work and issues Certificates for Payment.

If the architect does not agree with the contractor's claim of substantial completion because his own inspection indicates that the project is not in a state of completion so that the owner may utilize or occupy it, he amends the list of items to be corrected provided by the contractor and notifies him. A subsequent inspection is then scheduled, for which the contractor prepares a revised list of items to be completed or corrected.

The provisions of the AIA General Conditions relating to substantial completion leave the interpretation of this term to the architect. Generally, this means that any work left to be completed or corrected is of a relatively minor nature. Therefore, the contractor can complete or correct all that remains while the owner occupies the project. For example, a light fixture may have a cracked plastic diffuser, an electrical outlet may not be operable in one location, paint may be chipped and need retouching and HVAC equipment may be operating but need slight readjusting. In these cases, the owner could use the project while waiting for the contractor to receive replacement parts, touch up paint, adjust equipment, and so on. The architect should ensure that there is sufficient retainage held by the owner to cover all items to be completed or corrected after substantial completion.

The architect should make it clear that he will not make special inspections to determine the Date of Substantial Completion until there is reason to indicate that the project is in a sufficient state of completion that the owner may in fact occupy the work for the use for which it is intended. Often contractors will claim substantial completion prematurely in order to obtain the architect's inspections of their work to determine deficiencies.

This is the responsibility of the contractor's superintendent. In addition, an early start of the guarantee period is contrary to the owner's interests. Further, on the Date of Substantial Completion, the contractor is generally relieved of charges for any liquidated damages that may be a part of the contract.

Upon certification by the architect of substantial completion, the owner must make payment, reflecting an adjustment in retainage as provided in the Owner-Contractor Agreement. The amount due, including previous payments, is often an amount sufficient to bring the total payments to date up to ninety percent of the contract sum.

Note that the responsibilities of the owner and contractor for security, maintenance, heat, utilities, damages to the work and insurance are listed at the bottom of the AIA Certificate of Substantial Completion Form. Since these important responsibilities generally pass to the owner at this time, it is important to ensure that the owner recognizes the significance of this important document. Both the owner's and contractor's insurance counsel should review the document and determine insurance requirements and coverage prior to its execution. Further, the contractor should be required to obtain the consent of the surety company if bonds were provided for the project. In essence, much of the risk of loss shifts to the owner immediately after the time and date of substantial completion.

Paragraph 9.9.1 of the AIA General Conditions states that the owner may occupy any completed or partially completed portion of the work at any stage upon the condition that the portion utilized is designated by separate agreement with the contractor, consented to by the insurer and authorized by public authorities. Further, the owner and contractor must accept in writing the responsibilities assigned to each of them for payments, retainage, security, maintenance, heat, utilities, damage to the work, insurance, commencement of warranties and time for correction of deficiencies. Then, when the contractor considers the work substantially complete, the contractor submits a list of items to be corrected and the architect follows the provisions of paragraph 9.8.2 for determining substantial completion.

As outlined in the AIA General Conditions, the contractor's consent to such partial occupancy shall not be reasonably withheld. The owner and contractor must make a written agreement regarding the stage of progress of the work. If an agreement cannot be reached, the decision is made by the architect. Also, before partial occupancy the owner, architect and contractor inspect the area to be occupied in order to establish a written record of the condition of the work.

During the construction of a large project, the owner may wish to occupy a portion of the facility. For example, the office and administrative area of a manufacturing plant could be occupied well before the manufacturing area is completed. However, a number of serious problems can develop as a result of this partial occupancy. This could interfere with the contractor's work and therefore affect the construction schedule. The owner's and contractor's insurance coverages could be affected. Further, it could affect claims the owner may have for work that does not conform to the requirements of the Contract Documents. Therefore, the architect may wish to advise the owner of these potential problems related to partial occupancy since the number of claims and disputes generally increase as a result of such partial occupancy.

For instance, defective work found after occupancy often becomes disputed in regard to who is responsible for the problem. Equipment malfunctions are often claimed to be caused by improper maintenance by the owner. The security of the site and the responsibility of safety on the site are not clearly defined issues since the actions of either the owner's or contractor's personnel can affect the other party's personnel. The dates of the commencement of warranties may also become issues of dispute.

CERTIFICATE OF SUBSTANTIAL COMPLETION

AIA DOCUMENT G704

Distribution to:
OWNER ☒
ARCHITECT ☒
CONTRACTOR ☒
FIELD ☒
OTHER ☐

PROJECT: Typical Mfg. Co. Plant & Office
(name, address) 100 Industrial Blvd.
Hayward, California

ARCHITECT: ABC Architects

ARCHITECT'S PROJECT NUMBER: 87-116

TO (Owner):

William Jones, President
Typical Manufacturing Co.
950 Broadway Blvd.
Oakland, California

CONTRACTOR: Quality Construction Co.

CONTRACT FOR: Construction of Industrial Plant and Offices

CONTRACT DATE: May 1, 1988

DATE OF ISSUANCE: June 27, 1989

PROJECT OR DESIGNATED PORTION SHALL INCLUDE: Entire project, building and site

The Work performed under this Contract has been reviewed and found to be substantially complete. The Date of Substantial Completion of the Project or portion thereof designated above is hereby established as **July 1, 1989**

which is also the date of commencement of applicable warranties required by the Contract Documents, except as stated below.

DEFINITION OF DATE OF SUBSTANTIAL COMPLETION

The Date of Substantial Completion of the Work or designated portion thereof is the Date certified by the Architect when construction is sufficiently complete, in accordance with the Contract Documents, so the Owner can occupy or utilize the Work or designated portion thereof for the use for which it is intended, as expressed in the Contract Documents.

A list of items to be completed or corrected, prepared by the Contractor and verified and amended by the Architect, is attached hereto. The failure to include any items on such list does not alter the responsibility of the Contractor to complete all Work in accordance with the Contract Documents. The date of commencement of warranties for items on the attached list will be the date of final payment unless otherwise agreed to in writing.

ABC Architects		6/27/89
ARCHITECT	BY Frank Smith, Principal	DATE

The Contractor will complete or correct the Work on the list of items attached hereto within **thirty** days from the above Date of Substantial Completion.

Quality Construction Co.		6/28/89
CONTRACTOR	BY Robert Brown, President	DATE

The Owner accepts the Work or designated portion thereof as substantially complete and will assume full possession thereof at **8 AM** (time) on **July 1, 1989** (date).

Typical Manufacturing Co.		6/30/89
OWNER	BY William Jones, President	DATE

The responsibilities of the Owner and the Contractor for security, maintenance, heat, utilities, damage to the Work and insurance shall be as follows:

(Note—Owner's and Contractor's legal and insurance counsel should determine and review insurance requirements and coverage; Contractor shall secure consent of surety company, if any.)

Security, maintenance, heat, utilities, and insurance to be Owner's responsibility after 8 AM, July 1, 1989.

Final Punch List

The contractor notifies the architect that the work is ready for a preliminary final inspection to be performed for the purpose of determining the state of completion of the project. From the information gathered from this inspection the architect prepares a final punch list of work to be performed, corrected or completed before the project will be accepted. All work should be completed on the punch list prior to final inspection. In addition, the architect verifies that all items on the list attached to the Certificate of Substantial Completion have been corrected.

Recognize that the architect should make careful field observations at intervals appropriate to the stage of construction as the work progresses. Further, the architect should inform the contractor and owner in writing of deviations from the requirements of the Contract Documents as they are discovered, rather than waiting to place them on the final punch list. Therefore, if these procedures are followed and construction deficiencies are corrected on a regular basis throughout the Construction Phase, the number of items noted for correction on the final punch list will be minimized and the project closeout process will be completed in an expeditious manner.

As the contractor completes the items listed, he is required to submit to the architect all required operating instructions, a keying schedule and all keys, written guarantees, certificates of inspection, equipment test reports, maintenance stock, record drawings, and bonds. Upon receiving the contractor's written notice that all work has been completed, the architect checks the final punch list for the project to ensure that all items have been completed and corrected.

Upon checking the punch list at the project site, the architect may determine that some items of work still have not been completed or corrected. In this case, the process should be completed again with a new punch list at a later date until all listed items have been completed in accordance with the requirements of the Contract Documents. Every punch list that is prepared should be signed by the person that made the field inspection and prepared the punch list. Also, the time and date should be recorded on the form. Each item for completion or correction on the first list should be given a number and explained in sufficient detail so there will be no misunderstanding as to what is required before the item is considered corrected or complete. If necessary, references can be made to the specifications, drawings or other documents.

Each subsequent punch list should have only those items remaining to be completed or corrected listed on it. Items satisfactorily completed from the first list should be dropped off. However, the same item numbers that were assigned on the first list should be retained to ensure identification and continuity. Upon receiving notification from the contractor that these items have been corrected, items still requiring correction are reinspected and any tests that showed unsatisfactory results are conducted again. If items that were not on the first list are discovered later, they are simply added to the list and given consecutive numbers that follow the last number on the first list.

At this time the architect should verify that all temporary facilities have been removed from the site. In addition, he should verify that the building is thoroughly clean and all construction debris has been removed from the site.

The architect should ensure that all plumbing and mechanical equipment is operating freely and is free from vibration. Equipment producing objectionable noise or vibration should be adjusted, repaired, balanced, or replaced. All systems should operate without humming, surging or rapid cycling. Testing should include not only equipment, but also communication systems, life safety systems and other emergency devices. Often these items are tested by outside agencies. The architect observes the testing and reviews the test reports in these cases.

All operating instructions for equipment should have been delivered to the owner or posted as required in the specifications. In addition, if called for in the specifications, the architect should ensure that the contractor has instructed the owner's personnel in the use, operation and care of complex mechanical and electrical equipment. This is an important item in complex projects such as hospitals or industrial facilities for which maintenance personnel are required to oversee large amounts of new equipment.

The architect should verify that a copy of the keying schedule and all keys have been delivered to the owner. The keys should all be properly marked and tagged. Furthermore, all locksets should be checked through key operation. At this time, doors should be operated and closers checked to ensure that they function properly and swing in the proper direction.

The architect should check to see that all warranties and guarantees issued by appliance and equipment manufacturers have been forwarded to the owner. In addition, guarantees and warranties by subcontractors or suppliers should be forwarded to the owner and placed in his files. These guarantees are customarily prepared in triplicate, signed and transmitted to the owner, architect and contractor.

In addition, maintenance stock such as paint, carpeting, vinyl tile, and ceiling tile should have been properly stored in the maintenance storage area of the project. Quantities of these items should be as called for in the specifications.

Further, the architect should verify that completed and signed as-built drawings have been submitted by the contractor, if these were required by the owner. As-built drawings reflect conditions as actually built. Note that the architect may also be asked by the owner to provide a set of as- built drawings. This may be requested by the owner to be a part of the architect's contractual obligations that are included in the Owner-Architect Agreement or be requested by the owner after completion of the project. Recognize that the contractor may make changes during the construction of the project that deviate from the original Contract Documents. Such changes may entail items that are concealed such as routing of ducts, piping and electrical conduit.

For this reason, the original Contract Documents may no longer reflect actual conditions. Furthermore, the architect generally visits the site at intervals appropriate to the stage of construction and is not on the project site at all times. For this reason the architect is unaware of every deviation from the original documents and in addition, these deviations are now concealed. Recognize that the architect could incur potential liability by certifying drawings to be as-builts when he is not actually aware of concealed conditions. For example, during construction the contractor routes electrical conduit through a wall in a location other than that specified by the Contract Documents. Later, a maintenance worker drills into what "as-built" drawings certified by the architect show to be a typical wall. The worker drills into the conduit and is injured. The architect would almost certainly incur liability.

Therefore, if as-builts are required, the Contract Documents should require the contractor to record deviations from the original documents, sign these and transmit a set of marked up documents, reflecting actual conditions, to the architect at completion of the project. Further, the architect should clearly note on the drawings that these simply reflect a record of changes indicated by the contractor and are based only on this representation. In addition, the architect should include a statement in the

Owner-Architect Agreement or any subsequent agreement that such drawings are based on the representation of others and the architect disclaims any further responsibility for their accuracy. Also, these drawings should be referred to as "record drawings" and not "as-built drawings."

After the above noted items have been completed and all construction deficiencies corrected, the contractor notifies the architect, submits his final Application for Payment, and requests the final inspection. The contractor and his principal subcontractors generally accompany the architect and owner on their final inspection tour. If the work has been completed in accordance with the Contract Documents and no corrective measures are required, and all the contract obligations have been fulfilled, the owner accepts the project.

Final Payment to Contractor

When the work is ready for final inspection and acceptance, the contractor notifies the architect in writing and submits his final Application for Payment as outlined in paragraphs 9.10.1 and 9.10.2 of the AIA General Conditions.

The contractor makes his application for final payment on the same form as in the case of progress payments. Additional requirements with which the contractor must comply prior to the architect's issuing a final Certificate for Payment include the submittal to the architect of the Contractor's Affidavit of Release of Liens; a separate Affidavit of Release of Liens for all subcontractors, material suppliers and others who have lien rights against the property together with a list of the same; the Contractor's Affidavit of Payment of Debts and Claims stating that all payrolls, bills for material and equipment, and other work for which the owner might be held responsible have been paid; and the Consent of Surety Company to Final Payment. Furthermore, the contractor must provide a certificate stating that insurance which is required to remain in force after the final payment is in effect and will not be cancelled without 30 day's written notice. In addition, the contractor must submit a written statement that he knows of no reason that the insurance will not be renewable.

The Contractor's Affidavit of Release of Liens is typically made on the American Institute of Architects Document G706A. The Contractor's Affidavit of Payment of Debts and Claims is typically made on American Institute of Architects Document G706. These forms are designed expressly for this purpose. They greatly expedite proper evaluation of these documents and reduce possibility for errors or omissions.

In signing these documents, the contractor certifies that to the best of his knowledge, information, and belief, the release of liens submitted cover all persons who have lien rights against the owner's property arising out of the construction contract. The contractor must be required to list any exceptions to this general statement and furnish a lien bond to protect the owner against each exception. The contractor may be required by the owner to submit other data such as invoices and payment receipts. Such data should be named in the Supplementary Conditions.

After the contractor submits his final Application for Payment, supported by all the required documents called for in paragraph 9.10.2 of the AIA General Conditions, the architect makes a final check with proper governmental offices of the jurisdiction to verify that no liens have been filed against the property, the contract sum has been adjusted to reflect all additions and deductions included on change orders or liquidated damages, etc., and that all written guarantees and certificates of inspection have been delivered to the owner. In addition, the owner should be asked if he has any valid reason the certificate should not be issued.

If, upon making the final inspection, the architect finds the work fully completed in accordance with the Contract Documents, and all the contract obligations have been fulfilled, he issues a final Certificate for Payment. In so doing, he certifies that to the best of his knowledge, information and belief, and on the basis of his field observations and inspections, the work has been completed in accordance with the Contract Documents. Before acceptance, all work should be installed and complete and the workmanship should meet the standards of the specifications. Further, all systems and equipment should be operational and should have met the test requirements of the Contract Documents.

However, upon making the final inspection, there may be one or two minor items remaining on the final punch list that still have not been corrected or completed in accordance with the requirements of the Contract Documents. If the rest of the work has been completed satisfactorily, the architect notes the uncompleted items, estimates the cost of the work involved and informs the owner in writing. If a reduction in the retained percentage is contemplated through a partial release of the funds still held by the owner, the consent of the surety should be obtained if there are bonds on the project. A form for this purpose is AIA Document G707A, Consent of Surety to Reduction In or Partial Release of Retainage. Final payment of the retainage should be made only after the period for filing mechanics liens has elapsed and after deducting an amount that will adequately cover the cost of completing any items that still have not been corrected or completed in accordance with the Contract Documents. Some architects double the estimated cost of completing these items in order to ensure that the contractor will correct these items. Recognize that the Release of Liens that are required for final payment do not apply to the unfinished portion of the work.

Furthermore, work that was satisfactorily completed and accepted may be damaged during the owner's move-in. In addition, the owner's own work forces or separate contractors hired by the owner may damage previously accepted work. It will be the owner's responsibility to repair such damaged work. Therefore, repair costs for work damaged by the owner should not be withheld from the final payment to the contractor. If the owner requests that the contractor repair such damaged work, the contractor should be reimbursed and the procedures for Change Orders should be followed.

The date final payment is due is frequently thirty-five days after the Date of Substantial Completion. (It is desirable to withhold final payment until the period for filing mechanic's liens has elapsed. Check with local regulations for the exact time period for filing liens. These laws vary from state to state.) This is generally sufficient time for final completion of the work and correction of non-conforming items. This time period is binding only if the work is fully completed in accordance with the Contract Documents.

The architect should use caution in certifying release of the retained percentage. Its purpose is to guard the owner against mechanic's lien claims and to ensure that adequate funds remain to pay another contractor to correct or complete items that are not in accordance with the requirements of the Contract Documents should the contractor fail to complete those items.

As outlined in paragraph 4.3.5 of the AIA General Conditions, in making final payment to the contractor, the owner waives all claims except those from unsettled liens, defective work appearing after substantial completion, failure of the work to comply with the Contract Documents, and terms of special warranties. As outlined in paragraph 9.10.4 of the AIA General Conditions, in accepting final payment, the contractor waives all claims except those made in writing and unsettled at the time of the final Application for Payment. Any such claims made by the contractor should be clearly defined, since most of the potential disputes over decisions made by the architect are waived when the contractor accepts final payment.

CONTRACTOR'S AFFIDAVIT OF PAYMENT OF DEBTS AND CLAIMS

AIA Document G706

OWNER ☒
ARCHITECT ☒
CONTRACTOR ☒
SURETY ☒
OTHER

1. AIA copyrighted material has been reproduced with the permission of The American Institute of Architects under permission number 88015. Further reproduction is prohibited.
2. Because AIA Documents are revised from time to time, users should ascertain from the AIA the current edition of the Document reproduced herein.
3. Copies of the current edition of this AIA Document may be purchased from The American Institute of Architects or its local distributors.

TO (Owner)

Mr. William Jones, President
Typical Manufacturing Co.
950 Broadway Blvd.
Oakland, California

ARCHITECT'S PROJECT NO: 87-116

CONTRACT FOR: Construction of Industrial Plant and Offices

CONTRACT DATE: May 1, 1988

PROJECT: Typical Manufacturing Co. Plant and Offices
(name, address) 100 Industrial Blvd., Hayward, California

State of: California
County of: Alameda

The undersigned, pursuant to Article 9 of the General Conditions of the Contract for Construction, AIA Document A201, hereby certifies that, except as listed below, he has paid in full or has otherwise satisfied all obligations for all materials and equipment furnished, for all work, labor, and services performed, and for all known indebtedness and claims against the Contractor for damages arising in any manner in connection with the performance of the Contract referenced above for which the Owner or his property might in any way be held responsible.

EXCEPTIONS: (If none, write "None". If required by the Owner, the Contractor shall furnish bond satisfactory to the Owner for each exception.)

None

SUPPORTING DOCUMENTS ATTACHED HERETO:

1. **Consent of Surety to Final Payment. Whenever Surety is involved, Consent of Surety is required. AIA DOCUMENT G707, CONSENT OF SURETY, may be used for this purpose.**
   Indicate attachment: (yes X) (no).

The following supporting documents should be attached hereto if required by the Owner:

1. Contractor's Release or Waiver of Liens, conditional upon receipt of final payment.

2. Separate Releases or Waivers of Liens from Subcontractors and material and equipment suppliers, to the extent required by the Owner, accompanied by a list thereof.

3. Contractor's Affidavit of Release of Liens (AIA DOCUMENT G706A).

CONTRACTOR: Quality Construction Co.

Address: 300 First Ave.
Oakland, California

BY: Robert Brown, President

Subscribed and sworn to before me this
Fifteenth day of July 19 89

Notary Public: Susan Williams

My Commission Expires: Jan. 1, 1990

CONTRACTOR'S AFFIDAVIT OF RELEASE OF LIENS

AIA DOCUMENT G706A

OWNER
ARCHITECT
CONTRACTOR
SURETY
OTHER

[X]
[X]
[X]

TO (Owner)

Mr. Williams Jones, President
Typical Manufacturing Co.
950 Broadway Blvd.
Oakland, California

ARCHITECT'S PROJECT NO: 87-116

CONTRACT FOR: Construction of Industrial Plant and Offices

CONTRACT DATE: May 1, 1988

PROJECT: Typical Manufacturing Co. Plant and Offices
(name, address) 100 Industrial Blvd., Hayward, California

State of: California
County of: Alameda

The undersigned, pursuant to Article 9 of the General Conditions of the Contract for Construction, AIA Document A201, hereby certifies that to the best of his knowledge, information and belief, except as listed below, the Releases or Waivers of Lien attached hereto include the Contractor, all Subcontractors, all suppliers of materials and equipment, and all performers of Work, labor or services who have or may have liens against any property of the Owner arising in any manner out of the performance of the Contract referenced above.

EXCEPTIONS: (If none, write "None". If required by the Owner, the Contractor shall furnish bond satisfactory to the Owner for each exception.)

None

SUPPORTING DOCUMENTS ATTACHED HERETO:

1. Contractor's Release or Waiver of Liens, conditional upon receipt of final payment.

2. Separate Releases or Waivers of Liens from Subcontractors and material and equipment suppliers, to the extent required by the Owner, accompanied by a list thereof.

CONTRACTOR: Quality Construction Co.

Address: 300 First Ave.
Oakland, California

BY: Robert Brown, President

Subscribed and sworn to before me this

Fifteenth day of July 19 89

Notary Public: Susan Williams

My Commission Expires: Jan. 1, 1990

CONSENT OF SURETY COMPANY TO FINAL PAYMENT

AIA DOCUMENT G707

OWNER	[X]
ARCHITECT	[X]
CONTRACTOR	[X]
SURETY	[X]
OTHER	

1. AIA copyrighted material has been reproduced with the permission of The American Institute of Architects under permission number 88015. Further reproduction is prohibited.
2. Because AIA Documents are revised from time to time, users should ascertain from the AIA the current edition of the Document reproduced herein.
3. Copies of the current edition of this AIA Document may be purchased from The American Institute of Architects or its local distributors.

PROJECT: Typical Manufacturing Co. Plant and Offices
(name, address) 100 Industrial Blvd., Hayward, California

TO (Owner)

Mr. William Jones, President
Typical Manufacturing Co.
950 Broadway Blvd.
Oakland, California

ARCHITECT'S PROJECT NO: 87-116

CONTRACT FOR: Construction of Industrial Plant and Offices

CONTRACT DATE: May 1, 1988

CONTRACTOR: Quality Construction Co.

In accordance with the provisions of the Contract between the Owner and the Contractor as indicated above, the
(here insert name and address of Surety Company)

Standard Surety Co.   , SURETY COMPANY,
120 Commercial Dr., San Francisco, California
on bond of (here insert name and address of Contractor)

Quality Construction Co.   , CONTRACTOR,
300 First Ave., Oakland, California
hereby approves of the final payment to the Contractor, and agrees that final payment to the Contractor shall not relieve the Surety Company of any of its obligations to (here insert name and address of Owner)

Typical Manufacturing Co.   , OWNER,
950 Broadway Blvd., Oakland, California
as set forth in the said Surety Company's bond.

IN WITNESS WHEREOF,
the Surety Company has hereunto set its hand this **thirty first** day of **July** 19 **89**

Standard Surety Co.
_____
Surety Company

_____
Signature of Authorized Representative   John Doe

Bonding Officer
_____
Title

Attest:
(Seal):

NOTE: This form is to be used as a companion document to AIA DOCUMENT G706, CONTRACTOR'S AFFIDAVIT OF PAYMENT OF DEBTS AND CLAIMS, Current Edition

Mechanic's Lien Laws

Mechanic's lien laws vary from state to state. While they are generally similar, they differ in details. For this reason, the architect must be familiar with the laws of the state where the project is to be constructed. In addition, laws change from time to time by legislative action or court decision. Therefore, the architect should be up to date on the most recent laws and seek the advice of legal counsel as required regarding specific facts in a particular jurisdiction. The following general statements are consistent with lien laws in many states; however, local regulations must be checked in regard to mechanic's lien laws in all cases. The same holds true for stop notices and the Certificate of Occupancy which are discussed in the latter parts of this chapter.

A lien is a claim against a property. Mechanic's liens are claims imposed on a property for the value of labor and materials furnished for improvement of another's property. Since it is not possible for laborers or material suppliers to remove labor or materials incorporated into the structure, statutory regulations give a claimant the right to file a lien on the property or the construction funds. This provides security for the claim if it is substantiated in court. When a lien is perfected, the property is bound for the value of labor and materials furnished similar to the way a mortgage or deed-of-trust secures a loan.

In essence, a subcontractor, laborer or material supplier who has performed labor or furnished materials may file a lien on the property if not paid for his services by the prime contractor. Furthermore, in many states these parties may file liens on the owner's property, even though the owner has already made payment for their services to the prime contractor. Obviously, the prime contractor may also file a lien if not paid by the owner.

To protect his interests, the owner would like to see subcontractors and material suppliers that were listed as a part of the contractor's Application for Payment, to be paid by the contractor as soon as the contractor receives his payment. Payments to subcontractors and material suppliers should not be withheld by the contractor without justification as this can result in a mechanic's lien being filed on the owner's project.

The AIA General Conditions seek to protect the owner from this possibility in several instances. As outlined in paragraph 9.6.2, the contractor shall promptly pay each subcontractor. Also, paragraph 9.3.1.2 states that the contractor's Application for Payment may not include requests for payment of amounts related to a subcontractor or a material supplier if the contractor does not intend to pay the subcontractor or supplier because of a dispute.

Furthermore, protection is offered the architect from possible claims by the owner by paragraph 9.4.2. As outlined, the issuance of a Certificate for Payment does not constitute that the architect has reviewed copies of requisitions from subcontractors or suppliers and other data requested by the owner to substantiate the contractor's right to payment. Neither is the architect required to determine for what purpose the contractor has used money previously paid. In addition, as stated in paragraph 9.6.4, neither the owner nor architect have the obligation to pay or see to the payment of money to a subcontractor except as required by law. However, as outlined in paragraph 9.6.3, if practicable, the architect will furnish to a subcontractor on request, information on amounts applied for by the contractor and action taken for the portion of work done by the subcontractor.

To further protect the owner, legal procedures for perfecting claims have been established in every state. First, there is a limited time period in which liens can be filed after completion of the work. This time period varies from state to state. A mechanic's lien has to be filed within the specified time period after the last labor is furnished or the last material is delivered to the jobsite, or the right to file a lien is lost. The lien claim must be recorded with proper governmental authorities in the county where the property is located. In some states, the claimant must file suit to foreclose a mechanic's lien within a specific time period.

Secondly, in many states subcontractors and material suppliers must file a "Preliminary Notice" of their intent to file a lien with the owner, prime contractor and construction lender prior to actually filing a lien. The prime contractor and, in some cases, laborers need only to record a lien within a given time period and do not have to file "Preliminary Notice."

This "Preliminary Notice" must be filed within a given number of days after first performing labor or delivering materials to the jobsite. Late notice may cover labor or materials delivered within a specified time period prior to filing the notice. (This time period is 20 days in some states.)

Furthermore, the "Preliminary Notice" must contain an identification of the project, name and address of claimant, description and value of work performed or materials furnished, name of person who contracted for the labor or materials and a short statement. The statement informs the owner that if the claimant is not paid for his services, a lien will be filed on the property. The owner can then withhold final payment from the prime contractor until receiving sworn statements that all parties who filed "Preliminary Notice" have been paid. This is generally in the form of an Affidavit of Release of Liens from the contractor, all subcontractors and all material suppliers.

In addition to requiring Affidavits of Release of Liens and paid receipts, an Affidavit of Payment of Debts and Claims should be received prior to release of the retained percentage. This document states that the contractor has paid in full for all materials and equipment, work, labor and services performed and all known indebtedness for damages. This sworn statement offers the owner considerable protection that all laborers and material suppliers have been paid but is not an absolute guarantee that all laborers have been paid by their employers.

Therefore, it is desirable to withhold payment of the retained percentage until the period of time for filing liens has elapsed. This period of time generally starts on the date the owner files the Notice of Completion with the County Recorder. This is usually the same date as the Date of Substantial Completion. Note that if there is no Notice of Completion recorded, the specified time period for filing liens is often extended. In this case, the time period for withholding final payment should be adjusted accordingly.

When suits are filed to forclose mechanic's liens, a court may take the retained percentage due to contractor and use to pay parties with valid claims. Any additional amount required may be taken from bonds posted by the contractor. If funds are still insufficient, judgment may be obtained for sale of the property and the proceeds used to satisfy the liens.

Where there is a dispute as to validity of claims, final payment often need not be withheld from the contractor if he files a bond equal to 1 1/2 times the amount of the claim. Generally, suits must be filed to have disputed claims settled in court within a stipulated time period. In addition, liens may be settled by payment of claims and proper notification to the County Recorder.

A lien cannot be filed on public property. Material suppliers, laborers, and contractors are protected by filing a "stop notice" with proper governmental authorities. The stop notice places a claim on funds held by the owner or construction lender. The mechanic's lien places a claim on the property and improvements on the property and therefore may be used only on private projects. The stop notice may be used on both public work and private work. Stop notice regulations, like mechanic's lien laws, must be checked for each particular jurisdiction.

Generally, persons who may file mechanic's liens may file stop notices with the exception of the prime contractor. Upon receiving notification from a subcontractor or material supplier of not having been paid, the construction lender either is required to stop making further payments to the contractor or must assume the risk of proceeding with payments. A stop notice only attaches funds which have not been paid out by the owner to the prime contractor. The same rules for filing "Preliminary Notice" for mechanic's liens generally apply to stop notices. A suit to foreclose a stop notice must be filed within a given period. If judgment is made in favor of the claimant, the funds held by the owner or lender are used to settle the claim.

In public works projects, the "Preliminary Notice" must often be served within a stipulated period from the date of first delivering materials or furnishing labor, or the right to file a stop notice is lost. Service of the stop notice is usually to the head of the department which awarded the contract for construction or the public official who makes payments under the contract. Service on private projects is to the owner or construction lender.

If a Certificate of Occupancy or Occupancy Permit is required by a building code or zoning ordinance, the architect should assist the owner in obtaining it. The architect should notify the owner in writing of the availability of the building for occupancy. The date of this notification should coincide with the Date of Substantial Completion. Application for this permit is sometimes made by the architect as agent for the owner, but the contractor must show compliance with all legal construction requirements and inspections before the Certificate of Occupancy can be issued by the governmental agency.

The preceding paragraphs are general statements which do not apply to all jurisdictions. Local regulations should be checked in regard to Mechanic's Lien Laws, Stop Notices, and the Certificate of Occupancy. These laws vary from state to state. Furthermore, the explanatory material of this chapter is for study material only. The architect should not give assistance in any manner that can be construed to be legal advice. Filing, perfecting or defending claims of liens is a legal procedure. Both claimants and owners should be assisted by legal counsel if filing, perfecting or defending claims of lien is considered. to Mechanic's Lien Laws, Stop Notices, and the Certificate of Occupancy. These laws vary from state to state. Furthermore, the explanatory material of this chapter is for study material only. The architect should not give assistance in any manner that can be construed to be legal advice. Filing, perfecting or defending claims of liens is a legal procedure. Both claimants and owners should be assisted by legal counsel if filing, perfecting or defending claims of lien is considered.

Arbitration

During the course of construction, disagreements sometimes occur between the owner and contractor regarding requests by the contractor for extensions of time, claims for additional costs, and removal or correction of work which is not considered to be in accordance with the Contract Documents. If such disputes cannot be settled in a satisfactory manner, they must be decided by arbitration or the courts.

Disputes are often generated in the construction process. This is not necessarily due to flaws in the Contract Documents, but it is inherent in the construction process itself. For example, in order to ascertain whether the contractor's work is in accordance with the requirements of the Contract Documents, the documents have to be interpreted by the architect. This is a difficult task that obviously can lead to disputes. Further, the Contract Documents are highly complex. There are many variables that influence the rights, duties and responsibilities of the owner, architect and contractor. Therefore, it is difficult to define these rights, duties and responsibilities to cover all situations that may occur. For this reason, disputes and claims can result.

As outlined in paragraph 4.3.2 of the AIA General Conditions, claims, including those alleging an error or omission by the architect, must be made in writing and are referred initially to the architect. Further provisions of the document allow for appeal from decisions made at this level. The architect acts as a first level or quasi-arbitrator and attempts to settle any disputes through the claims resolution process outlined in article 4.4 of the AIA General Conditions. In acting in the capacity of first level arbitrator, the architect interprets the Contract Documents when so requested by either the owner of contractor in writing. In performing such services, the architect is often afforded certain protection from professional liability by immunity. In some cases, courts have ruled that the architect has immunity from liability for negligent conduct when such conduct is a result of the architect's responsibility to act as first level arbitrator of disagreements between the owner and contractor when so requested.

However, if the architect fails to exercise reasonable care or make a decision in good faith, such quasi-judicial immunity could be lost. For example, there have been many court cases where architects have been found negligent for certifying payments for obviously defective work or certifying payments far beyond the true percentage of completion. In these cases, claims of immunity have been rejected. Further, when the architect has failed to render a decision in a reasonable time, such inaction may be determined as delay to the project and the architect is not protected from liability by immunity. Recognize that the immunity applied to the architect's actions as first level arbitrator is quite limited. However, since expeditious decisions are required to keep the project moving, disputes are initially referred to the architect.

As outlined by the AIA General Conditions, the architect's role as first level arbitrator in the claims resolution process is as follows. References are to the paragraph numbers of the document.

4.3.3   A claim must be made within 21 days of the occurrence of an event giving rise to such claim. (See diagram below.)

4.4.1   The architect reviews the claim and takes one of 5 preliminary actions listed within 10 days of the claim. See (1) on diagram below.

1. Request additional data

2. Submit schedule indicating when action will be taken

3. Reject claim

4. Recommend approval

5. Suggest a compromise

4.4.3   If the claim has not been resolved, the claimant must take one of 3 actions listed within 10 days of architect's preliminary response. See (2) on diagram below.

1. Submit additional data

2. Modify the claim

3. Notify the architect that the initial claim stands

4.4.4   If the claim is still not resolved after consideration of the evidence, the architect will notify both the owner and the contractor in writing that a decision will be made within 7 days. See (3) on diagram below.

4.5.4.1 When a written decision by the architect states that "the decision is final and binding but subject to arbitration, and demand for arbitration must be made within 30 days", then failure to demand arbitration within 30 days results in the decision becoming final and binding. (Without this statement, contractor can wait until end of project to arbitrate.) See (4) on diagram below.

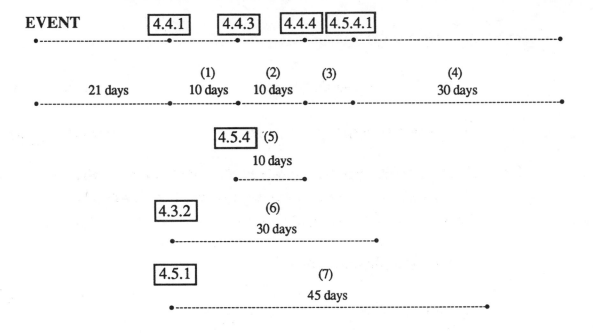

4.5.4 Arbitration may not be demanded earlier than: See (5) on diagram above.

1. The date the architect makes a final written decision on the claim.

2. The 10th day after the parties have presented evidence to the architect, if the architect has not made a final written decision by that date.

3. Any of the 5 events described in paragraph 4.3.2

4.3.2 The decision by the architect is not a condition precedent to arbitration in the event: See (6) on diagram above.

1. The position of the architect is vacant.

2. The architect has not received evidence or has failed to render a decision within the agreed time limits.

3. The architect has failed to take action under paragraph 4.4.4 within 30 days after the claim is made.

4. 45 days have passed after the claim has been referred to the architect. (Also see 4.5.1)

4.5.1 Arbitration may be commenced when 45 days have passed after the claim was referred initially to the architect and no decision has been rendered. See (7) on diagram above.

4.3.5 Final payment waives all claims not already made or preserved.

If a controversy cannot be resolved through the process outlined in articles 4.3, 4.4, and 4.5 of the AIA General Conditions, arbitration is generally the next and final procedure required to resolve the dispute. Arbitration is the hearing and settlement of a dispute between two parties arising from the discharge of contract obligations. The procedure may be initiated by either party to an agreement. This arbitration process provides a means of resolving disputes which cannot be settled through informal negotiations.

In general, arbitration is more expedient and less costly than judicial proceedings. In addition, it is suited to disputes in which technical questions rather than legal matters are the primary consideration. Furthermore, decisions are rendered by experts knowledgeable in construction and technical fields rather than by a jury composed of lay persons. However, the award is binding on both parties and there is usually no appeal procedure allowed. For this reason, some attorneys recommend limiting the value of a claim subject to arbitration to a certain dollar amount. Utilizing this concept, the cut-off for the maximum amount subject to arbitration often ranges between \$75,000 and \$200,000. Note that the AIA documents do not impose any limit on the amount subject to arbitration.

It should be noted that an award from an arbitration hearing is not binding on a third party that did not agree to participate in an arbitration hearing. The architect's professional liability insurance company is not required by law to be bound by an award from an arbitration hearing for liability imposed on the architect unless the company has specifically agreed to do so. For example, some insurance companies do not provide coverage to defend the architect in arbitration hearings nor will they pay arbitration awards. These companies prefer lawsuits since there is an appeal process. Therefore, the architect should check the terms of his professional liability insurance policy prior to using the AIA Documents since the AIA Documents include arbitration provisions. If the architect's insurance does not cover arbitration, these arbitration clauses should be modified or deleted from the documents.

The AIA General Conditions and Owner-Architect Agreement contain provisions for arbitration if efforts to resolve the dispute in an informal manner fail to settle the issue. After utilizing the claims resolution process and being unable to reach a satisfactory agreement, a party initiates arbitration by transmitting a written statement to the other party which outlines the following: his intention to arbitrate, the nature of the dispute, the sum involved, and the remedy sought. Two copies of the statement are then filed with the nearest Regional Office of the American Arbitration Association (AAA).

The defending party files a response to the statement with the AAA within seven days after notice of the action from the AAA. Failure to file a response is treated as a denial of the claim and does not delay the proceedings. Upon receiving the document initiating the arbitration process, the AAA assigns a staff member to administer the case.

The parties may agree to have a single arbitrator or to have a panel of three arbitrators. In the latter case, the tribunal often consists of an architect, an attorney and a contractor.

A list of names of prospective arbitrators for the tribunal panel is sent to both parties. Each party has the opportunity to reject any proposed arbitrator, number the remaining names in order of preference and return the list to the AAA. The panelists are then selected in regard to mutual choices of both parties.

The administrator then sets a time and place for the hearing, giving all parties five days notice. At the hearing, witnesses involved in the project are called and exhibits are introduced. Sometimes the arbitrators visit the construction site for inspections. In this case, both parties accompany the arbitrators at all times. Expert witnesses may also be utilized. In this case, a qualified expert's testimony is required because the complex matters involved in the arbitration hearing require a highly technical explanation of the issues.

Photographs and video recordings are extremely important in arbitration proceedings. The architect may wish to carry a camera on site visits and take photos of the project on a regular basis. Areas of potential dispute should be carefully photographed or video recorded in case a dispute develops later. Often by the time the claim is made, the work has already been covered. Video recordings often quickly communicate circumstances that might take hours of oral testimony to describe. Further, on site witnesses can often narrate facts while the video is being made which might be difficult to describe in oral testimony alone.

No statements may be made by either party to the arbitrators except in the presence of all arbitrators and all litigating parties. Transcripts of the proceedings are prepared if so requested by either party.

Generally, the complaining party presents his case first. The presentation should be made in a clear and logical manner describing the dispute, what is to be proved and the remedy sought. The hearing then proceeds somewhat like a court trial with the introduction of exhibits and testimonies. Upon commencement of the arbitration proceedings, delays may develop. Several hearings with lengthy periods of time between them may be required. The hearings close with a statement summarizing the evidence and a rebuttal by both sides regarding points made by the opposition. An award is then rendered by the arbitrators within thirty days from the closing date of the hearing. The award may be a cash settlement or a decision requiring one or both parties to perform certain actions to remedy the situation.

Claims subjected to arbitration originate from a variety of causes and generally involve relatively large sums of money. Job delay caused by the owner or another of his contractors often results in claims by a contractor for additional expenses. These extra costs are claimed by the contractor as a result of a delay to the project or some portion of it. Furthermore, claims for extra costs and time often occur when unforeseen subsurface conditions such as rock are encountered. Disputes then arise as to the exact amount to be paid for such extras. Errors and omissions also lead to many disputes regarding exact amounts of extra costs and extensions of time.

Many construction claims are in some way related to time. Since the contractor's original bid is based on his estimates of cost and time, "impact costs" or "consequential damages", resulting from alleged delays caused by the owner or architect are often the basis of the contractor's claim. Justification for such claims is based on the contractor's ability to demonstrate that he had incurred additional costs as a consequence of delays caused by the owner or the architect and that these delays had a substantial impact on job completion.

Final Comments

Architecture must possess aesthetic quality, be skillfully designed from suitable materials, and be useful and practical based on its function. The architect's responsibility is to provide leadership from conception to completion of the building process, to ensure that the project has been completed with consideration for human factors, technical care, and appropriateness to the nature of its use; and that it has been designed with due regard for environmental factors, so that the completed project is a source of satisfaction to the client and all who use it.

Bibliography

American Institute of Architects, "Architect's Handbook of Professional Practice," Volumes I, II, III and IV, published by the American Institute of Architects, Washington, D.C., 1987.

American Institute of Architects, "Lien Laws for Design Professionals: A Survey and Analysis," published by the American Institute of Architects, Washington, D.C., 1984.

American Institute of Architects, Project Delivery Approaches," published by Architectural Record and The American Institute of Architects, Washington, D.C., 1976.

Asken, G., "Resolving Construction Contract Disputes Through Arbitration," The American Arbitration Association, New York, New York, 1981.

Ayers, Chesley, "Specifications: for Architecture, Engineering and Construction," McGraw-Hill Book Company, New York, New York, 1984.

Clough, Richard H., "Construction Project Management," Wiley Interscience, New York, New York, 1979.

Collier, Keith C., "Construction Contracts," Prentice Hall, Englewood Cliffs, New Jersey, 1987.

Construction Specifications Institute, "Masterformat-Master List of Section Titles and Numbers," published by the Construction Specifications Institute, Alexandria, Virginia, 1983.

Construction Specifications Institute, "Manual of Practice," published by the Construction Specifications Institute, Alexandria, Virginia, 1985.

Cushman, Robert F., "Avoiding or Limiting Liability in Architectural Design and Construction," John Wiley and Sons, New York, New York, 1982.

De Goff, Robert A. and Friedman, Howard A., "Construction Management," Wiley Interscience, New York, New York, 1985.

Field, Robert C., Legal Aspects of Construction Seminar, seminar pamphlet entitled "Summary of Presentation--Mechanic's Liens and Stop Notices."

Fisk, Edward R., "Construction Engineer's Form Book," John Wiley and Sons, New York, New York, 1981.

Hauf, Harold, "Building Contracts for Design and Construction," John Wiley .and Sons, New York, New York, 1976.

Hohns, Murray, "Deskbook of Construction Contract Law," Prentice-Hall, Englewood Cliffs, New Jersey, 1981.

Hohns, Murray, "Preventing and Solving Construction Contract Disputes," Van Nostrand Reinhold Company, 1979.

Howell, Edward B., and Howell, Richard P., "Untangling the Web of Professional Liability," Design Professionals Insurance Co., San Francisco, California, 1980.

Jellinger, Thomas C., "Construction Contract Documents and Specifications," Addison-Wesley Publishing Company, Reading, Mass., 1981.

Kemper, Alfred M., "Architectural Handbook," John Wiley and Sons, New York, New York, 1979.

Lambert, Jeremiah and White, Lawrence, "Handbook of Modern Construction Law," Prentice-Hall, Englewood Cliffs, New Jersey, 1982.

Levy, Sidney M., "Project Management in Construction," McGraw-Hill Book Company, New York, New York, 1987.

Lewis, Jack, "Construction Specifications," Prentice-Hall, Englewood Cliffs, New Jersey, 1975.

Liebing, Ralph W., "Construction Regulations Handbook," John Wiley and Sons, New York, New York, 1987.

Liebing, Ralph W., "Systematic Construction Inspection," John Wiley and Sons, New York, New York, 1981.

Merritt, Frederick S., "Building Design and Construction Handbook," McGraw- Hill Book Company, New York, New York, 1982.

Rosen, Harold, "Construction Specification Writing," Wiley Interscience, New York, New York, 1981.

Rosenfeld, Walter, "Practical Specifier," McGraw-Hill Book Company, New York, New York, 1985.

Rothschild, Bernard B., "Construction Bonds and Insurance Guide," published by the American Institute of Architects, Washington, D.C., 1979.

Spencer, Whalen and Graham, "AIA Building Construction Legal Citator," published by the American Institute of Architects, Washington, D.C., 1984.

Bibliography

Sweet, Justin, "Legal Aspects of Architecture, Engineering and the Construction Process," West Publishing Company, St. Paul, Minn., 1985.

Walker, Edward and Rohdenburg, Theodor, "Legal Pitfalls In Architecture, Engineering and Building Construction," McGraw-Hill Book Company, New York,New York, 1979.

Wiley Law Publications Editorial Staff, "Construction Industry Contracts: Legal Citator and Case Digest," John Wiley and Sons, New York, New York, 1988.

Index

Index

Index

Index

Written Notice